The Psychology of Crimin[a]l Investigation

The contribution of psychological research to the prevention of miscarriages of justice and the development of effective investigative techniques is now established to a point where law enforcement agencies in numerous countries either employ psychologists as part of their staff, or work in cooperation with academic institutions. The application of psychology to investigation is particularly effective when academics and practitioners work together. This book brings together leading experts to discuss the application of psychology to criminal investigation.

This book offers an overview of models of investigation from a psychological and practical view point, covering topics such as investigative decision making, the presentation of evidence, witness testimony, the detection of deception, interviewing suspects and evidence-based police training. It is essential reading for students, researchers and practitioners engaged with police practice, investigation and forensic psychology.

Andy Griffiths is a Research Fellow at the University of Portsmouth, UK, Associate Tutor at the College of Policing, and international Consultant. He is both a former Senior Investigating Officer (SIO) and head of major crime for a UK police force, having completed 30 years' service specializing in interviewing and investigation, and during which he led numerous major crime investigations. During his police service he was awarded a PhD for his research on investigative interviewing and spent time as a Visiting Professor at John Jay College, New York.

Rebecca Milne is a Professor of Forensic Psychology at the Institute of Criminal Justice Studies, University of Portsmouth, UK, and Director of the Centre of Forensic Interviewing, an internationally recognised centre of excellence for investigative interviewing bringing together research, teaching and innovation. She is also a member of the UK National Police Chiefs' Council, Investigative Interviewing Strategic Steering Group, and a member of the UK Centre for Research and Evidence on Security Threats (CREST).

Issues in Forensic Psychology

Issues in Forensic Psychology is a book series which aims to promote forensic psychology to a broad range of forensic practitioners. It aims to provide analysis and debate on current issues and to publish and promote the work of forensic psychologists and other associated professionals.

The views expressed by the authors/editors may not necessarily be those held by the Series Editor or NOMS.

Edited by Richard Shuker, HMP Grendon

Research in Practice for Forensic Professionals
Edited by Kerry Sheldon, Jason Davies and Kevin Howells

Secure Recovery
Approaches to Recovery in Forensic Mental Health Settings
Edited by Gerard Drennan and Deborah Alred

Managing Clinical Risk
A Guide to Effective Practice
Edited by Caroline Logan and Lorraine Johnstone

Handbook on the study of Multiple Perpetrator Rape
A Multidisciplinary Response to an International Problem
Edited by Miranda A. H. Horvath and Jessica Woodhams

Forensic Practice in the Community
Edited by Zoë Ashmore and Richard Shuker

Supervision for Forensic Practitioners
Jason Davies

Transforming Environments and Rehabilitation
A Guide for Practitioners in Forensic Settings and Criminal Justice
Edited by Geraldine Akerman, Adrian Needs and Claire Bainbridge

The Psychology of Criminal Investigation
From Theory to Practice
Edited by Andy Griffiths and Rebecca Milne

For more information about this series, please visit: https://www.routledge.com/Issues-in-Forensic-Psychology/book-series/IFP

The Psychology of Criminal Investigation

From Theory to Practice

Edited by
Andy Griffiths and Rebecca Milne

Routledge
Taylor & Francis Group
LONDON AND NEW YORK

First published 2018 by Routledge

2 Park Square, Milton Park, Abingdon, Oxon OX14 4RN
605 Third Avenue, New York, NY 10017

Routledge is an imprint of the Taylor & Francis Group, an informa business

First issued in paperback 2021

Publisher's Note

The publisher has gone to great lengths to ensure the quality of this reprint but points out that some imperfections in the original copies may be apparent.

British Library Cataloguing in Publication Data
A catalogue record for this book is available from the British Library

Library of Congress Cataloging in Publication Data
A catalog record has been requested for this book

ISBN: 978-1-138-63941-6 (hbk)
ISBN: 978-0-367-48258-9 (pbk)

Typeset in Bembo
by Taylor & Francis Books

This book is dedicated to Dr Nina Westera,
12.12.1974–25.5.2014.

Figure 0.1 Nina Westera

Nina was one of our contributors and personified the ideology underpinning the collaboration between the practitioner world and academia – something that this book hopes to promote. Her personal journey commenced as a police officer in New Zealand, during which time she also studied for her PhD. After achieving this goal, she then moved into academia full-time where she felt she could make a greater difference. Sadly, Nina passed away due to illness before she was able to achieve everything we knew she would. Nevertheless, her memory and light will continue to shine, within us, and her celebrated work.

Contents

Figures

Contributors

Karl Ask is currently an associate professor of psychology at the University of Gothenburg, Sweden, and received his Ph.D. in psychology in 2006. He is a member of the Criminal, Legal and Investigative Psychology (CLIP) research unit. His research interests include judgment and decision-making, social cognition, and emotions. Over the past 15 years, he has studied decisions and judgments in the context of criminal investigations, with the aim of understanding (a) factors that contribute to errors and biases, (b) how decision-making quality can be improved, and (c) the roles of experience and personality characteristics in the investigative process. Much of this research has been carried out in international collaboration with police forces and educators, and he has been involved in basic and advanced training of police investigators.

Nathan Brooks is a Forensic Psychologist in full time private practice, based in Queensland, Australia. He has completed research in the area of investigative psychology and provides consultancy to the Department of Corrective Services.

Cliff Clark joined the UK police in 1990 and became involved in identification of suspects through artists impressions and then through the use of computer systems such as E-FIT. Clifford went onto Police training, covering general law, interviewing and identification issues, extending that to becoming a guest lecturer at Westminster and Leicester Universities. Clifford has trained with the Police in England and the FBI developing a range of skills in relation to identification issues, and completed his PhD in 2010 specialising in recall and recognition tasks in relation to facial composite tasks. Clifford's interest in interviewing techniques spread across a range of subjects including suspects, children, sexual offence victims and vulnerable adults, each having distinctive communication, memory, recall and recognition needs. Clifford moved to New Zealand in 2008 and developed experience with the New Zealand Police in relation to identification of online offenders, cyber investigations and latterly cyber security.

Mick Confrey is globally recognised as a subject matter expert in investigative interviewing, developed over a 30-year police career, latterly as Specialist Investigative Interview Advisor to Greater Manchester Police, UK. Mick advised on numerous cases, ranging from homicide to child exploitation, both nationally and internationally, and featured as the interview adviser on the highly acclaimed BBC/Open University documentary series 'Eyewitness', now used globally as a training aid for students of Forensic Psychology. On retiring from the police service Mick joined Intersol Global as their Operations Director, managing a group of specialist associates in adapting and delivering investigation and interview techniques internationally, to both the private and public sector. Mick has consulted and delivered training in Europe, North America, South America, Australasia, Asia and the Middle East, and is an expert witness.

Michael Davis is a Forensic and Clinical Psychologist in full time private practice. He is also an Adjunct Research Fellow with the Centre for Forensic Behavioural Science at Swinburne University of Technology, an Adjunct Senior Lecturer in the Department of Psychiatry at Monash University, and an Honorary Fellow in the Department of Psychiatry at The University of Melbourne, all Australia. His practice is divided between clinical-forensic assessment and providing behavioural investigative advice to police agencies in cases of violent and sexually violent crime.

Ivar Fahsing is an Assistant Professor and Detective Chief Superintendent with the Norwegian Police University College in Oslo. He previously worked with the Oslo Police and The National Criminal Investigation Service (Kripos) and has more than 15 years of operational experience with complex and serious investigations. He has published a number of books, articles and book chapters in several languages on eyewitness memory, investigative interviewing, organised crime, investigative expertise, decision-making and knowledge management. His PhD thesis from the University of Gothenburg, "The Making of an Expert Detective: Thinking and Deciding in Criminal Investigations," was published in 2016.

Mark Fallon is the author of *Unjustifiable Means*, and the founder of ClubFed, LLC, an international security consultancy firm. For more than 30 years, he served as a US national security professional, law enforcement specialist, and counterterrorism authority at the operational, policy, and executive level, and has been involved in some of the most significant counterterrorism operations in U.S. history. He served around the world in assignments as Deputy Assistant Director, Special Agent in Charge, Director of the NCIS Training Academy and Chief of the Counterintelligence Operations. In 2008, he was appointed as a US Homeland Security senior executive, and was the Assistant Director for Training at the Federal Law Enforcement Training Center. He is the Vice Chair of the International Association of

Chiefs of Police IMPACT Section, and a member of the US Government High Value Detainee Interrogation Group Research Committee.

Katarina Fritzon is an Associate Professor at Bond University, Australia and also a practising Forensic and Clinical Psychologist. She was formerly a member of the external expert panel providing behavioural investigative advice to the National Crime Agency, UK. Since moving to Australia in 2005, she has provided psychological assessment reports to legal bodies and tribunals including the Department of Immigration and Border Protection, WorkCover Queensland, Department of Communities, Child Safety and Disabilities, Criminal Courts and Family Courts. She has provided forensic treatment services for clients in high and medium secure forensic hospitals, and Corrections as well as in the community

Fiona Gabbert is a Professor of Applied Psychology, and Director of the Forensic Psychology Unit at Goldsmiths University of London. She has an international reputation for her research in the fields of suggestibility of memory and evidence-based investigative interviewing, where she seeks to develop innovative ways to improve the usability, credibility, and reliability of evidence from eyewitnesses (e.g., SAI© and SAW-IT™). Her work has set the agenda for new directions in the field of applied memory and cognition, and has had an important impact on police operational procedure and policy in the UK and internationally. Fiona chairs the Scientific Committee of the International Investigative Interviewing Research Group (iIIRG), and is an invited member of the Scientific and Professional Advisory Board of the British False Memory Society, as well as being an Honorary Member of the Centre for Memory and Law at City University, London.

Erik Mac Giolla is a Postdoc at the University of Gothenburg, Sweden. He received his Ph.D. in 2016 on the topic of true and false intentions. Since 2011 he has been a member of The research unit for Criminal, Legal and Investigative Psychology (CLIP). He has a broad interest in legal psychology, and has been involved in projects within the themes of eyewitness psychology, deception detection, and investigative interviewing

Pär Anders Granhag is a Professor of Psychology at University of Gothenburg, Sweden, long-term affiliate of the Norwegian Police University College (Oslo), and founding director for Criminal, Legal and Investigative Psychology (CLIP), one of legal psychology's leading units. His main areas of research are deception detection, interrogation and interactions in human intelligence contexts. He has authored/edited 8 books, 70+ chapters in edited volumes, published 160+ papers in international peer-reviewed journals, and been principal researcher for 25 full scale research projects. He has presented his research world-wide, and conducted missions for organizations such as the FBI, LAPD, Defence Intelligence (UK), UNHCR and the EC. He is the past president of the European Association of Psychology and Law (EAPL), and he is the founding director of the Nordic Network for research on Psychology & Law (NNPL). He is the Editor of the journal *Applied Cognitive Psychology*.

John G. D. Grieve CBE. QPM. BA (Hons). MPhil. Hon DL. is Professor Emeritus at London Metropolitan University and a Senior Research Fellow at University of Portsmouth, UK. During his 37-year police service he was Director of Intelligence at New Scotland Yard, London, UK, Director and Creator of the Race and Violent Crime Task Force and National Co-ordinator for Counter Terrorism Investigations. As an academic he has taught all over the globe, and his contributions to thinking, understanding and sharing knowledge have been made through 30+ academic journals, policy papers and books on Partnership and Engagement, Police Leadership, History of Policing and Investigation, Psychology and Investigations, Philosophy and Strategy of Investigations, Police Ethics, Intelligence, Critical Incidents, Community Impact, Corruption, Miscarriages of Justice, Institutional Racism, Counter Terrorism, Police Culture, Post Snowden Digital Surveillance. He currently researches the investigation of Non Recent Cases and retains an interest in Counter Terrorism, Investigative Strategy and Miscarriages of Justice.

Andy Griffiths is a Research Fellow at the University of Portsmouth, UK, Associate Tutor at the College of Policing, and international Consultant. He is both a former Senior Investigating Officer (SIO) and head of major crime for a UK police force, having completed 30 years' service specializing in interviewing and investigation, and during which he led numerous major crime investigations. Throughout his police career he also contributed to UK national policy and training on investigative interviewing, as a member of the national council advising all police forces. He was awarded his PhD for research on the effectiveness of training on real life major crime suspect and witness interviews and has numerous publications in this field. He has contributed to miscarriage of justice investigations in the USA, New Zealand and the UK on a *pro bono* basis, and lectured in many different countries.

Lorraine Hope is Professor of Applied Cognitive Psychology at the University of Portsmouth, UK and a member of the UK Centre for Research and Evidence on Security Threats (CREST). Her work focuses on the performance of human cognition in applied contexts, including memory and decision-making under challenging conditions. Over the past 15 years, her research has resulted in the development of innovative tools and techniques, informed by psychological science, for eliciting accurate and detailed information and intelligence in security, policing and intelligence contexts. She has published widely on memory and information elicitation topics and speaks regularly at academic and practitioner conferences. She is an elected member of the Governing Board of the Society for Applied Research on

Memory and Cognition (SARMAC), Associate Editor of British Psychological Society journal *Legal and Criminological Psychology* and Consulting Editor for the American Psychological Association *Journal of Experimental Psychology: Applied*.

Dean Jones served 30 years with Hampshire police (UK), including posts as Head of Major Crime and Director of Intelligence. He sat on the UK National Chief Officers steering group on Investigative Interviewing and developed one of the first Tactical Interview Managers courses. Dean also led the National Crime Faculty team, which developed the Senior Investigating Officer (SIO) and initial detective training programs. He has worked in Northern Ireland as an SIO on the Historical Enquiry Team and is now the Senior Forensic Pathology Manager overseeing the provision of forensic pathology services to police forces in England and Wales. He developed and delivers the 'Expert Witness' course for non-forensic organ specific and paediatric pathologists, and authored the current police policy on dealing with sudden and unexpected death. Dean is a Honorary Fellow at University of Portsmouth, and a part time tutor for Essex University.

Mark Kebbell is Professor of Forensic Psychology at Griffith University, Australia School of Applied Psychology. His expertise and research is in the area of Investigative Psychology particularly with regards the investigation and prosecution of serious crime. His previous work has included writing the guidelines for police officers in England and Wales (with Wagstaff) for assessing witness evidence, and developing risk assessment methods for suspected sex offenders for the Australian Federal Police and the Queensland Police Service. He has worked on 70+ criminal cases, principally involving murder or serious sexual assault, and has given expert evidence on numerous occasions including uncontested psychological evidence in an Old Bailey appeal case. He is a Registered Psychologist in Australia and a Chartered Forensic Psychologist in the United Kingdom. Academically, the quality of his work has been recognised by the award of a British Academy Postdoctoral Fellowship for Outstanding Younger Scholars. He is the Editor, with Professor Graham Davies, of the book *Practical Psychology for Forensic Investigations and Prosecutions* published by Wiley.

Becky Milne is a Professor of Forensic Psychology at the Institute of Criminal Justice Studies, University of Portsmouth, UK, and Director of the Centre of Forensic Interviewing, an internationally recognised centre of excellence for investigative interviewing bringing together research, teaching, and innovation. She is also a member of the UK Association of Chief Police Officers, Investigative Interviewing Strategic Steering Group and is a member of the UK Centre for Research and Evidence on Security Threats (CREST). The main focus of her work over the past 20 years concerns the examination of police interviewing and investigation; working with practitioners, and developing procedures that improve the quality of interviews of witnesses, victims, and suspects of crime across a number of countries. She works closely with the police (and other criminal justice organisations), creating novel interview techniques, developing training, running interview courses, and providing case advice. She received the Tom Williamson award for her outstanding achievements in the field of investigative interviewing in 2009.

Jordan Nunan is a doctoral researcher at the University of Portsmouth, funded by the Centre for Research and Evidence on Security Threats (CREST). He holds a distinction MSc in Crime Science, Investigation, and Intelligence and a first class BSc (Hons) in Criminology with Psychology. His doctoral research concerns memory encoding and retrieval techniques for covert policing and intelligence gathering, with a particular focus on Human Intelligence (HUMINT). He is also employed as a researcher at the University of Portsmouth, on a project exploring frontline communication at critical and major incidents, in particular, a focus on front-line briefings and information exchange captured through body worn cameras. Jordan is also a volunteer Special Constable with Hampshire Police.

Brendan O'Mahony is a Chartered Psychologist and a Registered Forensic Psychologist in England and Wales. He is a Specialist Member (psychologist) of The Parole Board for England and Wales. He also works in private practice completing expert witness reports for the criminal courts. He holds the Cardiff University Bond Solon Expert Witness Certificate. Dr. O'Mahony is a committee member of the Expert Witness Advisory Group at the British Psychological Society. He is a Registered Intermediary with the Ministry of Justice in London, a role in which he assesses and advises on the communication needs of vulnerable witnesses attending police interview or giving evidence at court. Dr. O'Mahony also works as an intermediary for vulnerable defendants at trial. He completed his professional doctorate at the Institute of Criminal Justice Studies, University of Portsmouth, UK, where he examined the experiences of defendant intermediaries. Dr. O'Mahony is a Visiting Fellow at the University of Portsmouth.

Martin O'Neill is Senior Lecturer in Criminal Investigation at Canterbury Christ Church University. He has a keen interest in all aspects of criminal investigation, including investigative decision making, training of detectives, death investigation, investigating sexual offences, and domestic abuse and stalking. He is currently engaged in research relating to an Advanced Detective Programme for police detectives, linked to an Undergraduate Degree from 2001 to 2006, and the application of a decision-making model to criminal investigations. Martin has recently authored a book entitled: *Key Challenges in Criminal Investigation*, which was published in February 2018.

Graham Pike is a Professor at The Open University with interests in forensic psychology, critical criminology and applied cognition, whose research focuses on issues of evidence, harm and evidence based practice within the criminal justice system; particularly in relation to eyewitness identification. He is Professor of Forensic Cognition at the Open University and Director of Research for the Centre for Policing Research and Learning. His research has led to changes in the PACE Codes of Practice and numerous guidelines for policing practice as well as development of the VIPER identification system and E-FIT and EFIT-V software. He has a passion for public engagement, whether it be producing Apps (see Photofit-me and OU Brainwave in the Apple and Android stores), TV programmes (e.g. www.bbc.co.uk/programmes/b00s6qdj) online courses and MOOCs (e.g. www.futurelearn.com/courses/forensic-psychology), blogs (oucriminology.wordpress.com) or participating in public lecture tours (see www.crimiknowledge.com). Twitter: @Graham_Pike

Sam Poyser is a Senior Lecturer in Criminology and Policing at York St. John University. After graduating from the University of Portsmouth with an MSc in Criminal Justice Studies (with Distinction), she went on to complete a PhD in Criminology and Criminal Justice which examined the role of the media in investigating miscarriages of justice. Her work in the field of investigation led to Sam being asked to act as an expert adviser to the BBC on the topic of miscarriages, television appearances and approaches from journalists relating to cases requiring reinvestigation. Sam has presented her research at conferences worldwide and has published widely on miscarriages and the lessons they present for practitioners. She has recently written a book on miscarriages for serving police officers and is drafting another examining miscarriages from a comparative perspective. Sam's research has recently expanded to include investigations into injustices committed against animals.

Lee Rainbow is the Head of Profession for Behavioural Investigative Advice within the National Crime Agency (NCA) and a member of the National Police Chief's Council (NPCC) Behavioural Science Committee. After gaining an MSc in Investigative Psychology in 1996 he subsequently worked within Cleveland Constabulary as a criminal intelligence analyst and Surrey Police as a behavioural science consultant before being employed by the National Crime Faculty as the first-ever full-time Behavioural Investigative Adviser. He has produced over 350 written reports in support of serious crime enquiries and has supported many of the most high profile cases in the United Kingdom, as well as cases in Europe and the Caribbean. He has played a leading role in the national coordination and governance of behavioural investigative advice within the United Kingdom and has contributed significantly to the enhanced professionalization of the discipline from both a tactical and strategic perspective.

Asbjørn Rachlew is currently a Police Superintendent at Oslo Police District, Norway, with previous assignments as a homicide detective, during which he was interview advisor to the team interviewing Anders Brevik after the 2011 Oslo terror attacks, and as a detective for the UN. Rachlew initiated and developed the first *Investigative Interviewing* training program in Norway (K.R.E.A.T.I.V), after completing his MSc in Investigative psychology at the University of Liverpool (1999) and later completed a Ph.D. at the University of Oslo (UiO) in 2009. He lectures on Criminal Investigation, Investigative Interviewing and Errors of Justice, and has also published and testified as an expert witness. He has been involved in Norway's Human Rights dialog with Vietnam and Indonesia for several years and is currently engaged by the Norwegian Centre for Human Rights (UiO) to continue the development of Investigative Interviewing and the operationalization of the presumption of innocence.

Kevin Smith is a Chartered Psychologist who currently works as the National Vulnerable Witness Adviser, at the UK National Crime Agency (NCA). He is regularly deployed operationally to develop interview strategies for victims and witnesses in complex cases. He also oversees the witness intermediary matching service. He previously completed 30 years service with the Metropolitan Police as a detective and sits on the National Police Chiefs' Council Strategic Steering Group for Investigative Interviewing, the Ministry of Justice Vulnerable and Intimidated Witnesses Working Group and the Intermediary Registration Board for England and Wales. He has numerous publications in the field of investigation and vulnerability.

Ian Stanier was awarded his PhD for research into UK information sharing pathologies and law enforcement intelligence failures and currently researches the HUMINT topics, covert evidence based policing, plus prison security. He was the UK lead for HUMINT Strategy for Counter-Terrorism policing and acted as advisor to HM Governments' Home Office on the review of the *Regulation of Investigatory Powers Act 2000* (UK). He has been responsible for the development of specialist intelligence in a number of operational arenas for UK policing, reviewed and developed policy on the *National Intelligence Model*, National Informant practice, and Prison Intelligence Officer practice, led on prison debriefing programmes, the enhancement of counter-terrorism tactics, and informant training nationally and internationally, including workshops in the Middle East, Eastern European and Africa. He has designed and delivered bespoke intelligence related courses in South East Asia, Australia, and Central America.

Zarah Vernham is an Early Career Researcher who completed her PhD in March 2015. She is a Senior Lecturer of Security and Investigations based in the Department of Psychology at the University of Portsmouth in the United Kingdom. She is also a member of the International Centre for

Research in Forensic Psychology within the same department. Zarah's PhD applied a 'collective interviewing' technique to the detection of deception in pairs or groups of suspects. Zarah continues to conduct research in the areas of detecting deception and investigative interviewing, but also conducts research within prisons and secure units to examine offending behaviours, offender expertise and offender risk assessment. Zarah regularly presents at conferences to both academics and practitioners. To date, she has 15 publications.

Adrian G. West is a Forensic Clinical Psychologist with a professional background in the assessment of mentally disordered offenders detained in high and medium secure psychiatric hospitals. He has advised the Police Service in the United Kingdom on major crime investigations for over 20 years.

Nina Westera began her career as an officer in the New Zealand Police, where she worked on the investigation of serious crime and implemented evidence-based policy and practice for interviewing witnesses and suspects. For this work, she was the recipient of the 2014 International Investigative Interviewing Research Group Practitioner Excellence Award. After leaving the police, Nina relocated to Australia, where she took up a postdoctoral fellowship at Griffith University. She then obtained a Research Fellowship at the Griffith Criminology Institute, and later a tenured position at Griffiths' School of Criminology and Criminal Justice. Nina's research interests included investigative interviewing, eyewitness testimony, and the criminal investigation and prosecution of sexual and violent offences. Throughout her career, she was heavily involved – both nationally and internationally – in educating and advising police officers, lawyers, judges, and other criminal justice sector professionals about eliciting eyewitness evidence. Shortly before she became ill, Nina was awarded an Australian Research Council Distinguished Early Career Research Award (DECRA) to continue her work on the investigation of adult sexual assault cases. She is profoundly missed

Foreword

In 1971, one year after graduating with a BSc in Psychology (with additional mathematical statistics) I was in a university laboratory conducting experimental research towards a PhD when the Head of Psychology invited me to assist his new research involving the police. I was very curious about this because at that time I was not aware that the police would be interested in psychology nor psychologists interested in policing. For the next two years I was employed full-time on a project investigating ways of improving police officers' memory of relevant information. Since then I have been fortunate to work with many police and investigative organisations and have witnessed around the world increasingly positive collaborations between growing numbers of investigators and of psychologists. Thus, I feel that it is very timely that this book on psychology's contributions to investigative practice has been published, especially involving editors who can combine decades of investigative experience (Andy – having achieved a PhD during his police service) with many years of sharing psychology with investigators and conducting a volume of quality research (Becky – having received honours from the police service and being a member of their relevant national committee).

A while prior to my writing of this foreword a friend of mine in the USA asked me whether the topic of "disputed confessions" often came up in the British cases that I work on in the role of an 'expert witness'. In my reply to her I said that in the last 20 years this occurred very rarely, due to the police here getting their act together (based on the findings of psychological research) in (i) developing the 'PEACE' method of investigative interviewing (in collaboration with myself and other psychologists) and (ii) investing substantially in training officers to employ this method.

Here in England, way back in 1990 I was commissioned (together with a Law Professor) by the government to draft the official guidance on how to interview child witnesses/victims (which became 'The Memorandum of Good Practice on Video Recorded Interviews with Child Witnesses for Criminal Proceedings'). In relation to this a series of meetings of interested parties was held in London. After one of these meetings the chairperson (a senior civil servant) telephoned me to say that he had reported back to the government minister that the meeting had gone well; however, the minister had just told the civil servant off for forgetting to mention one essential thing to me – which was that "Anything that you put in the guidance must be backed up by peer-reviewed, published research". To hear such words was highly pleasing to me. This is another reason why I happily accepted the invitation to write this foreword to a book that emphasises in a comprehensive way how the findings of quality research (and theory development) are contributing extensively to the conducting of crime investigations. Now is indeed a prime time for the present book to be published.

Professor Ray Bull
October 25, 2017
Fishbourne, UK

Introduction

Andy Griffiths and Rebecca Milne

The study of human behaviour related to crime and justice commenced more than 100 years ago when pioneer psychologists wrote about the reliability of witnesses and the confessions of suspects, in court cases (Munsterburg, 1908). As time passed psychologists gradually broadened their horizons to encompass all aspects of criminal behaviour and criminal investigation leading to the recognition of legal psychology by the American Psychological Association (APA) in 1984 (Grisso, 1991) as "professional practice by psychologists … in an activity primarily intended to provide professional psychological expertise to the judicial system"; and formation of the European Association of Psychology and Law (EAPL) in 1992 for the "promotion and development of research, improvements in legal procedures, teaching, and practice in the field of psychology and law (e.g., legal psychology, criminological psychology, forensic psychology)" (www.eapl.eu).

From its early observations of the trial process, the study of psychology within the legal domain has evolved, from not just *explaining* the phenomena observed in the trial process, but also to *suggesting* practical improvements to investigative techniques and judicial processes (e.g. changing the format of eye witness identification procedures, or amended interview techniques) through quality research and interaction with practitioners. Psychological intervention has tended to be hindsight driven with expert witness intervention in miscarriages driving research to identify a 'better way'. However, the contribution of psychological research in identifying, then preventing miscarriages of justice and developing effective investigative techniques is now established to a point where law enforcement agencies in numerous countries now either employ psychologists as part of their staff or work in co-operation with psychology departments of academic institutions.

In our view, the application of psychology to investigation is most effective when academics and practitioners work together. Indeed, this type of collaborative approach has recently been championed by the evolution of Evidence Based Policing (Sherman, 2013) as a distinct movement. However, it appears to us that investigative practice has been utilizing psychological theory for some years already. Indeed, the editors of this book began their work together in this way (Griffiths & Milne, 2006), by conducting joint research as a serving police officer and practically focused academic. We also knew of numerous similarly productive collaborations, but also situations where research and practice were not coordinated, or where research was not having an impact. We decided that the question of how much psychological research had been successfully incorporated into investigative practice was something that would interest a wider audience and so decided to produce this book, with each chapter deliberately created from both academic and practitioner contributions.

The first stage was to identify a team of practitioners and academics who could help us in this quest. In this we were incredibly lucky as friends and colleagues from across the world, interested in the same question, agreed to assist by writing their individual chapters. We are indebted to them for their diligence and commitment (please see the following section for more on the individual contributors). The development process led us to a realization that there were two levels of commentary relevant to the question. First, what we have termed the 'macro' level where the issues span the investigation process, and secondly, the micro level where the issues are specific to individual disciplines within the investigation process. Consequently, the book is structured in this way with the first set of chapters (1–5) dealing with the macro level and the following chapters (6–12) dealing with the micro level. The sections are then brought together in a conclusion written by the editors.

Deliberately, Chapter 1 discusses miscarriages of justice, the focal point of driving change in any criminal justice system, through the identification of failure. Every miscarriage represents a personal tragedy for the victim and the wrongly convicted. Therefore, it is imperative that society learns from these mistakes. The authors cover the main causes of miscarriages as a precursor to examining to what extent psychology has played a role in both the identification of and remedies to this problem. The chapter serves as an excellent introduction to the book, reminding the reader of the suffering caused by miscarriages and also how learning from psychological theory can limit the numbers of these cases in the future.

The second chapter is written by an author who is one of the new breed of practitioners, who have supplemented their careers as investigators with doctorate level study aimed at improving practice. The chapter examines the whole question of whether investigation is a science or a craft. The chapter examines the origins of investigation and its evolution. Yet the author is also critical of the lack of psychological influence in some areas and introduces the reader to one of the themes of the book: the influence of organizational culture on the evolution of practice, something that will reoccur.

Chapter 3 explores an area that encapsulates our challenge in putting this book together. The psychology behind how investigators make decisions transcends all areas of investigation and yet much of previous research has tended to focus on subject specific areas (e.g. false confessions, or identification). However, basic human traits dictate behaviour and affect the impartiality of investigations, sometimes through unconscious bias, other times through deliberate actions. The authors highlight the role of various cognitive biases, before exploring what psychology may have to offer for the future.

Investigation does not end with the arrest or charge of a suspect. It continues into the trial process where there needs to be a balance between honouring the presumption of innocence and presenting the prosecution evidence in the most effective way possible. Chapter 4 deals with this issue. The advent of the technological age has presented law enforcement and the justice process with the ability to utilize video records of testimony. The chapter examines the impact of psychological research in this area and argues that the use of technology overcomes some long-standing problems with not only the oral presentation of evidence but the way in which some evidence is gathered initially. However, in one of the recurring themes of this book, the chapter highlights the strength of cultural beliefs and heuristics within the criminal justice system that inhibit change and obstruct the development of policy and practice according to empirical research.

Vulnerability is the last of the 'macro' subjects that are covered by the first section of the book. The chapter is written from the perspective of the United Kingdom, where, since 1999, there has been a solid focus on this area with both legislation and guidance for investigators aimed at improving the experience of vulnerable people in the justice system. The chapter highlights the need to protect the vulnerable and facilitate their involvement in the justice system. This area is one where psychologists have been closely involved in both the development of the guidelines and implementation of the training, demonstrating the strength of positive multi-disciplinary collaborations.

Chapter 6 is the first chapter that focuses on a distinct area of investigation, discussing the impact of psychological theory on witness testimony. The chapter explores the issues that increase or decrease the reliability of eyewitness testimony and then discusses the role of interviewing as a variable in this formula, before exploring the conflict between investigative and criminal justice objectives that has been a feature of recent research on the utilization of psychological theory within real life practice. Identification evidence is one of the focal points of an investigation and has produced a wealth of research over many decades from numerous countries. Indeed, misidentification is one of the primary reasons for miscarriage of justice cases. Chapter 7 discusses the established theory and how practice has, or has not, developed. The chapter assesses the veracity of current criminal justice procedures and emphasises the need for a greater collaborative approach between researchers and practitioners.

The questioning of suspects is acknowledged as one of the most controversial areas of criminal justice. This controversy has resulted in a high level of research interest. Recent years have seen transformational change both in legislation and investigative practice in some countries, heavily influenced by psychological research, where psychology has moved from external critic identifying problems to collaborator developing solutions. Chapter 8 examines three different countries as case studies and also discusses how fundamental differences in culture are affecting change in the area of questioning suspects, even where research is convergent on 'what works'. Chapter 9 addresses an area that has been widely researched. Detecting deception has produced a rich seam of psychological research with strong and consistent results that contradict long held beliefs regarding non-verbal cues to deception. The chapter reviews the research, then discusses a tool developed from the research, that has been provided to investigators to help them in their task before discussing potential further uses for emerging research and the overall context.

Profiling is covered in Chapter 10 with an exploration of the reasoning underlying inferences that can be made from crime scene behaviour and describing the evolution of this investigation strand. Chapter 11 deals with the applicability of psychological research to intelligence, specifically investigative interaction with human sources of intelligence. This is an under researched area because access to data has been difficult due to confidentiality and the relative youth of the discipline. The authors discuss the applicability of research from other areas and highlight the need for further research informed by the lessons from other areas.

The final chapter in the book addresses what we believe to be a crucial element in the adoption of effective psychological theory by modern day investigators – that of training. The chapter discusses the relatively new concepts of Evidence Based Policing and Evidence Based Police Training and looks at three countries, providing evidence that there is a positive move towards training that incorporates empirical knowledge.

We are indebted to our contributors, each chapter has been produced by a combination of skilled practitioner and academic input, in line with our theme and designed to give the reader a realistic assessment of where psychological theory has impacted practice.

References

Griffiths, A., & Milne, R. (2006). Will it all end in tiers? In T. Williamson (ed.), *Investigative Interviewing: Rights, Research, Regulation*. Chichester, UK: Wiley, pp. 167–189.

Grisso, T. (1991). A developmental history of the American Psychology-Law Society. *Law and Human Behavior*, 15(3), 213–231, http://dx.doi.org/10.1007/BF01061710

Munsterburg, H. (1908). *On the Witness Stand: Essays on Psychology and Crime*. New York: McClure.

Sherman, L. (2013). *The Rise of Evidence Based policing: Targeting, Testing and Tracking*. http://cebcp.org/wp-content/evidence-based-policing/Sherman-TripleT.pdf. May 20. Accessed 1 June 2017.

Chapter 1

Miscarriages of justice

What can we learn?

Sam Poyser and John D. Grieve

Introduction

> "you've had your whole life ripped to shreds and you have been hugely damaged ... [these are] the ashes of what you had."
>
> (Barry George in BBC, 2015)

This statement, made by a victim of wrongful conviction in the UK, highlights the devastating impact of miscarriages of justice upon individuals who suffer them. Put simply, miscarriages destroy people's lives, erode public support for the Criminal Justice System (CJS) and are inimical to wider society (Gardner, 2015). However, they can also have positive impacts, serving as 'lessons to be learnt' concerning what went wrong in particular cases. The contribution of psychological research here has proved invaluable in revealing that most of these lessons relate to the police investigative process and potential weaknesses of that process and in helping to explain particular phenomena; such as why individuals might falsely confess (Brants, 2008). Psychologists have also advocated, and helped to implement, improvements to investigative processes aimed at reducing future incidences of miscarriages (Gudjonsson, 2003; Grieve, 2007). Nevertheless, much more remains to be learnt and to be done in terms of ongoing psychological research in this field.

This chapter will consider what we have, and can, learn from miscarriages of justice in England and Wales, chiefly as a result of psychological research. It will highlight what psychologists have discovered about the role of police investigative processes in causing miscarriages and how their research findings have helped to kick-start change agendas relating to those processes, which have in due course involved legislative, policy and practice reforms. Indeed, we will see that not only does the process of criminal investigation contribute to miscarriages; the lessons learnt from miscarriages due to the input of psychological research have contributed to the ways in which criminal investigations are conducted. The chapter will begin by considering 'What is a miscarriage of justice?' It will then highlight research, which reveals the causes of miscarriages, demonstrating as it does that many relate to police investigative processes. The chapter will next outline the contribution of psychological research to our understanding of the causes that are connected to police investigative processes, focussing specifically upon issues surrounding: i) the investigative process generally, including investigative philosophy, strategy and tactics; ii) interview practices involving suspects, victims and witnesses; and iii) identification procedures. Official responses to lessons learnt from psychological research and improvements made to investigative processes and techniques as a result are also discussed. The chapter ends by stressing that many opportunities remain for psychologists to conduct research in this area, so as to continue to work towards reducing miscarriages of justice.

What *is* a miscarriage of justice?

There is much disagreement concerning what the term 'miscarriage of justice' means. Definitions differ greatly, and are dependent upon individuals' perceptions and perspectives and the circumstances in which the phrase is used (Leverick and Chalmers, 2014). Interestingly, the word 'miscarriage' may have derived from Plato (whose mother was said to be a midwife) (Grieve, 2007) and, certainly, one of the most comprehensive definitions, that of Walker (1999: 33–4), suggests that the term refers to a failure to reach the end goal of 'justice'. However, where the State seeks to sanction an individual, the process is, by its very nature, coercive and unbalanced. Therefore, 'justice' might be said to be an instance in which that imbalance and coercion is minimised to tolerable levels; hence a 'miscarriage of justice' is a situation where this does not occur (Hall, 1994). Of major contention is whether the expression 'miscarriage of justice' encompasses both factual innocence (i.e. an individual did not commit the crime for which they were convicted) *and* procedural innocence (i.e. an individual committed the crime, but as their rights were violated during the justice process, they should not have been convicted) (Hall, 1994). However, in truth it is very difficult to identify the factually innocent (see Campbell, 2015).

The aforementioned discussion highlights the importance of the integrity of the *process* of justice as much as the result of that process. That process occurs not only in court-rooms but, for example, on streets (Weber and Bowling, 2012), and in police cars and police stations, where Walker (1999) suggests 'justice' is achieved when the State and its representatives give equal respect to individuals' rights. Therefore, a miscarriage of justice is a *breach* of an individual's rights (whether suspect, defendant, convict, victim or witness) by the State/State agencies. Walker (1999) also highlights that miscarriages can be institutionalised within laws *and/or* the result of laws being mis-applied/interpreted, as a recent Justice Committee report (2014) concerning Joint Enterprise Law exemplified.

Part of the process of justice involves criminal justice practitioners dealing with victims (and witnesses) of crime. Here, miscarriages can occur not only in situations where those practitioners have *done the wrong thing*, but where they have *not done enough/anything* in response to victimisation (Walker, 1999). This can include failure to: i) investigate crimes, ii) identify offenders, iii) press charges and iv) mount a robust prosecution case (Savage, Grieve and Poyser, 2007), resulting in the failure to hold offenders accountable.

Miscarriages of justice can also include failure to support, and poor treatment of, victims of crime/their families through, for example, neglecting to inform them of developments in their case (Savage et al., 2007). This can lead to secondary victimisation, as research by the Victims' Commissioner has recently highlighted (see Bowcott, 2015). Miscarriages may also be defined as failures on the part of the CJS and peripheral agencies to recognise, intervene and safeguard the public from 'known' risks or dangerous individuals (see for example the case of Carl Mills in Morris, 2015). Such miscarriages may lead to falling public confidence in the CJS and to individuals being less willing to engage with it (Hall, 1994). In addition to acknowledging high-profile wrongful convictions, any definition of a miscarriage of justice must also recognise the rather commonplace wrongful convictions obtained in the Crown Courts, regularly over-turned in the Court of Appeal and those obtained in magistrate courts, routinely overturned in Crown Courts (Naughton, 2013), particularly as the harms resulting from these miscarriages can be just as damaging as those caused by notorious miscarriages of justice (Ford, 1998).

Interestingly, Naughton (2014) who contends that the label 'miscarriage of justice' does not adequately represent all types of wrongful convictions, uses the concept of 'intent' to differentiate between '*miscarriages* of justice', which he argues are not caused by deliberate acts by individuals to transgress due process and '*abortions* of justice', which he suggests, are. Importantly, however, Naughton (2014) contends that at a structural level, miscarriages can *themselves* be viewed as abortions of justice, as they are *intended* by a crime control-oriented CJS that sees inherently unreliable forms of evidence, such as uncorroborated eyewitness testimony as admissible in court, despite psychological research (discussed shortly) warning that they render the innocent vulnerable to wrongful conviction. In reality, however, it is often difficult to ascertain whether mistake or malicious intent is behind the construction of individual miscarriages (Poyser and Milne, 2015). Clearly, whilst any comprehensive assessment of miscarriages of justice should include reference to as many definitions as possible, due to its particular focus, the following discourse will principally use the term to refer to wrongful conviction. Nevertheless, there are clearly copious complexities involved in seeking an all-encompassing definition, making further debate upon this issue, vital.

Miscarriages of justice: the contribution of research

Scholarly interest in miscarriages of justice has increased massively over the past 20 years or so (Radelet, 2013), however the first substantial study in this area was published by Borchard (1932). This detailed 65 miscarriages of justice (62 US and 3 UK cases) and crucially forced a change in academic thought on the issue, from questioning whether miscarriages *do* occur; to consideration of *why* they occur and how we can reduce them. Importantly, Borchard (1932) found that the main causes of miscarriages were: mistaken eyewitness identification, improperly obtained confessions, unreliable forensic science and expert evidence, witness perjury, inadequate defence representation and public pressure to solve horrific crimes – findings that have been reflected in almost every subsequent study. Most of the research that followed consisted of small-scale studies of similar case descriptions (see, for example, Frank and Frank, 1957; Radin, 1964; Huff, Rattner and Sagarin, 1986). This changed with the publication of Bedau and Radelet's (1987) large-scale study of 350 miscarriages in capital cases (1900–1985), which demonstrated that miscarriages were not the rarity once thought. From the mid-1990s onwards, such studies in the US permanently altered in nature, with the publication of research by Connors, Lundregan, Miller and McEwen (1996), which evidenced the ability of DNA testing to conclusively establish the prisoner's innocence in 28 cases. Subsequent research (Leo and Ofshe, 2001; Drizin and Leo, 2004), together with an ongoing database of DNA exonerations (Innocence Project, n.d.), in part spurred a series of enquiries into the legitimacy of the death penalty in the US (Leverick and Chalmers, 2014).

DNA evidence has not featured highly in most miscarriages of justice in the UK, making such studies impossible. Nevertheless, researchers have contributed to the scholarly analysis of miscarriages (Brandon and Davies, 1973; Walker and Starmer, 1999), with some work showing promise in terms of meeting Leo's (2010) call for the development of *theories* of miscarriages (see Naughton, 2013). In order to find research that has made the *biggest* impact in reducing miscarriages however, we must look to the 'specialised causes' literature (Leo, 2005: 210). Here, the research findings of psychiatrists and psychologists, working primarily in the US and UK on factors identified as causes of miscarriages, such as false confessions and erroneous eyewitness identification, are presented (see, for example, Gudjonsson, 2003; Horry et al., 2014). Such research confirms that these causes are comparable historically and globally (Radelet, 2013). Despite research highlighting a multiplicity of causes of miscarriages, studies worldwide indicate that the most frequent causes, are those linked to the police investigative process (Cutler, 2012). They include: i) reliance on circumstantial evidence; ii) fabrication of evidence; iii) non-disclosure of evidence; iv) unreliable cell confessions (Stevens, 2010); v) unreliable confessions due to external factors such as police pressure and/or internal factors, such as suspect vulnerabilities (Gudjonsson, 2003); and vi) unreliable victim and eyewitness identification and testimony (Forst, 2013).

Certainly, in the UK, many have asked 'What can we learn from miscarriages of justice?', resulting in attempts to address and reduce their causes. This is particularly the case in relation to psychological research, which has provided important information to help to explain such phenomena and suggest changes in legislation, policy and practice to improve the investigative process, with the aim of lessening future miscarriages. The following discussion outlines what we have, and can learn, from miscarriages of justice in the UK as the result of psychological research, and how subsequent reforms have worked to address and reduce their occurrence in a manner that Leo (2010) insists has not occurred in most other countries.

Miscarriages of justice and the investigative process: from building a case for conviction to building a case for convicting only the guilty

Although the responsibility for miscarriages of justice extends far and wide, the police investigative process plays a major role in their genesis (Savage and Milne, 2007). The contribution of the investigative process to causing injustice has been highlighted in many dreadful cases, including those of Timothy Evans and Derek Bentley, wrongly convicted and hanged for murder in the 1950s (Innocent, n.d.). However, the miscarriages which focussed a critical spotlight on the police investigative process more strongly than ever before were those associated with the Irish Republican Army's terrorist activities during the 1970s (May, 1994). In the case of the Birmingham Six, for example, suspects had not only been mentally and physically abused by police, evidence had been deliberately manipulated to fit in with the case that the police wished to present (Mullin, 1990). At face value, the miscarriages that resulted from such practices were caused by false confessions and fabrication of/tampering with evidence. However, stepping back from this, we might ask *why* confessions, for example, were such a focal concern of the investigative process in the first place. Clearly, the problems leading to these, and other miscarriages that came before and after them, go much deeper. Arguably, what most of these miscarriages have in common is that, from the early stages of their investigation, police officers *believed* they had the 'right' person and throughout the investigative process sought to confirm this belief. Potentially, these miscarriages were by-products of very human cognitive phenomena that led to problematic investigative decision-making (see Chapter 3, this volume) and ultimately inaction, incompetence and/or malfeasance (Findley and O'Brien, 2014).

Psychological research in this area has contributed to identifying how investigators make decisions, the factors that undermine the reliability of their decision-making and their contribution to causing miscarriages (Irving and Dunnighan, 1993; Ask and Granhag, 2005). In particular, it has established that the phenomenon most central to the miscarriages mentioned above is what has been called 'premature case closure' of police investigations. Psychologists initially alluded to this concept in relation to police interviewing, describing it as "the disposition to draw pre-emptive conclusions from information processed prior to conducting an interview" (Shepherd and Milne, 1999: 126). However, it is also applicable to the entire investigative process, whereby investigations which start with 'investigator openness' to consider many potential lines of inquiry, close, at an early stage, around a particular 'thesis' and accompanying suspect/s. Once this situation occurs, psychological research suggests that starting from the assumption that they have the guilty person, tunnel vision, belief perseverance and confirmation bias work in tandem towards 'successful' case construction, with detectives "selectively weav[ing] together available pieces of information … to produce a simplified [and] coherent story" (Sanders, Burton and Young, 2010: 368). Thus, premature closure operates around the logic of 'case construction' in that once a suspect is identified, the investigation alters from being a neutral, objective search, focussed upon 'What happened?', to being a search for information that supports suspicions that the suspect is the culprit (Maguire and Norris, 1992). In this situation, investigators have focussed on a particular conclusion and then filtered all information in a case through the 'tunnel-vision lens' provided by that conclusion. Through that filter, information supporting the conclusion is elevated in significance and deemed relevant and information which is inconsistent with the chosen theory is "overlooked or dismissed as irrelevant, incredible or unreliable" (Findley and Scott, 2006: 293). Indeed, psychological research has demonstrated how tunnel vision is both the *result* of fixation on a certain suspect (bias) and the *reason* for a one-sided search for more incriminating evidence or interpretation of evidence as incriminating (bias confirmation), even in the face of facts that point in the opposite direction (belief perseverance) (Ask, Rebellius and Granhag, 2008).

Importantly, as these problems that can undermine accuracy in the investigative process are caused by vulnerabilities underlying human cognition, they are unintentional. Thus, the investigator *unwittingly* assigns too much weight to evidence, which confirms their hypothesis, and too little to disconfirming evidence; and *inadvertently* clings to a belief in the face of evidence that discredits it (Findley and O'Brien, 2014). Additionally, another psychological phenomenon, namely 'groupthink', may also be operating here, in that investigators working as part of a close-knit team may seek to reduce conflict and promote consensus at the expense of questioning ideas and underlying assumptions (Orenstein, 2011). This may involve stifling dissent and self-censoring opinion that undermines the group's decisions (Tedlow, 2010). Clearly, in a police investigation this may exacerbate existing biases and undermine critical thinking, as recent revelations in Sweden's worst miscarriage of justice have demonstrated (see Crouch, 2015).

Certainly, the shift from considering *what happened* to *proving* it, presents a risk that investigators will overlook/minimise new evidence (perhaps calling into doubt the suspect's guilt) that contradicts an early theory of the case they have psychologically committed to (O'Brien, 2009). Psychological research has also established that when cognitive biases affect early evidence gathering and processing in this way, they can thereafter taint the *entire* process, impacting upon not only decisions made by police, but by other professionals involved in the case (Dror and Charlton, 2006). This can ultimately result in evidence against the suspect looking stronger than it actually is and may account for situations wherein innocent people find themselves in court with a compelling case against them. This problem arguably continues through to the appellate process where, considering that "the evidence and the State's resources have coalesced around a narrative of guilt which [frames] the case" (Findley and O'Brien, 2014: 40), to an appellate judge, the guilt hypothesis is particularly strong. Clearly, cognitive biases have implications for appellate review and evaluation of fresh evidence that the CJS convicted an innocent person, thereby overturning the version of events that everyone involved in the case had hitherto psychologically committed to (Nenkov and Gollwittzer, 2012).

Many miscarriages of justice seem to highlight that investigators in the cases operated on preconceived notions of guilt. In some cases, institutional cynicism around 'the usual suspect/s' (i.e. someone known to the police through previous convictions, is quickly focussed upon in their investigation) may have played a role (Poyser and Milne, 2015). Other psychological studies suggest that even 'inappropriate' emotional display in the accused early on in an investigation may lead investigators to adopt a mind-set that the suspect is guilty, causing them to neglect other investigative leads (Savage and Milne, 2007). Media, political and public pressure placed upon the investigation, particularly in child murder cases, may also be partly responsible. At times, this pressure can be almost unbearable, causing investigators to prioritise *speed* in bringing the case to a conclusion (Maguire, 2003) and creating a climate where the investigation can become 'ends' rather than 'means'-oriented. This may explain the alleged activities of officers in miscarriages associated with the child murders of Lesley Molseed and Carl Bridgewater (Innocent, n.d.). Clearly, environmental pressures may create the conditions for system failure, which, in the police investigative context, may be reflected in misconduct (Punch, 2003).

Allegations of misconduct appear in numerous miscarriages. Convinced of a suspect's guilt, the closed mind-set of investigating officers is sometimes pushed to the limit, with their activities proceeding beyond unintentionally constructing a case around a suspect, to intentional malfeasance/malpractice in suppressing, excluding and/or eradicating all that *does not* fit, and/or constructing evidence to ensure it *does* fit with the original 'guilt' narrative (Savage and Milne, 2007). Here, police may not only ignore the facts; they may demolish or invent them (Sanders et al., 2010). Some studies identify 'police malfeasance/malpractice' as featuring second only to eyewitness misidentification in wrongful convictions (Scheck, Neufeld and Dwyer, 2000). It also figures in some investigations, which fail to bring anyone to justice (Maguire, 2003: 376). There were allegations, for example, that such behaviour adversely affected the Stephen Lawrence murder investigation in 1993 (Peachey, 2012). This case also illustrates that premature investigative closure may also be a cause of miscarriages involving a failure to investigate a crime due to 'case denial', as here, officers whose investigative mind-set was arguably closed to the theory that the crime was racially motivated, failed to gather evidence with this in mind (Savage and Milne, 2007).

Clearly, psychological research has made major contributions to revealing cognitive weaknesses associated with investigative processes. Consequently, psychologists have made recommendations for improving and professionalising that process in the UK, aimed at minimising future miscarriages. In this way, the lessons learnt from miscarriages have helped to shape the investigative process of the future. This said, it was a specific miscarriage, namely the Lawrence case, which drove such recommendations through into policy and practice (Savage et al., 2009). In his inquiry into what could be learnt from the Lawrence miscarriage of justice, Sir William MacPherson (1999) identified several lessons relating to criminal investigation and made recommendations aimed at confronting the cognitive biases which had dominated it. Concerned with the quality of, and quality assurance measures absent throughout, the investigation into the murder, MacPherson's report emphasised the importance of review and oversight of the investigative process, so that if mistakes/miscalculations are made at one stage (such as those caused by cognitive biases), procedures are available to remedy them at later stages. Here, MacPherson was calling for greater openness in investigations (so as to counter the problem of premature case closure). He recommended that this should be achieved through conducting rigorous reviews of investigations and of the decision-making involved and that the Association of Chief Police Officers (ACPO) devise codes of practice to govern such reviews (Savage and Milne, 2007: 623).

Subsequently, the ACPO updated their policy guidelines on the investigation of major crimes through the *Murder Investigation Manual* (MIM) (see Chapter 3, this volume), with the aim of institutionalising formalised review of investigations (ACPO, 2006). The Professionalising the Investigative Process (PIP) programme (see also Chapter 12, this volume), launched by the ACPO in 2005, further aimed to enhance the investigative process through training and development of all police investigators (Centrex, 2005a). The Core Investigative Doctrine (CID) stated that this would be achieved through work-placed assessment and accreditation (Centrex, 2005b). The CID advises investigators to: challenge dubious assumptions, promote healthy scepticism, explain gut instincts, create, and be receptive to, the generation of alternative hypotheses, never rush to premature judgements regarding the meaning of material gathered and to test the 'null hypothesis' – i.e. to seek to disprove a theory (Centrex, 2005b: 23–63). Such advice is firmly rooted in the lessons learnt from miscarriages of justice.

The aforementioned discussion does not suggest that the task facing investigators has become simple. Indeed, it often remains extremely complex (Grieve 2014) and, therefore, we must certainly not assume 'problem solved'. As psychological research has highlighted, much of the investigative process is invisible, in terms of being behind closed-doors and cerebral. Therefore, challenges in ensuring that it is undertaken professionally will arguably remain (Stelfox, 2011). A doctrine alone cannot ensure the type of investigative mind-set which effective, fair investigation requires. Perhaps the analysis of lessons to be learnt from miscarriages of justice should feature in investigator training (Savage and Milne, 2007), because as recent miscarriages have demonstrated, cognitive biases continue to impede investigator decision-making. Indeed, as Barri White stressed when his murder conviction was recently quashed: "[After our arrest] it then became a selective investigation. They didn't look anywhere else [they] thought they had the right people" (Smith, 2013). Much remains to be learnt in this area, thereby providing continuing opportunities for psychological research. The same is true of the police interview process.

Miscarriages of justice and the police interview process

Whilst concern regarding the involvement of the police suspect interview process (see also Chapter 8, this volume) in contributing to miscarriages of justice did not begin with the Maxwell Confait murder investigation in 1972, it was this case that pinpointed the contribution of the interview process to causing them in the UK (Price and Caplan, 1977). Three youths were arrested, falsely confessed to Confait's murder and were found guilty at trial. However, in 1974 judges at the Court of Appeal quashed the convictions, labelling them as 'unsafe and unsatisfactory' and emphasising that the confessions upon which they were chiefly based had been extracted from the youths under improper police pressure (Williamson, 2007). Following the appeal, a public inquiry into the case established (from evidence provided by psychologists) that a flawed interview process coupled with the youths' psychological vulnerabilities had resulted in them falsely confessing (Fisher, 1977). These findings set the agenda for the subsequent Philips Commission (1981), which stressed the psychologically coercive nature of the police questioning process and found the Judges' Rules surrounding that process to be inadequate. Additionally, it highlighted the effects of custody on suspects (particularly the vulnerable) and sought reliability in terms of the information they provide during interviews (Steer, 1981). Changes to police practices and procedures were subsequently recommended based on the findings of psychological research into police working practices, authorised by the Commission. This research demonstrated that during interviews, police prioritised gaining a confession over searching for the truth of what happened in cases, and that this was leading to oppressive questioning and/or taking advantage of suspects' vulnerabilities (Baldwin and McConville, 1981; Irving, 1981; Irving and Hilgendorf, 1981; Softley, 1981).

Unfortunately, the widespread use of police threats and pressure during questioning continued, as later psychological research noted (Smith, 1983), thereby raising concerns about police conduct more generally. This was directly responsible for driving the enactment of the Police and Criminal Evidence Act (PACE) in 1984. PACE and its codes of practice provided a legislative foundation for the operation of police powers, suspects' rights and the regulation of custodial questioning designed to secure *fairness* and *transparency* in the process (Sanders et al., 2010). Section 66, covering detention, treatment and questioning of suspects in custody, aimed to protect suspects during the questioning process through ensuring their interviews were tape-recorded and that they were offered the right to free legal advice. It also moved to secure fair treatment of vulnerable, young and mentally disordered individuals and drove the later investigative interviewing agenda (Williamson, 2007). The establishment of another of Phillips' recommendations, the Crown Prosecution Service followed in 1985, removing the task of prosecuting offenders from the police (Scott, 2010).

Official recognition of the causes of miscarriages of justice had in part driven such reforms. However, they did not disburden the CJS of miscarriages or, as psychological research found, did they immediately improve the quality of police interviews. Interview quality remained poor and confession-focussed rather than searching for an accurate and reliable account of 'what happened' (McConville, Sanders and Leng, 1991; Baldwin, 1992), and miscarriages with causes similar to those revealed in the Confait case continued to occur (see Roberts, 2007). Clearly, individuals were still being negatively affected by poor police questioning and the safeguards in place to protect suspects were sometimes failing.

The exposure of poor suspect interviewing practices in many more miscarriages of justice during the 1980s and 1990s led to urgent calls for reform, indicating that lessons still needed to be learnt. This resulted in the establishment of the Runciman Commission (1993), which drew upon the findings of 22 research studies (see for example Irving and Dunnighan, 1993) examining the conduct, role and working practices of criminal justice practitioners. Its report revealed that although PACE had increased suspects' rights and introduced openness into the investigative process, gaining a confession remained investigators' priority. Changes in police interviewing practice and training were still required.

The latter came, to some extent, with the PEACE (a mnemonic for the Planning and Preparation, Engage and Explain, Account, Closure and Evaluation stages of an investigative interview: see Chapter 11, this volume, for an explanation of the stages) interviewing model (Milne and Bull, 1999). Developed by psychologists, this model recognised that information-gathering should play a core role in the planning and preparation for an interview, as well as the interview itself, and consisted of two interview types: i) 'conversation management' – for less co-operative interviewees (Shepherd, 1993) and ii) 'cognitive interview' – for more co-operative interviewees (Fisher and Geiselman, 1992).

The UK police subsequently trained over 120,000 officers in the PEACE model, training which a national evaluation found had (in combination with the recording of interviews) significantly improved the quality of suspect interviews (Clarke and Milne, 2001). Indeed, not only had officers' interviewing style improved (for example, there was a reduction in the use of leading questions), there was also more frequent provision of information as required by law, such as notifying the suspect of their right to legal advice. However, researchers also discovered that the listening skills of interviewing officers remained poor and that 10 per cent of interviews studied contained possible breaches of PACE (Sanders et al., 2010). Later psychological research concluded that ethical interviewing techniques emphasised by the PEACE model were commonly found in the police interviews analysed (Soukara et al., 2009) and that the PEACE model elicits a fuller account and, therefore, a better interview outcome (Walsh and Bull, 2010). Other research emphasised the need for refresher training (Griffiths and Milne, 2006). However, the fruits of psychological research in this area continued to ripen.

Following psychologists' national evaluation of police interviewing (Clarke and Milne, 2001), a five-tiered structure of interviewing skills, aimed at providing officers with theory-driven interview training specific to their career requirements and at developing other aspects of investigative interviewing (relating to vulnerable victims/witnesses and the supervision and monitoring of interviews), was developed (Griffiths and Milne, 2006). In 2007, this structure was incorporated into the PIP with the aim of increasing the professionalisation of all investigators. Subsequently, research has found that five-tier interview training has improved interviewing skills and resulted in the transmission of some of the best practice learnt to the wider workplace (Scott, 2010), with priority being placed upon an open-minded search for the truth and the collection of accurate information in investigative work more generally. Nevertheless, poor interviewing practices persist in some quarters, and though the introduction of PACE, PEACE and the five-tier training system has facilitated a change in the ethical conduct of interviews, many officers continue to believe that 'facts' are best secured in the form of a confession (Bearchell, 2010: 71). Therefore, even though improvements in the practice of police interviewing of suspects have been made, a confession focus and the allied risk of miscarriages occurring remain pressing concerns.

Interview processes with adult victims and witnesses

Recent research analysing victims' experiences of engaging with the CJS revealed that many felt it an experience worse than their "actual journey of being a victim" (Newlove, 2015). Crucial to any criminal investigation is the information provided by victims and witnesses. Criminal justice practitioners, particularly the police in their front-line public position, must not only treat victims and witnesses with respect they must conduct successful interviews with them so as to enable their voice to be heard; voices which contain information crucial to achieving justice in criminal cases. Conversely, poor interviews may lead to miscarriages of justice, which harm the victim of the wrongful conviction and the victim/witnesses of the original crime (Poyser and Milne, 2015).

Regrettably, psychological research examining interviews with adult victims and witnesses (see Chapter 6, this volume) has established that these are often poor in terms of their focus on statement-taking rather than trying to gather as much information as possible about the crime and very much police-led, sometimes benignly motivated in only supplying what they *think* the CJS needs (Shepherd and Milne, 2006). It has also found that the questioning techniques used are problematic, particularly relating to the use of leading questions, which can alter human memory (Milne and Bull, 1999). Since the introduction of the five-tier model of interviewing, additional psychological evaluations of police interviewing skills with victims and witnesses revealed that inexperienced frontline police officers, who conduct most witness interviews, felt under-trained, under pressure and ill-equipped to conduct a PEACE cognitive interview, despite receiving training (Dando, Wilcock and Milne, 2008). As witness interviews are not routinely recorded in England and Wales (unless involving vulnerable, intimidated and/or significant witnesses) (Ministry of Justice, 2011) this is of concern, particularly because, as recent miscarriages of justice have revealed, poor police questioning may result in unreliable witness testimony (see Morrison, 2013). Clearly, although in the UK psychological research has contributed to changing policy and practice in relation to victim/witness interviewing, through its recommendations for improvements to interviewing standards being incorporated into a national investigative interviewing strategy (ACPO, 2003), more work is required. A related area where psychological research is urgently required concerns the efficacy of police officers' contemporaneous handwritten statements (Westera, Kebbell and Milne, 2011). Indeed, it has been found that due to reliance on the interviewer's (fallible) memory of what was said (Conway, 2008), such statements (eventually presented in court as evidence) contain little detail (Rock, 2001) and many inaccuracies (McLean, 1995).

With the increased societal focus on the place of victims, and indeed witnesses, within the CJS (Newlove, 2015), the interviewing of these *key players* and their provision of accurate information regarding the criminal incidents they experience, is likely to gain heightened importance (Gabbert et al., 2016). Here, then, are favourable circumstances for psychologists and the CJS to join forces to help victims and witnesses impart reliable evidence, so as to achieve justice for all.

Miscarriages of justice and police procedures for eliciting eyewitness identification evidence

In 1976, Peter Hain, a victim a miscarriage of justice caused by erroneous witness identification, said: "We should not be blind as to the numbers … of people … that get gobbled up by the monster 'Mistaken Identity'" (in Robins, 2014: 129). Nearly 40 years on, this statement remains as pertinent as ever because, as research worldwide indicates, although each miscarriage is generally triggered by multiple factors, mistaken identification evidence continues to be *the* major cause (Huff and Killias, 2013). This is despite the many lessons learnt from psychological research (see also Chapter 7, this volume). Eyewitness identification is an influential component of the CJS, affecting virtually every aspect of the justice process, from the initial police investigation to trial, with most professionals viewing it as compelling evidence in criminal cases (Cutler, 2012). Psychological research has found, for example, that a positive identification can guide the police investigation towards/away from a suspect and that police officers believe that eyewitnesses are usually correct (Kebbell and Milne, 1998). Similarly, at trial, when a witness states "That's the person I saw", this is hugely compelling to a jury (Howitt, 2015). Identification evidence is, as psychological research has demonstrated, extremely fallible. However, it is also the second-most incriminating type of evidence after confession evidence (Kassin and Neuman, 1997), with wrongful convictions based upon such evidence being extremely difficult to rectify (Rowley, 2009).

The first records of miscarriages caused by mistaken eyewitness identification in England and Wales date back to 1735 (Shepherd, Ellis and Davies, 1982). However, it was not until 1860 that formal identification (ID) parades (i.e. placing a suspect amongst a group of his/her peers, and requesting that a witness see if they can identify the perpetrator of the crime) were introduced by the Metropolitan Police. Subsequently, procedures for such parades evolved, driven by the exposure of more miscarriages, including that of Adolf Beck who was wrongly convicted on two occasions (1896 and 1904) of defrauding women, having been erroneously identified by 10 out of 15 victims! (Naughton, 2013). The Court of Enquiry (1904) into Beck's case found that the ID parade was comprised of foils who did not resemble Beck! The Home Office subsequently revised the advisory codes of practice surrounding ID parades (Wilcock et al., 2008), and did so again in 1925 after an enquiry into another miscarriage, caused by mistaken identification, involving army officer Major Sheppard (Davies and Griffiths, 2008). These guidelines emphasised that foils should closely resemble the suspect and that s/he should be told that they may have a legal representative present during a parade. Still miscarriages caused by mistaken eyewitness identification continued, including those resulting in the innocent being hanged (see Robins, 2014).

The still *advisory* guidelines were revised once more in 1969 in response to miscarriages exposed in a communication from the National Council of Civil Liberties to the Home Office in which 15 wrongful convictions involving misidentification were detailed (Williamson, 2007). Circular (9/1969) stated that an officer of inspector rank or above with no knowledge of the case should conduct parades and witnesses should be instructed to say if they cannot make a positive identification (Wilcock et al., 2008). Unfortunately, however, miscarriages of this nature continued and crucially were beginning to attract media attention, thereby fuelling public controversy. These cases included that of Peter Hain, who later led the campaign 'Justice Against the Identification Laws' (JAIL) and that of George Davis (Poyser, 2012). However, it was the cases of Laszlo Virag and Luke Doherty, wrongly convicted in 1969 and 1972 respectively, that forced further change. When their convictions were quashed in 1974 on the basis of erroneous eyewitness identification, there was public outrage and a committee under Lord Devlin (1976), to review the law and procedures relating to ID parades, was established. The lessons learnt here would be those 'delivered' by 30 convictions based on mistaken identification including those previously mentioned, presented by the campaigning body JUSTICE (Robins, 2014). Devlin concluded that erroneous eyewitness identification evidence was a potent source of miscarriages and crucially requested that psychological research be conducted on it (Wilcock et al., 2008). Devlin's (1976) report recommended reforms including that: i) ID parades should be photographed for greater transparency and ii) if identification evidence was crucial in a case, judges should appraise the jury of any specific issues, such as if the witness viewed the crime in poor light. Devlin also urged that no one should be convicted on contested identification evidence alone; however, it remains the case today that a conviction can be secured on the uncorroborated evidence of a single eyewitness (Roberts, 2007).

Despite Devlin's recommendations, no action was immediately taken. However, in 1977 a landmark ruling in *R v Turnbull* (1976 63 Cr App R 132) resulted in specific guidelines being established governing the way a judge directs a jury when the evidence against a person rests on a disputed identification (Williamson, 2007). Under the Turnbull guidelines, many of Devlin's recommendations were realised in that judges were now *required* to warn juries to be cautious when relying on such evidence and to direct juries to relevant circumstances in which the crime occurred and the later identification took place (Sanders et al., 2010). In addition, police officers were also required to cover these issues when eliciting eyewitness accounts (Wilcock et al., 2008). Juries also had to be warned that a mistaken witness could nonetheless be a convincing one, and that many witnesses could all be mistaken. Seven years later *legislation* governing constructing and delivering ID parades came into force. PACE, 1984, Code D set out the procedures (revised since on several occasions) for the conduct of identification attempts, aiming to ensure that these were planned, monitored and properly recorded (Naughton, 2013). In addition, psychologists *did* respond to Devlin's request for more research to be conducted on eyewitness identification and their findings have resulted in more lessons being learnt and further improvements in procedures surrounding identification evidence, as outlined below.

The application of psychological research to this area

The 1970s in particular was a key phase in terms of Psychology's contribution to understanding witness identification performance, with ground-breaking work by Loftus (1979) in the US and Clifford and Bull (1978) in the UK. Through this, and subsequent studies, psychologists have shown that the roots of eyewitness fallibilities lie in human memory, which alters over time and is suggestible and susceptible to error (Thompson et al., 1998). More troubling is that their work since (including several meta-analyses), has consistently confirmed that eyewitnesses often perform at a level not better than chance (Memon, Hope and Bull, 2003). Psychological research has established that our ability to successfully remember a crime and identify its perpetrator, relies on three stages: i) perception and encoding of the crime, ii) retention of the information and iii) retrieval of that information (Wilcock et al., 2008) and that many factors, including i) social perceptions and demographic features of witnesses, ii) situational factors and iii) facets of interrogative situations, can influence any/all of these stages and therefore eyewitness performance in a) person descriptions and b) identification (Davies and Griffiths, 2008).

a) Person descriptions

Psychological research has demonstrated that many factors may affect eyewitness accuracy in providing person descriptions to police, whether in an initial emergency call (Ambler and Milne, 2006), a police interview (Milne and Bull, 1999) or whilst constructing facial composites (Wells, Charman and Olsen, 2005). These include factors relating to: i) *the witness themselves*, including age (Milne, 1999), gender (Sporer, 1996), ethnicity (Meissner and Brigham, 2001), and attitudes, experiences, expectations, prejudices and stereotypes (Chance, Goldstein and Sporer, 1996); ii) *conditions under which the crime was viewed*, including lighting (Sporer, 1996), stress levels of the witness/victim, the presence of a weapon at the scene (Steblay, 1992), witness involvement (Yuille and Tollestrup, 1992) and factors relating to attention paid to the event (Fruzzetti et al., 1992); and iii) *memory retrieval*, including time lapse between viewing the crime and giving a person description (Ellis, Davies and Shepherd, 1978), witness collaboration (Gabbert, Memon and Allan, 2003) and the way in which information about the crime is elicited from witnesses during a police interview. Here, the asking of leading questions (Milne and Bull, 1999) and repeating questions (Brown, Lloyd-Jones and Robinson, 2008) can affect the quality and quantity of person description.

As previously mentioned, tools developed by psychologists, such as the PEACE cognitive interview, have to some extent improved the quality and quantity of information gained from eyewitnesses during interviews (Milne and Bull, 1999). Psychologists have also suggested that such interviews are recorded electronically so as to ensure that all information reported is captured (Wilcock et al., 2008). Additionally, psychologists have stressed that because memory is malleable and fragile, it should be managed in the same way as a physical crime scene (to, as far as possible, preserve it and avoid contamination) (Wells and Loftus, 2001). However, presently this does not occur and therefore the risk of miscarriages caused by contaminated witness memory remains.

b) Person identification

Psychologists have discovered that many factors affect eyewitness accuracy in ID parades and have divided these into i) estimator variables (the effect of which on subsequent identification accuracy can only be estimated *after* a crime's occurrence and which, therefore, the police cannot control) and ii) system variables (that are under the control of the police) (Wells, 1978). The discussion below only briefly mentions estimator variables (see Chapter 6, this volume, for more detailed coverage of estimator variables as applicable to eyewitnesses) as psychological research on system variables has had more impact on criminal justice practice.

i) Estimator variables

Psychological research into the effect of estimator variables on eyewitness identification performance has been substantial, including two meta analyses (see Shapiro and Penrod, 1986; Narby, Cutler and Penrod, 1996). Such research has demonstrated that i) *witness factors* such as age (Valentine, Pickering and Darling, 2003), race (Meissner and Brigham, 2001), gender (Wright and Sladden, 2003), intelligence (Wojcikiewicz, 1990), personality (Hosch, 1994), occupation (Christianson, Karlsson and Persson, 1998), expectations and stereotypes (Kassin et al., 2001) and confidence (see Sporer et al., 1995; Brewer, 2006); ii) *perpetrator factors* such as race (Meissner and Brigham, 2001), gender (Shapiro and Penrod, 1986), distinctiveness of face (Valentine, 1991) and use of disguises (Patterson and Baddeley, 1977); and iii) *situational factors*, including stress and arousal (Deffenbacher et al., 2004), weapon presence (Loftus, Loftus and Messo, 1987), alcohol consumption (Dysart et al., 2002) and view of perpetrator (Shapiro and Penrod, 1986) may affect eyewitness accuracy (Dysart et al., 2002). These findings have permitted criminal justice practitioners to make more informed decisions on the impact of some estimator variables upon later identification performance (Wilcock et al., 2008).

ii) System variables

A lesson to be learnt from miscarriages of justice is that inadequate procedures used by the CJS are often responsible for mistaken identifications (Bedau and Radelet, 1987). Psychological research conducted on system variables has demonstrated the utility of one procedure over another, thereby helping to steer current UK legislation and guidelines and improve methods relating to ID parades (Wilcock et al., 2008). Examples of system variables include line-up construction, presentation and administration.

In relation to constructing line-ups, psychological research has demonstrated the importance of considering: i) numbers of suspects per parade – recommending one per parade; ii) size of parade – recommending that the larger the parade, the less likely the suspect will be identified by chance alone; and iii) bias in a parade – recommending that all foils should be *viable* alternatives to the suspect (Wells and Turtle, 1986). These recommendations have influenced PACE Code D, which stipulates that a parade must contain at least eight foils selected via the 'match to similarity of suspect method' (Darling, Valentine and Memon, 2008).

Regarding presentation of a line-up, psychological research has found little difference between live, video tape and photo line-ups in terms of witness performance (Shapiro and Penrod, 1986). However, as video parades are easier, cheaper, more convenient for witnesses and possibly fairer to suspects from all ethnicities (see Valentine, Darling and Memon, 2007), they are used in the UK. Psychological research has been unable to conclude whether, in order to reduce erroneous identifications, line-up members should be presented simultaneously or sequentially (as is the case in the UK) (Lindsay and Wells, 1985; Flowe, 2014). Therefore, further research is required.

Regarding administration of a line-up, the findings of psychological research suggest that line-ups should be administered double-blind, where the administrator is naïve to the suspect's identity and position (to avoid inadvertent transmission of cues to the witness) (Garrioch and Brimacombe, 2001). It has also established that line-up instructions given to witnesses should inform them that the perpetrator may not be there. This reduces erroneous identifications (Malpass and Devine, 1981) and is a requirement of PACE Code D.

What else could we learn?

Psychological research has made major contributions to our understanding of identification procedures and has guided legislation relating to line-ups, thereby making them fairer to witnesses and innocent suspects. However, before ending this discussion, we must also acknowledge psychological research concerning voice identification, which indicates that it is considerably error prone (Clifford, 1980; Philippon et al., 2007). Further research is also required to understand why vulnerable witnesses (due to, for example, their age or learning disabilities) are particularly prone to making false identifications from line-ups (Pozzulo, 2014; Wilcock and Bull, 2014). The CJS needs to urgently understand which investigative methods might aid their performance in target absent situations (Wilcock et al., 2008).

Further psychological research is also arguably required in order to understand why, despite the regulations/guidelines surrounding this area, criminal justice practitioners still sometimes fail to do what they are required to do. This includes judges failing to give correct Turnbull warnings (see Naughton, 2013) and police officers failing to comply with the regulations governing how they must obtain identification evidence. Indeed, as noted at Patrick Quinn's recent successful appeal: "Where a detailed regime regarding eyewitness identification is laid down in a statutory code … it is not for the police to substitute their own rules and procedures" (*R v Quinn*, p. 481 cited in Naughton, 2013: 90). Such miscarriages strengthen calls for psychologists to continue to conduct research in this area, where possible, through careful consideration of actual cases (Kebbell, Milne and Wagstaff, 1999).

Conclusion

Some errors – structural, systemic and even malign – are perhaps inevitable in all human systems and the CJS is no exception (Grieve, 2007). Miscarriages of justice are generated by a multitude of factors, which we can never rid the system of entirely (Forst, 2013). Nevertheless, we should take all steps possible in order to learn from our experiences and minimise their occurrence. As many of the causes of miscarriages relate to police investigative philosophy, strategy and tactics, and in particular interview and identification processes, most of these steps should arguably be centred on these issues. Certainly, there is an ongoing opportunity for criminal justice practitioners to learn many lessons from miscarriages of justice and to make appropriate changes to policy and practice in doing so. Psychological theory and research has, we have argued, made huge contributions to our understanding of some of the causes of miscarriages, thereby helping us to learn those lessons, which include the fact that: i) high-calibre pre-trial investigation and custodial questioning processes will reduce reliance on confession evidence and encourage a search for the truth; ii) good quality and more thorough questioning of victims and witnesses will enable them to provide their best evidence; iii) greater sensitivity in dealing with, and interviewing, vulnerable individuals, will permit them to give their best interview and identification evidence and iv) criminal justice practitioners' adherence to due process rules and regulations will ensure that the efforts of psychologists in these areas are not wasted. Psychological research has demonstrated, through its practical impact, that the risk of miscarriages of justice occurring can be minimised through such measures. Crucially however there remains much work to be done and a range of opportunities for psychologists to continue to identify weaknesses and propose reform based on scientific research of the kind that has been so valuable in reducing miscarriages to date. In addition, recent austerity measures must not be allowed to undermine the progress that psychology has helped to instigate (Grieve, 2014). After all, surely a civilised society is *morally obliged* to ask 'What can we learn from miscarriages of justice?' At the very least, it owes all the victims of its mistakes and malfeasance, this, so as to try to meet their appeal for "no one else [to] suffer what I've been through" (victim cited in Poyser, Nurse and Milne, in press).

References

ACPO (2003). Investigative interviewing strategy. National Steering Committee on Investigative Interviewing. Unpublished paper.

ACPO (2006). *Murder investigation manual.* London: National Centre for Policing Excellence.

Ambler, C. and Milne, R. (2006). Call handling centres – an evidential opportunity or threat? Paper presented at the Second International Interviewing Conference, Portsmouth, July.

Ask, K. and Granhag, P.A. (2005). Motivational sources of confirmation bias in criminal investigations: The need for cognitive closure. *Journal of Investigative Psychology and Offender Profiling*, 2, 43–63.

Ask, K., Rebellius, A. and Granhag, P.A. (2008). The elasticity of criminal evidence: A moderator of investigator bias. *Applied Cognitive Psychology*, 22, 1245–1259.

Baldwin, J. (1992). Video taping police interviews with suspects – an evaluation. Police Research Series Paper 1. London:The Home Office.

Baldwin, J. and McConville, M. (1981). *Confessions in Crown Court trials.* Research Study No 5, Royal Commission on Criminal Procedure. Cmnd 8092. London: HMSO.

BBC (2015). Barry George in protest over compensation rules. 23 February. Available from: http://www.bbc.co.uk/news/uk-31578422 [accessed 24 February 2015].

Bearchell, J. (2010). UK police interviews with suspects: A short modern history. In J. Adler and J. Gray (eds), *Forensic psychology: Concepts, debates and practice.* Cullompton, UK: Willan, pp. 58–71.

Bedau, H.A. and Radelet, M.L. (1987). Miscarriages of justice in potentially capital cases. *Stanford Law Review*, 40, 21–179.

Borchard, E.M. (1932). *Convicting the innocent: Sixty-five actual errors of criminal justice.* Garden City, NY: Doubleday.

Bowcott, O. (2015). Victims of crime let down by criminal justice system, reports finds. *The Guardian*, 27 January. Available from: http://www.theguardian.com/uk- news/2015/jan/27/victims-crime-let-down-criminal-justice-newlove [accessed 28 January].

Brandon, R. and Davies, C. (1973). *Wrongful imprisonment: Mistaken convictions and their consequences.* London: Allen & Unwin.

Brants, C. (2008). The vulnerability of Dutch criminal procedure to wrongful conviction. In R.C. Huff and M. Killias (eds), *Wrongful conviction: International perspectives on miscarriages of justice.* Philadelphia, PA: Temple University Press, pp. 157–181.

Brewer, N. (2006). Uses and abuses of eyewitness identification confidence. *Legal and Criminological Psychology*, 11, 3–23.

Brown, C., Lloyd-Jones, T. and Robinson, M. (2008). Eliciting person descriptions from eyewitnesses: A survey of police perceptions of eyewitness performance and use of interview techniques. *Special Edition European Journal of Cognitive Psychology.*

Campbell, D. (2015). Changes to compensation rules put the judicial system's fairness and integrity at risk. *The Guardian*, 23 February. Available from: http://www.theguardian.com/commentisfree/2015/feb/23/britain-refusing-compensate-victims-miscarriage-justice [accessed 24 February 2015].

Centrex (2005a). *Professionalising police investigation programme.* London: National Centre for Policing Excellence.

Centrex (2005b). *Core Investigative Doctrine.* London: National Centre for Policing Excellence.

Chance, J.E., Goldstein, A.G. and Sporer, S.L. (1996). The other-race effect and eyewitness identification. In R.S. Malpass and G. Koehnken (eds), *Psychological issues in eyewitness identification.* Hillsdale, NJ: Lawrence Erlbaum Associates, pp. 153–176.

Christianson, K.A., Karlsson, I. and Persson, L.G.W. (1998). Police personnel as eyewitnesses to a violent crime. *Legal and Criminological Psychology*, 3, 59–72.

Clarke, C. and Milne, R. (2001). *National evaluation of the PEACE investigative interviewing course*. London: Home Office.

Clifford, B. (1980). Voice identification by human listeners. *Law and Human Behaviour*, 4, 373–394.

Clifford, B.R. and Bull, R. (1978). *The psychology of person identification*. London: Routledge.

Connors, E., Lundregan, T., Miller, N. and McEwen, T. (1996). *Convicted by juries, exonerated by science: Case studies in the use of DNA evidence to establish innocence after trial*. Rockville, MD: National Institute of Justice.

Conway, M.A. (2008). *Guidelines on memory and the law: Recommendations from the scientific study of human memory*. Leicester, UK: British Psychological Society.

Crouch, D. (2015). Lawyers blame groupthink in Sweden's worst miscarriage of justice. *The Guardian*, Friday 5 June.

Cutler, B. (2012). *Convictions of the innocent: Lessons from psychological research*. Washington, DC: American Psychological Association.

Dando, C., Wilcock, R. and Milne, R. (2008). The cognitive interview: Inexperienced police officers' perceptions of their witness/victim interviewing practices. *Legal and Criminological Psychology*, 13, 59–70.

Darling, S., Valentine, T. and Memon, A. (2008). Selection of line up foils in operational contexts. *Applied Cognitive Psychology*, 22, 159–169.

Davies, G. and Griffiths, L. (2008). Eyewitness identification and the English courts: A century of trial and error. *Psychiatry, Psychology and Law*, 15(3), 435–449.

Deffenbacher, K.A., Bornstein, B.H., Penrod, S.D. and McGorty, E.K. (2004). A meta-analytic review of the effects of high stress on eyewitness memory. *Law and Human Behaviour*, 28, 687–786.

Devlin, LordP. (1976). *Report to the Secretary of State for the Home Department of the Departmental Committee on Evidence of Identification in Criminal Cases*. 26 April 1976. London: HMSO.

Drizin, S.A. and Leo, R.A. (2004). The problem of false confessions in the post-DNA world. *North Carolina Law Review*, 82, 891–1007.

Dror, I.E. and Charlton, D. (2006). Why experts make errors. *Journal of Forensic Identification*, 56(4), 600–616.

Dysart, J.E., Lindsay, R., MacDonald, T.K. and Wicke, C. (2002). The intoxicated witness: Effects of alcohol on identification accuracy. *Journal of Applied Psychology*, 87, 107–175.

Ellis, H.D., Davies, G.M. and Shepherd, J.W. (1978). A critical examination of the photoFIT system for recalling faces. *Ergonomics*, 21, 297–307.

Findley, K.A. and O'Brien, B. (2014). Psychological perspectives: Cognition and decision making. In A. Redlich, J.R. Acker, R.J. Norris and C.L. Bonventre (eds), *Examining wrongful convictions: Stepping back, moving forward*, Durham, NC: Carolina Academic Press, pp. 35–53.

Findley, K.A. and Scott, M.S. (2006). The multiple dimensions of tunnel vision in criminal cases. *Wisconsin Law Review*, 291, 291–397.

Fisher, Henry, Sir (1977). *Report of an Inquiry by the Hon. Sir Henry Fisher into the circumstances leading to the trial of three persons on charges arising out of the death of Maxwell Confait and the fire at 27, Doggett Road, London SE6*. London: HMSO.

Fisher, R. and Geiselman, R. (1992). *Memory-enhancing techniques for investigative interviewing: The cognitive interview*. Springfield, IL: Thomas.

Flowe, H.D. (2014). Emergence of the 'Simultaneous Superiority Effect' – A curious paradigm shift in eyewitness identification research. Invited talk, Nottingham Trent University.

Ford, R. (1998). Motorists awarded conviction payouts. *The Times*, 25 June.

Forst, B. (2013). Wrongful convictions in a world of miscarriages of justice. In C.R. Huff and M. Killias (eds), *Wrongful conviction and miscarriages of justice: Causes and remedies in North American and European criminal justice systems*. London: Routledge, pp. 15–43.

Frank, J. and Frank, B. (1957). *Not guilty*. New York: Doubleday.

Fruzzetti, A.E., Toland, K., Teller, S.A. and Loftus, E.F. (1992). Memory and eyewitness testimony. In M. Gruneberg and P. Morris (eds), *Aspects of memory, 1: The practical aspects*. New York: Routledge, pp. 18–50.

Gabbert, F., Memon, A. and Allan, K. (2003). Memory conformity: Can eyewitnesses influence each other's memories for an event? *Applied Cognitive Psychology*, 17, 533–543.

Gabbert, F., Hope, L.Carter, E., Boon, R. and Fisher, R. (2016). Communicating with witnesses: The role of initial witness accounts within the investigative process. In G. Oxburgh, T. MykelbustT. Grant andR. Milne (eds), *Communication in investigative and legal contexts: A handbook*. Chichester: Wiley.

Gardner, B. (2015). Theresa May to order probe into collapse of police corruption trial. *The Telegraph*, 9 February. Available from: http://www.telegraph.co.uk/news/uknews/crime/11401999/Theresa-May-to-order-probe-into-collapse-of-police-corruption-trial.html [accessed 12 March 2015].

Garrioch, L. and Brimacombe, A.A. (2001). Line up administrators' expectations: Their impact on eyewitness confidence. *Law and Human Behaviour*, 25, 299–315.

GrieveJ. (2007). Behavioural sciences and the law: Investigation. In D. Carson, R. Milne, F. Pakes, H. Shalev and A. Shawyer (eds), *Applying psychology to criminal justice*. Chichester, UK: Wiley, pp. 39–64.

GrieveJ. (2014). *The Stephen Lawrence Inquiry: A case study in policing and complexity*. In A. Pyecroft and C. Bartollas (eds), *Applying complexity theory*. Bristol: Policy Press, pp. 141–158.

Griffiths, A. and Milne, R. (2006). Will it all end in tiers? Police interviews with suspects in Britain. In T. Williamson (ed.), *Investigative interviewing: Rights, research and regulation*. Cullompton, UK: Willan, pp. 167–189.

Gudjonsson, G.J. (2003). *The psychology of interrogations and confessions*. Chichester, UK: Wiley.

Hall, A. (1994). It couldn't happen today? In M. McConville and L. Bridges (eds), *Criminal justice in crisis*. Aldershot, UK: Edward Elgar, pp. 313–321.

Horry, T., Halford, P., Brewes, N., Milne, R. and Bull, R. (2014). Archival analyses of eyewitness identification test outcomes: What can they tell us about eyewitness memory? *Law and Human Behaviour*, 38(1), 94–108.

Hosch, H. (1994). Individual differences in personality and eyewitness identification. In J.D. Read, D.F. Ross and M.P. Togilia (eds), *Adult eyewitness testimony: Current trends and developments*. New York: Cambridge University Press, pp. 328–347.

Howitt, D. (2015). *Introduction to forensic and criminal psychology* (5th edition). London: Pearson.

Huff, R.C. and Killias, M. (eds). (2013). *Wrongful convictions and miscarriages of justice: Causes and remedies in North American and European criminal justice systems*. London: Routledge.

Huff, C.R., Rattner, A. and Sagarin, E. (1986). Guilty until proven innocent: Wrongful conviction and public policy. *Crime and Delinquency*, 32, 518–544.

Innocence Project (n.d.) [online]. Available from: http://www.innocenceproject.org/ [accessed 13 March 2015].

Innocent (n.d.) [online]. Available from: http://www.innocent.org.uk/ [accessed 13 March 2015].

Irving, B. (1981). *Police interrogation: A case study of current practice*. Royal Commission on Criminal Procedure. London: HMSO.

Irving, B. and Dunnighan, C. (1993). *Human factors in quality control in CID investigations*. Royal Commission on Criminal Justice. London: HMSO.

Irving, B. and Hilgendorf, L. (1981). *Police interrogation: The psychological approach*. Royal Commission on Criminal Procedure. London: HMSO.

Justice Committee (2014). *Justice Committee – Fourth Report. Joint Enterprise: Follow-up*, 10 December 2014. London: House of Commons.

Kassin, S.M. and Neuman, K. (1997). On the power of confession evidence: An experimental test of the fundamental difference hypothesis. *Law and Human Behaviour*, 21, 469–484.

Kassin, S.M., Tubb, V.A., Hosch, H.M. and Memon, A. (2001). On the general acceptance of eyewitnesss testimony research. *American Psychologist*, 56, 405–416.

Kebbell, M. and Milne, R. (1998). Police officers' perceptions of eyewitness performance in forensic investigations. *Journal of Social Psychology*, 138(3), 323–330.

Kebbell, M., Milne, R. and Wagstaff, G. (1999). The Cognitive Interview: A survey of its forensic effectiveness. *Psychology, Crime, & Law*, 5, 101–115.

Leo, R.A. (2005). Rethinking the study of miscarriages of justice: Developing a criminology of wrongful conviction. *Journal of Contemporary Criminal Justice*, 21(3), 201–223.

Leo, R.A. (2010). From false confession to wrongful conviction: Seven psychological processes. *Journal of Psychiatry and the Law*, 38, 9–56.

Leo, R.A. and Ofshe, R. (2001). The truth about false confessions and advocacy scholarship. *The Criminal Law Bulletin*, 37, 293–370.

Leverick, F. and Chalmers, J. (2014). Causes of wrongful conviction. In J. Chalmers, F. Leverick and A. Shaw (eds), *Post-corroboration safeguards review report of the academic expert group*. Edinburgh: The Scottish Government, pp. 30–43.

Lindsay, R.C. and Wells, G.L. (1985). Improving eyewitness identifications from line-ups: Simultaneous versus sequential line up presentation. *Journal of Applied Psychology*, 70, 556–564.

Loftus, E. (1979). *Eyewitness testimony*. Cambridge, MA: Harvard University Press.

Loftus, E.F., Loftus, G.R. and Messo, J. (1987). Some facts about 'weapon-focus'. *Law and Human Behaviour*, 11, 55–62.

Macpherson of Cluny, SirW. (1999) The Stephen Lawrence Inquiry. Cm 4262–4261. London: HMSO.

Maguire, M. (2003). *Criminal investigation and crime control*. In T. Newburn (ed.), *Handbook of policing*. Cullompton, UK: Willan, pp. 363–393.

Maguire, M. and Norris, C. (1992). *The conduct and supervision of criminal investigations*. Royal Commission on Criminal Justice Research Report 5. London: HMSO.

Malpass, R.S. and DevineP.G. (1981) Eyewitness identification: Line-up instruction and the absence of the offender. *Journal of Applied Psychology*, 66, 482–489.

MayJ. (1994) *Report of the Inquiry into the circumstances surrounding the convictions arising out of the bomb attacks in Guildford and Woolwich in 1974*. London: HMSO.

McLean, M. (1995). Quality investigation? Police interviewing of witnesses. *Medicine, Science and the Law*, 35, 116–122.

McConville, M., Sanders, A. and Leng, R. (1991). *The case for the prosecution: Police suspects and the construction of criminality*. London: Routledge.

Meissner, C.A. and Brigham, J.C. (2001). Thirty years of investigating the own-race bias in memory for faces: A meta-analytic review. *Psychology, Public Policy and Law*, 7, 3–35.

Memon, A., Hope, L. and Bull, R. (2003). Exposure duration effects on eyewitness accuracy and confidence. *British Journal of Psychology*, 94, 339–354.

Milne, R. (1999). False testimony. In R. Milne and R. Bull (eds), *Investigative interviewing: Psychology and practice*. Chichester: Wiley, pp. 91–110.

Milne, R. and Bull, R. (1999). *Investigative interviewing: Psychology and practice*. Chichester: Wiley.

Ministry of Justice (2011). *Achieving best evidence in criminal proceedings: Guidance on interviewing victims and witnesses and on achieving special measures*. London: Home Office.

Morris, S. (2015). South Wales agencies heavily criticised over triple murderer Carl Mills. *The Guardian*. Thursday 26 February. http://www.theguardian.com/uk-news/2015/feb/26/south-wales-agencies-heavily-criticised-over-triple-murderer-carl-mills [accessed 1 March 2015].

Morrison, S. (2013). Second ordeal for Sam months after jail release. *The Independent*. Tuesday 25 June. http://www.independent.co.uk/news/uk/crime/second-ordeal-for-sam-hallam-months-after-jail-release-8673738.html [accessed 1 March 2015].

Mullin, C. (1990). *Error of judgement: The truth about the Birmingham bombings*. Dublin: Poolbeg.

Narby, D.J., Cutler, B.L. and Penrod, S.D. (1996). The effects of witness, target and situational factors on eyewitness identification. In S.L. Sporer, R.S. Malpass and G. Kohnken (eds), *Psychological issues in eyewitness identification*. Mahwah, NJ: Erlbaum, pp. 23–52.

Naughton, M. (2013). *The innocent and the criminal justice system: A sociological analysis*. Basingstoke, UK: Palgrave.

Naughton, M. (2014). Criminologizing wrongful convictions. *British Journal of Criminology*, 45(2), 165–182.

Nenkov, G.Y. and Gollwitzer, P.M. (2012). Pre versus post-decisional deliberation and goal commitment: The positive effects of defensiveness. *Journal of Experimental Social Psychology*, 48(1), 106–121.

Newlove, B. (2015). Victims still let down by justice agencies. 27 January 2015. http://victimscommissioner.org.uk/baroness-newlove-victims-still-let-down-by-justice-agencies/ [accessed 10 February 2015].

O'Brien, B. (2009). Prime suspect: An examination of factors that aggravate and counteract confirmation bias in criminal investigations. *Psychology, Public Policy and Law*, 15, 315–334.

Orenstein, A. (2011). Facing the unfaceable: Dealing with prosecutorial denial in post-conviction cases of actual innocence. *San Diego Law Review*, 48(1), 401–446.

Patterson, K.E. and Baddeley, A.D. (1977). When face recognition fails. *Journal of Experimental Psychology: Human Learning and Memory*, 3, 406–417.

Peachey, P. (2012). After 19 years, Stephen Lawrence police face corruption investigation. *The Independent*. Retrieved December 30, 2012 from http://www.independent.co.uk/news/uk/crime/after-19-years-stephen-lawrence-police-face-corruption-investigation-7738003.html [accessed 15 March 2015].

Penrod, S., Read, D. and Cutler, B.L. (1995). Choosing, confidence and accuracy: A meta-analysis of the confidence-accuracy relation in eyewitness identification studies. *Psychological Bulletin*, 118, 315–327.

Philippon, A.C., Cherryman, J., Bull, R. and Vrij, A. (2007). Earwitness identification performance: The effect of language, target, deliberate strategies, and indirect measures. *Applied Cognitive Psychology*, 21(4), 417–556.

Philips, Sir C. (1981). *The Royal Commission on Criminal Procedure*. Cmnd 8092. London. HMSO.

Poyser, S. (2012). Calling for renewed media interest. In J. Robins (ed.), *Wrongly accused: Who is responsible for investigating miscarriages of justice?*London: Waterlow, pp. 46–50.

Poyser, S. and Milne, R. (2015). No grounds for complacency and plenty for continued vigilance: Miscarriages of justice as drivers for research on reforming the investigative interviewing process. *Policing and Society*, 88(4), 265–280.

Poyser, S., Nurse, A. and Milne, R. (in press). *Miscarriages of justice*. Bristol: Policy Press.

Pozzulo, J. (2014). Person description and identification by child witnesses. In R. Lindsay, D. Ross, J. Read and P. Toglia (eds), *Handbook of eyewitness psychology volume 2*. New York: Psychology Press, pp. 283–307.

Price, C. and Caplan, J. (1977). *The Confait confessions*. London: Marion Boyars.

Punch, M. (2003). *Control in the police organisation*. London: MIT press.

Radelet, M. (2013). Foreword. In R.C. Huff and M. Killias (eds), *Wrongful convictions and miscarriages of justice: Causes and remedies in North American and European criminal justice systems*. London: Routledge, pp. xv–xviii.

Radin, E.D. (1964). *The innocents*. New York: Morrow.

Roberts, P. (2007). Law and criminal investigation. In T. Newburn, T. Williamson and A. Wright (eds), *Handbook of criminal investigation*. Cullompton, UK: Willan, pp. 92–145.

Robins, J. (2014). *The first miscarriage of justice*. London: Waterside.

Rowley, S. (2009). Wrongful conviction throws spotlight on unreliability of eyewitness evidence. *The Guardian*, Tuesday 18 August. http://www.theguardian.com/uk/2009/aug/18/eyewitness-evidence-wrongful-conviction [accessed 15 March 2015].

Rock, F. (2001). The genesis of a witness statement. *Forensic Linguistics*, 8, 44–72.

Runciman, Viscount of Doxford, CBE. FBA (1993). *The Royal Commission on Criminal Justice*. Cm 2263. London: HMSO.

Sanders, A., Burton, M. and Young, R. (2010). *Criminal justice*. Oxford: OUP.

Savage, S. (2007). *Police reform: Forces for change*. Oxford: OUP.

Savage, S., Grieve, J. and Poyser, S. (2007). Putting wrongs to rights: Campaigns against miscarriages of justice. *Criminology and Criminal Justice*, 7(1), 83–106.

Savage, S., Grieve, J. and Poyser, S. (2009). Lawrence as a miscarriage of justice. In J. Grieve, N. Hall and S. Savage (eds), *Policing and the legacy of Lawrence: Policy and practice a decade on from the Lawrence Inquiry*. Cullompton, UK: Willan, pp. 25–40.

Savage, S. and Milne, R. (2007). Miscarriages of justice. In T. Newburn, T. Williamson and A. Wright (eds), *Handbook of criminal investigation*. Cullompton, UK: Willan, pp. 610–627.

Scheck, B., Neufeld, P. and Dwyer, J. (2000). *Actual innocence: Five days to execution and other dispatches from the wrongly convicted*. New York: Doubleday.

Scott, A. (2010). *Forensic psychology*. London: Palgrave Macmillan.

Shapiro, P.N. and Penrod, S. (1986). Meta-analysis of facial identification studies. *Psychological Bulletin*, 100, 139–156.

Shepherd, E. (1993). Ethical interviewing. *Issues in Criminological & Legal Psychology*, 18, 46–56.

Shepherd, J.W., Ellis, H.D. and Davies, G. (1982). *Identification evidence: A psychological evaluation*. Aberdeen: Aberdeen University Press.

Shepherd, E. and Milne, R. (1999). Full and faithful: Ensuring quality practice and integrity of outcome in witness interviews. In A. Heaton-Armstrong, D. Wolchover and E. Shepherd (eds), *Analysing witness testimony*. London: Blackstone Press, pp. 124–145.

Shepherd, E. and Milne, R. (2006). Have you told the management about this? Bringing witness interviewing into the 21st century. In A. Heaton-Armstrong, E. Shepherd, G. Gudjonsson and D. Wolchover (eds), *Witness testimony: Psychological, investigative, and evidential perspectives*. Oxford: Oxford University Press, pp. 131–152.

Smith, D.J. (1983). *Police and people in London: A survey of Londoners*. London: Policy Studies Institute.

Smith, V. (2013). 1m compensation for men who were wrongly jailed for teenager's murder. *The Mirror*, 27 September. Available from: http://www.mirror.co.uk/news/uk-news/barri-white-keith-hyatt-line-2308185 [accessed 21 March 2015].

Softley, P. (1981). *Police interrogation: An observational study in four police stations*. Research Study No. 4, Royal Commission on Criminal Procedure. Cmnd 8092. London: HMSO.

Soukara, S., Bull, R., Virj, A., Turner, M. and Cherryman, J. (2009). What really happens in police interviews of suspects? Tactics and confessions. *Psychology, Crime and Law*, 15, 493–506.

Sporer, S. (1996). Psychological aspects of person descriptions. In S. Sporer, R. Malpass and G. Kohnken (eds), *Psychological issues in eyewitness identification*. Mahwah, NJ: Erlbaum, pp. 53–86.

Sporer, S.L., Penrod, S.D., Read, D. and Cutler, B.L. (1995). Choosing, confidence and accuracy: A meta-analysis of the confidence-accuracy relation in eyewitness identification studies. *Psychological Bulletin*, 118, 315–327.

Steblay, N.M. (1992). A meta-analytic review of the weapon focus effect. *Law and Human Behaviour*, 16, 413–424.

Steer, D. (1981). *Uncovering crime: The police role*. Research Study No. 7, Royal Commission on Criminal Procedure. Cmnd 8092. London: HMSO.

Stelfox, P. (2011). Criminal investigation: Filling the skills gap in leadership, management, and supervision. *Policing*, 5(1), 15–22.

Stevens, D.J. (2010). *Introduction to American policing*. Sudbury, MA: Jones and Bartlett.

Tedlow, R.S. (2010). *Denial: Why business leaders fail to look facts in the face and what to do about it*. New York: Portfolio.

Thompson, C.P., Hermann, D.J., Read, J.D., Bruce, D., Payne, D. and Toglia, M. (eds). (1998). *Eyewitness memory: Theoretical and applied perspectives*. Mahwah, NJ: Erlbaum.

Valentine, T. (1991). A unified account of the effects of distinctiveness, inversion and race in face recognition. *The Quarterly Journal of Experimental Psychology*, 43, 161–204.

Valentine, T., Darling, S. and Memon, A. (2007). Do strict rules and moving images increase the reliability of sequential identification procedures. *Applied Cognitive Psychology*, 21, 933–949.

Valentine, T., Pickering, A. and Darling, S. (2003). Characteristics of eyewitness identification that predict the outcome of real line-ups. *Applied Cognitive Psychology*, 17, 969–993.

Walker, C. (1999). Miscarriages of justice in principle and practice. In C. Walker and K. Starmer (eds), *Miscarriages of justice: A review of justice in error*. London: Blackstone Press, pp. 31–62.

Walker, C. and Starmer, K. (eds). (1999). *Justice in error*. London: Blackstone Press.

Walsh, D. and Bull, R. (2010). What really is effective in interviews with suspects? A study comparing interviewing skills against interviewing outcomes. *Legal and Criminal Psychology*, 15, 305–321.

Weber, L. and Bowling, B. (2012). *Stop and search: Police power in global context*. London: Routledge.

Wells, G.L. (1978). Applied eyewitness testimony research: System variables and estimator variables. *Journal of Personality and Social Psychology*, 36, 1546–1557.

Wells, G.L. (1985). Verbal descriptions of faces from memory: Are thy diagnostic of identification accuracy? *Journal of Applied Psychology*, 70, 619–626.

Wells, G.L., Charman, S.D. and Olsen, E.A. (2005). Building face composites can harm line- up identification performance. *Journal of Experimental Psychology: Applied*, 11, 147–156.

Wells, G.L. and Turtle, J.W. (1986). Eyewitness identification: The importance of line-up models. *Psychological Bulletin*, 99, 320–329.

Westera, N., Kebbell, M. and Milne, R. (2011). Interviewing witnesses: Will investigative and evidential requirements ever concord? *British Journal of Forensic Practice*, 13, 103–113.

Wilcock, R. and Bull, R. (2014). Improving the performance of older eyewitnesses on identification procedures. In M. Toglia, D. Ross, J. Pozzulo and E. Pica (eds), *The elderly eyewitness in court*. New York: Psychology Press, pp. 118–134.

Wilcock, R., Bull, R. and Milne, R. (2008). *Criminal identification by witnesses: Psychology and practice*. Oxford: Oxford University Press.

Williams, A. (2015). *Forensic criminology*. London: Routledge.

Williamson, T. (2007). Psychology and criminal investigation. In T. Newburn, T. Williamson and A. Wright (eds), *Handbook of criminal investigation*. Cullompton, UK: Willan, pp. 68–91.

Williamson, T., Milne, R. and Savage, S. (2009). *International developments in investigative interviewing*. Cullompton, UK: Willan.

Wojcikiewicz, J. (1990). Decoding of memory traces as a function of witness' intelligence. *Forensic Science International*, 46, 83–85.

Wright, D.B. and Sladden, B. (2003). An own gender bias and the importance of hair in face recognition. *Acta Psychologia*, 114, 101–114.

Yuille, J.C. and Tollestrup, P.A. (1992). A model of the diverse effects of emotion on eyewitness memory. In S.A. Christianson (ed.), *The handbook of emotion and memory*. Hillside, NJ: Erlbaum, pp. 201–306.

Chapter 2

The art and science of investigation

Martin O'Neill

> In the story of progress, art always precedes science. Mankind meets its problem first by learning from experience. As an understanding of underlying forces becomes necessary, a science is developed. This is the history of every profession. This is the story of the development of police practice.
>
> Valentine (1935, p. v)

Introduction

The historical development of detective practice in the UK is well traced in academic literature and it is possible to discern strong influences upon it as time progressed (Shpayer-Makov, 2011). In the early days of the New Police, detectives were small in number and chosen from the ranks of uniformed constables, having demonstrated some aptitude for that type of work (Beattie, 2012). A number had been Bow Street Runners whilst others had experience on the street as some of the first uniformed police officers (Beattie, 2012). The men (there were no early female detectives) learnt their craft on the job and whenever successful were lauded for innate qualities that set them apart from their peers. Unfortunately, because of this, a particular cultural view of detectives emerged – that detective work could not be learnt other than in the field, and that only an exclusive few could perform it well (if they had the requisite innate qualities). Early myths were fuelled by a rising crime fiction genre that stressed the artistic qualities of successful sleuths (Shpayer-Makov, 2011). Attempts to suggest that crime investigation was a role that required specialist training were often rebuffed. Successive committees on the police up to the 1920s disagreed with suggestions that detectives required any more training than their uniformed colleagues (Tong, Bryant & Horvath, 2009). It was not until the 1930s that real inroads were made. Detective training became the norm, detective departments were rationalised, and the use of science within investigations was encouraged throughout the UK (paralleled in the USA by the introduction the Chicago crime laboratory and a new Polygraph test to herald in a new scientific era). Though the craft metaphor was prevalent, the acceptance that science could play an important role in criminal investigations represented a move away from the practice of the 'dark arts' of detection. Since that time, detective work has developed into a specialism, despite the turmoil of widespread corruption, multiple high profile miscarriages of justice and other unsavoury scandals. This is so despite academic research in both the USA and the UK that directly challenged the impact that detectives had upon crime detection (for instance, Greenwood, Chaiken & Petersilia, 1977; Bottomly & Coleman, 1981). Despite several incarnations over the years (such as increased systemisation of the work together with increased centralisation and considerable legal changes), it is remarkable that little was written in relation to criminal investigation best practice (Morris, 2007; Moore & Rubin, 2014). The UK Professionalising the Investigative Process programme (PIP) (2005) not only provided for different levels of qualification for investigators depending upon the level of criminal investigation undertaken, but also a set of National Occupational Standards (NOS) and an Integrated Competency Framework (ICF) (James & Mills, 2012). In addition, for the first time a Core Investigative Doctrine (CD) was produced by capturing good practice from practitioners, built up over many years of investigative experience (Stelfox, 2009; McGrory & Treacy, 2012).

These developments can be seen as a move away from art and craft to a more rational, scientific approach. However, it is not possible to suggest that one (science) has completely replaced the others (art and craft), particularly in the minds of practitioners. Indeed, modern practice seemingly involves a mixture of all three approaches (Reppetto, 1978; Tong & Bowling, 2006; Innes, 2003; O'Neill, 2011). This chapter will trace some of the historical developments that demonstrate a move towards professionalisation of criminal investigations, and will articulate the art craft science debate in light of this perceived direction. Aspects of PIP will also be discussed, taking into consideration claims made about the process, CD and its impact on investigative practice.

Surprisingly, the quotation at the beginning of the chapter derives from a text-book on criminal investigation, written in 1935 (Soderman & O'Connell 1935). Yet it does suggest that what has been occurring in the policing field is a natural process mirroring other professions. Following a period of denial that detective work was anything other than common sense policing, observers began to recognise that a shift in emphasis was required in order to harness scientific principles to aid criminal investigations. This linked to a growing acknowledgement that criminal investigation was much more complex than initially thought. Little was known of the particular skills required to investigate crime effectively (Beattie, 2012). Many early detectives were from working class backgrounds and barely literate (Morris, 2007), and they often learnt their trade through on the job experience. Criminal investigation relied upon the individual flair, craft, experience and guile of individuals, and detectives in early years undertook their investigative task with very little assistance from the sciences (Ramsland, 2014). Detective work was intended to be another facet of general police work, and therefore capable of being undertaken by 'citizens in uniform' performing their role whilst representing the people. Detectives were seen as requiring only common sense and their role one that anyone could perform (Stelfox, 2007).

The first training academy in the Metropolitan Police was not opened until 1902, and very little was taught to fledgling detectives prior to that time. This encouraged the idea that crime investigation, like policing itself, was not something that could be "learned from books", but a craft that had to be learned from experience on the streets and from other experienced officers (Manning, 1977; Hobbs, 1988; Savage & Milne, 2007; Stelfox, 2007). Others considered it to be a fairly pragmatic simple task to perform, suggesting that the large majority of cases were straightforward and easy to solve (Morris, 2007). Even when in 1834 there was public disquiet about perceived lack of effectiveness of police investigations into serious crime, Commissioners Rowan and Mayne responded to a Metropolitan Policing Committee by insisting that investigative work required no specialist detective department because it could be performed adequately by existing members of the uniformed branch (Beattie, 2012). Only eight years later, following several reported investigative controversies (such as a poor investigation into a murder by Daniel Goode), was a small detective branch formed.

The 1920 Desborough Committee Report did little to support claims that detective work was a specialist role, recommending that detectives did not need any more training or education than their uniformed colleagues in order to be able to investigate crime: The caveat being that there was adequate training for police constables across the country (Desborough Committee, 1920). According to the Committee Report, detective practices could be learned from experience (Tong, Bryant & Horvath, 2009). Various textbooks and memoirs also fostered the idea that the investigation of crime was both an art and a craft. Good detectives were those who had innate qualities making them ideal for the job, and they honed these by experience in the field (Soderman & O'Connell, 1935; Shpayer-Makov, 2011). The description of investigation as an art in criminal investigation text books in the USA in the 1970s was criticised for perpetuating a myth that did not withstand scrutiny (Greenwood, Chaiken & Petersilia, 1977). Arguably some of these ideas persist in modern thinking, although this will be discussed later.

Police detectives had little in the way of scientific knowledge to assist them in the early years. Although there is evidence that science in the classic sense was used to assist cases (i.e. medical evidence, toxicology), the forensic use of fingerprints did not begin until 1902 (Ramsland, 2014), and the use of DNA did not enter into policing until 1987 with the conviction of Colin Pitchfork for the double murders of Linda Mann in 1983 and Dawn Ashworth in 1986 (Wambaugh, 2011). Though there is some evidence of the use of science, fingerprints and technology to assist in the detection of crime pre and post 1919, it was not until the Departmental Committee on the Police reported (1938) that the systematic use of forensic science was encouraged (Moore & Rubin,

2014). Seizing upon good practice, the Committee sanctioned the promulgation of material to all police officers, encouraging them to be aware of the importance of the use of science within investigations (Moore & Rubin, 2014). It is surprising, then, to discover that as far back as 1936 the Home Office produced a document entitled "Scientific aids to criminal investigation: An instructional pamphlet for the use of police officers" (Home Office, 1936). Numbering 38 pages, the pocket sized pamphlet discussed such matters as examination of crime scenes, searching for material, judging the value of scientific material and how to handle and package evidence. The document states:

> It has been shown on many occasions, especially in recent years, that the scientist can often render valuable assistance to the police if he is afforded an opportunity to examine articles connected with the scene of a crime. Any evidence a scientist can give is, of course, additional to the evidence available from other sources; its role is, not to take the place of other evidence, but to corroborate and supplement it.
>
> (Home Office, 1936, p. 3)

The same Departmental Committee recommended that all detectives received specialist training, suggesting that the prevailing state of affairs was unsystematic, ill conceived, badly coordinated and in need of modernisation. Detectives were to learn from experienced colleagues, training was to be standardised, science was to be harnessed and all newly trained detectives were to be issued with the pamphlet. Eight week courses for detectives and six week courses for detective sergeants began to appear (Moore & Rubin, 2014).

Of course, the craft of detective work was strengthened by these pronouncements (Williamson, Newburn & Wright, 2007). The changes did, however, promise a more systematic approach to crime scenes, a more thorough investigation, a more coordinated approach and the seeds of a doctrine for investigation (Moore & Rubin, 2014). Yet ideas of detective work as art and craft still persisted, not only because the mythology was embraced by practitioners themselves, who were happy to view themselves in such a light, but also because the public perception of the skills and abilities required to be a successful detective was fuelled by media images in books, on TV and in film (Morgan, 1990), as well as by memoirs of famous detectives undoubtedly spiced up for public consumption (Shpayer-Makov, 2011). Popular myths surrounding detective work were exposed following the publication of seminal research in the USA in the 1970s. The RAND study (Greenwood et al., 1977) exploded many myths surrounding detective work, suggesting that it did little to solve crimes. What mattered, according to the report, was the initial response to crimes undertaken by patrol officers and the information forthcoming from members of the public. Routine detective effort made little inroad into detecting crime, and was ultimately fruitless in all but a minority of cases. Following the RAND publication, questions were raised as to whether large numbers of detectives could be reassigned. If they were ineffective as investigators and patrol was more effective, then perhaps a large number could be moved to patrol duties. Greenwood et al. (1977) made it clear that they felt that detective work should no longer be shrouded in mystery, and they criticised prominent criminal investigation textbooks of the time, such as O'Hara (1970) for continuing to describe criminal investigation in such a manner (Greenwood et al., 1977). The O'Hara preface observed: "The investigation of crime is after all not a science but an art whose secrets are not likely to be captured in any great part between the covers of a book" (O'Hara, 1970, p. 1). This, Greenwood et al. (1977) suggested, promoted the idea that it was a practice without definition, and one that could only be performed by those with innate qualities to undertake it. Greenwood et al. (1977) advocated a more scientific approach to management, processes, procedures and resource allocation of investigations, based upon effectiveness. Whilst it would be easy to suggest that RAND was US research and thus not relevant to the UK, the findings of RAND in relation to investigative effectiveness were echoed in the UK by studies such as Crust (1975), Zander (1979), Steer (1980), Bottomly and Coleman (1981), Banton (1985) and latterly Burrows and Tarling (1987). The most significant difference appears to be that the studies in the USA defined "case clearance" as when an arrest was made (as this point is much closer to charge there), whereas in the UK this has never been the measure. Through Home Office Counting Rules (Home Office, 2016) a detection is judged as the point at which a charge or summons is laid or, in more modern times, when any other criminal justice outcome is applied (i.e. caution, reprimand). Either perspective has tended to ignore the importance of case building and case management with regard to the investigative process (with notable exceptions such as McConville, Sanders & Leng, 1991). An arrest of an individual is not the end of the investigative process in the UK. Much investigative effort is required in order to ascertain whether an arrested individual is responsible for a crime, and the case building function is often minimised as somehow unimportant to investigative work. It can often be the most important and challenging part of an investigation (Stelfox, 2007; Brodeur, 2010).

Reppetto (1978) set out to assess organisational responses to the RAND publication. He sought to establish whether there had been a decline in detective numbers since RAND. Far from discovering a decline, a rise was evident. He noted how RAND had suggested that detective effort could significantly affect outcomes post charge (i.e. in what the UK would now call the case management phase) and that proactive units were more effective in combatting crimes such as burglary and robbery (providing staff were well resourced and supported by the organisation). Differences in departments suggested to Reppetto that a distinction could be drawn between the art, craft or science practiced, depending upon the seriousness of the crime and the type of investigative activities undertaken to combat it. Borrowing from Wilson's 1978 study of FBI and DEA agents, Reppetto contended that there were at least five types of investigator working in the USA at that time. He identified:

1 Detectives – in the truest sense, working regionally or nationally dealing with high profile crime investigations (i.e. FBI officers working mostly in a reactive manner),
2 Detectives engaged in neighbourhood level crime investigations (working in a reactive manner),
3 Intelligence officers or analysts,
4 Administrative detectives – usually preparing cases or conducting local, anti-crime patrol, and
5 Instigators/undercover officers working in a proactive fashion to combat crime (i.e. DEA officers).

Reppetto (1978) observed that RAND had failed to take into account different detective roles, nor did it take account of contrasting contexts and nuances within which investigators worked. Wilson (1978) found that the FBI primarily worked in a traditional manner – by reacting to and investigating crime – whereas DEA operatives were more proactive, sometimes resorting to undercover work in order to bring drug dealers to justice. Reppetto (1978) argued that investigators at 2, 3 and 4 were more reliant upon the craft model. They were usually recruited from patrol officers and learnt their trade on the job. Reppetto proposed that those at number 1 reflected the scientific approach. He justified this on the basis that they were usually directly employed, had a college education and were highly trained. Investigators at number 5 were more akin to the art paradigm. What he did not do was identify why these dimensions reflected the different roles. Moreover, he did not elaborate on what facets characterised each dimension. Wilson (1978) suggested that narcotics agents needed to have artful skills in both acquiring reliable information and in persuading others to engage in criminal activity (usually in an undercover capacity).

Tong and Bowling (2006) preferred to situate the debate in terms of art, craft, science being ideal types, with no one type being mirrored in reality or prevailing over any other. However, they did caution that the art craft distinction is wont to see the investigator as unaccountable, individualistic and much more representative of the mythical sleuth who has innate abilities and has learnt their trade on the job. The artist and craftsmen are seen as anathema to learning the science of investigation because much of it in their world is incapable of explanation or learning in any other manner than from experience. For Tong and Bowling (2006), science connotes a more systematic, methodical approach, harnessing science to assist in bringing offenders to justice. More recent studies suggest that practitioners view criminal investigation as a mixture of all three (Innes, 2003; O'Neill, 2011). However, as Westera, Kebbell, Milne and Green (2014) point out, no studies explore what attributes represent each dimension, nor does any research deconstruct the qualities identified as key to effective investigation so that each can be described accurately. Westera et al. (2014) utilise their study of Australian detectives to formulate a description of the dimension often cited as the most important in any sphere of investigation: communication (Wilson, 1978; O'Neill & Milne, 2014). They go on to suggest that the same process could be utilised with all identified skills and abilities to produce an explicit catalogue of the skills required, together with accurate descriptions.

So, what does inhabit the separate dimensions of art, craft and science?

Art

The art of investigative work appears to connote the use of innate qualities such as intuition, creativity, imagination and flair (Tong & Bowling, 2006), as well as abilities to acquire and persuade (Wilson, 1978). These qualities tend to invoke the romantic notion of the detective solving cases by instinct rather than by the use of any systematic approach. That is, being able to "feel" a case. A modern incarnation of this type of character is Adrian Monk (an American Crime series detective), although interestingly his feel for cases appears to be exacerbated by his OCD tendencies and thus his ability to use acute observational skills to detect even the smallest clue. Notwithstanding that some cases in real life might be solved by individual brilliance or that some are enhanced by some creative masterstroke on the part of an investigator, there is no known research that demonstrates how often this happens within detective work. Doubtless, there are investigator memoirs that lay claim to such insightful moments, but these would need to be treated with some caution.

There is research to suggest that intuition is more likely to be acute observational skill rather than some innate ability. Often practitioners asked to explain the phenomenon describe it as a hunch or gut feeling when in fact it can be more mundane. Rossmo (2008) recounts the story of Juan Fangio when he won the Formula One world title in 1950. Somehow, entering into a bend in the rain, Fangio inexplicably slowed down and avoided ploughing into vehicles that had crashed further round the bend. Because he had slowed, Fangio was able to drive round the stationary vehicles, avoid crashing, and win the championship. When asked why he had slowed, Fangio initially described it as intuition. Later, he was able to recount how he had noticed several factors, all in a fractional time frame, that led him to believe something had happened – such as the roar of the crowd and the position of their heads as he entered the bend (Fangio noticed that they were looking away from him rather than at him, as was usual when he entered that bend; they were, in fact, looking at the crash). These clues led to his actions, rather than intuition (Rossmo, 2008). In the same way, where police officers describe making arrests as a result of a hunch or gut feeling, more in depth exploration might reveal something more tangible unfolding. Whatever the nature of intuition, Kahneman (2003) contrasted intuitive thought with rational thinking. Whilst intuitive thinking is automatic and happens in circumstances where there is little time for deliberation, it is unfortunately likely to be prone to errors. Rational thinking on the other hand takes place in circumstances where more time and information is available to a decision-maker. There are many police tasks undertaken where intuitive thinking may be dominant, and necessary, such as responding to emergencies. In the process of criminal investigation, however, rational thinking is likely to be more effective and as such it is important that it is given primacy in detective training and education. Wright (2013) recently found that intuition was central to the development of homicide detectives' hypothesis generation in a number of case vignettes. She found that they were accurate in two thirds of cases and concluded that intuitive ability was linked to the detectives' contextual experience and knowledge of homicide investigations. Wright suggested that intuition was a cognitive process that could be developed in the training of homicide detectives in the future.

Creativity is another oft cited area in the art dimension; described in relation to criminal investigation as "behaviours and activities that are directed at developing novel solutions that work for the investigation" (Dean, Fahsing, Gottschalk & Solle-Saether, 2008, p. 176).

This dimension may contain both flair and imagination. Dean et al. (2008) identified four thinking styles utilised by detectives in Norway (the method style, the challenge style, the skill style and the risk style). Although the authors saw creativity as part of every investigation, they identified that it was most utilised by detectives within the skill and risk styles. These styles were usually reflected in experienced practitioners, and they were often applied when traditional investigative methods had proved ineffective. This tends to suggest investigative creativity is situated in both the art and craft dimension. Whilst this area is ripe for further research, it is difficult to assess at this time whether the interest in investigative creativity is in fact necessary or whether it reflects a concern to cling to mythological aspects of detective practice. Fox (2014) recently reported that Senior Investigating Officers (SIOs) in the UK lamented the lack of freedom to act creatively within investigations due to the constraints of investigative practice enshrined in guidance such as the Murder Investigation Manual (MIM), the Major Incident Room Standard Administrative Procedures (MIRSAP) and Core Investigative Doctrine (CD). An analysis of MIM and CD would suggest that an SIO has significant discretion to employ strategies within an investigation, and that the list of strategies available are not identified as the *only* strategies available. In both the MIM and CD investigators are only constrained by the law and their own imaginations. Creativity is often described as the ability to think outside the box. However, this is clearly dependent upon a detective's perception of the size of the box in the first place. CD encourages investigators to be creative when other investigative strategies have proved fruitless, and to look at the problem in another way. It also suggests that intuition in the form of hunches and gut feeling can be acceptable if the reasons for them are recorded appropriately

(Savage & Milne, 2007). What CD does not do, however, is elaborate upon the nature of investigative creativity or intuition, which are relatively under researched in the investigative domain.

Craft

Described by Sherman (2015) as a somewhat smothering paradigm, 'craft culture' dominates policing. It is little surprise that craft ideas dominate traditional views of detective work also. These views overlap in some ways with considerations of detectives as artists. Willis (2013) notes that whilst the notion of craft is wedded to culture, it still has much to offer, especially at a time when there is considerable focus upon the dichotomy of craft and science, when the two could perhaps be blended together. Hobbs' classic 1988 study of East End detectives observed how detectives used guile, manipulation and other craft-like tendencies in an entrepreneurial manner, reflective of the nature of East End tradesmen. Others have noted the power of reputation in distinguishing successful detectives, with 'good thief takers' and more experienced detectives elevated to a higher level of kudos (Tong & Bowling, 2006). Being able to use 'ways and means' to achieve results, utilising on the job experience to find novel solutions, using common sense and being able to negotiate with witnesses, suspects, informants, supervisors and managers, are all arguably facets of the craft domain. Yet, like the artistic qualities described above, these facets are by definition indicative of a rare few investigators, and they imply that no amount of training or education can effectively replicate them. That 'experience on the job' assumes an elevated status is not a surprise. However, it does lead to an assumption that the detective will only learn good lessons from peers as opposed to bad lessons – something that is not always certain. That is not to suggest that detectives themselves have steadfastly held this same opinion regarding craft supremacy. We have already seen that historically there was a reluctance to accept that detective work was a specialism, but that a slow realisation allowed for extra training, and the appliance of scientific concepts to aid criminal investigations. When crime investigation was less complex, craft was much less of a concern (Stelfox, 2009).

Interestingly, Sherman (2015) (like Valentine in 1935) absolves policing from charges of being the *only* profession ever to have been dominated by craft culture. The medical profession also began as an artistic and craft-like endeavour, and Sherman provides an example where prevailing practices were resistant to change in relation to the treatment of scurvy on board ships, despite available evidence indicating a better method (Sherman, 2015). Despite the elevation of 'on the job' experience as indicative of craft ability, a recent study by Fahsing and Ask (2016; see also Chapter 3, this volume, for more on this study) suggests that experience alone is insufficient, and by implication, development programmes for detectives (such as PIP) may play a pivotal role in professional development.

Science

The science dimension may contain many facets. This chapter will focus upon four.

i) Science in the classic sense that is utilised within criminal investigation

This would encompass fingerprints, toxicology, medicine, pathology, biology, chemistry and so on. These sciences have influenced criminal investigations significantly (Ramsland, 2014). As a result of the importance of this type of evidence to securing convictions, the manner in which evidence is obtained at crime scenes, now in itself resembles scientific practice. From the early days of detective work, when great detectives like Vidocq saw the need to protect scenes and keenly observe every detail, science has been able to assist in finding evidence not visible to the human eye, taking advantage of science and the maxim "every contact leaves a trace" (Locard, 1928; Edwards, 1977). So too have the same scientific advancements made investigators acutely aware of the need to secure, protect and preserve evidence in such a way that it is not contaminated. Police training asserts the importance of continuity of evidence from the crime scene to the lab, in order to prevent problems arising in court (Fraser, 2007). The rise of the application of forensics to investigations has led to significant possibilities to bring to justice those responsible for crime. Fingerprints and DNA have been credited with bringing a new scientific era to criminal investigation. Police investigators must not only be aware of these fruitful investigative avenues for their cases, but they must marshal resources and assimilate the results of those activities within their investigations (Stelfox, 2009). Whilst the harnessing of science within criminal investigations (and policing in general) has grown, some commentators apply a more cautionary tone, because it is still underused in volume crime investigation (Ludwig & Fraser, 2014), and could produce lazy investigations in the absence of forensic material (Innes, 2010).

ii) Science used to inform crime management practices

> Criminal investigation is the scientific collection, examination and preservation of evidence. Because it is a costly and resource-intensive procedure, a thorough investigation cannot be applied to all reported crimes. Hence, the strategic categories of volume and serious crime are used to determine where and how investigation resources are allocated.
>
> (Harfield, 2008, p .67)

As the above definition of criminal investigation makes clear, the public police simply do not have the resources to investigate every crime. In addition, it is also fairly apparent that cases are often solved when there is a good initial response, where scenes are managed effectively, and where suspects are identified quickly, either by name, good physical description, or detailed modus operandi. A number of research studies in the UK and the USA concluded that investigative effort was often wasted on cases that had little chance of success from the outset

(Greenwood et al., 1977; Bottomley & Coleman, 1981). As a result, crime management systems evolved that screen crimes at the point of report. If the crime is deemed high volume and there are no leads, it will be filed without an officer even attending the scene. In other cases crime scenes will be visited, and the attending officer will report what has been discovered from victims, witnesses and the locale. A further screening process will take place, utilising solvability factors in order to determine whether the crime should be allocated to an investigator for secondary investigation (Volume Crime Investigation Manual (VCIM); ACPO, 2001). These structures and processes are designed to ensure that investigative effort is not wasted on cases perceived to have little chance of success. The twin concepts of solvability and level of crime can sometimes conspire to ensure that some cases are filed early that could also be solved with further investigative effort. Linking crime management systems to investigative work and the classification of art, craft and science, it is arguable that few of these attributes are required of an investigator when crimes are allocated that have already been assessed as more likely to be solved. The image of the sleuth hunting for clues during a crime investigation is consigned to history, with an image more consistent with what Reppetto (1978) would call an administrative detective. That said, no such screening process occurs in serious or major crime cases.

iii) Science used to inform investigative practice

Stelfox (2009) identifies that different academic disciplines can and do inform investigative practice, ranging from law through to psychology, sociology, criminology and the classic sciences. In the area of investigative interviewing (see also Chapters 6 and 8 this volume), much has been learnt from the field of psychology (Williamson, 2007). This has informed practice in terms of victim, witness and suspect interviewing (Shepherd & Griffiths, 2013; O'Neill & Milne, 2014; Westera et al., 2014). These changes were not practitioner led, but were imposed upon practice following a wealth of examples of malpractice and miscarriages of justice (Bull, 2014).

A new paradigm has recently emerged presenting opportunities for research to inform investigative practice. The rise of evidence based policing (EBP), based upon the medical model, has promised much in areas such as hotspot policing (Braga & Weisburd, 2010; Neyroud & Weisburd, 2014; Stanko & Dawson, 2016). Despite criticisms relating to the narrow focus of EBP and reliance upon gold standard Random Control Trials (RCT) (Thacher, 2001; Greene, 2014; Willis, 2013; Stanko & Dawson, 2016), Sherman (2015) suggests that there must be a valuing of science within the police service, a good understanding of scientific methods and, more crucially, good leadership within the service to appreciate the benefits that science can bring. He suggests that the crucial factor is the blending of craft and science. Stanko and Dawson (2016) posit that scientific evidence should be utilised where it fits best within a profession. In their view, clear risks in policing and investigations lie in areas such as mental health, vulnerable victims and the investigation of crime, and these are the areas that should be researched as a priority. Complementing these thoughts, there are pressing issues relating to risk assessments in domestic abuse cases, stalking, the treatment of victims of rape and serious sexual assault (in particular where they have mental health or other vulnerability issues), threat to life assessments and investigative decision-making, all of which demand research (O'Neill, 2018, in press).

What is apparent in the discussions around EBP and appropriate research methodologies is that opinions vary. A mixed method approach favoured by Stanko and Dawson (2016) has attractions, whilst a purely RCT driven methodology risks ostracising some important empirical research (Thacher, 2001). As Willis (2013) suggests, a middle ground is possible by developing a more constructive relationship between craft and science. After all, as Stanko and Dawson (2016) point out, craft and science both have at their heart an aim to achieve successful outcomes. Harnessing the two in order to find best evidence is in the interests of both police and researchers. Sherman (2015) concedes that science (and EBP) is not designed to ignore the craft of policing, but to complement it. He asserts that the craft could utilise EBP, particularly where slow thinking (as elucidated by Kahneman, 2011) is engaged. Much of criminal investigation involves (or should involve) slow thinking, so it is essential that EBP research extends to criminal investigation matters described above, by using the most appropriate methodology (this may or may not be RCT). EBP promises much for the future in relation to criminal investigation research and the 'scientific' approach. Criminal investigation after all is still very much an under researched area (Stelfox, 2009; Brodeur, 2010).

iv) The application of the scientific method to investigative decision making

Arguably one of the biggest failures of the police service is to elucidate a clear decision-making protocol for criminal investigations (see also Chapter 3 this volume), bearing in mind how often it has been suggested as the root of many investigative failures (Rossmo, 2008). Suffice to say that guidance such as CD does not operationalise investigative decision-making practice, while the National Decision Model lacks any empirical evidence to suggest its utility In a criminal investigation context.

Having considered the separate dimensions of art, craft and science, as they relate to criminal investigation, it is important to acknowledge that these ideal types were formulated prior to the inception of PIP in the UK. It could be reasoned that, bearing in mind the preceding backdrop, efforts would be made to assert the prevalence of the scientific investigator, albeit recognising that the art and craft dimensions would play some part (West, 2001; Phillips, 2003). The next subsection will review aspects of PIP with a critical eye. Before doing so, it is important to make clear that some steps have been made toward professionalising investigations, particularly in relation to the uniform investigation of crime, and the structure of professional development of investigators. However, do all aspects of the process withstand closer scrutiny?

The PIP programme and the professional investigator (England and Wales)

A growing recognition of the complexities of policing, together with a realisation that omni-competence was not appropriate in the twenty-first century investigation of crime heralded a new era for crime investigation and a proposed move toward professionalisation (Police Reform Act, 2002; HMIC, 2004; Stelfox, 2009). A sea change in investigative development was signalled in 2005 with the creation of the PIP programme designed to professionalise investigations (Savage & Milne, 2007; Stelfox, 2009; McGrory & Treacy, 2012). The programme aimed to embed new standards into investigative practice and introduced levels of qualification depending upon the type of investigations that an investigator would encounter (see Chapter 12 for more on PIP levels). PIP level one was for priority and volume crime investigations (mainly uniformed constables). Level two encompassed serious and complex crime investigations undertaken by detective constables, detective sergeants and detective inspectors, as well as several other specialist investigative roles (i.e. specialist child abuse investigations). PIP level three was for the management of major crime investigations at SIO level, whereas PIP level four was for SIOs in overall command of linked, series, cross border major crimes (Stelfox, 2009; McGrory & Treacy, 2012).

In theory, investigators were required to qualify in order to practice at a particular level, and once qualified, would have to undergo a process of Continuing Professional Development (CPD) to periodically requalify. In this process, even those undertaking volume crime investigations were required to qualify in order to investigate (they would usually do this during their probationary training). At the same time, underpinning knowledge, CD, was developed. This guidance aimed to provide a corpus of knowledge in relation to criminal investigations – in effect providing a resource for investigators to use when investigating any crime (Centrex, 2005). The doctrine was created in consultation with both practitioners and academics. It was described thus:

> This Practice Advice is a strategic overview of the investigative process, providing a framework for investigative good practice. Its purpose is to provide investigators with the skills and knowledge they require to conduct investigations in a competent manner, inspiring confidence in the investigator and the wider criminal justice system.
>
> (Centrex, 2005, p. 6)

The document was described as "practice advice", as opposed to a mandatory policy. Describing it as "advice" rather than making it mandatory for practitioners is questionable practice. Anecdotal evidence suggests that several Forces were slow to utilise CD for this very reason. Whether a document is able to provide investigators with "skills" is also questionable. That said, CD needs to be seen in conjunction with the PIP process as a whole, which for instance, suggested skill development at phase two of the Initial Crime Investigator Development Programme (ICIDP).

CD was divided into two parts. Part One described the principles underlying investigations, together with the knowledge required to effectively perform an investigative role. Part Two detailed the process of investigation describing a typical investigation and its attendant stages (Centrex, 2005). CD was described as a vehicle that would provide impetus for a future research agenda, and as something that would constantly be honed as new knowledge was discovered (Centrex, 2005, p. 16). The general consensus appeared to be that one had to start somewhere if one was building a knowledge base for investigations. Like the Murder Investigation Manual (MIM), designed to provide a starting point for major crime SIOs, CD promised to do the same in relation to all crime. PIP was designed to transform the process of investigation from a craft to a science, an interesting perspective bearing in mind the preceding discussions (James & Mills, 2012).

Training was to comprise three main learning phases in the ICIDP. A pre learning phase where officers were required to learn the law relating to criminal investigation and subsequently pass a National Investigator Examination in order to attend the second phase; a skills phase taught over a period of successive weeks; and finally a competence related assessment in the workplace, where investigators were to be tutored by tutor detective constables, and required to submit a portfolio of evidence to prove practical application of the principles, measured against set criteria (Savage & Milne, 2009; ACPO, Centrex, 2005). From an outward perspective, this rhetoric sounds very positive, and no doubt some advances have been made in professional practice as a result of PIP. Indeed, there is some support for the programme in recent research (Fahsing & Ask, 2015; also see Chapter 3 this volume). In terms of investigator training at PIP level 2 (ICIDP), recent years have seen a gradual decline in the number of weeks at the skills phase stage. Although the number of training weeks is not necessarily indicative of any drop in standards, proponents of the PIP regime would point to the fact that law is now dealt with adequately by phase one of the programme. They would also argue that modern investigators are constantly required to keep up to date with essential e-learning that is accessible via the National Centre for Applied Learning Technologies (NCALT). Others might suggest that a paucity of time spent on decision-making, miscarriages of justice, IPCC cases, and even CPIA is suggestive at worst of an ignorance of the importance of the issues, or at best an exercise in risk management.

The advent of PIP intended to signal a new era in investigative development and practice: but rather than signalling mere structural change, it needed to create behavioural change, championing as it did an open minded search for the truth, ethical values, planning and preparation, and an investigative mindset. However, setting out doctrine is necessary but not necessarily sufficient to change ingrained practice (Savage & Milne, 2007). James and Mills (2012) conducted a small study of PIP in one police force. They found evidence of cultural and organisational influences that appear to militate against the rhetoric of PIP. According to their research, some old cultural values still pervade. Despite PIP, some officers were still being mentored by detectives who put greater emphasis upon someone's face "fitting" rather than their qualifications. One respondent suggested that ICIDP was easy to pass, and that it produced investigators without the same abilities as before (before is not defined). The same respondent complained that historically investigators had to pass a selection process prior to becoming a trainee detective and that the new process allowed anyone to become a detective irrespective of their capabilities. In relation to organisational factors, whilst the Home Office had scrapped performance criteria, respondents made it clear that in reality these were still being used by managers. At a time when local CID was suffering from lack of resources (as opposed to specialist detective units such as the major crime department), respondents made it clear that the last thing required were performance criteria likely to encourage corner cutting with consequent detrimental effect upon quality of service and effectiveness. Indeed, it was suggested that volume crime investigations were undertaken poorly for this very reason. There are echoes here of the poor resourcing of general CID found by Chatterton (2008). The snapshot produced by this study is not a comforting one. Would it be optimistic to assume that the climate has changed in the last few years and that it is different now? This question demonstrates why it is important to establish by independent research whether the PIP programme really does represent a move toward professionalising investigative practice. As Stelfox (2007) has suggested, changes needed to occur within management and supervisory capacities for the rhetoric to become a reality, otherwise much of the process becomes a tick box exercise where real change does not occur. Some of the issues discussed above indicate some doubt about the process.

CD was replaced in 2012 by Authorised Professional Practice (APP). Not all of CD made it to the pages of APP. This is an example of a general move away from 'technical' guidance towards a more discretionary approach, espousing the importance of professional judgment and the use of the National Decision Model (NDM). Again, it is beyond the scope of this chapter, but research would be useful to understand the use made of the NDM by investigative practitioners, together with its effectiveness in improving practical decision making. This model appears to have no evidence base for its use. Another aspect of this current trend is the move away from publishing force policies toward the promulgation of memoranda of understanding instead. The technical details of force policies are replaced by broader principles, with the accent upon professional judgment. For professional judgment must we also imply 'individual responsibility' as opposed to organisational responsibility? A similar idea was suggested by the Home Office in relation to PACE Codes of Practice, but thankfully this was never implemented (Zander, 2012).

Are these proposed changes genuinely influenced by a wish to be more professional or do they represent cost cutting in an era of austerity? Is the professional agenda merely a rhetorical device, designed to placate the public: an outward facing cosmetic exercise to appease? Moreover, is it just repackaged 'business as usual' or worse? In 2013, the College of Policing issued a press release on its website relating to a forthcoming review of PIP training. It was not clear whether the review was an independent review. It read:

> The way investigators are trained will also change. The system will move away from investigators attending courses and conferences and instead focus on operational experience, peer learning, workplace observations and e-learning. This new way of working will ensure investigators' time is best used while reducing the cost of development for police forces.
>
> (CoP, 2013)

This appears to be little more than a confirmation of the prevalence of the craft model of investigation, based upon financial considerations rather than research. Does this announcement lead one to believe that professionalism is really at the heart of PIP policy and practice? What of the move from craft to science heralded by the inception of the PIP process?

In the same vein, CoP is now championing Higher Education involvement in police training, and a consideration that officers would need, like other professions, to obtain a degree to join the police service and higher qualifications to progress. Is this all in the name of professionalisation, or is the real reason rooted in the savings likely to result in such a move? There is an opportunity for police training to be provided by Higher Education at the cost of the student, thus freeing up the organisation's financial obligations toward training staff. Whilst it is accepted that this is what happens in other professions, such as medicine, law, nursing and teaching, policing appears to suffer from a lack of agreement as to what the necessary elements of a policing degree would entail. How will it be possible to blend an academic policing programme with the training required for a front line police officer? How much of an academic degree would be taken up by the practical training that would be required? All of these are very important questions that need answering. The answers to them go to the heart of the idea of policing as a profession and directly affect the idea of the professionalisation of investigation. All of this against a backdrop that suggests a lack of evidence base for the switch (Paterson, 2011).

Conclusion

The foregoing discussion has identified a potential discrepancy between the rhetoric and the reality of investigative development and practice. On the one hand, conventional wisdom would describe a more professional structure for the development of investigators, a move from art and craft to a more scientific perspective and a now evidence based focus. Practitioners have suggested a blending of art craft and science, a position far removed from early detective practice and development. Yet what little research there is does not tend to support the rhetoric. The PIP process appears to be suffering from age-old cultural obstacles, and little independent evidence exists to suggest that the framework, the training or some of the practical guidance issued is appropriate for modern practice. Against this backdrop, CoP have determined without evidence that the NDM is appropriate for investigative decision making, and have indicated a return to the dominance of the craft model for the development of investigators of the future. The decision to engage with Higher Education has also been criticised for lacking any evidence base. The rise of EBP is a welcome development if it can grasp the nettle of engaging research that matters in the field of criminal investigation. Whenever criminal investigation practice is discussed inside or outside of the police organisation, credibility problems will arise if there is little evidence to underpin practice, training, and development. This chapter has identified some key areas in the investigative field, where research would be welcome in the modern era: risk assessments, vulnerability, mental health, decision making (NDM and its applicability), the effectiveness of investigative training under the banner of PIP and the effectiveness of the PIP process itself. EBP promises much, and if researchers can blend craft and science and overcome the naturally pessimistic culture, then some genuinely useful discoveries about the nature of what constitutes investigative best practice might be found. Such research must also overcome, or at least be cognisant of, political and policy agendas and demonstrate integrity and boldness in accurately reporting findings, even if sometimes those findings do not match those agendas.

References

ACPO (2000). *MIRSAP Manual: Major Incident Room Standard Administrative Procedures.*

ACPO (2001). *Volume Crime Investigation Manual.* London: ACPO Crime Committee.

ACPO (2006). *Murder Investigation Manual.* Wyboston, UK: NPIA.

ACPO, Centrex (2005, 2012). *Practice Advice on Core Investigative Doctrine* (2nd edn). Wyboston, UK: Association of Chief Police Officers and National Policing Improvement Agency.

Banton, M. (1985). *Investigating Robbery.* Aldershot, UK: Gower.

Beattie, J.M. (2012). *The First English Detectives: The Bow Street Runners and the Policing of London, 1750–1840.* Oxford, UK: Oxford University Press.

Brodeur, J.P. (2010). *The Policing Web.* Oxford, UK: Oxford University Press.

Bottomley, K. & Coleman, C. (1981). *Understanding Crime Rates.* Farnborough, UK: Gower.

Braga, A.A. & Weisburd, D. (2010). *Policing Problem Places: Crime Hot Spots and Effective Prevention*. Oxford, UK: Oxford University Press.

Bull, R. (2014). *Investigative Interviewing*. New York: Springer.

Burrows, J. & Tarling, R. (1987). The investigation of crime in England and Wales. *The British Journal of Criminology*, 27(3), 229–251.

Chatterton, M. (2008). *Losing the Detectives: Views from the Front Line*. Surbiton, Surrey: Police Federation of England & Wales.

CoP (2013) College of Policing press release relating to a forthcoming review of PIP training. College of Policing.

Crust, P.E. (1975) 'Criminal investigation project'. Home Office Police Research Services Unit (unpublished).

Dean, G., Fahsing, I.A., Gottschalk, P. & Solli-Saether, H. (2008). Investigative thinking and creativity: An empirical study of police detectives in Norway. *International Journal of Innovation and Learning*, 5(2), 170–185.

Desborough, Lord (1920). *Report of the Committee on the Police Service of England and Wales*. London: HMSO.

Edwards, S. (1977). *The Vidocq Dossier: The Story of the World's First Detective*. Boston, MA: Houghton Mifflin Company.

Fahsing, I. & Ask, K. (2016). The making of an expert detective: The role of experience in English and Norwegian police officers' investigative decision-making. *Psychology, Crime & Law*, 23(3), 1–21.

Fox, J. (2014). Is there room for flair in criminal investigation? *Journal of Homicide and Major Incident Investigation*, 9(1), 2–18.

Fraser, J. (2007). The application of forensic science to criminal investigation. In T. Newburn, T. Williamson & A. Wright (eds), *Handbook of Criminal Investigation*. Cullompton, UK: Willan Publishing, pp. 381–403.

Greene, J.R. (2014). New directions in policing: Balancing prediction and meaning in police research. *Police Research, Justice Quarterly*, 31(2), 193–228. doi:10:1080/07418825.2013.840389.

Greenwood, P.W., Chaiken, J.M. & Petersilia, J. (1977). *The Criminal Investigation Process*. Toronto: D.C. Heath.

Harfield, C. (2008). Criminal investigation. In T. Newburn & P. Neyroud (eds), *The Dictionary of Policing*. Cullompton, UK: Willan Publishing, pp. 67–69.

HMIC (2004). *Modernising the Police Service: A Thematic Inspection of Workforce Modernisation – The Role, Management and Deployment of Police Staff in the Police Service of England and Wales*. London: HMIC.

Hobbs, D. (1988). *Doing the Business: Entrepreneurship, the Working Class, and Detectives in the East End of London*. Oxford: Clarendon Press.

Home Office (1936). *Scientific Aids to Criminal Investigation*. London: Home Office.

Home Office Counting Rules (2016). Available at: https://www.gov.uk/government/uploads/system/uploads/attachment_data/file/489732 /count-general-january-2016.pdf

Innes, M. (2003). *Investigating Murder: Detective Work and the Police Response to Criminal Homicide*. Oxford, UK: Oxford University Press.

Innes, M. (2010). The art, craft and science of policing. In P. Cane & H. Kritzer (eds), *The Oxford Handbook of Empirical Legal Research*. Oxford: Oxford University Press, pp 11–36.

James, A. & Mills, M. (2012). Does ACPO know best: To what extent may the PIP programme provide a template for the professionalization of policing? *The Police Journal*, 85, 133–149.

Kahneman, D. (2003). A perspective on judgment and choice: Mapping bounded rationality. *American Psychologist*, 58(9), 697–720.

Kahneman, D. (2011). *Thinking Fast and Slow*. Harmondsworth, UK: Penguin Books.

Locard, E. (1928). Dust and its analysis: An aid to criminal investigation. *Police Journal*, 1, pp. 177–192.

Ludwig, A. & Fraser, J. (2014). Effective use of forensic science in volume crime investigations: Identifying recurring themes in the literature. *Science & Justice*, 54(1), 81–88.

Manning, P.K. (1977). *Police Work: The Social Organization of Policing* (pp. 344–345). Cambridge, MA: MIT Press.

McConville, M., Sanders, A. & Leng, R. (1991). *The Case for the Prosecution: Police Suspects and the Construction of Criminality*. London: Routledge.

Mcgrory, D. & Treacy, P. (2012). The Professionalising Investigation Programme. In M.R. Haberfield, C.A. Clarke & D.L. Sheridan (eds), *Police Organisation and Training*. New York: Springer, pp. 113–136.

Morgan, J.B. (1990). *The Police Function and the Investigation of Crime*. Brookfield, VT: Avebury.

Morris, B. (2007). History of criminal investigation. In T. Newburn, T. Williamson & A. Wright (eds), *Handbook of Criminal Investigation*. Cullompton, UK: Willan Publishing, pp. 15–41.

Moore, C.R. & Rubin, G.R. (2014). Civilian detective doctrine in the 1930s and its transmission to the Military Police in 1940–1942. *Law, Crime and History*, 1–30. Available at: https://kar.kent.ac.uk/41318/7/Colin%20R%20%20Moore%20and%20Gerry%20R%2 0%20Rubin%20FINAL.pdf

Neyroud, P. & Weisburd, D. (2014). Transforming the police through science: The challenge of ownership. *Policing*, 8(4), 287–293.

O'Hara, C. (1970). *Fundamentals of Criminal Investigation*. Springfield, IL: Charles Thomas.

O'Neill, M. (2018, in press). *Key Challenges in Criminal Investigation*. Bristol, UK: Policy Press.

O'Neill, M. (2011). What makes a successful volume crime investigator? Unpublished PhD thesis, University of Portsmouth.

O'Neill, M. & Milne, B. (2014). Success within criminal investigations: Is communication still a key component? In R. Bull (ed.), *Investigative Interviewing*. New York: Springer, pp. 123–146.

Paterson, C. (2011). Adding value? A review of the international literature on the role of Higher Education in police training and education. *Police, Practice and Research*, 12(4), 286–297.

Philips, Sir C. (1982) *Royal Commission on Criminal Procedure* (Cmnd 8092). London: HMSO.

Phillips, D. (2003) The route to professionalism. *Policing Today*, 9, 5–6.

Police Reform Act 2002. London: HMSO.

Ramsland, K. (2014). *Beating the Devil's Game: A History of Forensic Science and Criminal Investigation*. Harmondsworth, UK: Penguin.

Reppetto, T.A. (1978). The detective task: The state of the art science craft? *Police Studies: The International Review of Police Development*, 1(3), 5–10.
Rossmo, K.D. (2008). *Criminal Investigative Failures*. Boca Raton, FL: CRC Press.
Savage, S.P. & Milne, B. (2007). Miscarriages of justice. In T. Newburn, T. Williamson & A. Wright (eds), *Handbook of Criminal Investigation*. Cullompton, UK: Willan Publishing, pp. 610–627.
Sherman, L.W. (2015). A tipping point for "totally evidenced policing": Ten ideas for building an evidence-based police agency. *International Criminal Justice Review*, 25(1), 11–29.
Shepherd, E. & Griffiths, A. (2013). *Investigative Interviewing: The Conversation Management Approach*. Oxford, UK: Oxford University Press.
Shpayer-Makov, H. (2011). *The Ascent of the Detective: Police Sleuths in Victorian and Edwardian England*. Oxford, UK: Oxford University Press.
Soderman, H. & O'Connell, J.J. (1935). *Modern Criminal Investigation*. London: Bell.
Stanko, E. & Dawson, P. (2016). *Police Use of Research Evidence: Recommendations for Improvement*. New York: Springer.
Steer, D. (1980). *Uncovering Crime: The Police Role*. The Royal Commission on Criminal Procedure Study No 7 (Cmnd 8092). London: HMSO.
Stelfox, P. (2007). Professionalising criminal investigation. In T. Newburn, T. Williamson & A. Wright (eds), *Handbook of Criminal Investigation*. Cullompton, UK: Willan Publishing, pp. 628–652.
Stelfox, P. (2009). *Criminal Investigation: An Introduction to Principles and Practice*. Cullompton, UK: Willan Publishing.
Thacher, D. (2001). Policing is not a treatment: Alternatives to the medical model of police research. *Journal of Research in Crime and Delinquency*, 38(4), 387–415.
Tong, S. & Bowling, B. (2006). Art, craft and science of detective work. *The Police Journal*, 79(4), 323–329.
Tong, S., Bryant, R.P. & Horvath, M.A. (2009). *Understanding Criminal Investigation*. Chichester, UK: John Wiley & Sons.
Valentine, J. (1935). Introduction. In H. Soderman & J.J. O'Connell, *Modern Criminal Investigation*. London: Bell.
Wambaugh, J. (2011). *The Blooding*. New York: Open Road Media.
West, A. (2001). A proposal for an investigative science course. Any takers! *Police Research and Management*, 5, 13–22.
Westera, N.J., Kebbell, M.R., Milne, B. & Green, T. (2014). Towards a more effective detective. *Policing and Society: An International Journal of Research and Policy, 26(1)*.
Williamson, T. (2007). Psychology and criminal investigation. In T. Newburn, T. Williamson & A. Wright (eds), *Handbook of Criminal Investigation*. Cullompton, UK: Willan Publishing, pp. 68–92.
Williamson, T., Newburn, T. & Wright, A. (2007). The future of criminal investigation. In T. Newburn, T. Williamson & A. Wright (eds), *Handbook of Criminal Investigation*. Cullompton, UK: Willan Publishing, pp. 652–657.
Willis, J.J. (2013) *Improving Police: What's Craft Got to Do with It? Ideas in American Policing. The Police Foundation*. Available online at: http://www.policefoundation.org/docs/library.html
Wilson, J.Q. (1978). *The Investigators: Managing FBI and Narcotics Agents*. New York: Basic Books.

Wright, M. (2013). Homicide detectives' intuition. *Journal of Investigative Psychology and Offender Profiling*, 10(2), 182–199.

Zander, M. (1979). Investigation of crime: a study of cases tried at the Old Bailey. *Criminal Law Review*, April, 203–219.

Zander, M. (2012). *PACE (The Police and Criminal Evidence Act 1984): Past, Present and Future*. LSE Law, Society and Economy working papers, 1/2012, London School of Economics Law Department. Available at: http://www.lse.ac.uk/collections/law/wps/

Chapter 3

Investigative decision making

Karl Ask and Ivar Fahsing

Introduction

The ultimate aim of a criminal investigation is to provide reliable, complete, and relevant information about an event or series of events. In theory, this may seem like a straightforward endeavour, but in reality investigations are complicated by a number of practical constraints. For instance, not all relevant information is there to be found in the first place; a criminal may not leave any detectable traces at the crime scene, and there may not be any witnesses to the event. Moreover, information tends to decay over time; whether left as physical traces or encoded in human memory, relevant information may no longer be available by the time investigators try to retrieve it. Furthermore, and most critical to this chapter, there are no universal standards as to what is to be considered reliable, complete, and relevant information. Instead, this depends very much on the individuals who conduct the investigation and the hypotheses those individuals entertain in their minds. It is thus obvious that psychology in general, and particularly the psychology of decision making, is relevant to how investigative decision making can be improved.

Progress in the research field of investigative decision making has been spurred on by numerous discoveries of miscarriages of justice (see Chapter 1, this volume). A recent notorious example can be found in the multiple murder convictions of Sture Bergwall (formerly known as Thomas Quick). In the period between 1994 and 2001, Bergwall was convicted of eight murders in Sweden and Norway to which he had confessed while in forensic psychiatric care. These convictions were passed despite the fact that Bergwall's confessions were the only tangible evidence of his guilt, and despite the fact that the confessions were often incomplete and inconsistent, many times blatantly at odds with known facts in the case. In 2008, Bergwall retracted his confessions, claiming he had confessed to the crimes during a period of severe mental illness and that he had reaped benefits from the confessions in the form of therapeutic attention and access to potent sedative medication. Following the retractions, Bergwall has been exonerated from all eight charges due to the absence of incriminating evidence. In 2015, the official reports of commissions on the

Bergwall cases in Sweden and Norway, respectively, were presented (Justitiedepartementet, 2015; Riksadvokaten, 2015). In both reports, it was concluded that the wrongful convictions can be traced in part to poor decision making on the part of the investigative team (which consisted largely of the same individuals in all the cases). Specifically, investigators focused narrow-mindedly on a single hypothesis (i.e., that of Bergwall being guilty) and failed to consider alternative possibilities and search for potentially exonerating evidence. In fact, the cases had most of the characteristics of the compendium of psychological phenomena popularly known as 'tunnel vision' (Findley & Scott, 2006).

Cases such as the example above have taught us that one of the most crucial skills of criminal investigators is the ability to generate, entertain, and test investigative hypotheses in a systematic and impartial manner.[1] Moreover, there is a striking resemblance between accounts of different notorious criminal investigative failures (e.g., the 'Yorkshire Ripper' and 'Dr Death' investigations, the Soham murders, the murder of Stephen Lawrence), suggesting that their causes cannot be attributed mainly to inadequately performed investigative actions (e.g., interviews, lineups), but rather to errors in investigators' underlying decision making (Macpherson, 1999; McGrory & Treacy, 2012; Roycroft, Brown, & Innes, 2013). In this chapter, we first briefly review how psychological research has contributed to our understanding of biases and errors in criminal investigations. Then, we review important policy changes with relevance for investigative decision making and evaluate them in light of the current knowledge about human decision making. Finally, we turn to what we identify as the most promising contributions that psychology can offer to improve investigative decision making in the future.

Psychology and investigative decision making

Most of the current academic knowledge about the nature of criminal investigation comes not from psychological research but from research conducted within a criminological or sociological approach (e.g., Burrows & Tarling, 1987; Greenwood, Chaiken, & Petersilia, 1977; Innes, 2003). This line of research has had the purpose of providing an accurate account of actual police practice, and the data presented are typically of a descriptive character. For instance, comparisons between different types of crime in terms of clear-up rates and typical investigative strategies are common (Burrows & Tarling, 1987; Greenwood et al., 1977). Particularly noteworthy is the seminal work by Martin Innes (2003), who conducted extensive observational field studies of detectives' work in homicide investigations. From this research, we have learned a great deal about how investigations typically proceed and about the challenges that investigators face in the complex reality of policing. While this type of descriptive knowledge is important in its own right, it tells us little about *why* certain obstacles to successful investigative decision making occur and what can be done to prevent them.

To draw reliable causal conclusions (i.e., what causes what), and to develop effective countermeasures, experimental methods are required, and that is a domain for which psychological science is particularly well suited. Over the past couple of decades, psychologists have conducted experimental research to understand why a range of investigative biases and errors take place. This research has tended to focus on a particularly pernicious and ubiquitous tendency of human thinking – confirmation bias (Ask & Granhag, 2005). Confirmation bias has two expressions: (a) the tendency of decision makers to primarily search for evidence that supports a currently held hypothesis (while failing to seek evidence inconsistent with the hypothesis); and (b) the tendency to interpret ambiguous information predominantly as support for the hypothesis (while disregarding alternative interpretations). Confirmation bias can do a lot of damage in criminal investigations, where the ideal is to conduct a fair and objective test of multiple hypotheses. Experimental psychology research has documented a range of factors that increase the risk of investigative confirmation bias and has widened our understanding of how investigators, despite the best of intentions, can arrive at blatantly inaccurate conclusions. Among the identified risk factors are circumstances that frequently characterize investigators' work environment, such as time pressure, results-oriented occupational norms, and emotion-provoking events (Ask & Alison, 2010).

Although there is now a growing body of experimental research into the workings of criminal investigation, it is by no means easy to translate that knowledge into changes in actual police practice. Canter and Youngs (2009) discuss several ways in which the cultures of the police organization and the scientific community differ. For instance, the preferred methodology (due process vs. scientific method) and the scope of explanation (individual case vs. general trends) differ markedly. These differences may explain, at least partly, why psychological research has had a rather limited impact on policy changes with regard to investigative decision making. It may be that police investigators' predominant focus on legal requirements and case-specific facts makes general scientific knowledge about human decision making seem irrelevant to day-to-day police work. Hence, it remains an important challenge to bridge the gap between the reality of policing and the academic nature of psychological research. It should be noted, however, that great advances have been made in translating psychological research into practice in other specific aspects of criminal investigation, like witness testimony (see Chapter 6, this volume) and suspect interviewing (see Chapter 8, this volume), and that the domain of investigative decision making may well follow suit. Because that progress is rather modest thus far, we will spend most of this chapter examining policy changes that have taken place without much involvement of psychological research, and describing areas where we believe psychological research may play a key role in the future.

Policy changes: where is psychology?

As mentioned earlier, psychological research has had little impact on past reforms regulating specifically how investigative decision making occurs in practice. It is nonetheless useful to examine the most relevant policy changes in light of psychological knowledge, because this can help identify their likely consequences and any issues to be addressed in future reforms.

A crucial milestone was the first UK Royal Commission on Criminal Procedure (1978–1984), which appointed Barrie Irving to examine the current practice of interrogation in England and Wales. The abuse of police powers and over-reliance on confession evidence at the time clearly permeated police work outside of the interviewing room too. The Commission resulted in the Police and Criminal Evidence Act (1984), setting out a core framework of police powers and safeguards around stop and search, arrest, detention, investigation, identification, and interviewing detainees (Irving & Hilgendorf, 1980). Around the same time, the so-called Byford Report (1982) looked into the investigation of the murders committed by Peter Sutcliffe, more commonly known as "the Yorkshire Ripper". Sir Byford found that the 6-year enquiry, involving several different police forces, suffered from difficulties with the organizing and processing of the vast amount of gathered information, as well as poor decision making relating to the early elimination of Peter Sutcliffe as a suspect. The problems identified in this enquiry accelerated the introduction of the computer software HOLMES (Home Office Large Major Enquiry System) into major incident rooms in England and Wales (Harris, 2008). From a psychological perspective, such decision support systems are indispensable as they counteract the well-known problem of information overload, which quickly appears as large quantities of data accumulate (Bryant, 2009). The observations regarding faulty decision making made in those early reports, however, appear to have had little impact on the responses that followed in the British police organization; the research and development that actually took place after the first Royal Commission mainly concerned the introduction of computer systems and improved methods for investigative interviewing (Williamson, 2007; see also Chapter 8, this volume).

The next British Royal Commission on Criminal Justice (1993) focused even more on deficits in the supervision of criminal investigations, and for the first time investigators' decision making was mentioned explicitly. Barrie Irving, again involved in the Commission, argued for the need to improve officers' reasoning and decision making by challenging the "common sense" about criminals and crimes, and the "working rules about causation, about suspicion and guilt … [which] are passed from experienced to inexperienced officers" (Irving & Dunningham, 1993, p. 17). These conclusions were supported by other studies under the same Commission, which found that although new legislation was in place and all suspect interviews were now being recorded, very little had changed for the better and the researchers "found no evidence of formal or informal quality control systems designed to minimise error" (Royal Commission on Criminal Justice, 1993, p. 20). To address these shortcomings, the Commission recommended a number of changes, including external revision of ongoing cases; increased disclosure of documents to the defence lawyer; overhaul of the detective training; a clearer distinction between the role of general police officers and detectives; increased use of the HOLMES system; formal debriefs; and the introduction of policy files in all major inquiries, documenting the outset of the investigation, its lines of enquiry, any critical decisions made, and any restrictions made due to limited resources.

The Association of Chief Police Officers (ACPO) and the British Police Service have clearly attempted to make up for the, more or less, continuous critique over the past 35 years. The Home Office established their own research series in the early 1990s and the ACPO has introduced a series of manuals aiming to implement a model for investigation in England and Wales (e.g., ACPO, 2000, 2012). This is clearly illustrated by the following excerpt from the *Murder Investigation Manual* (ACPO, 2000), which presents itself as

> constructed around a model of murder investigation developed within the police service, but based upon a scientific model. The model fully recognises the core activities which occur during the course of a murder investigation, whilst promoting the principles that all investigations should be:
>
> - intelligence led
> - underpinned by research and analysis
> - managed through the application of theory and logic
> - dynamic and capable of rapid response.
>
> Importantly, the model not only describes the investigative process, but it seeks to discipline the mind of an SIO [Senior Investigating Officer]. It is suggested that, if SIOs can train their minds to manage murder investigations using the model, the outcome will be an ethical and professionally led investigation.
>
> (ACPO, 2000, p. 15)

Additionally, there has been a drive to improve the competence of all police officers and staff tasked with conducting investigations through the introduction of the Professionalising Investigation Programme (PIP; McGrory & Treacy, 2012) as explained in Chapter 2. Moreover, full-scale exercises in so-called Hydra decision-making simulation suites are compulsory to all PIP levels, both operative and strategic. Hydra is a high-fidelity immersive simulation training system designed to facilitate the development of operational decision-making skills, cooperation, and review (Eyre, Crego, & Alison, 2008). It can be specifically tailored to develop the strategic and critical decision-making skills of Senior Investigating Officers (SIOs; Alison & Crego, 2008). As a part of the recent reforms, all investigations that are defined as *major crime enquiries* are subject to the requirement of documenting decision logs, policy files, and written reviews (ACPO, 2012). The implementation of PIP was reviewed by Flanagan (2008), who concluded that it had established a body of knowledge for investigative practice and delivered a recognizable framework to professionalize investigation which had been previously absent. According to Flanagan, it had provided the opportunity to "deliver the right people, with the right skills in the right place at the right time" (p. 6).

It is indeed likely that these combined initiatives to improve detectives' accountability and operational decision making have improved the overall quality of investigative work in England and Wales. However, this assumption has never been scientifically tested against other potential approaches, models, or methods. The available research from the Home Office Research Series show that there has been no research on investigative decision making since the research series first was established in 1992. The *Murder Investigation Manual* (ACPO, 2000) is presented more or less as a silver bullet to ensure successful and ethical investigations in critical and major incidents. Unfortunately, however, instead of expressing awareness and humility toward this highly complex task, the publication seems to uphold an existing culture of overconfidence within the organization. It is a paradox that while influential researchers in human decision making identified criminal justice as a particularly risky arena already in the early 1970s (Tversky & Kahneman, 1974), the ACPO manuals do not at all promote knowledge based on decision-making research. In fact, although the words "scientific" and "science" appear frequently throughout the *Murder Investigation Manual*, there are no references to actual scientific work in it or any indication that the advocated model of investigation is supported by empirical evidence. It is therefore not possible to assess the degree to which the guidelines are inspired by available research. Reading between the lines of the *Manual*, however, it becomes clear that the model itself has never been scientifically tested (Tong, Bryant, & Horvath, 2009). This discrepancy was highlighted by the National Head of Investigative Practice in England and Wales at the time, Peter Stelfox, who depicted the science of cognition and the field of criminal investigation as *reluctant bedfellows* (Stelfox & Pease, 2005). In order to guide future practice and policy, previous qualitative research (e.g., Innes, 2003) and changes in working procedures should be followed up with controlled experimental research on how to facilitate professional and evidence-based practices (Sherman, 2015).

Despite the apparent lack of scientific evidence for the advice given in previous reforms in England and Wales, no other government or police service in the world has so openly stated a need for a change in policy when it comes to investigative decision making (Home Office, 2001). Despite a number of high-profile cases of serious miscarriage of justice in other European countries (e.g., Fahsing & Rachlew, 2009; van Koppen, 2008), we are not aware of any policy developments towards standardized investigative methods or accreditation of detectives that match the scope and investment seen in the British police. Instead, the materials produced by ACPO and the Home Office today serve as a standard toward which police services in many other parts of the world aspire (Westera, Kebbell, Milne, & Green, 2016). While this is arguably much better than allowing police forces to operate without any standards, we believe that future platforms for investigative decision making need to be rooted more firmly in the knowledge base arising from over 50 years of research on human decision making.

The future: how can psychology help investigative decision making?

Based on our own experience from research and development in policing, and on observations from other areas of applied decision making, we believe what is needed to improve criminal investigative practice is concrete, practical interventions that draw on solid scientific knowledge. It is to such interventions we turn next. Historically, there are many examples of how psychological science can help improve decision making in applied domains, such as medicine, financial decision making, and engineering (Zsambok & Klein, 1997). Through sound practitioner–researcher collaboration, systems have been developed that improve decision making with real and tangible consequences (e.g., increased survival rates as a result of improved medical decisions; Gigerenzer & Todd, 1999). Although psychological knowledge has not been transferred to the investigative decision-making domain to the same extent, we see great potential for this in the future. Below we will address four areas that we have identified as particularly promising.

Training and education

Awareness and insight into decision theory is the first step toward better methods, systems, and safeguards in any organization (Tversky & Koehler, 1994). Awareness of relevant psychological phenomena is therefore essential and should be a part of any curriculum for police officers and detectives. Today, a number of textbooks offer applied perspectives on judgment and decision making in the criminal investigative process (e.g., Alison & Crego, 2008; Rossmo, 2009). In Norway, where the police education is offered at a university level (a 3-year Bachelor's degree in policing), such literature has been on the curriculum for more than 10 years. In England and Wales, where the basic police training is shorter and more practically oriented (typically compulsory foundation training for 25 weeks followed by a 2-year probation period; Metropolitan Police, 2014), recruits may be less likely encounter this body of research at an early stage of their careers. So are experienced detectives generally aware of relevant psychological phenomena? At present there is no conclusive answer to that question. In a recent interview study, however, experienced

Norwegian detectives and PIP-accredited English SIOs both expressed familiarity with at least some of the factors which may compromise optimal decision making, and the consensus among the Norwegian and English respondents regarding these factors was very high (Fahsing & Ask, 2013). This result indicates that beliefs corresponding to the available decision-making literature can be achieved based on either of two distinctly different epistemological foundations – one more academically oriented (Norway) and the other more practically oriented (England). The findings do not show, however, whether detectives are exceptionally well aware of decision-making phenomena or whether their expressed beliefs simply reflect common-sense knowledge (no comparison with the beliefs of laypeople was made).

The awareness displayed among specialized crime detectives may seem reassuring. However, numerous studies have shown that whilst knowledge, skills, and abilities are typically interlinked, they are not the same thing; awareness of cognitive biases and knowledge of decision theory does not necessarily make one a good decision maker or protect one against cognitive biases (Gigerenzer & Todd, 1999; Gilovich, Griffin, & Kahneman, 2002). What is needed to improve performance is active de-biasing countermeasures, in combination with skills and abilities developed through extensive training and feedback (Ericsson, Prietula, & Cokely, 2007). A good example of a countermeasure against the confirmation bias is the 'consider-the-opposite' technique (Lord, Lepper, & Preston, 1984). In short, the technique works by forcing decision makers to consider why their focal hypothesis might be wrong early in the hypothesis-testing process. Although we are not aware of any studies testing its effectiveness among experienced detectives, O'Brien (2009) showed that mock investigators (college students) became less biased in their information search and inferences as a result of the technique. Interestingly, the *Murder Investigation Manual* (ACPO, 2000) and the *Core Investigative Doctrine* (ACPO, 2012), while not specifically referring to psychological research, offer some recommendations similar to those that can be derived from relevant research findings. For instance, Jones, Grieve, and Milne (2008) describe how SIOs in murder investigations are to document the relevant hypotheses that can be identified in the case and subsequently seek to *disprove* each one; the one that remains after such attempts at falsification is probably the strongest theory.

In an attempt to investigate how differences in training and education may influence investigators' decision-making skills, we recently conducted a study comparing the hypothesis-testing abilities of Norwegian and English police officers at different levels of experience (Fahsing & Ask, 2016). As mentioned previously, the paths toward detective expertise are distinctly different in the two countries: Norwegian investigators initially undergo an extensive, academically oriented basic education, but receive no standardized training to develop and maintain detective expertise (Politidirektoratet, 2013). English detectives, on the other hand, receive little academic training initially, but subsequently undergo an elaborate training and accreditation programme, including frequent quality assurance measures (e.g., policy logs, case reviews). When testing the ability to generate relevant investigative hypotheses and investigative actions, we observed a huge effect of experience in the English sample; the experienced English investigators (SIOs who had undergone the entire PIP programme) vastly outperformed English novice police officers and performed markedly better than their Norwegian counterparts. In the Norwegian sample, however, we did not observe any beneficial effect of experience, but the Norwegian novices performed significantly better than their English counterparts (Fahsing & Ask, 2016).

Our cross-national comparison suggests that some aspects of investigative decision making are susceptible to system differences. It seems that experience may be conducive of improved decision-making skills, but only when developed under favourable conditions. Thus, lengthy experience alone does not guarantee sound decisions. On the other hand, academically oriented basic police training seems neither sufficient nor necessary for achieving expert performance, but may provide a solid foundation that guarantees an adequate performance early in investigators' careers. Although our results indicate that the reforms put in place in England and Wales may benefit detectives' decision making, it must be kept in mind that differences in performance between countries may also stem from differences in variables like crime rates, operational routines, professional status, and culture. More tightly controlled experimental studies are necessary to elucidate the unique contribution of different policy changes.

It is impossible to talk of education and training without stressing the importance of feedback. Repeated and realistic feedback is fundamental to developing any skill, and the more complex the task the more training and feedback is needed (Klein & Hoffmann, 1993). In countries like Norway, where the number of homicides occurring each year is small (23 homicides in 2015; Kripos, 2015), the opportunities for individual officers to receive extensive feedback on homicide investigations through their daily duty are quite rare and unsystematic. The aviation industry has tackled the individual need for extensive training, and the fact that most critical incidents occur very rarely, through the use of realistic flight simulators and the development of mandatory checklists for use in the cockpit (Graham, 2004). The simulators are now so realistic that airline crews can be trained to handle critical situations, which many of them will never experience in real life. In order to implement similar systems in the investigative domain, research is needed to identify (a) the most critical operations in real-life environments, and (b) the best way to train and evaluate these operations in simulated environments. Both simulations and so-called electronic debriefs (where senior officers anonymously communicate their experiences from critical events) have been used successfully in England and Wales to identify critical operations in the police management of critical incidents (Eyre, Crego, & Alison, 2008). Furthermore, recent research demonstrates how simulations might improve operational decision making in life-saving terrorism operations (van den Heuvel, Alison, & Crego, 2012). Ideally, simulation training of investigative decision making and academic research can be combined in fruitful ways. Participation in research experiments provides an excellent opportunity for detectives to get first-hand experience and receive immediate feedback on factors that influence decision making. At the same time, researchers can systematically manipulate critical factors and evaluate their influence on decision making in a realistic setting and with a relevant sample of participants, who are otherwise difficult to recruit for research purposes.

Procedures and models

The most valuable instrument for any detective is their ability to think and analyze information in as rational a manner as possible in sometimes very demanding situations. Though there are a myriad of checklists and methods available on how to reliably collect information during an investigation, there are very few models available that guide detectives' thinking and decision making. As concluded by Stelfox and Pease (2005), "there is no commonly-accepted corpus of knowledge within the police service which informs officers' actions in the process of detection" (p. 192). It should therefore be a paramount goal of research in this area to develop evidence-based, normative models of thinking that help investigators avoid the most common decision-making errors.

A common decision-making failure, identified both in experimental research and in investigations of criminal cases, is the decision maker's failure to identify all plausible alternatives before they start evaluating and integrating information to arrive at a final choice. Accordingly, it has been suggested that one of the most effective strategies for reducing judgmental biases is to force individuals to systematically consider alternatives – a debiasing strategy recommended already by the seventeenth-century philosopher Francis Bacon (Lord et al., 1984). This Baconian approach to probability builds on the assumption that regardless of how many favourable results there are for a hypothesis, it only takes one unfavourable result to disprove it. The procedure thus encourages the decision maker to also generate evidence that supports alternative outcomes, resulting in a more balanced and objective evaluation of the relevant evidence at the time of judgment. A systematic consideration of all the competing options should lead people to use a more thorough and qualitatively better judgmental process (Hirt & Markman, 1995). Translated to criminal investigations, the Baconian approach is closely related to Zuckerman's (1989) recommendation that "the fact-finder has to follow a mental procedure of progressive elimination of explanations consistent with innocence" (p. 134). A number of subsequent studies have proven this strategy effective for reducing the negative effects of several known cognitive sources of error, such as for example confirmation bias (Lord et al., 1984), hindsight bias (Sanna & Schwarz, 2003), and overconfidence (Koriat, Lichtenstein, & Fischhoff, 1980). The effect of the 'consider-the-alternatives' strategy has been demonstrated to go beyond the task at a hand (Hirt, Kardes, & Markman, 2004) and to stimulate creative thinking and analytical problem-solving in general, by invoking persistent changes in mind-sets (Markman, Lindberg, Kray, & Galinsky, 2007).

A similar approach is advocated in the British Criminal Procedure and Investigations Act (1996) code of practice: "where a criminal investigation is conducted, the investigator must take all reasonable steps for the purposes of the investigation and pursue *all reasonable lines* of enquiry, whether these point towards or away from the suspect" (section 23[1]; emphasis added). The fundamental legal obligation to impartially consider both incriminating and exculpatory evidence, embedded in principles from early Roman law, is a norm in the criminal justice system of most modern democracies (Stumer, 2010) and can only be understood as a caution against fast and frugal decision making in criminal cases. This caution, however, has not yet been incorporated into any scientifically validated model prescribing how investigators should go about generating and testing investigative hypotheses.

A prescriptive model of reasoning must take as its starting point the *type* of reasoning to which it is intended to apply. Solving crime is probably best characterized as a task of abductive logic (Simon, 2012). Abduction is the cognitive process of identifying the best possible explanation (out of several competing options) for a set of observations, and is characteristic of tasks like medical diagnosis, scientific discovery, and discourse comprehension (Josephson & Josephson, 1994). In the context of criminal investigation, the competing explanations are different narrative accounts of what has occurred (e.g., a missing person has run away, has been kidnapped, has committed suicide, etc.), and the set of observations to be explained includes any information with relevance to the event (e.g., physical traces, witness reports, etc.).

In an attempt to describe and facilitate this abductive process, Fahsing (2014) presented the Investigative Cycle (see Figure 3.1). The model seeks to describe both the questions any investigation ideally should answer (who did what, how, where, when and why?) and how these can be explored in a systematic process involving six interlinked steps: (1) collecting data; (2) checking the data for relevance, accuracy, and reliability; (3) connecting data from different sources; (4) constructing all relevant competing explanations/hypotheses; (5) considering all explanations, gauging them against available data, and identifying information gaps; and (6) consulting others to feed in new knowledge and to challenge one's own views. This process should be iterated as long as there is legally obtainable information available and a perceived need to explore or strengthen the case construction (Dean, Fahsing, Glomseth, & Gottschalk, 2008).

Another proposed tool that may facilitate a systematic approach to hypothesis testing is the Analysis of Competing Hypotheses (ACH) method. Originally designed for use by practitioners within the intelligence field (Heuer Jr., 1999), ACH uses a matrix to display the weighting of alternative explanations and conclusions for a given problem (see Figure 3.2). Drawing on the fundamental investigative principle of cross-checking information from different sources

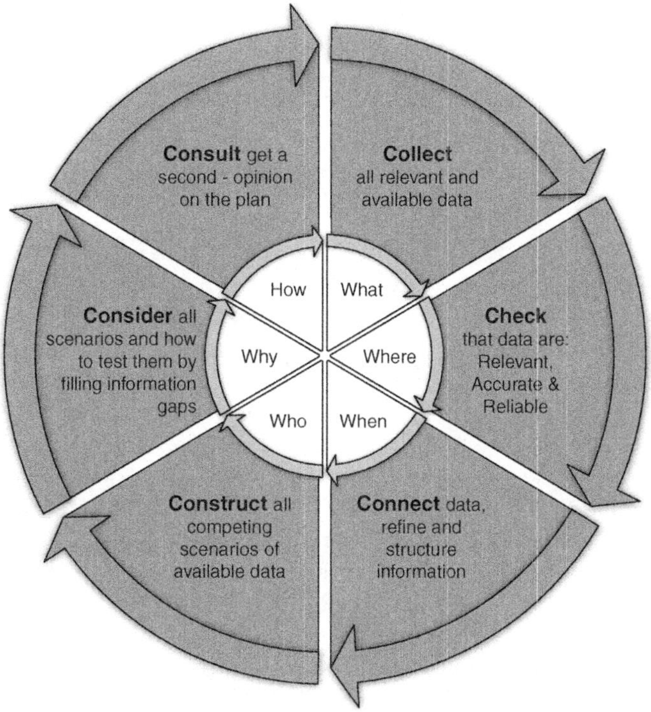

Figure 3.1 The Investigative Cycle model (Fahsing, 2014), intended to describe and facilitate the process of abductive reasoning in criminal investigations

(Gordon & Hayward, 1968; Dean, 2005), ACH makes explicit what evidence is used, how evidence is considered, and how it relates to all the competing hypotheses in the case. In a first step, all possible alternative hypotheses are generated. To uphold the legally required presumption of innocence, a null hypothesis (H_0) assuming that the suspect has not committed the crime must be among the hypotheses considered. Second, the items of evidence with the greatest probative value with regard to a given hypothesis are identified. Third, particular focus is placed on identifying evidence that may disprove or weaken a given hypothesis. The latter step aligns the ACH method with the scientific ideal of "falsification" (Townsley, Mann, & Garrett, 2011) and aids investigators in achieving the standard burden of proof in criminal cases. Because the considered hypotheses are mutually competitive, the weakening of one hypothesis necessarily entails the strengthening of others. Hence, the progressive elimination of explanations consistent with innocence helps rule out any reasonable doubt that may prevent the conviction of a guilty perpetrator.

The Investigative Cycle (Fahsing, 2014) and the ACH method (Townsley et al., 2011) have not yet been subject to empirical testing, and their practical

	H_0	H_1	H_2
Evidence 1	Consistent	Consistent	N/A
Evidence 2	Inconsistent	Consistent	Inconsistent
Evidence 3	Inconsistent	Consistent	Consistent

Figure 3.2 An example Analysis of Competing Hypotheses matrix that uses a colouring scheme for evidence evaluation to facilitate interpretation

value for improving investigators' decision making is therefore not known. We present them here, however, as examples of the type of condensed and pragmatic guidelines that may be necessary to bridge the current gap between available scientific knowledge and operational routines in detective work. The tradition for checklists and models is strong within the police. This is evident in the ACPO manuals (e.g., ACPO, 2000, 2012) and in investigation handbooks written by detectives (e.g., Cook & Tattersall, 2014). To boost the impact of any prescriptive model, its presentation should be tailored to the modes of instruction already established in the field. It is important to keep in mind that a structured model of investigative decision making would not automatically solve any crimes; the quality of decisions will ultimately depend on the reasoning abilities of the individual detective. Instead, the model would help the detective to engage in a deeper and more systematic processing of information than would otherwise be the case. To summarize, while some practical procedures to aid decision making have been recommended by researchers (Ask, 2006; Fahsing, 2014), by the ACPO (2012), and recently by the Norwegian Prosecutor General (Riksadvokaten, 2015), their actual debiasing effects in investigative settings have not been evaluated scientifically. This should be a priority of future research in the area.

Decision support systems

The limited capacity of the human mind to store and process information is often painfully obvious. This is especially true when decision makers need to make sense of vast and constantly changing bodies of data, as is often the case in complex criminal investigations (Bryant, 2009). Without external aids for storing and systematizing information, much of modern-day policing would not be possible. For instance, investigations of organized crime today often span across several continents and contain information about thousands of suspects. The coordination of such massive inquiries has been made possible largely by technological innovations over the past 40 years. This is a development that is likely to proceed at an increasing rate in the future, and one to which psychologists may bring important contributions.

The need to sift through and reduce the complexity of large quantities of data is addressed by so-called decision support systems. Typically, such systems not only encode and store information, but importantly present the information in a form that will assist investigators in making the right decisions (Canter & Youngs, 2009). Many decision support systems make use of the fact that humans often find it easier to make sense of information presented visually rather than verbally. For instance, graphical illustrations feature prominently in software developed to aid the task of *geographical profiling* (i.e., predicting a perpetrator's most likely residence or base location), where prioritized search areas are typically indicated by coloured regions on a map (e.g., Dragnet; Canter & Youngs, 2009). A related use of decision support systems is for the purpose of *crime linking*, which is the process of identifying multiple crime instances likely to have been committed by the same perpetrator(s). Computer-based implementations of complex computational algorithms, drawing on statistics of previously solved crimes, can offer investigators guidance as to which crimes display the highest probability of having a common offender. Hence, many investigative decision support systems existing today can undoubtedly provide valuable *input* for decisions; that is, they can generate a meaningful and structured information basis on which decisions can be made. However, systems intended to aid the actual decision *process* – how decision alternatives are generated and chosen – are still very rare.

Interestingly, the process of abductive reasoning, which characterizes much of investigative work, is a central feature also in the development of artificial intelligence (Reiter, 1987). Today, so-called expert systems dominate many professional fields to the degree that we would not be able to operate without them (Liao, 2005). Modern weather forecasting, for example, would be entirely impossible without the predictive power of complex computer simulations (Edwards, 2001). Much like crime investigators, weather forecasters are faced with the abductive-reasoning task of identifying the most likely scenario (future weather) based on a particular set of observations (past and current weather). Initial attempts to exploit the power of artificial intelligence for investigative purposes have been made by Keppens and colleagues (Keppens & Schafer, 2004; Keppens & Zeleznikow, 2003), who have designed computational algorithms for evidence evaluation based on abductive logic. Combining such algorithms with large-scale evidence databases, like the Scottish Phoenix database (Linden & Campbell, 2010), may in the future help investigators with the demanding task of generating and selecting among multiple plausible crime scenarios. Possibly, the same algorithms and databases can be exploited to generate large-scale, realistic decision-making simulations. In sum, while still in its infancy, the introduction of artificial intelligence has the potential to transform both procedures and training in criminal investigation.

Police culture and organization

Psychologists can help structuring investigators' work environment in ways that optimize conditions for sound decision making and minimize the risk of error. A good place to start would be the incentive structure characteristic of much police work. Police authorities are characterized by a specific occupational culture with social norms that place a premium on decisiveness and efficiency

(Mortimer & Shepherd, 1999). Moreover, most of the performance indicators that are being used to evaluate the quality of crime investigations are quantitative, implying that achieving an acceptable throughput of cases is of paramount importance. As would be predicted from the scientific literature on cultural and organizational psychology (e.g., Hofstede, 2001), these norms affect the values and goals held by crime investigators and how they approach individual cases (Ask, Granhag, & Rebelius, 2011). Researchers have noted a 'confession culture' in criminal investigation departments, where the motivation to achieve incrimination and closure risks taking precedence over truth-finding and impartiality (Mortimer & Shepherd, 1999).

To combat the systemic fostering of an overly confession- and incrimination-oriented culture, a two-pronged approach to organizational changes of the incentive structure of criminal investigation departments is necessary: First, the predominant focus on incrimination and closure needs to be shifted so that investigative work is rewarded on the merit of its soundness in addition to its outcome.[2] Investigators need to be confident that a thorough and unbiased investigation is considered equally as important as the speedy identification and prosecution of a suspect. This requires the introduction of alternative performance indicators which do not focus on the mere throughput of cases but rather on the manner in which those cases were handled. Second, measures can be taken to encourage self-evaluation and constructive criticism within the police organization. Such measures include peer-reviewing of recent cases to enable constructive feedback and critical learning opportunities. Importantly, such reviews should focus not only on the outcome of the case (i.e., whether the perpetrator was detected), but also on whether the case was processed in an unbiased and systematic manner. The latter aspect is crucial, because sometimes even biased and sloppy detective work leads to the successful solving of simple cases (so-called 'self-solvers'; Innes, 2003), whereas even the most skilled detectives, using the most thorough of methods, may fail to solve complex crimes. With an emphasis on qualitative performance indicators, the latter type of investigation would receive the more favourable evaluation. Another measure to the same end would be to appoint 'devil's advocates' – individuals who are encouraged to identify weaknesses and competing perspectives in current cases. This may be colleagues within the same police department, or better yet, someone from outside the organization. Importantly, the devil's advocate should be an individual without personal investment in the case and with a status and personality makeup that make them comfortable voicing criticism. Interestingly, some of the organizational changes implemented through the PIP programme in England and Wales (e.g., case reviews, decision logs) have most likely had the effect of encouraging self-evaluation, although the measures were not introduced as a result of psychological research.

Another area where psychological research may help concerns the identification of individuals with the optimal set of cognitive and social characteristics for the job as detective. To date, this is a largely unexplored area. A few scattered studies have been conducted, suggesting some relationships between personality and the performance of investigative tasks. For instance, Ask and Granhag (2005) found that detectives with a higher need for cognitive closure (i.e., the desire to quickly arrive at conclusions and to avoid uncertainty) were somewhat less likely to identify inconsistencies in the evidence regarding a homicide. Moreover, Alison and colleagues (2013) found that detectives who performed better at a measure of fluid intelligence were also more capable of withstanding the debilitating influence of time pressure on hypothesis generation in criminal cases. In contrast, however, Fahsing and Ask (2017) recently failed to observe any relationship between hypothesis-generation performance and measures of cognitive ability administered at the commencement of the basic training of police officers in Norway. In light of the scarce and somewhat inconsistent findings, it seems a more systematic research programme would be necessary to identify a personality profile which is predictive of skillful performance across a range of investigative tasks. It should be noted that most existing measures of reasoning ability are designed to measure varieties of inductive and deductive reasoning (Stanovich, 2011). These tests may not adequately capture the type of abductive reasoning necessary to successfully carry out investigative tasks. Hence, to truly capture the role of individual differences in the detective profession, it may be necessary to devise measures of reasoning ability that more accurately reflect the decision environment of criminal investigations.

Related to detectives' personality characteristics is the challenge of constructing investigative teams with an optimal combination of skills and individual thinking styles. We believe this is also an area where psychological research may be of assistance in the future. Considering previous research demonstrating the negative consequences of an excessively homogenous group composition (Parks & Sanna, 1999), it is likely that criminal investigations would benefit from a well-balanced mix of personal strengths and competencies. To return to the example of need for cognitive closure (NFC), one could predict that high- and low-NFC team members would contribute uniquely to the team's productivity; high-NFC members by promoting the momentum necessary for successful investigations (e.g., by preventing decision inertia; Alison & Crego, 2008), and low-NFC members by promoting the thoroughness and reflectiveness necessary to avoid premature conclusions. Apart from being useful at the recruitment stage, knowledge about productive team compositions would be informative as to how senior managers can best organize their existing staff resources.

A final organizational aspect that may prevent bias and decision-making errors concerns the allocation of investigative tasks among team members. It is well established in the psychological literature that personal investment in a hypothesis or explanation greatly increases the risk for partiality and wishful thinking (Nickerson, 1998). The amount of personal investment rises with every step taken in a particular favoured direction. Hence, it may not be optimal that the same individual detectives are involved in the execution of most or all of the steps in an investigation. Instead, a potential safeguard against personal investment could be to separate investigative steps through a process of bifurcation; for instance, some team members can be actively involved in the generation of hypotheses, whereas other members are responsible for the actual testing of those hypotheses. An additional means to the same end would be to introduce *blinding* where feasible; for instance, forensic analysts should ideally be unaware of investigators' dominant hypothesis when examining criminal evidence (MacLean & Dror, 2016).

Conclusions

In this chapter, we have reviewed the past and current relationships between psychological research and investigative decision-making practice. From a historical perspective, there is very little evidence that psychological theory or research has been consciously incorporated into official reforms and guidelines regarding how investigators should process information and make investigative decisions. Nonetheless, the beginning of this century has witnessed some developments in the police profession which resonate well with established findings in psychology. These include the requirements for systematic documentation and review introduced with the PIP programme in England and Wales. Considering research on the debiasing potential of systematic scrutiny and accountability, the PIP programme has likely contributed to an increase in the overall quality of investigative decisions. Empirical support for this assumption has just recently started to emerge.

Because of the scarcity of research–practice interplay in the past, we have spent a great part of this chapter identifying key areas of investigative decision making where psychological research has the potential to contribute in the future. These areas include the incorporation of psychological knowledge in the education and training of detectives, in the development of procedures and decision aids, and in structural changes at the organizational level that may facilitate unbiased and successful decision making. Our personal experiences from psychological research and from police practice tell us that both areas are ripe for a closer and more productive exchange in the future. The psychological literature, on one hand, is rich in relevant knowledge applicable to the decision-making challenges that investigators face on a daily basis; past successful applications of psychology in other practitioner environments (e.g., medicine, financial decision making, engineering) demonstrate the feasibility of this approach. The detective community and police organizations, on the other hand, have expressed a need for evidence-based methods and are becoming increasingly open to researcher–practitioner collaboration. Hence, we expect and welcome an increase in psychologically informed developments in investigative decision making in the near future.

Notes

1 Admittedly, the conduct of criminal investigations involves decisions other than those pertaining to investigative hypotheses (e.g., media strategy, resource allocation, team

management). Most such decisions have received considerably less research attention, however, and are beyond the scope of this chapter. Moreover, they have been treated extensively elsewhere (e.g., Alison & Crego, 2008).

2 Interestingly, a similar movement is currently underway in scientific research, where the traditional reward system has been clearly biased toward the recognition of "statistically significant" research findings (at the expense of well-conducted research with "null findings"). A number of measures have been implemented by the scientific community (e.g., pre-registration of studies), to ensure that research is published on the merit of its theoretical and methodological soundness rather than the "statistical significance" of its outcome (Nosek, Spies, & Motyl, 2012).

References

ACPO. (2000). *Murder investigation manual.* Wyboston, UK: Association of Chief Police Officers.

ACPO. (2012). *Practice advice on core investigative doctrine* (2nd ed.). Wyboston, UK: Association of Chief Police Officers.

Alison, L., & Crego, J. (2008). *Policing critical incidents: Leadership and critical incident management.* Cullompton, UK: Willan Publishing.

Alison, L., Doran, B., Long, M. L., Power, N., & Humphrey, A. (2013). The effects of subjective time pressure and individual differences on hypotheses generation and action prioritization in police investigations. *Journal of Experimental Psychology: Applied,* 19, 83–93.

Ask, K. (2006). Criminal investigation: Motivation, emotion and cognition in the processing of evidence (doctoral dissertation). University of Gothenburg, Department of Psychology, Gothenburg, Sweden. Retrieved from hdl.handle.net/2077/676

Ask, K., & Alison, L. (2010). Investigators' decision making. In P. A. Granhag (ed.), *Forensic psychology in context: Nordic and international perspectives* (pp. 35–55). Cullompton, UK: Willan.

Ask, K., & Granhag, P. A. (2005). Motivational sources of confirmation bias in criminal investigations: The need for cognitive closure. *Journal of Investigative Psychology and Offender Profiling,* 2, 43–63.

Ask, K., Granhag, P. A., & Rebelius, A. (2011). Investigators under influence: How social norms activate goal-directed processing of criminal evidence. *Applied Cognitive Psychology,* 25, 548–553.

Bryant, R. P. (2009). Forms of reasoning and the analysis of intelligence in criminal investigation. In S. Tong, R. P. Bryant, & M. Horvath (eds.), *Understanding criminal investigation* (pp. 35–49). Chichester, UK: Blackwell-Wiley.

Burrows, J., & Tarling, R. (1987). The investigation of crime in England and Wales. *British Journal of Criminology,* 27, 229–251.

Byford, S. L. (1982). *Report into the case of Peter Sutcliffe.* London, UK: Home Office.

Canter, D., & Youngs, D. (2009). *Investigative psychology: Offender profiling and the analysis of criminal action.* Chichester, UK: Wiley.

Cook, T., & Tattersall, A. (2014). *Blackstone's senior investigating officers' handbook.* Oxford, UK: Oxford University Press.

Dean, G. (2005). The 'Cross+Check' system: Integrating profiling approaches for police and security investigations. *Journal of Police and Criminal Psychology,* 20, 20–43.

Dean, G., Fahsing, I. A., Glomseth, R., & Gottschalk, P. (2008). Capturing knowledge of police investigations: Towards a research agenda. *Police Practice and Research,* 9, 341–355.

Edwards, P. N. (2001). Representing the global atmosphere: Computer models, data, and knowledge about climate change. In C. A. Miller & P. N. Edwards (eds.), *Changing the atmosphere: Expert knowledge and environmental governance* (pp. 31–65). Cambridge, MA: MIT Press.

Ericsson, K. A., Prietula, M. J., & Cokely, E. T. (2007). The making of an expert. *Harvard Business Review*, 85, 1–8.

Eyre, M., Crego, J., & Alison, L. (2008). Electronic debriefs and simulations as descriptive methods for defining the critical incident landscape. In L. Alison & J. Crego (eds.), *Policing critical incidents* (pp. 24–53). Collumpton, UK: Willan Publishing.

Fahsing, I. A. (2014). How can we operationalize the presumption of innocence? Paper presented at the 7th Annual Conference of the International Investigative Interviewing Research Group, Lausanne, Switzerland.

Fahsing, I. A., & Ask, K. (2013). Decision making and decisional tipping points in homicide investigations: An interview study of British and Norwegian detectives. *Journal of Investigative Psychology and Offender Profiling*, 10, 155–165.

Fahsing, I. A., & Ask, K. (2016). The making of an expert detective: The role of experience in English and Norwegian police officers' investigative decision-making. *Psychology, Crime & Law*, 22, 203–223.

Fahsing, I. A., & Ask, K. (2017). In search of Indicators of Detective Aptitude: Police recruits' logical reasoning and ability to generate investigative hypotheses. *Journal of Police and Criminal Psychology*. doi:10.1007/s11896-017-9231-3.

Fahsing, I. A., & Rachlew, A. A. (2009). Investigative interviewing in the Nordic region. In T. Williamson, B. Milne, & S. P. Savage (eds.), *International developments in investigative interviewing* (pp. 39–65). Cullompton, UK: Willan.

Findley, K. A., & Scott, M. S. (2006). The multiple dimensions of tunnel vision in criminal cases. *Wisconsin Law Review*, 2, 291–397.

Flanagan, R. (2008). *The review of policing: Final report*. London, UK: HMIC.

Gigerenzer, G., & Todd, P. M. (1999). *Simple heuristics that make us smart*. New York: Oxford University Press.

Gilovich, T., Griffin, D., & Kahneman, D. (eds.). (2002). *Heuristics and biases: The psychology of intuitive judgment*. New York: Cambridge University Press.

Gordon, T. J., & Hayward, H. (1968). Initial experiments with the cross-impact matrix method of forecasting. *Futures*, 1, 100–116.

Graham, C. (2004). Advanced airway management in the emergency department: What are the training and skills maintenance needs for UK emergency physicians? *Emergency Medicine Journal*, 21, 14–19.

Greenwood, P. W., Chaiken, J. M., & Petersilia, J. (1977). *The criminal investigation process*. Lexington, MA: Heath.

Harris, E. C. (2008). The investigation of murder in France and England: A comparative account (unpublished doctoral dissertation). London School of Economics and Political Science, London, UK.

Heuer, Jr., R. J. (1999). Psychology of intelligence analysis. Langley, VA: Central Intelligence Agency. Retrieved from https://www.cia.gov/library/center-for-the-study-of-intelligence/csi-publications/books-and-monographs/psychology-of-intelligence-analysis/art7.html

Hirt, E. R., Kardes, F. R., & Markman, K. D. (2004). Activating a mental simulation mind-set through generation of alternatives: Implications for debiasing in related and unrelated domains. *Journal of Experimental Social Psychology*, 40, 374–383.

Hirt, E. R., & Markman, K. D. (1995). Multiple explanation: A consider-an-alternative strategy for debiasing judgments. *Journal of Personality and Social Psychology*, 69, 1069–1086.

Hofstede, G. (2001). *Culture's consequences: International differences in work-related values*. Beverly Hills, CA: Sage.

Home Office. (2001). *Policing a new century: A blueprint for reform*. London, UK: Home Office.

Innes, M. (2003). *Investigating murder: Detective work and the police response to criminal homicide*. Oxford, UK: Oxford University Press.

Irving, B., & Dunningham, C. (1993). *Human factors in the quality control of CID investigations: A brief review of relevant police training*. London, UK: HM Stationery Office.

Irving, B., & Hilgendorf, L. (1980). *Police interrogation: A case study of current practice*. London, UK: HM Stationery Office.

Jones, D., Grieve, J., & Milne, B. (2008). The case to review murder investigations. *The Journal of Homicide and Major Incident Investigation*, 2, 51–70.

Josephson, J. R., & Josephson, S. G. (eds.). (1994). *Abductive inference: Computation, philosophy, technology*. New York: Cambridge University Press.

Justitiedepartementet. (2015). *Rapport från Bergwallkommissjonen* (Statens Offentliga Utredningar 2015:52). Stockholm: Fritzes offentliga publikationer.

Keppens, J., & Schafer, B. (2004). "Murdered by persons unknown": Speculative reasoning in law and logic. In T. Gordon (ed.), *Legal knowledge and information systems* (pp. 109–118). Amsterdam: IOS Press.

Keppens, J., & Zeleznikow, J. (2003). A model based reasoning approach for generating plausible crime scenarios from evidence. Paper presented at the 9th International Conference on Artificial Intelligence and Law.

Klein, G. A., & Hoffmann, R. (1993). Seeing the invisible: Perceptual/cognitive aspects of expertise. In M. Rabinowitz (ed.), *Cognitive science foundations of instruction* (pp. 203–226). Mahwah, NJ: Lawrence Erlbaum Associates.

Koriat, A., Lichtenstein, S., & Fischhoff, B. (1980). Reasons for confidence. *Journal of Experimental Psychology: Human Learning and Memory*, 6, 107–118.

Kripos. (2015). *Nasjonal drapsoversikt 2015*. Oslo: Kripos. Retrieved from https://www.politi.no/vedlegg/lokale_vedlegg/kripos/Vedlegg_3500.pdf

Liao, S.-H. (2005). Expert system methodologies and application: A decade review from 1995 to 2004. *Expert Systems with Applications*, 28, 93–103.

Linden, W., & Campbell, P. (2010). The Phoenix Database: Homicide analysis, action learning and knowledge sharing. *The Journal of Homicide and Major Incident Investigation*, 6, 3–21.

Lord, C. G., Lepper, M. R., & Preston, E. (1984). Considering the opposite: A corrective strategy for social judgment. *Journal of Personality and Social Psychology*, 47, 1231–1243.

MacLean, C. L., & Dror, I. E. (2016). A Primer on the psychology of cognitive bias. In C. Robertson & R. Kesselheim (eds.), *Blinding as a solution to bias* (pp. 13–22). Cambridge, MA: Academic Press.

Macpherson, W. (1999). *The Stephen Lawrence Inquiry*. London, UK: The Secretary of State for the Home Department by Command of Her Majesty.

Markman, K. D., Lindberg, M. J., Kray, L. J., & Galinsky, A. D. (2007). Implications of counterfactual structure for creative generation and analytical problem solving. *Personality and Social Psychology Bulletin*, 33, 312–324.

McGrory, D., & Treacy, P. (2012). The Professionalising Investigation Programme. In M. R. Haberfeld, C. A. Clarke, & D. L. Sheehan (eds.), *Police organization and training: Innovations in research and practice* (Vol. 1, pp. 113–137). New York: Springer.

Metropolitan Police. (2014). *New police constables*. London, UK: Metropolitan Police. Retrieved from http://content.met.police.uk/Site/newpoliceconstables

Mortimer, A., & Shepherd, E. (1999). Frames of mind: Schemata guiding cognition and conduct in the interviewing of suspected offenders. In A. Memon & R. Bull (eds.), *Handbook of the psychology of interviewing* (pp. 293–315). Chichester, UK: Wiley.

Nickerson, R. S. (1998). Confirmation bias: A ubiquitous phenomenon in many guises. *Review of General Psychology*, 2, 175–220.

Nosek, B. A., Spies, J. R., & Motyl, M. (2012). Scientific Utopia: II. Restructuring incentives and practices to promote truth over publishability. *Perspectives on Psychological Science*, 7, 615–631.

O'Brien, B. (2009). Prime suspect: An examination of factors that aggravate and counteract confirmation bias in criminal investigations. *Psychology, Public Policy, and Law*, 15, 315–334.

Parks, C. D., & Sanna, L. J. (1999). *Group performance and interaction*. Boulder, CO: Westview Press.

Politidirektoratet. (2013). *Etterforskningen i politiet 2013*. Oslo, Norway: Politidirektoratet.

Reiter, R. (1987). A theory of diagnosis from first principles. *Artificial intelligence*, 32, 57–95.

Riksadvokaten. (2015). Norsk politi og påtalemyndighets behandling av straffesakene mot Sture Bergwall: Hva kan vi lære? (3/2015). Oslo, Norway: Riksadvokaten. Retrieved from http://www.riksadvokaten.no/filestore/Dokumenter/2015/Riksadvokatenspublikasjoner3_2015.pdf

Rossmo, D. K. (ed.). (2009). *Criminal investigative failures*. Boca Raton, FL: CRC Press.

Royal Commission on Criminal Justice. (1993). *Report CM 2263*. London, UK: HMSO.

Royal Commission on Criminal Procedure. (1981). *Report CMND 8092*. London, UK: HMSO.

Roycroft, M., Brown, J., & Innes, M. (2013). Reform by crisis: The murder of Stephen Lawrence and a socio-historical analysis of developments in the conduct of major crime investigations. In M. Rowe (ed.), *Policing beyond Macpherson* (pp. 148–164). Cullompton, UK: Willan.

Sanna, L. J., & Schwarz, N. (2003). Debiasing the hindsight bias: The role of accessibility experiences and (mis)attributions. *Journal of Experimental Social Psychology*, 39, 287–295.

Sherman, L. W. (2015). A tipping point for "totally evidenced policing": Ten ideas for building an evidence-based police agency. *International Criminal Justice Review*, 25, 11–29.

Simon, D. (2012). *In doubt: The psychology of the criminal justice process*. Cambridge, MA: Harvard University Press.

Stanovich, K. E. (2011). *Rationality and the reflective mind*. New York: Oxford University Press.

Stelfox, P., & Pease, K. (2005). Cognition and detection: Reluctant bedfellows? In M. J. Smith & N. Tilley (eds.), *Crime science: New approaches to preventing and detecting crime* (pp. 194–210). Cullompton, UK: Willan.

Stumer, A. (2010). *The presumption of innocence: Evidential and human rights perspectives*. Haywards Heath, UK: Bloomsbury Publishing.

Tong, S., Bryant, R. P., & Horvath, M. A. (2009). *Understanding criminal investigation*. Chichester, UK: Wiley.

Townsley, M., Mann, M., & Garrett, K. (2011). The missing link of crime analysis: A systematic approach to testing competing hypotheses. *Policing: A Journal of Policy and Practice*, 5, 158–171.

Tversky, A., & Kahneman, D. (1974). Judgment under uncertainty: Heuristics and biases. *Science*, 185, 1124–1131.

Tversky, A., & Koehler, D. J. (1994). Support theory: A nonextensional representation of subjective probability. *Psychological Review*, 101, 547–567.

van den Heuvel, C., Alison, L., & Crego, J. (2012). How uncertainty and accountability can derail strategic "save life" decisions in counter-terrorism simulations: A descriptive model of choice deferral and omission bias. *Journal of Behavioral Decision Making*, 25, 165–187.

van Koppen, P. J. (2008). Blundering justice. In R. N. Kocsis (ed.), *Serial murder and the psychology of violent crimes* (pp. 207–228). New Jersey, NJ: Humana Press.

Westera, N. J., Kebbell, M. R., Milne, B., & Green, T. (2016). Towards a more effective detective. *Policing and Society: An International Journal of Research and Policy*, 26, 1–17.

Williamson, T. (2007). Psychology and criminal investigations. In T. Newburn, T. Williamson, & A. Wright (eds.), *Handbook of criminal investigation* (pp. 68–91). Cullompton, UK: Willian.

Zsambok, C. E., & Klein, G. (eds.). (1997). *Naturalistic decision making*. Hillsdale, NJ: Lawrence Erlbaum Associates.

Zuckerman, A. A. S. (1989). *The principles of criminal evidence*. New York, NY: Oxford University Press.

Chapter 4

Presentation of evidence

Nina Westera and Mark Kebbell

Introduction

How police gather information during the investigation has a direct influence on what evidence is presented to key decision makers such as investigators, prosecutors and jurors. In this chapter we explore what psychology can tell us about how police can best preserve the information they collect to produce the most reliable (accurate) and credible (believable) evidence. How the evidence is presented is also important because it is not the evidence that matters per se, but the perceptions of those who review the evidence and decide on the outcome of a case. It is therefore imperative that, when collecting evidence, investigators are aware of the factors that influence perceptions of how that evidence will be perceived later on. Because police are gatekeepers of the evidence process, failing to gather evidence in this way will prevent lawyers, judges and jurors from being presented with the best evidence possible.

We address two of the main sources of evidence to criminal investigations: accounts from eyewitnesses and suspects (Greenwood, Chaiken, & Petersilia, 1977; Kebbell & Wagstaff, 1997). A large body of psychological research on factors that influence the reliability and credibility of this type of evidence have direct implications for investigative practice. We specifically focus on when this evidence is captured on video because police are increasingly capturing evidence in this way (e.g. with body cameras, handheld electronic devices and recordings at the police station). Police video recording witness and suspect interviews is likely to have a major influence on how evidence is presented because the evidence collection process becomes part of the evidence. For instance, the body camera recording of a victim's initial account to police (and the officer's interview that elicits that account) may be played to a jury or judge, which means police interview practice forms part of the evidence.

An implication of video recording these interviews is that the lines between investigation (ideally the impartial collection of information for fact-finding) and prosecution (presenting the prosecution's evidence to persuade jurors or judges) are blurred. This can create ethical difficulties for police because, although the objectives of these two phases often overlap, sometimes they conflict. For example, during the investigation one imperative of investigators may be to gather as much information as possible about the description of the alleged offender so that the offender can be identified, but at trial the identity of the offender may not be under dispute making this evidence irrelevant. An assumption we therefore make is that the investigator's primary objective is to gather reliable and relevant information for the investigation in a fair way and that this includes, where possible, the investigator fairly representing the credibility of the witness or suspect. This means, for example, not making a witness or suspect look more credible than is warranted. We suggest that where investigative needs clash with prosecutorial preferences, investigative needs take priority.

In this chapter we adopt a practical focus by highlighting where possible how the evidence-base suggests police and criminal justice professionals can adapt their practices to ensure a fair representation of a witness's or suspect's evidence is captured and presented. We examine the decision makers in a holistic way by considering how, if this video is played as evidence, it might affect every key decision maker in the outcome of an investigation or prosecution – investigators, suspects, lawyers, and judges and jurors. While each of these decision makers has their own knowledge, biases and experiences, there are also commonalities in how they perceive information due to the underlying processes of human cognition. We therefore explore the commonalties, but outline the differences where the evidence-base allows starting with the factors that influence the reliability of the evidence, and then the factors that influence the credibility of the evidence. It is important to note that the distinction between reliability and credibility is somewhat arbitrary as the two often overlap and are sometimes indistinguishable from each other.

The reliability of the evidence presented

Police video recording the witness or suspect interview provides those who assess evidence with the potential to review more reliable evidence than was previously possible because they can see how evidence is collected without it being 'filtered' by the investigator (Shepherd & Milne, 2006). This type of record is in contrast to the traditional way of capturing the account of a witness or a suspect where the investigator produces a written statement of what was said at interview. The traditional method meant that written statements were assessed by some people in the decision-making process such as police and lawyers, whereas others, such as judges and jurors, saw the witness or suspect in person. This meant there were often discrepancies in perceptions between written accounts and accounts given in person.

Memory and cognition research provides the evidence-base for the improved reliability of video recording witness and suspect interviews. Memory itself is not like a video recording. It does not capture and preserve a pure recording of events. Rather memory is a reconstructive process that is influenced by the person's knowledge, biases, expectations and other experiences (Baddeley,

Eysenck, & Anderson, 2009). This is true for all people – children and adults, witnesses and suspects. When these research understandings are applied to the how interviews are recorded and presented, there are three main factors that mean a video recorded interview is likely to be more reliable than a written statement or evidence given some time after the interview.

1. Fresher account

By recording the interview on video police investigators are capturing a fresher account than a witness or suspect giving evidence months and sometimes years later. Memory fades over time as people forget information (Ebbinghaus, 1913; Read & Connolly, 2007). This is especially true for 'fine grain' details about the event when compared with coarser details (Rubin & Wenzel, 1996). For example, the detail of what a person was wearing is more likely forgotten than whether the actual event occurred. As memory fades the ability and opportunity for memory to become contaminated or distorted increases. Information from other sources, such as media reports about the event, co-witness discussions, psychological therapy and even a person's expectations about how an event should occur, may overwrite or become integrated into a person's memory for the crime event (French, Garry, & Kazuo 2008; Loftus & Banaji 1989; Tuckey & Brewer, 2003). A person may also misattribute the source of information or the temporal details of the event. For example, they may be mistaken about the timing of the offence or mix-up what the offender was wearing on one occasion with another. Together these factors mean that video recording the earlier account means decision makers can have the opportunity to review more reliable and complete evidence than evidence testimony given later in court.

An example of the difference in the content of the evidence presented in the video recorded interview conducted by police compared with live oral evidence presented in court months later was a study we conducted with adult sexual assault complainants in New Zealand (Westera, Kebbell, & Milne, 2013a). We compared the transcripts of 10 complainants' police video interviews with the same complainants' live evidence-in-chief in terms of the evidentially relevant details that went towards establishing consent (e.g., "I told him I didn't want him near me") and what happened during the commission of the alleged offence (e.g., from "he pushed me onto the bed" until "he rolled over and fell asleep"). Over two thirds of these details in police interview were never reported by the complainant in evidence-in-chief. A small number of inconsistencies between the police interview and live evidence were also found (which may indicate the information was less reliable). These findings suggest that the use of video recorded evidence could provide jurors and judges with substantially more (relevant) evidence than a witness's recollection months later.

Changes in memory over time are not confined to detail; the confidence that witnesses have in their account can also change over time. Jurors use confidence to predict accuracy. For instance, a witness who says, "he punched me twice, I'm sure of it!" is more likely to be believed than a witness who says, "he might have punched me twice, I'm not sure" (Wells, Ferguson, & Lindsay, 1981). Research shows that confidence can increase or decrease over time depending on what feedback the witness receives and this reduces the relationship between confidence and accuracy (Wixted, Mickes, Clark, Gronlund, & Roediger III, 2015). Consequently, recording the confidence a witness has at the time of an interview allows for changes in confidence over time to be observed.

The use of mobile devices means that accounts can be captured soon after the offending has occurred. As a general rule this provides an opportunity for investigators to improve the quality of information because in most cases the sooner an investigator captures the witness's or suspect's account on video the more reliable the account. There are some exceptions. For example, the psychological state of the witness may be influenced by intoxication, trauma or tiredness and the environment may not be conducive to concentration because of distractions, interruptions and the presence of the offender. In these situations interviewers will need to balance these factors with timeliness when deciding when to conduct and video record the interview (Milne & Bull, 1999).

2. First-hand account

Another benefit of video recording the interview is that is allows decision makers to view a first-hand account of what happened in contrast to a written statement that is the interviewing officer's interpretation of what the witness or suspect said at interview. With written statements the interviewer questions the witness or suspect and reproduces the responses given in the form of a written statement. The interviewee is then given an opportunity to read the statement, make additions and corrections, and endorse it as an accurate record of the interview. The limitations of an interviewer's memory mean it is an impossible task for the officer to remember and reproduce a 'verbatim record' of the witnesses' or suspects' accounts. For example, Köhnken, Thurer, and Zoberbier (1994) found 31 interview statements written by the interviewer immediately after the interview contained only about two thirds of the information reported by the witness. Further, statements also mean that the demeanour of the witness or suspect is not available to assist fact-finders in determining how much weight they place on this evidence.

The reconstructive nature of memory means that when processing the information the interviewer may unconsciously use heuristics (assumptions in memory) to fill in the gaps in his or her memory and misreport what was said (Bower, Black, & Turner, 1979). Confirmation bias means the interviewer is more likely to remember information that supports their preconceptions of what happened, and disregard information that does not (Nickerson, 1998; see Chapter 2 for more on investigator bias). For example, Rock (2001) found that when the audio recording of an interview was compared with the written statement resulting from it, contradictory information and the degree of the witness's uncertainty about central facts were often missing. Police video recording the interview rather than taking a written statement can therefore provide more reliable evidence for decision makers.

Recognising these benefits has led many lawyers to call for this change (Heaton-Armstrong & Wolchover, 1992). Prosecutors, who have access to these first-hand accounts, perceive this truer record improves their ability to decide how best to present the witnesses evidence (Westera, Kebbell, & Milne, 2014; Westera & Powell, 2015). For example, Sanders, Creaton, Bird and Weber (1996) found that many witnesses with intellectual disabilities appeared far more competent in their written statements than in fact they actually were, potentially allowing cases to go to trial with no chance of a jury being able to deliver a 'guilty' verdict but proving distressing to both the complainant and defendant. Nevertheless, there is the drawback of decision makers having to view a recording that will take longer than reading a statement, which may be seen as an obstacle by police and lawyers who already have a large workload (Westera et al., 2012, 2014). There is some evidence to suggest lawyers tend to rely on the, often unreliable and always incomplete police statement or summary of interview to avoid viewing the materials (Baldwin & Bedward, 1991; HMCPSI & HMIC, 2007). However, we argue that reviewing the interview is an opportunity to increase early resolutions and improve case outcomes, and so is likely to save time in the long run.

3. Transparency in how evidence is elicited

The reconstructive nature of memory means one of the key factors influencing the reliability of the information provided by a witness is how that information is elicited. Decision makers should place less weight on information resulting from leading than from non-leading questions (Clifford & Scott, 1978; Fisher & Geiselman, 1992; Loftus & Palmer, 1974). For example, when a witness has disclosed that they were punched, the leading question "he punched you in the face, didn't he?" is less likely to result in reliable information than the specific question "where did he punch you?" This is because we use cues as well as our actual experience to help recall information. A witness may therefore draw inferences from questions asked by the interviewer, which may lead to errors in what a witness or suspect remembers and contaminate how he or she later recalls events. Generally speaking, the more a witness or suspect (motivated to tell the truth) is encouraged to control his or her memory recall process, the more reliable the memory recall. Decision makers should place the most weight on information elicited from non-leading open questions that do not restrict the answers given (e.g. "tell me what happened"; Fisher & Geiselman, 1992; Milne & Bull, 1999; Powell et al., 2005). More specific, restrictive questioning the may result in decreased accuracy due to social compliance (e.g. "what colour were his eyes?"; Hutcheson, Baxter, Telfer, & Warden, 1995;

Lipton, 1977). With a transparent record of how information was elicited at interview, decision makers can make more accurate judgments about the reliability of this account information (Heaton-Armstrong & Wolchover, 1992; Powell et al., 2005; Westera, Kebbell, & Milne, 2013b).

This added transparency of the account means that how police carry out interviews will have an impact on how well the evidence is perceived. Coercive and accusatory behaviour may result in decision makers placing less weight on the evidence obtained or the interview being ruled inadmissible. Leading or suggestive questioning may also lead to decision makers placing more weight on the witness's or suspect's account (Ruva & Bryant, 2004). For example, prosecutors and police rated the account of a sexual assault complainant as less reliable when police used leading questioning compared with open-ended questioning (Westera et al. 2011, 2014).

The use of mobile technology means officers are now capturing witness and suspects accounts at the scene soon after (and sometime during) the offending in less controlled conditions and exposing frontline interviewing practices whereas, previously, recorded interviews were conducted in a specially designed room at the police station with a specially trained interviewer. While this approach may alleviate judges' and lawyers' concerns by seeing the whole process, especially with suspects, as to what police do in any 'pre-interview interview' prior to return to the recording facilities of the station (Schollum, 2005) it does mean that first response officers' practices may be under greater scrutiny. These officers are generally least equipped to conduct these interviews – they have minimal experience, only basic interview training and are dealing in wide variety of high-pressure situations (Westera & Powell, 2016). In other words, those least equipped to conduct these interviews are doing them in some of the most demanding conditions. There appears to be a great need for first responders to be able to interview effectively and it doesn't appear that their current training meets this need.

In sum, video recording interviews is the best way to ensure investigators meet their primary fact-finding objective of gathering reliable information for the investigation. Since the early 1990s many, but not all, police services have responded by introducing video or at least audio recording of suspect interviews (Baldwin, 1993; Geller, 1993; Schollum, 2005). Concerns about the reliability of child witnesses have led to the mandatory recording of these interviews around the same time period in many countries (Advisory Group on Video Recorded Evidence, 1989; Davies, Wilson, Mitchell, & Milsom 1995; Goodman et al., 1998). The same is not true for adult witnesses, who seldom have this opportunity despite similar potential benefits to reliability (some exceptions exist for witnesses to serious crime). Video recording more interviews for a wider variety of witness provides an effective means of increasing the reliability of the evidence collected.

For the benefits of the improved reliability of video recording witness and suspect interviews to be fully realised, a number of changes also need to happen in the criminal justice process more generally. With suspect interviews, only some countries play the entire interview (e.g., New Zealand, Australia), whereas in other countries only excerpts are played (e.g., England and Wales). With witness interviews, legislation enabling the video to be played as a witness's evidence is only available in some countries with certain types of vulnerable witnesses such as children, intellectually disabled adults and intimidated witnesses (e.g., England and Wales, some jurisdictions in Australia, New Zealand; Australian Law Reform Commission, 2010; Criminal Justice System, 2007; Mahoney et al., 2007). Further, in those countries, legal professionals often continue to rely on live evidence processes rather than playing the video (Burton, Evans, & Sanders, 2006; Kingi & Jordan, 2009; Stern, 2010). Part of this low uptake may be due to a traditional approach to courtroom practices, which assumes 'an adult is perfectly capable of giving evidence' (Stern, 2010; Westera et al., 2013a). More than 40 years of memory research suggests this not the case (Read & Connolly, 2007).

The credibility of the evidence presented

Whilst we know a great deal about collecting reliable evidence via video recording, we are less clear about how video-recorded evidence affects the credibility. This is partly because the research on how video recorded evidence influences credibility is not well developed and partly because credibility is a complex phenomenon. First, it is important to note that the *perceived* credibility or believability of someone who reports an event does not necessarily relate to the accuracy or truthfulness of that report. Still, some common themes arise when the use of video recording is examined in light of what is known about the factors that influence credibility judgements. Some of these factors may be diagnostic of *actual* credibility whereas others may lead to errors in credibility assessment. Next we discuss these factors and how they may influence the credibility of interviewee accounts when presented on video.

1. Accuracy

As we have mentioned video recorded evidence is likely to be more accurate than alternatives such as statements. Still though, evidence will not be perfect. Researchers have found that true and false memories can both appear detailed and coherent, and the witness may be confident that they are true (Ceci, Huffman, Smith, & Loftus, 1994; Loftus & Pickrell, 1995; Porter, Yuille & Lehman, 1999). The non-verbal cues of the interviewee captured in the video are unlikely to be helpful in determining if that interviewee is deliberately being inaccurate (i.e., lying; Bond & DePaulo, 2006; Vrij, Granhag & Porter, 2010). Some evidence-based tools have been developed to assist with ascertaining if the account is given is truthful (e.g., statement validity testing in Criterion Based Content Assessment (CBCA); but the high error rates of this test and disputes between experts in the field about its utility suggest it does not achieve a standard expected by the courts in many countries, see Vrij, 2005).

Consequently, a more useful means of determining the credibility of the account is examining how the information provided by the interviewee fits with the other evidence. A more reliable account is more likely to be corroborated with other evidence, which is turn will make the witness or suspect more credible (although there is always the possibility that due to an absence of evidence a genuine account may be unable to be corroborated). Access to a more accurate and complete account from interviewees (as provided by the video record) is likely to enable investigators, lawyers, judges and jurors to make more diagnostic credibility judgments as they compare and contrast this account with the whole body of evidence. Strength of evidence is the strongest predictor of conviction (Devine et al., 2001). Clear contradictions between the interviewee's account and other evidence (discussed in more detail in the next section on 'inconsistency') about relevant issues to proving the alleged offending are likely to be one of the most important factors for decision makers to rely on when deciding case outcome. This even extends to suspects, for example, Kebbell, Alison, Hurren, and Mazerolle (2010) found that suspects were more likely to make admissions if evidence against them was strong and emphasised. Therefore, more detailed evidence, as collected by video recording, may increase the likelihood of admissions.

2. *Inconsistency*

Video recording the interview may also affect the consistency of the evidence presented to decision makers. Consistency between accounts and with other evidence can be diagnostic of credibility, but not always. It is important to know that inconsistencies can commonly arise in an interviewee's account due to the reconstructive nature of memory rather than through fault or deceit of the witness or suspect (Fisher, Brewer, & Mitchell, 2009). Memory is recollected in different ways at different times and is a product of the retrieval conditions present at each time (e.g., the types of questions asked, the environmental context; Tulving, 1972). This means over the course of an interview or between multiple interviews a witness is likely remember new details, miss out details or even provide contradictory details. As a result of this feature of memory, and because the video is likely to capture more information, there is an increased chance that inconsistencies within a witness's account will occur. But because memory is componential, an error for one aspect of a complex event, does not mean that the witness will be wrong about other aspects of the event (Fisher et al., 2009). Further when the issue is not reliability but truthfulness, liars are often highly consistent in the details that they give (see Vrij et al., 2010).

Despite these robust findings, police, lawyers and lay people are likely to rate a witness as less credible or reliable overall if they are inconsistent in one part of their evidence (Berman, Narby, & Cutler, 1995; Leippe & Romanczyk, 1989;

Oeberst, 2012; Potter & Brewer, 1999). A common tactic lawyers use and misuse is the value placed by decision makers on consistency as a means to discredit a witness (Wigmore, 1974). Advocacy guidance recommends lawyers use cross-examination to highlight minor inconsistencies in the evidence and infer that the entire evidence of the witness is not credible (Evans, 1995). In one of the only studies to examine how this plays out in the courtroom, Zydervelt and colleagues (2016) found that this line of cross-examination was used with 71 per cent of complainants in the sexual assault cases examined.

The research on inconsistencies has implications for investigators, lawyers and judges in deciding whether to present evidence via video recorded interview. First, police video recording the interview, as opposed to producing a written statement, is a fairer process for the witness or suspect. This is because the recording is a more accurate account. The alternative, a statement, may mean that lawyers may unfairly cross-examine a witness on inconsistencies made by the police in making the statement, rather than the witness's account. Second, when the witness or suspect gives live evidence (regardless of how the police interview is recorded) they are again generating a new memory record of the events. This process by its very nature is likely to contain inconsistencies when compared with the account that the witness gave during the police interview. These discrepancies may have occurred naturally due to memory decay or repeated recall attempts (see Read & Connolly, 2007). Presenting the video as evidence therefore can remove some of the natural memory errors that occur over time. However, the extra detail captured on the video recorded interview is likely to create more opportunities for inconsistencies to be generated. In the written statement process, police would filter what information went into the statement and what did not on the basis of perceived relevance. Capturing the whole interview on video produces a purer account but also means more details will be captured. This process is therefore likely to generate more avenues for cross-examination on inconsistencies. Interviews and surveys of lawyers and judges suggest this is a major concern with the use of video interviews as evidence with complainants of sexual assault (Stern, 2010; Westera et al., 2014). In sum, though, using the video recorded interview will reduce the number of inconsistencies generated by the criminal justice process, but may lead to more minor inconsistencies within the interview (which are unlikely to be diagnostic of credibility).

3. Detail, vividness and coherence

Detail may both enhance and reduce perceived credibility. The extra detail captured by the video may in itself improve credibility ratings. Jurors have been found to rate more detailed or gruesome accounts, even when the details are peripheral to the alleged offending, as more credible (Bell & Loftus, 1988; Bright & Goodman-Delahunty, 2006; Wells & Leippe, 1981). For example, Bell and Loftus (1989) found mock jurors rated the account of an eyewitness to a robbery as more credible when they provided details of the type of chocolate (Milk Duds) and drink (Diet Pepsi) that was stolen than when they did not. However, in contrast to this finding, Borckardt, Sprohge, and Nash (2003) found no effect for trivial details, but cross-examination on these details when incorrect made the witness less credible. Bright and Goodman-Delahunty (2006) found jurors who saw gruesome photographs of injuries compared with those that did not, felt more emotional about the evidence (including anger towards the defendant) and were more likely to convict. The video may capture a more detailed and emotionally arousing account given its proximity to the crime.

High levels of detail may diminish interviewee credibility and the ability of decision makers to systematically analyse the evidence. Lawyers and judges have expressed concerns that some interviewing practices – unstructured, overly long, repetitive, rambling – reduce the coherence of the video-evidence and therefore the credibility of adult sexual assault complainants (Stern, 2010; Westera, Powell, & Milne, 2015). A lack of coherence has been found to reduce juror credibility ratings of a witness (Klettke, Graesser, & Powell, 2010; Pennington & Hastie, 1993). This may be particularly problematic with interviewees who are experiencing trauma because they are often less able to report what happened coherently (Brewin, 2007; Shepherd et al., 1999). More research is required to examine if high levels of detail throughout the account, especially about contextual details rather than the narrative of the event, may make an account less coherent and therefore less credible. It is cognitively demanding for a witness or a suspect to recall high levels of detail. Vrij and Granhag (2012) suggest using this to the interviewer's advantage may aid with deception detection by encouraging detail and asking unexpected questions of a suspect (e.g., where did you and your friend sit in the restaurant; see also Vrij et al., 2010).

But, on other hand, if a witness or suspect becomes tired from recalling high levels of detail this may impede his or her ability to concentrate and reliably recall information from memory (Fisher & Geiselman, 1992). This is especially the case if the witness or suspect has to recall events that happened over long periods of time or finds the interview process emotionally demanding because high levels of stress can impede cognitive performance (Deffenbacher et al., 2004; Yerkes & Dodson, 1908). Reviewing a highly detailed account is cognitively demanding for decision makers in the process. This may lead them to only superficially evaluate the evidence at the expense of more reliable systematic analysis (Chaiken, 1980; Chaiken, Liberman, & Eagly 1989; Petty & Cacioppo, 1986). For example, they may rely on how emotional the interviewee is or on stereotypes about that particular interviewee rather than the content of the evidence.

The video recording of interviews is likely to influence how police carry out interviews. Avoiding the generation of unnecessary details that are not central to the investigation or to evidence may create an account that is more diagnostic of credibility and easier to process for investigators, lawyers, suspects, judges and jurors but there are risks of police having a more targeted approach to interviewing. Officers may be more open to bias and resort to more closed and leading questions known to reduce the reliability of an interviewee's responses. Safeguards may help to reduce bias, such as being open-minded to alternate hypotheses, and having the skills in how to ask open-ended questions to elicit this information in a reliable way may help with this process (Powell, Fisher, & Wright, 2005). Researchers have begun to define what is and is not relevant to different types of investigations, based on the perceptions of investigators and prosecutors, by examining the type of information targeted in cross-examination and what factors predict case outcome (e.g., Burrows, Powell, & Anglim, 2013; Zydervelt et al., 2016). The findings of these studies coupled with how police can skilfully use forensically safe questioning to elicit this type of information will help to inform interviewing protocol for different types of witnesses.

4. *Medium of the record*

With witnesses, usually victims of sexual assault, lawyers and judges have raised concerns that using the video recorded police interview as evidence is less credible than live evidence because of the distance between the witness and the jury (Pipe & Henaghan, 1996). Researchers have examined this issue and generally found that the same witness giving video recorded evidence is viewed less positively than if presenting live evidence. Children giving video interview evidence are perceived as providing less confident and convincing statements than children testifying live, are regarded as less honest and evoke less empathy (Goodman et al., 2006; Landström & Granhag, 2010; Landström, Granhag, & Hartwig, 2005; Landström, Granhag & Hartwig, 2007). But this does not appear to influence the (poor) ability of jurors to determine accuracy or honesty (Landström et al., 2005, 2007; Goodman et al., 2006).

Only a few experimental studies have examined the effectiveness of using video interviews of adults as evidence when compared with live evidence. Two small scale studies simulating trials with mock juries have found no differences in guilt judgments (Ellison & Munro, 2014; Taylor & Joudo, 2005). In comparison Landström and colleagues (2005) found that individual mock jurors gave higher ratings for appearance in terms of eloquence and pleasantness of an adult witness to an accident in the live condition than in the video condition. However, they found no differences in jurors' judgments about the quality of the testimony or ability to assess veracity.

Studies with suspects have focused on how the angle of the camera can influence judgments of guilt (Lassiter et al., 2001, 2002). People are prone to attributing causality to more salient or noticeable stimuli; a phenomenon known as illusionary causality. Lassiter (2001) tested this phenomenon with suspect interviews by examining what influence the position of a suspect would have on mock juror judgments about the suspect's blameworthiness of the crime and voluntariness of the interview. In a series of studies he consistently found that mock jurors were more likely to perceive the suspect as guilty and the statement voluntary if the suspect was the direct focus of the camera rather than in a more neutral frame (e.g., focused on the interviewer and suspect). This led Lassiter (2002) to recommend that a balanced viewpoint is adopted by the camera that contains a view of both the suspect and the interviewer. Interestingly, Landström and Granhag (2008) examined the camera angle of judgments about child witnesses and found jurors in the close-up condition viewed the child more critically than those with a more distant view.

Together these findings suggest that police should set up interview rooms in such a way that jurors can get a clear picture of the interviewee; that is, with a camera angle that is not too close and set up in a neutral position. Although video evidence may reduce positive perceptions of the interviewee for jurors, this should be balanced against the other benefits of video interview such as the increased reliability and completeness of the account.

5. Demeanour and behaviour

Little is known about how an earlier video recorded account compared with a courtroom rendition influences judgments about the interviewee's demeanour and behaviour. It is likely that capturing the interview on video soon after or during the alleged offending will show the witness or a suspect in a different state compared with the formal and controlled environment of the courtroom months or years later (or the absence of demeanour completely in a written statement). For example, crime statistics suggest that at the time of the interview witnesses or suspects may be intoxicated, aggressive or distressed (Australian Bureau of Statistics, 2015). They may also behave differently in the less formal environment of the interview compared with at a trial (e.g., casual language, dress) or if they know they are being video recorded. There is also the possibility the video will capture other evidence in addition to the interviewee's account such as injuries or damage to clothing. These factors could all influence the credibility of the account (and the extent to which it is corroborated), but research is needed to explore these possibilities.

We do know that deception detection based on non-verbal cues present in this interview that indicate anxiety are unlikely to be reliable regardless of the time frame (Bond & DePaulo, 2006; Vrij et al., 2010). Other aspects of the interviewee's demeanour may influence credibility. For example, investigators, lawyers and judges perceive adult sexual assault complainants may present a more emotional (and therefore more credible) account on the video than in live courtroom evidence (Stern, 2010; Westera, et al., 2011, 2013b). Researchers have found that mock jurors rate rape complainants as less credible if they do not display emotion (Dahl et al., 2007; Rose, Nadler, & Clark, 2006; Wessel, Drevland, Eilersten, & Magnussen, 2006). However, the expectations of those accessing the evidence may also impact on this process (Dahl et al., 2007). For example, fact finders may expect a witness to have heightened emotion at the time of the interview and if he or she does not this may make the witness appear less credible.

Social factors may also make the earlier account more credible in cases where the motivations of witnesses and suspects change over time. For example, an analysis of 216 domestic violence cases heard in specialist family violence courts in England and Wales found that during the criminal justice process 50 per cent of complainants retracted their statements given to police (Robinson & Cook, 2006). It is well known that many victims withdraw from this process as a result of fear, shame, a lack of confidence in police, concerns about their children or reconciliation with the offender (Epstein, 1999). Capturing the interview on video may therefore provide credible evidence of what occurred that would not otherwise be available and evidence that may be corroborated by the video through the physical evidence such as injuries and torn clothing (Westera & Powell, 2015).

Conclusion

Advances in technology mean we are capable of recording their accounts, cheaply, conveniently and accurately. Video recording the interview offers the opportunity to bring decision makers closer to the actual crime and the ability to observe what investigators observe when responding to that alleged crime. However, more research is required to systematically examine the influence of these features on judgments about credibility. Psychological research clearly shows that recording these interviews on video and presenting this video as evidence will provide police, lawyers, judges and jurors with the most reliable evidence possible. Now the onus is on police to record these interviews and policy makers, lawyers and judges to enable and promote the use of these videos as evidence. Victims, witnesses and suspects are central to most investigations and prosecutions and it is time to let their voices be heard directly.

References

Advisory Group on Video Recorded Evidence. (1989). *Report of the Advisory Group on Video Recorded Evidence*. London: Home Office.

Australian Law Reform Commission. (2010). *Family violence – a national legal response*. Retrieved from http://www.alrc.gov.au/26.%20Reporting,20%Prosecutionand%20Pretrialprocesses

Baddeley, A., Eysenck, M. W., & Anderson, M. C. (2009). *Memory*. East Sussex, UK: Psychology Press.

Baldwin, J., & Bedward, J. (1991). Summarising tape recordings of police interviews. *Criminal Law Review*, 671–679.

Bell, B. E., & Loftus, E. F. (1988). Degree of detail of eyewitness testimony and mock juror judgments. *Journal of Applied Social Psychology*, 18(14), 1171–1192.

Bell, B. E., & Loftus, E. F. (1989). Trivial persuasion in the courtroom: The power of (a few) minor details. *Journal of Personality and Social Psychology*, 56(5), 669–679.

Berman, G. L., Narby, D. J., & Cutler, B. L. (1995). Effects of inconsistent eyewitness statements on mock-jurors' evaluations of the eyewitness, perceptions of defendant culpability and verdicts. *Law and Human Behavior*, 19(1), 79–88.

Borckardt, J. J., Sprohge, E., & Nash, M. (2003). Effects of the inclusion and refutation of peripheral details on eyewitness credibility. *Journal of Applied Social Psychology*, 33(10), 2187–2197.

Bright, D. A., & Goodman-Delahunty, J. (2006). Gruesome evidence and emotion: Anger, blame, and jury decision-making. *Law and Human Behavior*, 30(2), 183–202.

Burrows, K. S., Powell, M. B., & Anglim, J. (2013). Facilitating child witness interviewers' understanding of evidential requirements through prosecutor instruction. *International Journal of Police Science and Management*, 15, 263–272.

Burton, M., Evans, R., & Sanders, A. (2006). *Are special measures for vulnerable and intimidated witnesses working? Evidence from the criminal justice agencies*. London: Home Office.

Ceci, S. J., Huffman, M. L. C., Smith, E., & Loftus, E. F. (1994). Repeatedly thinking about a non-event: Source misattributions among preschoolers. *Consciousness and Cognition*, 3(3), 388–407.

Criminal Justice System. (2007). *Achieving best evidence in criminal proceedings: Guidance in interviewing victims and witnesses, and using special measures*. London: Home Office.

Deffenbacher, K. A., Bornstein, B. H., Penrod, S. D., & McGorty, E. K. (2004). A meta-analytic review of the effects of high stress on eyewitness memory. *Law and Human Behavior*, 28, 687–706.

Devine, D., Clayton, L. D., Dunford, B., Seying, R., & Pryce, J. (2001). Jury decision making: 45 years of empirical research on deliberating groups. *Psychology, Public Policy and Law*, 7, 622–727.

Ebbinghaus, H. (1913). *Memory: A contribution to experimental psychology* (H.A. Ruger & C.E. Bussenius, Trans). New York: US Teachers College Press.

Evans, K. (1995). *Advocacy in court: A beginner's guide* (2nd ed.). London: Blackstone.

Fisher, R. P., Brewer, N., & Mitchell, G. (2009). The relation between consistency and accuracy of eyewitness testimony: Legal versus cognitive explanations. In T. Williamson, R. Bull, & T. Valentine (eds), *Handbook of psychology of investigative interviewing: Current developments and future directions* (pp. 121–136). Chichester, UK: John Wiley and Sons.

Fisher, R. P., & Geiselman, R. E. (1992). *Memory enhancing techniques for investigative interviewing: The cognitive interview*. Springfield, IL: Thomas.

French, L., Garry, M., & Kazuo, M. (2008). You say tomato? Collaborative remembering leads to more false memories for intimate couples than for strangers. *Memory*, 16, 262–273.

Goodman, G. S., Tobey, A. E., Batterman-Faunce, J. M., Orcutt, H. K., Thomas, S., Shapiro, C., et al. (1998). Face-to-face confrontation: Effects of closed-circuit technology on children's testimony and jurors' decisions. *Law and Human Behavior*, 22, 165–203.

Goodman, G. S., Myers, J. E. B., Qin, J., Quas, J. A., Castelli, P., Redlich, A. D., & Rogers, L. (2006). Hearsay versus children's testimony: Effects of truthful and deceptive statements on jurors' decisions. *Law and Human Behavior*, 30, 363–401.

Greenwood, P. W., Chaiken, J. M., & Petersilia, J., 1977. *The criminal investigation process*. Lexington, MA: The Rand Corporation.

Heaton-Armstrong, A., & Wolchover, D. (1992). Recording witness statements. *Criminal Law Review*, 160–172.

HMCPSI, & HMIC. (2007). *Without consent: A report on the joint review of the investigation and prosecution of rape cases*. London: HM Crown Prosecution Service Inspectorate & HM Inspectorate of Constabulary.

Hutcheson, G. D., Baxter, J. S., Telfer, K., & Warden, D. (1995). Child witness statement quality: Question type and errors of omission. *Law and Human Behavior*, 19, 631–648.

Kebbell, M., Alison, L., Hurren, E., & Mazerolle, P. (2010). How do sex offenders think the police should interview to elicit confessions from sex offenders? *Psychology, Crime & Law*, 16(7), 567–584.

Kebbell, M., & Wagstaff, G. F. (1997). Why do the police interview eyewitnesses? Interview objectives and the evaluation of eyewitness performance. *The Journal of Psychology*, 131, 595–601.

Kingi, V., & Jordan, J. (2009). *Responding to sexual violence: Pathways to recovery*. Wellington: Ministry of Women's Affairs.

Köhnken, G., Thurer, C., & Zoberbier, D. (1994). The cognitive interview: are interviewers' memories enhanced, too? *Applied Cognitive Psychology*, 8, 13–24.

Landström, S., & Granhag, P. A. (2008). Children's truthful and deceptive testimonies: How camera perspective affects adult observers' perception and assessment. *Psychology, Crime & Law*, 14(5), 381–396.

Landström, S., & Granhag, P. A. (2010). In-court versus out-of-court testimonies: Children's experiences and adults' assessments. *Applied Cognitive Psychology*, 24, 941–955.

Landström, S., Granhag, P. A., & Hartwig, M. (2007). Children's live and videotaped testimonies: How presentation mode affects observers' perception, assessment and memory. *Legal and Criminological Psychology*, 12, 333–347.

Landström, S., Granhag, P. A., & Hartwig, M. (2005). Witnesses appearing live versus on video: Effects on observers' perception, veracity assessments and memory. *Applied Cognitive Psychology*, 19, 913–933.

Lassiter, G. D., Geers, A. L., Munhall, P. J., Handley, I. M., & Beers, M. J. (2001). Videotaped confessions: Is guilt in the eye of the camera? *Advances in Experimental Social Psychology*, 33, 189–255.

Lassiter, G. D., Geers, A. L., Handley, I. M., Weiland, P. E., & Munhall, P. J. (2002). Videotaped interrogations and confessions: A simple change in [illegible] perspective alters verdicts in simulated trials. *Journal of Applied Psychology*, 87(5), 867–874.

Leippe, M. R., & Romanczyk, A. (1989). Reactions to child (versus adult) eyewitnesses: The influence of jurors' preconceptions and witness behavior. *Law and Human Behavior*, 13(2), 103–132.

Lipton, J. P. (1977). On the psychology of eyewitness testimony. *Journal of Applied Psychology*, 62, 90–95.

Loftus, E. F., & Palmer, J. C. (1974). Reconstruction of automobile destruction: An example of the interaction between language and memory. *Journal of Verbal Learning and Verbal Behavior*, 13, 585–589.

Loftus, E. F., & Pickrell, J. E. (1995). The formation of false memories. *Psychiatric Annals*, 25(12), 720–725.

Mahoney, R., McDonald, E., Optican, S., & Tinsley, Y. (2007). *The Evidence Act 2006: Act and analysis*. Wellington, New Zealand: Brookers.

Milne, R., & Bull, R. (1999). *Investigative interviewing: Psychology and practice*. Chichester, UK: Wiley.

Nickerson, R. F. (1998). Confirmation bias: A ubiquitous phenomenon in many guises. *Review of General Psychology*, 2, 175–220.

Oeberst, A. (2012). If anything else comes to mind ... better keep it to yourself? Delayed recall is discrediting – unjustifiably. *Law and Human Behavior*, 36(4), 266–274.

Pipe, M. E., & Henaghan, M. (1996). Accommodating children's testimony legal reforms in New Zealand. *Criminal Justice and Behavior*, 23, 377–401.

Porter, S., Yuille, J. C., & Lehman, D. R. (1999). The nature of real, implanted, and fabricated memories for emotional childhood events: Implications for the recovered memory debate. *Law and Human Behavior*, 23(5), 517–537.

Potter, R., & Brewer, N. (1999). Perceptions of witness behaviour-accuracy relationships held by police, lawyers and mock-jurors. *Psychiatry, Psychology and Law*, 6(1), 97–103.

Powell, M. B., Fisher, R. P., & Wright, R. (2005). Investigative interviewing. In N. Brewer & K. Williams (eds), *Psychology and law: An empirical perspective* (pp. 11–42). New York: Guilford.

Read, J. D., & Connolly, A. (2007). The effects of delay on long-term memory for witnessed events. In M. P. Toglia, J. D. Read, , D. R. Ross, & R. C. L. Lindsay (eds.), *Handbook of eyewitness psychology: Volume I. Memory for events* (pp. 117–155). New York: Lawrence Erlbaum Associates.

Rock, F. (2001). The genesis of a witness statement. *Forensic Linguistics*, 8, 44–72.

Rose, M. R., Nadler, J., & Clark, J. (2006). Appropriately upset? Emotion norms and perceptions of crime victims. *Law and Human Behavior*, 30, 203–219.

Rubin, D. C., & Wenzel, A. E. (1996). One hundred years of forgetting: A quantitative description of retention. *Psychological Review*, 103, 734–760.

Ruva, C. L., & Bryant, J. B. (2004). The impact of age, speech style, and question form on perceptions of witness credibility and trial outcome. *Journal of Applied Social Psychology*, 34, 1919–1944.

Sanders, A., Creaton, J., Bird, S., & Weber, L. (1996). *Witnesses with learning disabilities*. London: Home Office.

Schollum, M. (2005). *Investigative interviewing: The current situation*. Wellington: New Zealand Police.

Shepherd, E., & Milne, R. (2006). 'Have you told management about this?' Bringing witness interviewing into the twenty-first century. In A. Heaton-Armstrong, E. Shepherd, G. H. Gudjonsson, & D. Wolchover (eds), *Witness testimony: Psychological, investigative and evidential perspectives* (pp. 131–152). Oxford: Oxford University Press.

Stern, V. (2010). *The Stern Review*. London: Home Office.

Taylor, N., & Joudo, J. (2005). *The impact of pre-recorded video and closed circuit television testimony by adult sexual assault complainants on jury decision-making: An experimental study*. Canberra: Australian Institute of Criminology.

Tuckey, M. R., & Brewer, N. (2003). The influence of schemas, stimulus ambiguity, and interview schedule on eyewitness memory over time. *Journal of Experimental Psychology: Applied*, 9, 101–118.

Tulving, E. (1972). Episodic and semantic memory. In E. Tulving & W. Donaldson (eds), *Organization of memory* (pp. 382–403). Oxford, UK: Academic Press.

Vrij, A. (2005). Criteria-based content analysis: A qualitative review of the first 37 studies. *Psychology, Public Policy, and Law*, 11(1), 3–41.

Vrij, A., & Granhag, P. A. (2012). Eliciting cues to deception and truth: What matters are the questions asked. *Journal of Applied Research in Memory and Cognition*, 1(2), 110–117.

Vrij, A., Granhag, P. A., & Porter, S. (2010). Pitfalls and opportunities in nonverbal and verbal lie detection. *Psychological Science in the Public Interest*, 11(3), 89–121.

Wells, G. L., Ferguson, T. J., & Lindsay, R. C. (1981). The tractability of eyewitness confidence and its implications for triers of fact. *Journal of Applied Psychology*, 66, 688–696.

Wells, G. L., & Leippe, M. R. (1981). How do triers of fact infer the accuracy of eye-witness identifications? Using memory for peripheral detail can be misleading. *Journal of Applied Psychology*, 66(6), 682–687.

Wessel, E., Drevland, G. C. B., Eilersten, D. E., & Magnussen, S. (2006). Credibility of the emotional witness: A study of ratings by court judges. *Law and Human Behavior*, 30, 221–230.

Westera, N., Kebbell, M. R., & Milne, R. (2011). Interviewing rape complainants: Police officers' perceptions of interview format and quality of evidence. *Applied Cognitive Psychology*, 25, 917–926.

Westera, N., Kebbell, M. R., & Milne, B. (2013a). It is better, but does it look better? Prosecutor perceptions of using rape complainant investigative interviews as evidence. *Psychology, Crime and Law*, 19, 595–610.

Westera, N., Kebbell, M., & Milne, B. (2013b). Losing two thirds of the story: A comparison of the video recorded police interview and live evidence of rape complainants. *Criminal Law Review*, 4, 290–308.

Westera, N., & Powell, M. (2015). Improving communication: Beyond the cognitive interview for adult eyewitnesses. In G. Oxburgh, T. Grant, T. Myklebust, & B. Milne (eds), *Communication in investigative and legal contexts* (pp. 337–358). Chichester, UK: Wiley.

Westera, N. J., Powell, M. B., & Milne, B. (2015). Lost in the detail: Prosecutors' perceptions of the utility of video recorded police interviews as rape complainant evidence. *Australian and New Zealand Journal of Criminology*, doi:10.1177/0004865815620705

Westera, N., & Powell, M. B. (2015). Prosecutors' perceptions of the utility of video-recorded evidence with rape complainants. *Criminal Law Journal*, 39, 198–207.

Wigmore, J. H. (1974). *Evidence in trials at common law*. Boston, MA: Little, Brown & Company.

Wixted, J. T., Mickes, L., Clark, S. E., Gronlund, S. D., & RoedigerIIIH. L. (2015). Initial eyewitness confidence reliably predicts eyewitness identification accuracy. *American Psychologist*, 70(6), 515–526.

Yerkes, R. M., & Dodson, J. D. (1908). The relation of strength of stimulus to rapidity of habit-formation. *Journal of Comparative Neurology & Psychology*, 18, 459–482.

Zydervelt, S., Zajac, R., Kaladelfos, A., & Westera, N. (2016). Lawyers' strategies for cross-examining rape complainants: Have we moved beyond the 1950s? *British Journal of Criminology*, doi:10.1093/bjc/azw023

Chapter 5

Vulnerability and criminal investigations

Kevin Smith and Brendan O'Mahony

Introduction

The word 'vulnerable' has its origins in the Latin vulnerare 'to wound'. Most modern dictionary definitions of the word tend to focus on situations in which a person is "exposed to the possibility of being attacked or harmed" (*Compact Oxford English Dictionary*, 2005) but some have extended the definition to include the impact of social influences such as being "open to persuasion, temptation, censure etc." (*Collins Concise English Dictionary*, 2012). Both definitions are relevant in the legal settings in which forensic psychologists work; the vulnerability of the victim with its focus on exposure to attack or harm can certainly affect the extent of an offender's sentence. For example, "culpability will be greater … where an offender targets a vulnerable victim (because of their old age or youth, disability or by virtue of the job they do)" (Sentencing Guidelines Council, 2004). In addition, concerns have been expressed over the past 30 years about the potential lack of reliability of the information obtained in some police interviews with vulnerable victims, witnesses and suspects where they might be susceptible to interrogator pressure (Gudjonsson, 2010). It is also the case that interviewees can be vulnerable to miscommunication through cultural and language issues (O'Mahony, Marchant and Fadden, 2015).

In practice, the way in which vulnerability is defined depends on the purpose for which the concept is used and the language. The concept of 'vulnerability' may translate vaguely in other languages, for example, Dutch (Mergaerts, Van Daele and Vervaeke, 2016) and anecdotally, at the time of writing, there is some discussion amongst academics and practitioners in the UK about the negative connotations of the word 'vulnerability'. Where it is used in statute law and secondary legislation it focuses on groups of people who may be thought of as vulnerable on the basis of age, disability or disorder and, in some jurisdictions, circumstances (e.g. the nature of the relationship between a victim and a suspected offender). Where it is used by practitioners who have face-to-face contact with people, it tends to focus on the various factors to be considered when assessing the extent to which any given individual is vulnerable (e.g. their mental state). These definitions are not mutually exclusive; it is rather the case that they occur at different levels of analysis. Law operates at a societal level in that it prescribes the rules governing behaviour in general, whereas the role of practitioners who have face-to-face contact with people is usually to assess and, sometimes, to treat or support the individual. Psychologists who practise their craft in the justice system have to work with both definitions simultaneously, though the emphasis given to either is likely to depend on the context in which they work. After exploring these contexts this chapter will consider how the police and the courts have utilised outside expertise and developed innovative ways to adapt practices so that the environment is better managed, the questioning of vulnerable persons is more appropriate and miscommunication is, therefore, less likely. In essence, the argument advanced here is that the need to identify and to take account of vulnerability at every stage of the process, from the investigation to the trial, is extremely important to giving vulnerable people fair access to justice and to making the system as effective and efficient as possible.

Legal definition of vulnerability

'Vulnerability' is defined in different ways by different jurisdictions. It is often the case that children are regarded as vulnerable, although the age at which childhood is thought to end can vary a little. While some jurisdictions focus exclusively on children in their definitions of vulnerability, other jurisdictions include certain vulnerable groups of adults. When vulnerable groups of adults are included in the definition, they often focus on factors that might be thought of as, to some extent, inherent such as mental health, learning disability and physical disability. Some jurisdictions go on to include situational factors such as the type or circumstances of the offence (for example, sexual offences, domestic abuse) in their definition of vulnerability.

In England, Wales and Northern Ireland, for example, a vulnerable witness is defined as:

- A child under 18; or
- A witness of any age whose quality of evidence is likely to be diminished as a result of a
  - mental disorder (as defined in the legislation);
  - "significant impairment of intelligence and social functioning" (commonly taken to mean a learning disability, for example; Ministry of Justice, 2011); or
  - physical disability.

The legislation in England, Wales and Northern Ireland[1] goes on to separately define 'intimidated' witnesses as those whose quality of evidence is likely to be diminished as a result of fear or distress over testifying when taking a number of factors into account including the nature of the alleged offence, the social and cultural background of the witness, their ethnic origins, domestic or employment circumstances, religious beliefs or political opinions or any inclination that the suspected offender or their associates might have to intimidate or to threaten them.

While the criminal law in England, Wales and Northern Ireland limits the definition of vulnerability when it is applied to witnesses to the kind of inherent characteristics that might have an impact on the individual's ability to communicate effectively, designating those who may be regarded as vulnerable by the situation as 'intimidated', the law in Scotland includes inherent and situational elements in a single definition of vulnerability. It would be a mistake to think of these differences in the definition as ideological, they are in fact pragmatic. Vulnerable witnesses in England, Wales and Northern Ireland are eligible for the full range of 'special measures' set out in the legislation, including giving their evidence-in-chief by means of a previously video-recorded interview, the assistance of an intermediary (see below) and the use of aids to communication (e.g. speech synthesizers). Intimidated witnesses in England, Wales and Northern Ireland are eligible for most of the same special measures except for the assistance of an intermediary or aids to communication. At the time of writing, there were no statutory provisions in Scotland for either intermediaries or aids to communication (though access to such provisions in Scotland is in principle possible via the courts' inherent common law powers). The effect of this is that there is no need to draw a distinction between inherent and situational vulnerability in Scottish law.

Vulnerability is defined with reference to suspected offenders in England, Wales and Northern Ireland as:

- Any suspected offender under 17 and, in England and Wales, to a lesser extent, between 17 and 18; and
- A suspected offender of any age who either
    - has a 'mental disorder' or
    - is 'otherwise mentally vulnerable' (applies to any person who because of "their mental state or capacity, may not understand the significance of what is said, of questions or of their replies" (Note 1G to Code C of the Codes of Practice to the Police and Criminal Evidence Act 1984 and the Codes of Practice to the Police and Criminal Evidence (Northern Ireland) Order 1989).

As in the case of witnesses, practices in Scotland are similar to those in England, Wales and Northern Ireland in that they make special provision for suspected offenders under 16 and, to a lesser extent, for suspected offenders aged 16 or 17 years. There is currently no statutory definition for vulnerable adult suspected offenders in Scotland (Scottish Government, 2011a). In practice, however, adult suspects are treated as vulnerable if they appear unable to communicate properly with the police as a result of a mental disorder, including a personality disorder or a learning disability (Scottish Parliament Information Centre briefing 15/27 20th May 2015 "Criminal Justice [Scotland] Bill: Update").

Although the law in England, Wales and Northern Ireland explicitly defines vulnerability in respect of suspected offenders with reference to the inherent characteristics of age, mental disorder and mental capacity, it acknowledges the possibility of situational vulnerability when it refers to people being 'otherwise mentally vulnerable' as a result of their 'mental state'. This could perhaps include issues due to life adversity, neuroticism and compliance (Drake, 2010). The emphasis on mental disorder, mental capacity and mental state and its potential impact on understanding, means that some assessment of the individual's communication and cognitive needs is necessary.

Assessment, safeguards and provisions can only be made if an individual has been highlighted as potentially vulnerable in the first place. The proverbial problem is just this; spotting vulnerable individuals (for example, Young, Goodwin, Sedgwick and Gudjonsson, 2013). Thus developing screening tools at all stages of the criminal justice system is essential. Work to date has, however, focussed primarily on prison settings (Murphy, Gardner and Freeman, 2015; Silva, Gough and Weeks, 2015). That many people with cognitive impairment and other mental health issues become very good at masking their difficulties makes it harder for professionals to identify any issues within the custodial setting.

Even when police officers are made aware of issues of vulnerability they may implement a hierarchy of need to determine whether to secure the services of an 'appropriate adult' to assist the suspect, where anxiety and depression may be viewed at the lower end of the scale (Dehaghani, 2016). In these circumstances, an 'appropriate adult' is likely to be a professional who is independent of the police, although in some situations the appropriate adult could be a relative, guardian or someone responsible for the suspect's care who is not involved in the case. In England and Wales, the role of an appropriate adult in the context of an interview is to advise the suspect, observe whether the interview is conducted properly and fairly and to facilitate communication between the suspect and the interviewer. For more information about the appropriate adult role see Code C of the Codes of Practice to the Police and Criminal Evidence Act 1984 (Home Office, 2017) with particular reference to paragraphs 1.7 and 11.17. Research has found that experienced interviewing officers have reported how they tailor an investigative interview to meet the needs of a suspect with a mental disorder but inexperienced interviewers may have less knowledge of the cognitive factors impacting on the investigative interview (Oxburgh, Gabbert, Milne and Cherryman, 2016). Oxburgh, Gabbert, Milne and Cherryman also raise concerns about the implementation of the safeguards afforded by securing the services of an appropriate adult when police officers hold negative perceptions.

Psychological definitions of vulnerability

'Risk' tends to be a central feature of psychological definitions of 'vulnerability'. Bull (2010, p. 5) rightly points out that "around the world, there is no generally agreed definition of the word 'vulnerable' as it applies to witnesses in the investigative setting". It could be argued that this is so because the nature and the extent of the perceived risk depends on the jurisdiction. For example, in England, Wales and Northern Ireland adults with a physical disability or disorder are viewed as 'vulnerable' if it is likely to have an adverse impact on the quality of their evidence whereas in Scotland they are not, unless they also have either a mental disorder or a learning disability. One of the consequences of this is that in England, Wales and Northern Ireland witnesses who are deaf but who have not, for one reason or another, developed sufficient competence in British Sign Language are viewed as 'vulnerable' by statute law whereas in Scotland they are not (although the flexibility of Scottish common law is such that they are unlikely to be denied access to justice). On the other hand, as noted above, Scottish definitions include situational vulnerability whereas English, Welsh and Northern Irish definitions consist solely of the inherent characteristics of youth and disability or disorder to draw a distinction between the kind of special measures available to different groups of witnesses. What each of the jurisdictions in the United Kingdom has in common is the psychological notion that vulnerability can increase the risks to the reliability of the evidence of witnesses. The effect of this is that psychologists have been influential in developing interview protocols that set out to manage the risk by encouraging a process in which techniques such as active listening and open-ended questioning are used (for example, Home Office, 1992; Ministry of Justice, 2011; Scottish Government, 2011b; Department of Justice, 2012).

The focus on groups that seems to dominate when vulnerable witnesses are considered arises because the law in all the jurisdictions in the United Kingdom is concerned with giving them access to various special measures intended to be of assistance when they give evidence. In contrast, the focus on the individual that tends to dominate when suspected offenders are considered largely comes about because of a focus on how best to assess their fitness to be interviewed. It comes as no surprise then that when considered mainly, though not exclusively, from the perspective of suspected offenders during police interviews, psychological definitions of vulnerability tend to be broader than legal definitions in that they are framed in terms of social, emotional, cognitive, situational and physiological factors (Gudjonsson, 2003). These vulnerabilities make it more difficult for interviewees to participate in police interviews because they make it harder to cope with the situation by impairing their ability to make decisions, understand questions and the implications of their answers and to provide detailed accurate and coherent answers to questions (Gudjonsson, 2010). In some circumstances such difficulties could of course give rise to false confessions. Thus, where the focus is on the assessment of the individual, vulnerability amounts to "psychological characteristics or mental state which render a witness prone, in certain circumstances, to providing information which is inaccurate, unreliable or misleading" (Gudjonsson, 2006, p. 68) so that vulnerability represents a potential risk to the evidence rather than being a definitive marker of unreliability (Gudjonsson, 2010). A concern with the accuracy, completeness and coherence of evidence is also central to the way the legislation in respect of vulnerable witnesses has been drafted in England and Wales (see section 16[5] Youth Justice and Criminal Evidence Act 1999). In the case of witnesses it is about fairness by means of access to special measures; in the case of suspected offenders it is about fairness in the right to liberty and security that is recognised in Article 5 of the European Convention on Human Rights (Gudjonsson, 2010). Given that fairness for a vulnerable witness is about access to special measures and that fairness for a vulnerable suspect is about the way in which they are treated by the police it is hardly surprising that focusing on witnesses lends itself to an approach that puts more emphasis on groups than is the case when the focus is on suspected offenders.

Expert psychological evidence relating to admissions made in police interviews was first accepted in the Court of Appeal in 1991 (Davies and Gudjonsson, 2013). The expert witness must give a fair and accurate presentation of the psychological knowledge underpinning their testimony when giving an opinion to the court (Crighton, 2013). The term 'mental disorder' is perhaps more readily defined than the more loosely worded 'otherwise mentally vulnerable' and the criminal justice system may benefit from an expert psychological opinion about the impact on other factors such as environmental issues that might have made a detainee vulnerable in the absence of a defined mental disorder. However, as argued by Dehaghani (2016) the courts have a responsibility to both understand the breadth of the term 'vulnerability' in the custodial setting and to ensure that the services of an appropriate adult safeguard are secured to support the suspect as intended in the police station.

Case study

The second author (O'Mahony) recalls a case where a detainee who made admissions during the police interview was subsequently found to have impaired levels of cognitive functioning, albeit the expert witnesses were not in agreement as to the exact level of the cognitive impairment. There was no appropriate adult present at the police station and the detainee had declined legal advice prior to the first police interview. Vulnerability must be considered in terms of whether the detainee was making an informed decision to decline legal advice if he had not had the benefit of discussing the issue with an appropriate adult. With the benefit of hindsight an expert witness can examine what happened, both in terms of the environment and the trajectory towards the police interview, which may have impacted on the detainee's level of mental vulnerability. In this case the experts for the prosecution and defence all agreed that the detainee did not meet the criteria for mental disorder. The court appeared to be keenly focused on whether the defendant met the criteria for intellectual disability and having been advised that this was not the case, the court appeared less concerned about whether the defendant was 'otherwise mentally vulnerable' at the time of police interview(s). The court was then left in the position of deciding whether having impaired levels of verbal comprehension and working memory, together with other factors such as the time and distance spent travelling to the police station and the time of day at which the interview(s) was conducted (evening), made this individual mentally vulnerable, as was argued by one expert witness. The suspected offender was found to be functioning at the borderline level (IQ 70s range) although the court accepted there were difficulties with agreeing the exact level of his cognitive functioning. One expert witness argued that distance travelled prior to interview, together with a relatively lengthy assessment of his 'fitness to be detained' and an interview with a medical practitioner immediately prior to the police investigative interview, all needed to be considered when evaluating mental vulnerability. The impact of (any) fatigue on impaired cognitive functioning and subsequent decision-making and comprehension needed to be evaluated. On detention, the detainee was given his rights by the sergeant in charge of the custody office in what appeared to be a relatively busy custodial environment, and perhaps at a pace of delivery by the sergeant that the detainee might have had difficulty comprehending. Additionally, the police interview in which admissions were made was almost two hours in duration without breaks. In these circumstances, the experts and the court had to carefully evaluate what was said during the police interview together and how it was said (in terms of pace, intonation etc.) and the court found itself in the unenviable position of ruling on whether the detainee was mentally vulnerable at the time of interview.

This example illustrates that there are some difficulties with categorical legal definitions where a detainee may find him or herself on the margins of what is accepted as a defined vulnerability. In such circumstances it can be difficult to convince the court that the detainee was actually mentally vulnerable as a result of their situation. This is particularly the case if the police forensic medical examiner or other healthcare practitioner in the custody facility has assessed the detainee as being 'fit to be interviewed'. It is essential that medical and healthcare practitioners employed in this role have a full understanding of the impact that fatigue and impaired levels of cognitive functioning may have on expressive and receptive vocabulary and in the second author's experience this is not always the case. It is imperative that the forensic medical examiner or healthcare practitioner has expertise in appraising impaired cognitive functioning when advising interviewing officers and the court about issues relating to fitness to be interviewed. In such instances it is surely the case that, a medical practitioner who has specialised in forensic learning disabilities or a healthcare practitioner trained specifically in learning disabilities is a fundamental requirement when these decisions are made. In practice, however, it is, of course, extremely difficult to have access to every type of specialist in the police station.

Vulnerable witnesses

It was, perhaps, the Cleveland Inquiry (Butler-Sloss, 1988) that first drew widespread public attention to the impact of poor interview practices on the alleged victims of child abuse in England. The report drew attention to the mind-set of the interviewers in assuming that there was something to disclose in the interview and the consequential view that the child must be in 'denial' when they did not disclose anything. The areas of agreement by professionals reported by the Cleveland Inquiry (*The Therapeutic Journal*, 2011) included the following:

- Interviews should not be referred to as 'disclosure' because doing so assumes that abuse has taken place;
- Interviews should be approached with an open mind;
- Open-ended questions should be mainly used; and
- Interviewers should be trained.

Concerns about the mind-set of some interviewers are reflected today in the psychological concept of confirmation bias (see Chapter 3, this volume), which refers to looking for or interpreting evidence through the lens of pre-existing beliefs (Nickerson, 1998) and can have a negative impact on the types of questions asked by poor interviewers (Powell, Hughes-Scholes and Sharman, 2012). More recent police guidance recommends that investigators should adopt an 'investigative mind-set' amounting to a disciplined and critical approach to going about the business of investigation (ACPO, 2005, 2009). Such an approach is consistent with the framework advocated today in the guidance for interviewing victims and witnesses. This framework has its origins in the *Advisory Group on Video-Recorded Evidence* that was set up by the Home Office in 1988, 17 days before the publication of the Cleveland Inquiry Report. The report of the Advisory Group, commonly referred to as the 'Pigot Report' after its chairman, His Honour Judge Thomas Pigot QC, was published a year later (Home Office, 1989). It made a number of recommendations that included making video-recorded interviews with some vulnerable witnesses admissible as evidence-in-chief during a trial provided that they were conducted in accordance with a memorandum of good practice. The Advisory Group went on to endorse the 'stepwise' approach to interviewing advocated by John Yuille (for example, Yuille, Hunter, Joffe and Zaparniuk, 1993), though not the approach that he developed for analysing interviews, Statement Validity Analysis (for example, Yuille and Farr, 1987).

The law in England and Wales was subsequently amended to allow for the playing of video-recorded interviews as evidence-in-chief in respect of children under 17 who were witnesses to sexual offences and children under 14 who were witnesses to violent offences. A policy steering group was set up to develop some guidance in respect of interviewing these witnesses, as recommended by the Advisory Group. Professor Graham Davies of the British Psychological Society and Professor Ray Bull of the Department of Psychology at Portsmouth Polytechnic (later the University of Portsmouth) were influential in this group and much is owed to them today for the contribution that they made to the development of the *Memorandum of Good Practice on Video Recorded Interviews with Child Witnesses for Criminal Proceedings* (Home Office, 1992; and see Davies, Bull and Milne, 2015 for further reading). The *Memorandum of Good Practice* recommended a four phase approach to interviewing based on stepwise, as follows:

1 Rapport;
2 Free narrative account;
3 Questioning; and
4 Closing the interview.

Stepwise and the *Memorandum of Good Practice* adopt an approach to interviewing that begins with rapport building in order to reduce anxiety, followed by an attempt to initiate a free-narrative account by means of an open-ended prompt, active listening to sustain the account and then questioning in order to develop and clarify the account. This approach is supported by research suggesting that anxiety can result in increased susceptibility to suggestion (Vallano and Compo, 2011) and the observation that open-ended questions are more likely to result in accurate, detailed and relevant accounts from witnesses (Su-Lin, Powell and Guadagno, 2014).

Five years after the publication of the *Memorandum of Good Practice* the United Kingdom government set up an interdepartmental working group to review the provision for vulnerable and intimidated witnesses in the criminal justice system for England and Wales. The terms of reference for the group included the identification of measures likely to improve the treatment of vulnerable and intimidated witnesses at every stage of the criminal justice process. The working group published their recommendations a year later in *Speaking up for Justice* (Home Office, 1998). Their recommendations included:

- The development of a *Memorandum of Good Practice* for vulnerable adult witnesses;
- An extension to the legislation to allow video-recorded interviews with vulnerable adult witnesses to be played as evidence-in-chief followed by the further extension of the provision to witnesses who are vulnerable by circumstances; and
- The use of communication aids and intermediaries to assist witnesses to give their best evidence where necessary.

These recommendations led to the development of the interview advice set out in *Achieving Best Evidence in Criminal Proceedings: Guidance for Vulnerable or Intimidated Witnesses, including Children* (Home Office, 2002) and the remaining recommendations were legislated for as 'special measures' intended to assist witnesses in court.

When it comes to communication, the assistance of an intermediary is, perhaps, the most significant of the special measures available to vulnerable witnesses. The role of an intermediary is to facilitate communication between a vulnerable witness with a communication need and the police during an interview and/or the court to help them give their best evidence. Intermediaries can help to explain the questions asked and the answers given "as far as necessary to help the witness but without changing the substance of the evidence" (Ministry of Justice, 2015). The Ministry of Justice in England and Wales and the Department of Justice in Northern Ireland have set up registered intermediary schemes. In England and Wales the scheme is limited to victims and witnesses, in Northern Ireland the scheme also applies to suspected offenders who are interviewed by the police and to defendants when they give evidence in court. Registered intermediaries are professionals such as speech and language therapists, psychologists, occupational therapists, teachers, social workers and experienced sign-language specialists from the deaf community. In essence, they work by assessing a victim, witness and, in the case of Northern Ireland, a suspect or defendant's, communication needs then by helping to plan the interview and participating in it and/or by assisting the court in a ground rules hearing prior to the commencement of a trial and when evidence is given during it (O'Mahony, 2010; O'Mahony, Smith and Milne, 2011).

Achieving Best Evidence (ABE) has been revised twice since it was first published, in 2007 and 2011, and a further edition is anticipated in due course. The model of interviewing advocated by ABE in England and Wales is reflected in Northern Ireland in *Achieving Best Evidence in Criminal Proceedings: Guidance on Interviewing Victims and Witnesses, the use of Special Measures and the Provision of Pre-Trial Therapy* (Department of Justice, 2012). Similar guidance is recommended in Scotland by *Joint Interviewing Child Witnesses in Scotland* (Scottish Government, 2011b). For further reading about interview strategies for vulnerable witnesses see Smith and Milne (in press).

Vulnerable suspects and defendants

Unfortunately, developments in respect of interviewing vulnerable suspects have not followed vulnerable witnesses, despite research findings consistently indicating that a significant number of suspected offenders in police custody are vulnerable (Gudjonsson, Clare, Rutter and Pearse, 1993) and that a significant proportion of the prison population has learning disabilities and/or mental health issues (Eysenck and Gudjonsson, 1989; Eysenck and Gudjonsson, 2008).

The only requirements in England and Wales are contained in the Codes of Practice to the Police and Criminal Evidence Act 1984, which simply place an obligation on the police to secure the services of an appropriate adult during an interview for the following reasons:

- to advise the person being interviewed;
- to observe whether the interview is being conducted properly and fairly; and
- to facilitate communication with the person being interviewed.

Various inadequacies in the use of appropriate adults have, however, been highlighted for a number of years (for example, Medford, Gudjonsson and Pearse, 2003 and National Appropriate Adult Network, 2015). For example, the relative inactivity of appropriate adults during the custody process, including the interview, and a substantial lack of appropriate adult provision for vulnerable adults in many parts of England and Wales.

The overall guidance on interviewing victims, witnesses and suspected offenders follows the PEACE framework (**P**reparation and planning, **E**ngage and explain, **A**ccount, **C**larification and **c**hallenge, **c**losure and **E**valuation) as recommended by the College of Policing (see https://www.app.college.police.uk/app-content/investigations/investigative-interviewing/#peace-framework) and discussed more fully in Chapters 6 and 8. There is, however, no *specific* guidance on the interviewing of vulnerable suspects beyond the general principle that "people with clear or perceived vulnerabilities should be treated with particular care, and extra safeguards should be put in place" (ACPO, 2009). Of particular concern is the absence of any guidance on how to best challenge the accounts of vulnerable suspects in the police station (O'Mahony, Milne and Grant, 2012).

Communicating with vulnerable victims, witnesses, suspects and defendants

A great deal of work has been and continues to be conducted into the memory recall and the interviewing of children who are developing within standard parameters (see, for example, Goodman and Melinder, 2007). Some work has been done on interviewing children with learning disabilities (for example, Henry and Gudjonsson, 2007; Henry, Bettenay and Carney, 2011) but the literature is far more limited when it comes to interviewing adults with learning disabilities, mental health issues and physical disabilities or disorders. This may be the case for a number of reasons including the following:

- The sheer range of disorders and disabilities that can have an impact on communication;
- The variable impact of many disorders and disabilities on communication (for example, variations along the autistic spectrum); and
- Ethical considerations.

Such research as has been conducted into interviewing adults with learning disabilities has largely focussed on their suggestibility in terms of being more susceptible to misleading questions (Bowles and Sharman, 2014; Antaki, Young and Finlay, 2002), the positive contribution made by training in terms of avoiding leading and suggestive questions (Agnew, Powell and Snow, 2006), the value of the cognitive interview in interviewing children with a mild learning disability (Milne and Bull, 1996) and the use of the cognitive interview with adults on the autistic spectrum (Richards and Milne, in preparation).

With the possible exception of the impact of trauma on memory recall, research into interviewing witnesses with mental health issues is even more limited. Research into traumatic memory such as is summarised in the *Guidelines on Memory and the Law* (British Psychological Society, 2010) is very helpful in that it sensitises interviewers to the potential impact of trauma on memory. Work on the management of the kind of behaviours that can be associated with trauma in investigative interviews such as dissociation is, however, still very much in its infancy. Overall, research examining interviews with victims, witnesses and suspected offenders with learning disabilities and mental health issues tends to look at these factors as being one of the four types of psychological vulnerability that might, in some circumstances, lead to them providing unreliable information during an interview (for example, Gudjonsson, 2006).

There is a general lack of research focussing on victims, witnesses and suspected offenders with physical disorders, possibly because the range of physical disabilities that could have an impact on communication is even wider than it is for learning disabilities or mental health issues. Some of the wider research on interviewing may, however, be relevant to conducting such interviews. For example, research highlighting the potential that forced-choice questions have towards eliciting misleading responses from witnesses (e.g. Gee, Gregory and Pipe, 1999) should be borne in mind when developing an interview plan for witnesses whose disabilities mean that they can only respond in terms of yes/no to a series of forced-choice questions (as was the case in with one of the witnesses with quadriplegic cerebral palsy in *R v Watts* [2010] EWCA Crim 1824).

Good practice guidance

The research referred to in this chapter up until this point suggests that vulnerability can lead to victims, witnesses and suspects being more easily misled in police interviews. It follows that the techniques used in these interviews should seek to reduce the pressure on interviewees to conform to the perceived wishes of the interviewer. This could be assisted, for example, by being explicit about ground rules such as encouraging a witness to tell the interviewer if they do not understand a question or do not know the answer to it (Ministry of Justice, 2011). It is also important that the kind of questioning used in such interviews should be neither leading nor misleading.

In advance of further research into the interviewing of witnesses who are vulnerable by disorder or, disability, it is necessary to follow the good practice guidance that has been developed from the experience of clinicians and practitioners and informed by research findings where available. Such guidance is freely available on the internet from reputable sources such as the Ministry of Justice for England and Wales, the Scottish Government, the Department for Justice in Northern Ireland and the National Autistic Society (for example, Ministry of Justice, 2011; Scottish Government, 2011c; Department of Justice, 2012; and the National Autistic Society, 2011). A good example of this kind of guidance can be found in some of the 'toolkits' on an internet site hosted by the Advocacy Training Council (for England and Wales) known as the 'Advocate's Gateway'. The toolkits relevant to this chapter at the time of writing relate to questioning children and young people (including the additional factors involved in communicating with children under seven), the general principles involved in planning to question a vulnerable person or someone with communication needs, and some of the specific considerations involved in communicating with witnesses and defendants with:

- Learning disabilities;
- Autistic spectrum disorder (including memory and sensory issues);
- 'Hidden' disabilities (specific language impairment, dyslexia, dyspraxia, dyscalculia and attention deficit disorder); and
- Mental disorder.

The toolkits covering the questioning of people who are deaf and the use of communication aids are also relevant.

While the toolkits were developed with barristers and court in mind the principles of communication on which they are based are equally applicable to investigative interviews. The general principles they set down for communicating with vulnerable people (witnesses and defendants) are as follows:

- Speak slowly and calmly, give the interviewee enough thinking time to process questions and do not be tempted to interrupt them or to fill the pause with another question;
- Look out for possible misunderstanding and, if necessary ask the interviewee to explain what they think is meant in their own words; and
- Be alert to a loss of concentration.

When asking questions:

- Tailor the questions to the interviewee's needs and abilities;
- Follow a logical, chronological order, questions that jump around in time can be confusing;
- Signpost changes of subject;

- Keep questions short and simple, ask about one idea at a time using simple common words that are familiar to the interviewee;
- Use concrete rather than abstract concept words;
- Use who/what/where questions in preference to why/how questions because 'why' and 'how' tend to involve abstract concepts and to rely on a capacity to identify the motives for behaviour. 'Why' questions can also be interpreted as shifting blame onto the interviewee; and
- Use people's names, and the names of places and objects rather than using pronouns.

Avoid:

- Using the present tense when talking about past events;
- Questions that include the phrase 'do you remember ...?' because this sort of question requires complex processing, particularly when the interviewee is asked about what they told someone else rather than about the incident;
- Forced-choice questions because they create opportunities for error when the correct alternative may be missing;
- Leading questions; and
- Repetition because the interviewee might conclude that their first answer was wrong.

Important though verbal communication is within the criminal justice system, it is important to acknowledge that there are some vulnerable people for whom spoken language is either very limited or is not their primary means of communication at all. There are a variety of circumstances in which this might be the case including:

- People who can only respond in terms of "yes" or "no" to a question;
- Sign-language users;
- Symbol system users;
- People for whom visual cues or supports are needed to scaffold communication; and
- People suffering from trauma and prone to dissociation.

Interviewees who can only respond in terms of "yes" or "no" to a question

Having said that forced-choice questions should be avoided, there are some witnesses for whom forced-choice questions are the only option. For example, *in R v Watts* [2010] EWCA Crim 1824 one of the witnesses "could only communicate by movements of her eyes. In order to signify 'yes' she would raise them upwards towards the ceiling. In order to say 'no' she would move them, and to an extent move her head, from side to side". In these circumstances, the only thing that can be done is to present the topics to the interviewee in a logical and chronological order. As a means of ensuring that the alternatives are properly considered during the interview, the forced-choice questions in each topic area should then be ordered so that those least likely to lead to a positive response are presented before those more likely to result in a positive response. Where there are only two options the least likely possibility should be presented to the interviewee first. For example, in situations where it has already been established that there was only one offender, that the offender was an adult and, given the wider circumstances of the allegation, that a female perpetrator is most likely, "was it a man?" should be asked before "was it a woman?". Where there are a number of options (e.g. a list of names once it has been established that the offender was someone in a group of people known to the interviewee such as family, carers or friends) the most likely possibility should be presented to the interviewee second or third last in order to reduce the chances of them giving a positive response to the final question in the sequence simply because all the other options have been exhausted. It is accepted that this form of communication has its limitations and it should, therefore, only be used when there is no other viable alternative but it is a practical solution to a problem that could otherwise see some very vulnerable victims of crime denied access to justice and exposed to further abuse.

Sign-language users

Some vulnerable interviewees may use sign language to communicate, either as an alternative to verbal communication or to augment verbal communication. The most common form of sign language in the United Kingdom is British Sign Language (BSL) but it is not the only form of sign language in use. Other forms of sign language used by the deaf community include Irish Sign Language, French Sign Language, Australian Sign Language, American Sign Language etc. It is also important to remember that, like spoken English, there are regional variations in the way that BSL is used and that a BSL interpreter familiar with one regional variation may take time to acclimatise to some of the ways in which it is used in another. BSL is commonly used as an alternative to verbal communication by people from the deaf community who were born deaf, though it can be used by some people with acquired deafness. Unless they are also deaf, people with learning disabilities who also sign[2] may be using Makaton to either augment verbal communication or as an alternative to it. Makaton is a form of communication that includes signs and symbols (see next section for symbols). While Makaton shares many signs with BSL it uses the same grammar as spoken English (the grammar used by BSL is spatial whereas English grammar is linear). Whatever the case, it is important to understand what sign language is being used by the interviewee and how well they are using it. Where an interviewee's use of sign language is under developed or idiosyncratic the services of a specialist such as a registered intermediary in England, Wales or Northern

Ireland should be considered. Relevant case law in respect of the use of intermediaries with deaf witnesses can be found in English and Welsh case law in *R v AI, TA and FA* [2013] EWCA Crim 1308.

Symbol system users

Some interviewees with physical or learning disabilities use symbols to communicate. The symbols may be organised on a board, in a book or on cards. There are a number of symbols systems that include Makaton, Rebus, Bliss, Picture Communication Symbols (PCS) and Picture Exchange Communication symbols (PECs). Not all users have access to a comprehensive set of symbols that extend to parts of the body. In these circumstances it may be necessary to increase the user's lexicon by introducing new symbols to them when conducting an interview about physical assault or a sexual offence. This obviously needs to be done with considerable care in a neutral context far removed from the alleged offence(s).

People for whom visual cues or supports are needed to scaffold communication

Drawings, pictures, photographs, symbols, dolls, figures, models, writing (e.g. speech bubbles or on post it notes), visual timetables and social stories (e.g. Gray and White, 2000) can be used to assess a vulnerable interviewee's communication skills, to prepare them for an interview and to initiate and/or support their account. It is, perhaps, when they are used to initiate and support an account that their use may be at its most controversial and it is important to be aware of the research surrounding their use for these purposes (e.g. Poole, Bruck and Pipe, 2011). For this reason it is essential that the interview plan is clear about the following:

- Why it is necessary to use visual supports (even if it seems obvious to the interviewer);
- When they are to be used in the interview (i.e. to initiate an account or to support it);
- How they are going to be used in the interview (protocol for introducing them and managing their ongoing use).

People suffering from trauma and prone to dissociation

As noted earlier in this chapter, research on the impact of trauma on communication during investigative interviews is limited. Such research as has been conducted tends to largely focus on the impact of trauma on memory (for example, Safer, Christianson, Autry and Osterlund, 1998). There is a notable lack of research into the management of trauma during an investigative interview although one recent paper focussed on the needs of traumatised victims during police investigative interviews. Risan, Binder and Milne (2016) have identified three themes that must be considered by interviewers. Firstly, interviewers must become aware of the interviewees' capacity to cope with distress by attending to nonverbal cues. Secondly, the interviewer should communicate acceptance of managing the difficult emotions that may emerge during interview. Finally, the interviewer must also assist in regulating distress by helping the interviewee feel safe and grounded in the interview room. Reactions to trauma during an interview could include elements of avoidance, hyper-vigilance and dissociation. It is the last of these elements, dissociation, that is of most concern to the authors of this chapter. Dissociation can cover a range of behaviours that include being mentally detached from the process (e.g. as may be suggested by a fixed gaze) and, in extremis, Dissociative Identity Disorder (DID) (see O'Mahony, Milne and Smith, 2016) and, if one accepts the ICD-10[3] classification, conversion disorders such as Psychogenic Non-Epileptic Seizures (PNES). The authors of this chapter are currently collaborating on an exploratory study of the communication needs in investigative interviews of witnesses who have a diagnosis of Dissociative Identity Disorder. It may be the case that the findings can be extrapolated to other interview scenarios where interviewees dissociate or present with other complex trauma.

Conclusion

This chapter argues that in practice the meaning of 'vulnerability' depends on the purpose for which it is used. When it is used in relation to the criminal justice system, vulnerability is initially defined with reference to groups. The main emphasis for victims, witnesses, suspected offenders and defendants alike is on a kind of inherent vulnerability stemming from age, disability or disorder but we should remain mindful of other issues including life adversity and language and culture. Situational vulnerability is acknowledged in respect of victims and witnesses in England, Wales and Northern Ireland although the designation here is one of intimidation rather than vulnerability. The only jurisdiction to take account of situational factors in the definition of vulnerability for victims and witnesses is in Scotland. Situational vulnerability is, however, acknowledged in respect of suspected offenders in England, Wales and Northern Ireland in that it could contribute towards or result in someone being 'otherwise mentally vulnerable' if their understanding is impaired as a result of their 'mental state'. In practice, the definitions of vulnerability used by the criminal justice systems of the United Kingdom effectively serve as screening tools to assist practitioners to identify people who might be vulnerable; an assessment of the individual (either by the police or a specialist) is needed to establish whether and to what extent they are actually vulnerable. When the term 'vulnerability' is used in the context of an investigative interview it refers to the possibility that a person who is defined as 'vulnerable' may not understand what is said or be able to communicate effectively. The emphasis here is on the risk to any evidence that arises from interacting with the vulnerable person.

As a result of the risks posed by vulnerability to evidence in the criminal justice system, guidance influenced by research has been developed for investigative interviews with vulnerable witnesses throughout the United Kingdom. Although this guidance establishes some useful principles and provides a useful framework for interviewing victims and witnesses, further research is needed into the techniques that might be used to communicate with people who are vulnerable by virtue of disorder or disability. In advance of this research it is necessary to follow the good practice guidance that has been developed from the experience of clinicians and practitioners and informed by research findings where available.

Whilst accepting that there can be difficulties in identifying some categories of vulnerable witnesses and suspects prior to the police interview, there is no excuse for not implementing safeguards when vulnerability has been identified. Yet it seems to be the case that safeguards such as the support of an appropriate adult for vulnerable suspects are still disregarded on many occasions by those charged with implementing them. The court is the arbiter when issues of vulnerability are later highlighted as part of the prosecution or defence case and it is not beyond feasibility that negative perceptions, cynicism and subjectivity may also be at play in the courtroom as it has been found to be the case in the police station. It seems to be the case that psychological research and legal research have operated in isolation from each other for too long now and it is time for a combined approach from these disciplines (and others) to better manage vulnerability in investigative interviews. A starting point would be to gather data on the number of court judgements made annually about the inadmissibility of investigative interviews with witnesses and suspects. The analysis of vulnerability made by the court and the reasoning behind each judgement could then be evaluated from a psychological and a legal perspective.

Notes

1 The legislation referring to vulnerable and intimidated witnesses in England and Wales can be found in the Youth Justice and Criminal Evidence Act 1999. In Northern Ireland it can be found in the Criminal Evidence [Northern Ireland] Order 1999.
2 It is important to note that not everybody with a learning disability uses sign language; whether or not it is used often depends on the severity of the learning disability and the nature and extent of the communication impairment that arises from it.
3 ICD 10 is the 10th revision of the International Statistical Classification of Diseases (ICD) and related health problems.

References

ACPO (2005) *Core Investigative Doctrine*, London, Association of Chief Police Officers.
ACPO (2009) *National Investigative Interviewing Strategy*, London, Association of Chief Police Officers.

Agnew, S., Powell, M. and Snow, P. (2006) An Examination of the Questioning Styles of Police Officers and Caregivers when Interviewing Children with Intellectual Disabilities, *Legal and Criminological Psychology*, 11, 35–53.

Antaki, C., Young, N. and Finlay, M. (2002) Shaping Client's Answers: Departures from Neutrality in Care-Staff Interviews with People with a Learning Disability, *Disability and Society*, 17, 435–455.

Bowles, P.V. and Sharman, S.J. (2014) The Effect of Different Types of Leading Questions on Adult Eyewitnesses with Mild Intellectual Disabilities, *Applied Cognitive Psychology*, 28, 129–134.

British Psychological Society (2010) *Guidelines on Memory and the Law: Recommendations from the Scientific Study of Human Memory*, Leicester, British Psychological Society.

Bull, R. (2010) The Investigative Interviewing of Children and other Vulnerable Witnesses: Psychological Research and Working/Professional Practice, *Legal and Criminological Psychology*, 15, 5–23.

Butler-Sloss, E. (1988) *Report of the Inquiry into Child Abuse in Cleveland 1987*, CM 413, London, Her Majesty's Stationery Office.

Crighton, D. (2013) Expert Witness Work-Time to Step up to the Plate, *The Psychologist*, 26(7), 486–487.

Davies, G.M. and Gudjonsson, G.H. (2013) Psychologists in the Witness Box, *The Psychologist*, 26(7), 496–497.

Davies, G., Bull, R. and Milne, R. (2015) Analyzing and Improving the Testimony of Vulnerable Witnesses Interview under the 'Achieving Best Evidence' Protocol, in P. Radcliffe, G.H. Gudjonsson, A. Heaton-Armstrong and D. Wolchover (eds), *Witness Testimony in Sexual Cases: Evidential, Investigative and Scientific Perspectives*, Oxford, Oxford University Press.

Dehaghani, R. (2016) He's Just Not That Vulnerable: Exploring the Implementation of the Appropriate Adult Safeguard in Police Custody, *The Howard Journal of Crime and Justice*, 55(4), 396–413.

Department of Justice (2012) *Achieving Best Evidence in Criminal Proceedings: Guidance on Interviewing Victims and Witnesses, the use of Special Measures and the Provision of Pre-Trial Therapy*, Belfast, Department of Justice.

Drake, K.E. (2010) Interrogative Suggestibility: Life Adversity, Neuroticism and Compliance, *Personality and Individual Differences*, 48, 493–498.

Eysenck, H.J. and Gudjonsson, G.H. (1989) *The Causes and Cures of Criminality*, London, Plenum Press.

Gee, S., Gregory, M. and Pipe, M.-E. (1999) 'What Colour is your Pet Dinosaur?' The Impact of Pre-Interview Training and Question Type on Children's Answers, *Legal and Criminological Psychology*, 4, 111–128.

Goodman, G.S. and Melinder, A. (2007) Child Witness Research and Forensic Interviews of Young Children: A Review, *Legal and Criminological Psychology*, 12, 1–19.

Gray, C. and White, A. L. (2000) *My Social Stories Book*, London, Jessica Kingsley.

Gudjonsson, G.H. (2003) Psychology Brings Justice: The Science of Forensic Psychology, *Criminal Behaviour and Mental Health*, 3, 159–167.

Gudjonsson, G.H. (2006) The Psychological Vulnerabilities of Witnesses and the Risk of False Accusations and False Confessions, in A. Heaton-Armstrong, E. Shepherd, G. Gudjonsson and D. Wolchover (eds), *Witness Testimony. Psychological, Investigative and Evidential Perspectives*, Oxford, Oxford University Press.

Gudjonsson, G.H. (2010) Psychological Vulnerabilities During Police Interviews. Why are they Important? *Legal and Criminological Psychology*, 15, 161–175.

Gudjonsson, G.H., Clare, I.C.H., Rutter, S. and Pearse, J. (1993) *Persons at Risk During Interviews in Police Custody: The Identification of Vulnerabilities*, Research Study No. 12, The Royal Commission on Criminal Justice, London, Her Majesty's Stationery Office

Henry, L., Bettenay, C. and Carney, P.J. (2011) Children with Intellectual Disabilities and Developmental Disorders, in M.E. Lamb, D.J. La Rooy, L.C. Malloy and C. Katz (eds), *Children's Testimony: A Handbook of Psychological Research and Forensic Practice* (second edition), Chichester, John Wiley and Sons.

Henry, L. and Gudjonsson, G.H. (2007) Individual and Developmental Differences in Eyewitness Recall and Suggestibility in Children with Intellectual Disabilities, *Applied Cognitive Psychology*, 21, 361–381.

Home Office (2017) *Code C, Codes of Practice to the Police and Criminal Evidence Act 1984*, London, Home Office, available at https://www.gov.uk/government/uploads/system/uploads/attachment_data/file/59254 7/pace-code-c-2017.pdf (accessed 5 September 2017).

Home Office (1989) *Report of the Advisory Group on Video Evidence*, London, Home Office.

Home Office (1992) *Memorandum of Good Practice on Video-Recorded Interviews with Child Witnesses for Criminal Proceedings*, London, Home Office.

Home Office (1998) *Speaking up for Justice: Report of the Interdepartmental Working Group on the Treatment of Vulnerable or Intimidated Witnesses in the Criminal Justice System*, London, Home Office.

Home Office (2002) *Achieving Best Evidence in Criminal Proceedings: Guidance on Interviewing Victims and Witnesses, and using Special Measures*, London, Home Office.

Medford, S., Gudjonsson, G.H. and Pearse, J. (2003) The Efficacy of the Appropriate Adult Safeguard During Police Interviewing, *Legal and Criminological Psychology*, 8, 253–266.

Mergaerts, L., Van Daele, D. and Vervaeke, G. (2016) Vulnerable Suspects in Criminal Proceedings: Exploring 'Vulnerability' and the Role of the Criminal Defence Lawyer in the Pre-Trial Investigation. Paper presented to the International Investigative Interviewing Research Group, London.

Milne, R. and Bull, R. (1996) Interviewing Children with Mild Learning Disability with the Cognitive Interview, in N. Clark and G. Stephenson (eds), *Investigative and Forensic Decision Making: Issues in Criminological Psychology*. Leicester, British Psychological Society.

Ministry of Justice (2007 and 2011) *Achieving Best Evidence in Criminal Proceedings: Guidance on Interviewing Victims and Witnesses, and Guidance on using Special Measures*, London, Ministry of Justice.

Ministry of Justice (2015) *Code of Practice for Victims of Crime*, London, Ministry of Justice.

Murphy, G.H., Gardner, J. and Freeman, M.J. (2015) Screening Prisoners for Intellectual Disabilities in Three English Prisons, *Journal of Applied Research in Intellectual Disabilities*; early view at http://onlinelibrary.wiley.com/doi/10.1111/jar.12224/abstract (accessed 23 January 2016).

National Appropriate Adult Network (2015) *There to Help: Ensuring Provision of Appropriate Adults for Mentally Vulnerable Adults Detained or Interviewed by Police*, London, National Appropriate Adult Network.

National Autistic Society (2011) *Autism: A Guide for Criminal Justice Professionals*, London, National Autistic Society.

Nickerson, R.S. (1998) Confirmation Bias: A Ubiquitous Phenomenon in Many Guises, *Review of General Psychology*, 2, 175–220.

O'Mahony, B.M. (2010) The Emerging Role of the Registered Intermediary with the Vulnerable witness and Offender: Facilitating Communication with the Police and Members of the Judiciary, *British Journal of Learning Disabilities*, 38, 232–237.

O'Mahony, B.M., Smith, K. and Milne, R. (2011) The Early Identification of Vulnerable Witnesses Prior to an Investigative Interview, *British Journal of Forensic Practice*, 13(2), 114–123.

O'Mahony, B.M., Milne, R. and Grant, T. (2012) To Challenge, or not to Challenge? Best Practice when Interviewing Vulnerable Suspects, *Policing*, 6(3), 301–313.

O'Mahony, B.M., Marchant, R. and Fadden, L. (2015) Vulnerable Individuals, Intermediaries and Justice, in Gavin Oxburgh, Trond Myklebust, Tim Grant and Rebecca Milne (eds), *Communication in Investigative and Legal Contexts: Integrated Approaches from Forensic Psychology, Linguistics and Law Enforcement*, Chichester, UK: Wiley Blackwell.

O'Mahony, B.M., Milne, R. and Smith, K. (2016) Can an Intermediary Effectively Facilitate Communication During an Investigative Interview where the Witness has Dissociative Identity Disorder? Symposium paper presented to the International Investigative Interviewing Research Group, London.

Oxburgh, L., Gabbert, F., Milne, R. and Cherryman, J. (2016) Police Officers' Perceptions and Experiences with Mentally Disordered Suspects, *International Journal of Law and Psychiatry*, 49(A), 138–146.

Poole, D.A., Bruck, M. and Pipe, M-E. (2011) Forensic Interviewing Aids: Do Props Help Children Answer Questions About Touching? *Current Directions in Psychological Science*, 20(1), 11–15.

Powell, M.B., Hughes-Scholes, C.H. and Sharman, S.J. (2012) Skill in Interviewing Reduces Confirmation Bias, *Journal of Investigative Psychology and Offender Profiling*, 9, 126–134.

Richards, J. and Milne, R. (forthcoming) The Cognitive Interview and its use for People with Autism Spectrum Disorder: Can we Create an ASD Friendly Version?, in *The Wiley Handbook of Autobiographical Memory, Autism Spectrum Disorders and the Law*.

Risan, P., Binder, P.-E. and Milne, R. (2016) Regulating and Coping with Distress During Police Interviews of Traumatised Victims, *Psychological Trauma: Theory, Research, Practice and Policy*, 8(6), 736–744.

Safer, M.A., Christianson, S.-A., Autry, M.W. and Osterlund, K. (1998) Tunnel Memory for Traumatic Events, *Applied Cognitive Psychology*, 12, 99–117.

Scottish Government (2011a) *The Carloway Review: Report and Recommendations*, Edinburgh, Scottish Government.

Scottish Government (2011b) *Joint Interviewing Child Witnesses in Scotland*, Edinburgh, Scottish Government.

Scottish Government (2011c) *People with Learning Disabilities and the Criminal Justice System*, Edinburgh, Scottish Government.

Sentencing Guidelines Council (2004) *Overarching Principles: Seriousness*, London, Sentencing Guidelines Secretariat.

Silva, D., Gough, K. and Weeks, H. (2015) Screening for Learning Disabilities in the Criminal Justice System: A Review of Existing Measures for use within Liaison and Diversion Services, *Journal of Intellectual Disabilities and Offending Behaviour*, 6(1), 33–43.

Smith, K. and Milne, R. (in press) Vulnerable Witnesses, in H. Norton and P. Cooper (eds), *A Fair Trial: A Practical Guide to Managing Vulnerability in the Criminal Justice System*, Oxford, Oxford University Press.

Su-Lin, B.Y., Powell, M.B. and Guadagno, B. (2014) The Association Between Investigative Interviewers' Knowledge of Question Type and Adherence to Best Practice Interviewing, *Legal and Criminological Psychology*, 19, 270–281.

The Therapeutic Journal (2011) *The Cleveland Report: by Judge Elizabeth Butler-Sloss*, [internet] available at: http://www.thetcj.org/child-care-history-policy/the-clevela nd- reportby-judge-elizabeth-butler-sloss (accessed 5 September 2017).

Talbot, J. (2008) *No One Knows: Prisoners' Voices, Experiences of the Justice System by Prisoners with Learning Disabilities and Difficulties*, London, Prison Reform Trust.

Vallano, J.P. and Compo, N.S. (2011) A Comfortable Witness Is a Good Witness: Rapport-Building and Susceptibility to Misinformation in an Investigative Mock-Crime Interview, *Applied Cognitive Psychology*, 25, 960–970.

Young, S., Goodwin, E.J., Sedgwick, O. and Gudjonsson, G.H. (2013) The Effectiveness of Police Custody Assessments in Identifying Suspects with Intellectual Disabilities and Attention Deficit Hyperactivity Disorder, *BMC Medicine*, 11:248.

Yuille, J.C. and Farr, V. (1987) Statement Validity Analysis: Systematic Approach to the Assessment of Children's Allegations of Sexual Abuse, *British Columbia Psychology*, Fall, 19–27.

Yuille, J., Hunter, R., Joffe, R. and Zaparniuk, J. (1993) Interviewing Children in Sexual Abuse Cases, in G.S. Goodman and B.L. Bottoms (eds), *Child Victims, Child Witnesses: Understanding and Improving Children's Testimony*, New York, Guilford.

Chapter 6

Witness testimony

Fiona Gabbert, Lorraine Hope and Mick Confrey

Introduction

Obtaining detailed and reliable information from victims and witnesses is essential for criminal investigations. From the outset of the investigatory process, witness testimony often directs the allocation of resources while in the latter stages of an investigation it plays a central role in legal decision-making (Ridley, Gabbert, & La Rooy, 2013; Shepherd & Griffiths, 2013; St-Yves, 2015). Competent forensic investigative interviewing effectively transforms information and intelligence into high quality evidence which should (i) lead to reliable prosecutions and (ii) mitigate the risk of miscarriages of justice. However, investigative interviewing is a multi-faceted skill to master, and demands a sound understanding of memory and communication processes, as well as knowledge of the many cognitive, social and environmental factors that may affect the content and accuracy of witness or suspect accounts. As such, skilled interviewing is not intuitive, and is not easily learned on the job (Powell, 2013). Poor investigative interviewing, as a result of inadequate training, motivation and/or a lack of resources, leads to incomplete witness testimony at best, and unreliable or biased evidence at worst. It not only denies victims and witnesses the justice they deserve by limiting the usability, credibility and reliability their testimony, but also runs the risk of wasted time and resources on false leads. In sum, poor interviewing practice exerts a heavy price at a societal level, nationally and internationally, producing a spectrum of injustice ranging from the misuse of resources funded by the taxpayer through to miscarriages of justice and failure to dispense appropriate justice to the guilty.

In this chapter we first outline some of the key factors that typically increase or decrease the reliability of eyewitness testimony before exploring the role of the investigative interview in eliciting reliable information and evidence from witnesses and victims. Finally, we discuss the often competing agendas concerning witness testimony pertaining to practitioner objectives and legal requirements in the course of an investigation.

Reliability of eyewitness memory

Many contextual factors affect the testimony provided by eyewitnesses, irrespective of whether that testimony is elicited in the course of an interview (i.e. recall) or an identification procedure (i.e. recognition). Some factors affecting witness and suspect testimony are present at the encoding or witnessing phase, others are more closely associated with the post event phase – including the interview context. A useful distinction between these factors was introduced by Wells (1978) who differentiated between *estimator variables* and *system variables*. Although introduced to distinguish between factors affecting eyewitness identifications, this distinction equally applies to interviewing practice. System variables are factors that are (or could be) under the control of the criminal justice system. With respect to investigations, system variables, therefore, reflect the practice that investigators use to elicit evidence, such as the procedures or techniques used to obtain identifications or witness accounts. In the case of recognition procedures, system variables include identification test factors such as pre-lineup instructions, lineup composition and presentation method. In the case of interview procedures, system variables include the interviewing approach used to elicit information from the suspect or witness with high quality procedures likely to produce high quality testimony and low quality procedures likely to produce, at best, limited information and, at worst, inaccurate information or entirely false accounts (e.g. false confessions; see Chapter 1 this volume for more on system variables).

In contrast, estimator variables are not under the control of the criminal justice system. Within the context of an investigation, estimator variables are factors that may affect the nature and quality of the evidence a witness or victim is able to provide. For example, estimator variables can be features of the encoding context (e.g. level of stress, type of incident, viewing conditions) or the witness (e.g. witness age, race, vulnerability, intoxication). While these factors can (sometimes) be manipulated in research and effects on memory accuracy can broadly be established under controlled laboratory conditions, such factors cannot be controlled for actual witnessed incidents. Therefore, the impact of such factors on witness accuracy has to be considered in a *post-hoc* manner by investigators. A review of all the factors likely to affect the accuracy of testimony is beyond the scope of this chapter. Instead, we focus on a small number of estimator variables likely to affect witness testimony (fear and stress, retention interval, and exposure to post-event information), before exploring investigative interviewing as a key system variable.

Fear and stress

The level of stress or fear a witness experiences during encoding, and the effect that such emotional reactions will have on subsequent memory performance, varies according to the nature of the incident and the individual witness.

However, the typically damaging effect of acute stressors at encoding on both recall and recognition is well-established in animal and human laboratory research (e.g. DeQuervain, Roozendaal, Nitsch, McGaugh, & Hock, 2000; Kuhlmann, Piel, & Wolf, 2005; Salehi, Cordero, & Sandi, 2010) and also in research conducted in police and military training environments (e.g. Morgan et al., 2004; Taverniers, Taylor, & Smeets, 2013). With respect to recall, individuals exposed to high levels of stress usually report fewer details than those in control conditions (e.g. Hulse & Memon, 2006; Stanny & Johnson, 2000) and can show increased susceptibility to misinformation and error (e.g. Hope, Lewinski, Dixon, Blocksidge, & Gabbert, 2016). Similarly, with respect to recognition, Morgan, Southwick, Steffian, Hazlett, and Loftus (2013) tested identification accuracy across 800 military personnel during a stressful prison camp phase of Survival School training. When asked to identify the person who had interrogated them, 50 per cent of personnel who viewed a perpetrator absent lineup made an incorrect identification. Impaired identification performance has also been observed among police officers placed in challenging physical contexts (e.g. physical exertion; see Hope, Lewinski, Dixon, Blocksidge, & Gabbert, 2012).

Other unpredictable factors in the encoding context can affect memory performance. For instance, the presence of a weapon has been shown to impair identification performance: the so-called "weapon focus effect". Fawcett, Russell, Peace, and Christie's (2013) meta-analytic review of the weapon focus effect confirmed a small to moderate negative effect of weapon presence on identification accuracy, but noted that this effect was also moderated by situational factors (such as exposure duration, retention interview, level of threat, etc.). The complex factors underpinning memory impairment as a result of stress and arousal can be difficult to disentangle in applied contexts. However, research suggests that the degree or level of stress experienced is critical, with high levels of stress likely to result in impaired memory (Deffenbacher, Bornstein, Penrod, & McGorty, 2004; for reviews see Finsterwald & Alberini, 2014; Hope, 2016).

Retention interval

Delays between witnessing an incident and being formally interviewed by police are commonplace (Kebbell & Wagstaff, 1999). Within the psychological research literature, it has long been observed that delay systematically reduces the amount of information that can be recalled (Ebbinghaus, 1885/1913; Rubin & Wenzel, 1996; see also Tuckey & Brewer, 2003). Empirical studies of eyewitness memory have also observed the deleterious effect of delay on memory, noting that the completeness of eyewitness testimony *decreases* as the delay between witnessing an incident and recall *increases* (see Penrod, Loftus, & Winkler, 1982; Wixted & Ebbesen, 1991, 1997). Delaying recall also selectively reduces access to detailed information (e.g. Begg & Wickelgren, 1974; Reyna & Kiernan, 1994) because more fine-grained or detailed information decays more rapidly than coarse or gist-level information (Fisher, 1996; Goldsmith, Koriat, & Pansky, 2005; Koriat, Levy-Sadot, Edry, & de Marcas, 2003). These qualitative changes to memory over a delay also mean that people become more suggestible over time (e.g. Loftus, Miller, & Burns, 1978; Underwood & Pezdek, 1998). This is because when memory fades, individuals are less likely to notice, and reject, discrepant post-event information that is encountered (Loftus, 2005; Wright & Villalba, 2012). Demonstrating this, a recent study by Horry, Colton, and Williamson (2014) observed a large effect of delay on both discrepancy detection and a person's ability to accurately identify the source of their memory (e.g. discriminating between something personally experienced versus a suggested item of information). This finding confirms the importance of securing eyewitness statements as soon as possible after an event, when witnesses are best able to differentiate between information that was personally seen and information obtained from secondary sources.

Identification accuracy is also likely to be negatively affected by a delay between the witness encoding the suspect and identification. Research demonstrates that increased delay between the event and the identification test is associated with poorer identification performance. A meta-analysis of 128 studies of face recognition suggests there is a linear decline in the correct identification of previously seen faces after a delay (Deffenbacher, Bornstein, McGorty, & Penrod, 2008; Shapiro & Penrod, 1986). However, recent research suggests that the type of the identification task should be taken into account (Wetmore, Neuschatz, Gronlund, Wooten, Goodsell, & Carlson, 2015). Specifically, Wetmore et al. (2015) found that both immediately and following a delay, show-ups (where a single suspect is presented to a witness in person or via a photograph) never resulted in better accuracy than a lineup (where the suspect is presented alongside a number of matching 'foils'). In sum, unbiased lineups, presented to witnesses with minimal delay, secure more reliable identification evidence.

Post-event misinformation

Over the past 40 years research has consistently demonstrated that eyewitness recall can be influenced by information encountered after the original incident was encoded (see review by Frenda, Nichols, & Loftus, 2011). There are many ways in which a witness might be exposed to misleading post-event information (PEI); for example, inaccurate news reports, information from co-witnesses, suggestive or misleading questions from journalists or inexperienced investigators. A delay between witnessing an incident, and reporting memories about it, increases the opportunity that witnesses will be exposed to other, non-memorial information. This phenomenon has been called the 'misinformation effect' (Loftus, 1979, 2005).

Research on the misinformation effect has systematically demonstrated that misleading post-event suggestions introduced after an eyewitness event are highly likely to contaminate eyewitness memory (Loftus, 2005). In a typical experimental paradigm, participants view a (simulated) complex and forensically relevant event, such as a traffic accident or theft. Misinformation is typically introduced in the form of leading questions or additional information from a news report or other source. After exposure to the misinformation, participants are tested on their memory for the witnessed event. Participants who receive misinformation are likely to report the misleading suggestions, rather than the events they actually witnessed. The effect of misleading PEI on memory accuracy is now well documented (see Chrobak & Zaragoza, 2013; Frenda et al., 2011).

Closely related to the misinformation paradigm is the effect of co-witness discussion on 'memory conformity' (Gabbert & Hope, 2013), which refers to people's memories for an event becoming similar following a discussion. The difference between memory conformity studies and more general misinformation studies is that in the former misleading post-event information is usually encountered in the social context of a discussion with an apparent co-witness. Both social and cognitive factors can play a role in susceptibility to memory conformity, meaning that exposure to misleading PEI during discussions with others constitutes a particularly powerful form of suggestion. Understanding the potential effects of co-witness influence on the accuracy of witness accounts is important in investigative contexts. Crimes often have more than one eyewitness (Valentine, Pickering, & Darling, 2003; Wright & McDaid, 1996), and surveys completed by real eyewitnesses reveal that discussion between witnesses is common. For example, Paterson and Kemp (2006) found that a majority (86 per cent) of witnesses to real incidents admitted to having discussed what they had seen with a co-witness who was also present. Although these witnesses may have shared the same experience, their individual perceptions of *and* memory for the event may differ for many reasons, including naturally occurring differences in attention paid to various details of the event, differences in spatial or temporal location at the scene, or perceived differences in memory ability (Gabbert, Memon, & Wright, 2006). When two witnesses discuss their memories, their individual descriptions of what they saw increase in similarity. This effect is strongest, but certainly not reliant on, the co-witness being a prior acquaintance, such as a friend or partner (Hope, Ost, Gabbert, Healey, & Lenton, 2008).

Few studies have explored the impact of co-witness information on subsequent *identification* performance. However, if a witness has information about the identification decision made by a co-witness, either because they have been deliberately given this information or encountered it inadvertently, their own identification decision may be influenced. For example, Levett (2013) observed that witnesses who overheard that their co-witness had chosen from the lineup were more likely to choose themselves than those who heard no information about the co-witness decision or heard the co-witness had rejected the lineup. Witnesses who heard co-witness decisions were also influenced by the confidence expressed by their co-witness in that decision. Levett's (2013) research is particularly relevant to a UK case study illustrating how witnesses' recognition decisions can be vulnerable to suggestion. Here, a witness central to the Jill Dando murder investigation (April, 2001) became increasingly confident that the main suspect, Barry George, was responsible for the crime after discussing the identification procedure with another witness who had identified George. This witness, who had not felt confident enough to make an identification originally, subsequently revealed that, following discussions with the other witness, she felt "95 per cent sure" that George was the man she had seen at the crime scene (Cathcart, 2002).

In sum, both recall and recognition are vulnerable to suggestion from non-memorial sources. Any delay prior to eliciting evidence from eyewitnesses can increase the risk of memory contamination, simply because witnesses have more time in which to encounter items of new and/or misleading PEI. When contamination occurs in the context of a forensic investigation there can be serious and costly implications as (i) the evidence obtained from key witnesses might be contaminated and (ii) similar accounts across multiple witnesses as a result of cross-contamination may mistakenly be interpreted as corroboration. Both erroneous information and false corroboration have the potential to lead to misdirected lines of enquiry and, ultimately, to miscarriages of justice. While the police might not be able to control the estimator variables discussed above, they are able to exert control over how to most appropriately elicit evidence from an eyewitness via an investigative interview. Research has examined how best to support witnesses and facilitate retrieval in a range of contexts (e.g., engaging with reluctant or intimidated witnesses), and from a range of witnesses (including children, the elderly, and those with mental or personality disorders). Investigative interviewing then is a vital skill for any investigating officer. The role of interviewing as a key system variable is explored in full below.

Investigative interviewing: applying research to practice

Although witness testimony is sometimes compromised by unavoidable contextual factors at encoding (such as stress), the way in which interviews are conducted can have also have a significant impact on the reliability of witness accounts. It is unfortunate then, that many police investigators receive minimal, and limited, training on how to conduct investigative interviews, resulting in avoidable errors, continued use of techniques that have limited effectiveness, and failure to use interview practices that have proven effectiveness. For example, evaluations of police interviews have shown that interviewers ask too many closed-ended questions (e.g. How tall was the robber?), too few open-ended questions (e.g. Describe the robber), and often interrupt witnesses in the middle of their narrative descriptions (Dando, Wilcock, & Milne, 2008). Recent findings suggest that poor interview practice is still prevalent; Gabbert, Hope, La Rooy, McGregor, Ellis, and Milne (2016) examined real-life interview data for interviews conducted by almost 100 UK frontline police officers to identify common challenges and training needs, and found an absence of any rapport or trust-building attempts in 93 per cent of cases, an absence of explaining expectations of the witness in 83 per cent of cases, an over-reliance on closed questions, and an 'interviewer-led' structure (where the questioning related to the interviewer's agenda, rather than being based upon what the interviewee had said); this last finding is also seen in earlier research (Griffiths, Milne, & Cherryman, 2011). This is despite the introduction of the PEACE model of interviewing (in England, Wales, and Northern Ireland) in the early 1990s to promote best practice interviewing. PEACE is a mnemonic acronym for the recommended phases of the interview process (*P*reparation and planning, *E*ngage and explain, *A*ccount, *C*larify and challenge, and *E*valuation of the interview).

Research suggests that the continued use of sub-optimal interviewing techniques reflects a training issue (Dando et al., 2008; Hewitt, 2001). For example, Dando and colleagues (2008) investigated the interviewing practice of 200 non-specialist frontline officers from five UK police forces, with an average of 2 years' service. All officers reported investigating a large number of crimes, including conducting 'interviews' with victims and witnesses often at the scene of an incident. Respondents reported that their training did not equip them sufficiently to conduct interviews when on duty. At best only a couple of days training were allocated to learning how to interact with victims and witnesses of crime and this training typically occurred in a limited environment using colleagues as interviewees. Similar findings have been reported by Hewitt (2001). Training provision of investigative interview skills has been further negatively impacted by austerity measures imposed in many countries.

The provision of investigative interview training for more specialised officers is also limited – with worrying knock-on effects. While the Cognitive Interview (CI; Fisher & Geiselman, 1992) is generally recognised as 'gold-standard' in terms of its effectiveness in eliciting 'best evidence' from co-operative witnesses, survey data reveal it to be a demanding procedure for interviewers to learn, understand, and administer (Dando, Wilcock, Behnkle, & Milne, 2011; Kohnken, Milne, Memon, & Bull, 1999; La Rooy, Lamb, & Memon, 2011). A direct and alarming consequence of this general perception of the CI is that interviewers frequently report that they do not use the technique at all despite it being one of the only evidence-based witness interview procedures currently available and incorporated in investigative interviewing training curricula (Dando, Wilcock, & Milne, 2008, 2009; Wright & Holliday, 2005). This is a concern, because when trained appropriately, and used by interviewers who fully understand and engage with the key cognitive and social principles, the CI is associated with the increased reporting of evidentiary information provided and a reduction in the use of inappropriate questioning during interviews (Memon, Meissner, & Fraser, 2010).

In response to the need for appropriate investigative interviewing training for frontline officers who typically receive minimal training with respect to communicating with victims, witnesses or suspects, researchers have recently developed a 'Structured Interview Protocol', designed to complement the PEACE interview framework (Gabbert et al., 2016). Specifically, the protocol, and associated training, incorporates the most recent, and most effective, interview techniques into each of the stages of PEACE. As such, it promotes best practice interview skills to elicit high quality, reliable evidence via effective research-based guidelines and techniques. For example, for the 'Engage & Explain' stage of PEACE, the protocol draws from a broad theoretical understanding of memory and human interaction, as well as from more specific empirical research on building rapport, and influencing reporting thresholds (amongst other relevant research), to produce guidelines on how to effectively engage and build trust with a victim/witness, and how to best set expectations for the interview context. Further, for the 'Account' stage of PEACE, the protocol draws from theoretical work on memory and metamemory (including source monitoring), as well as from empirical research on the use of specific question types (Oxburgh, Myklebust, & Grant, 2010), as well as focusing techniques such as eye-closure (Perfect, Andrade, & Eagan, 2011; also, see below), and the use of 'don't know' responses (Scoboria & Fisico, 2013). Results of laboratory and field trials to date indicate that the Structured Interview Protocol promotes high quality, efficient, and effective interview performance via skilled use of rapid rapport techniques, enhanced 'engage and explain' skills, and a clear increase in appropriate question types used in a structured manner (Gabbert et al., 2016).

Other tools and techniques that have been introduced to support frontline police officers include those that help focus a witness's attention on what was seen. For example, simply asking a witness to close their eyes when recounting their memories can help them block out distractions from the environment and focus on their mental image of the witnessed event (see Perfect, et al., 2011; Vredeveldt & Perfect, 2014). In a series of experiments, Vredeveldt and colleagues have found benefits of eye-closure for memory of events across a variety of conditions (see Vredeveldt, Tredoux, Nortje, Kempen, Puljevic, & Labuschagne, 2015). Similarly, asking witnesses to produce a detailed sketch plan of what they have seen can help them focus on aspects of their memory as they draw (see Dando et al., 2009).

A further interview tool that has been introduced to support frontline officers, especially those responding to large-scale incidents, is that of the Self-Administered Interview (SAI©; Gabbert, Hope, & Fisher, 2009). The SAI© is an evidence-based investigative tool that can be used to elicit comprehensive initial statements from multiple witnesses, quickly and efficiently. It takes the form of a standardised protocol of clear instructions and questions that enable witnesses to provide their own statement. The SAI© was developed to address the serious challenge faced by investigators when a large-scale incident occurs for which there are numerous eyewitnesses. Any of these witnesses may hold potentially vital information about the incident and descriptions of the perpetrators i.e. information that will provide both critical leads for the investigation or compelling evidence in a trial. However, investigators may not have the resources in terms of time, expertise, or personnel to conduct interviews with many witnesses shortly after an incident. Early stage development and testing of the SAI© revealed that the SAI© recall tool elicited significantly more information from witnesses with high accuracy rates (Gabbert et al., 2009). Furthermore, the initial completion of an SAI© increased the amount of information provided by witnesses in a delayed interview (Hope, Gabbert, Fisher, & Jamieson, 2014). Subsequent research also showed that witnesses who complete an SAI© are more resistant to misleading information encountered after an incident (Gabbert, Hope, Fisher, & Jamieson, 2012). This is because, despite the fallibility of memory, a good original memory for an event can offer some protection against exposure to misleading PEI. Specifically, when a strong memory trace is present there is an increased likelihood that individuals notice, and reject, discrepant information (Loftus, 2005; Loftus, Levidau, & Duensing, 1992). The 'SAI© effect' has been replicated and extended by researchers. For example, Gawrylowicz, Memon, and Scoboria (2014) found that not only does the SAI© facilitate recall and prevent forgetting, but it equips witnesses with transferable skills they can use during future retrieval of new events. Since 2009 the SAI© development team has worked closely with both UK and international police forces on the evaluation and implementation of the SAI© with real witnesses. To date, the SAI© has made an important contribution to a number of live investigations by providing detailed initial accounts, enabling the efficient prioritisation of witnesses, and facilitating the identification of additional witnesses, in a range of criminal incidents.

Further research-based investigative interview tools and techniques include those that have been developed to target specific challenges, such as differentiating who did what, and when, in crimes featuring multiple perpetrators. For example, the Timeline Technique (Hope, Mullis, & Gabbert, 2013) is a self-administered recall and reporting technique designed to optimise an interviewee's ability to recall a particular time period in sequence, identify people involved, and link those people with their specific actions. Episodic memory is temporally ordered and temporal context plays an important role in the retrieval process (Howard & Kahana, 1999; Kahana, 1996; Kahana, Howard, & Polyn, 2008; Unsworth, 2008). Research on the Timeline Technique suggests that its use to elicit information about an episodic event works to elicit more (i) person-description detail, (ii) person-action detail (iii), sequence detail and (iv) verbatim detail than requesting a free report at no cost to accuracy (Hope et al., 2013). The technique uses a 'timeline' of the relevant time period to provide a structure for remembering. Additional retrieval support is delivered through the use of instructions and interactive materials. As such the Timeline Technique provides witnesses with an intuitive organising structure that facilitates flexible reporting while reducing processing demands. The timeline reporting format likely reduces working memory load; reduces pressure to maintain correct sequence/inhibit information recalled at the wrong time in a linear narrative; and works to maximise cuing of associated memories. As the technique is self-directed any inadvertent influence of the interviewer on the interviewee's account is eliminated. On-going work is exploring the use of the Timeline Technique in combination with other non-linear approaches (e.g. sketching) in order to maximise the amount and accuracy of output using multi-modal interview formats (MMIF; Hope et al., 2016; Kontogianni, Hope, Taylor, Vrij, & Gabbert, in submission; see also Fisher, Schreiber Compo, Rivard, & Hirn, 2014).

Other emerging work in the field of investigative interviewing includes the development of novel cognitive mnemonics to facilitate retrieval, such as the 'guided peripheral focus' mnemonic (Columb & Ginet, 2012), the 'category clustering recall' mnemonic (Paulo, Albuquerque, & Bull, 2016), and the 'self-generated cues' mnemonic (Wheeler & Gabbert, 2017). Columb and Ginet (2012) refer to their 'guided peripheral focus' mnemonic as a cognitive aid that can be used towards the end of an interview if required; i.e., if the amount of information collected previously, using other mnemonics from the Cognitive Interview, has been poor. The technique encourages witnesses to (i) divide the memory of the event into a set of main actions; (ii) form a mental image of each main action he/she has remembered; (iii) close their eyes to help access the mental images; and (iv) transfer the focus from the retrieval of central elements to the recall of peripheral ones (i.e. peripheral focus). Across two studies, Columb and Ginet observed the benefit of this mnemonic in enhancing the completeness of statements.

More recently Paulo et al. (2016) explored whether their technique of 'category clustering recall' has similar benefits in facilitating retrieval. This mnemonic is based upon the rationale that recalling in 'category clusters' might be effective because it is compatible with the way in which we use semantic categories to encode, organise, and recall information (Dalrymple-Alford & Aamiry, 1969; Manning & Kahana, 2012; Robinson, 1966). The technique involves asking people to organise their recall into seven information categories (person details; person location details; object details, object location details; action details, conversation details; and sound details). To test the technique, participants watched a mock robbery video and were interviewed 48 hours later with either (i) an enhanced cognitive interview; (ii) a revised enhanced cognitive interview, with category clustering recall instead of the change order mnemonic; or (iii) a revised enhanced cognitive interview, with category clustering recall conjunctly used with 'eye-closure' and additional open-ended follow up questions. Participants interviewed with category clustering recall reported more information without compromising accuracy (eye-closure and follow up questions were not found to further benefit recall).

A further retrieval technique that has proven to be effective is the use of 'self-generated' memory cues (Wheeler & Gabbert, 2017). The rationale for this mnemonic is based upon Anderson's (1983) spreading activation theory, Tulving and Thomson's (1973) cue overlap theory and Nairne's (2002) cue distinctiveness theory, all of which support the idea that the quality of the overlap between encoded information and retrieval cue predicts the likelihood of successful retrieval. A self-generated cue is defined as any detail salient to the individual, and generated by the individual themselves, which is intended to facilitate more complete retrieval of a target memory. Initial findings by Wheeler and Gabbert (2017) show that self-generated cues enhanced the recall performance of mock witnesses. Specifically, they produced significantly more accurate information overall than either standard 'mental reinstatement of context' instructions or free recall alone, with no corresponding increase in the amount of inaccurate information reported. These findings were replicated in a second study, with a different (live) event (Wheeler & Gabbert, 2017; Study 2).

That investigative interview techniques continue to be developed and refined is testament to how important the quest for eliciting reliable witness testimony is deemed to be, and rightly so. The new retrieval techniques and mnemonics outlined above represent a promising step towards developing effective methods of incorporating witness-led cueing techniques into investigative interviewing contexts. Regardless of which investigative interview technique is used, the goal is to gather usable, credible, and reliable evidence. Increasingly, this evidence must not only be useful for the initial investigative purposes, but must also be of particular quality for presentation in Court. The different agendas that are at play when, and the tensions between them, are outlined in the next section.

Practitioner objectives and legal requirements

In criminal court cases within the UK adversarial system, there are two opposing parties: the defence representing the accused and the prosecution representing the complainant. Despite the growth of forensic science in providing evidence to the Court for either party, the majority of criminal court cases involve witnesses giving their testimony. This testimony is generally based on the information originally obtained from the witness during a police interview. There is no 'ownership' of witnesses; either party can call witnesses to give evidence in support of their case. The party calling the witness will normally lead the witness through their testimony, known as the evidence in chief, before then making the witness available to the other party for cross-examination. An exception to this is where provisions have been made for the visual or audio recording of police interviews with young persons, and other witnesses who are deemed vulnerable or intimidated by legal definition. In such cases, the recorded interviews (or edited versions) are played in Court as the evidence in chief, and the witness is protected by special measures during any cross-examination. It is also possible for vulnerable or intimidated witnesses to record on video their cross-examination before the trial (see also Chapter 5, this volume). Here, both the recorded evidence in chief and the recorded cross-examination are played at trial so the witness does not need to be present at the trial (see Ministry of Justice, 2016). These protective measures (Youth Justice and Criminal Evidence Act, 1999; as amended by the Coroners and Justice Act, 2009) have led to a marked improvement in young, vulnerable, or intimidated witnesses gaining access to justice. However, the majority of witness evidence presented at Court is generally the testimony of older or non-vulnerable witnesses. This evidence, presented in the courtroom, is based on their written evidential statement, prepared by the police from information gathered during a police interview. Oddly, whilst the taking of notes by police during a witness interview is recommended, and expected, the law does not require it. This lack of legislative rules for the gathering of the majority of witnesses' information, before it is distilled into the evidential product, will be explored in this section.

In England and Wales, the Police and Criminal Evidence Act (PACE, 1984) lays down strict rules in simple terms for the interviewing of suspects, including that all interviews (with the rare exception of urgent interviews) with suspects must be recorded (either audio or visual); the suspect be given access to legal advice; and that, prior to the interview, the suspect be given a warning known as the Caution. Since the introduction of PACE (1984) in England and Wales, police have become very adept at adhering to these rules and as a result the suspect interview is rarely challenged in Court. When the police do breach these rules, it is likely that the interview will be deemed inadmissible in any subsequent Court proceedings. For example, in the well publicised case of *R v Christopher Halliwell* (Bristol Crown Court, 3 February, 2012; 9 May, 2012), the defendant's confession to murder was deemed inadmissible due to "wholesale and irretrievable breaches" of PACE, much to the surprise of the general public. Similarly, in the USA, crime suspects have the protection of the more complex warning established by the *Miranda v Arizona* 1966 case, in which the Supreme Court issued guidance to the police on warnings they must give to suspects, based on the Fifth Amendment. The application of these Miranda rights varies from state to state in relation to its application. However, failure to deliver the warning can lead to any interrogation being excluded.

These 'rules' for interviewing/interrogating suspects are laid down for the police to follow, and – importantly – allow an argument as to the admissibility of any interview in any subsequent Court proceedings. Conversely, the rules for the interviewing of victims of, and eyewitnesses to, crime have yet to be legislated for. The police, when tasked with the interview of a witness to crime, are only equipped with guidance. In England and Wales that guidance is in the form of the Ministry of Justice publication; *Achieving Best Evidence (ABE) in Criminal Proceedings: Guidance on Interviewing Victims and Witnesses and Guidance on Special Measures* (2011). The courts, through arguments and decisions established in previous hearings, also offer guidance. A good example of this is the case of *R v Turnbull* (1977); here, in response to widespread concern at the time regarding cases relying wholly or substantially on visual identification of the defendant(s), the Court provided guidelines to future interviewing officers and decision makers on points to cover with the witness to ensure the identification of the suspect is correctly established. These include: (i) the amount of time the witness observed the alleged offender(s), (ii) the distance between the witness and the alleged offender(s), (iii) the visibility at the time, (iv) any obstructions in the view, (v) did the witness have prior knowledge of the alleged offender(s), (vi) any other reason the witness had to remember who they saw, (vii) the time passed between the incident observed and the witness describing/identifying the person to the police and (viii) any errors or discrepancies between the description given and the alleged offender(s) actual appearance. This process is referred to by the mnemonic ADVOKATE, and is included in all police training in England and Wales, and beyond.

From a policing perspective, the ABE publication (see Chapter 5, this volume) is regarded as *guidance* to police and others with the task of carrying out interviews with victims and witnesses. Interestingly though, the defence community increasingly sees ABE not only as guidance, but rather as a *requirement* for police practice, and regularly challenges police officers regarding their adherence to the recommended procedure. The ABE guidance advises that victims and witnesses should be interviewed using a phased interview (such as PEACE) or a Cognitive Interview (CI; Fisher & Geiselman, 1992), whilst also outlining the special requirements to consider when interviewing vulnerable and young persons to obtain their testimony, and the legislation covering the presentation of their testimony subsequently, during trial (Youth Justice and Criminal Evidence Act, 1999, as amended by Coroners and Justice Act, 2009). Further guidance to the police is provided in the form of the Ministry of Justice *Code of Practice for Victims of Crime* (2013) and the Ministry of Justice *Witness Charter* (2013).

It is in the context of this abundance of guidance, but lack of clear and simple legislation, that the interviewer must strike a balance and attempt to service three separate agendas at the same time. The first agenda concerns ensuring that the victim or witness is handled with empathy and respect, whilst also managing their expectations of the judicial system. The second agenda is that of effective policing, through gaining not only evidence of the actions of the suspect to present to legal decision makers, but also sufficient information to apprehend the suspect, and sufficient intelligence to target police resources to protect the public in future. The third agenda is that of the legal decision makers in (i) making a decision based on the available evidence (obtained in part from the interviews conducted with victims and witnesses) to bring a suspect before the Court or not, and (ii) making the decision (again in part based on the same interviews) in Court as to a defendant's guilt or innocence. Police attempts to manage this difficult, multi-agenda, task often can lead to confusion about what the interviewer is attempting to achieve. For example, when police investigators interview a witness, an integral part of the interview concerns not only the actions of the suspect at the time of the crime, but also the identification and apprehension of the suspect. When this evidence is presented in the courtroom, there may be little interest in how the police came to apprehend the suspect. Instead, witness's information concerning the actions of the defendant at the time of the crime is likely to be the focus. This disjoint has led to frustration (on the Court's behalf) regarding the length and structure of any visually/ audio-recorded interviews that are played as evidence in chief. In England and Wales this issue was addressed by the National Police Chief's Council *Advice on the Structure of Visually Recorded Witness Interviews* (3rd edition, 2015). This document recognises the challenges facing the interviewer in managing the three agendas and offers practical advice in how to conduct the interview to address each party's needs. One suggestion is to cut the unnecessary recording of the important victim/witness agenda rapport building stage, providing there is no witness vulnerability or requirement to prove to the Court the witness's awareness of truth and lies. The interviewer then, to satisfy the decision-makers' agenda, focuses first on the evidential information, before finishing by addressing the police agenda in gaining case specific information to enable the apprehension of the suspect. At around the same time, Leveson's *Review of Efficiency in Criminal Proceedings* (2015), suggests that

> After a first general investigative interview conducted in accordance with best practice (taken from the ABE practice guide), in most cases, there should be a second, far shorter interview, ordered, chronologically presented and directed only to the relevant material … it is this interview that should be presented as examination in chief.
>
> (p. 66)

Such a suggestion should be considered carefully as there has (apparently) been little consideration or examination of the likely psychological or memorial implications of such a second interview.

In sum, there is a mismatch between the goals of the initial interviewer (who wants to gather information to lead an investigation), and the goals of legal decision-makers at Court (who want to evaluate evidence, rather than being presented initial information and intelligence). The balancing of the different agendas is clearly an area that requires attention. In the majority of cases, the onus is on the police to accurately distil into paper statement format, the (often lengthy) initial interviews conducted with victims and witnesses. This process, of extracting selected elements from the interviews that are deemed to be of evidential value to legal decision-makers, has the potential to result in a miscarriage of justice. The multi-purpose nature of the investigative interview clearly remains an issue demanding a solution that adequately addresses the needs of all parties, victims, witnesses, investigators, and decision-makers and ensures a fair investigative and trial process for the defendant.

The future; research-based policing

The burgeoning academic interest in forensic and investigative psychology has generated increased opportunities for police investigators to harness this growing area of knowledge, to increase their own understanding of science-based practice, and in doing so, enhance their skills. What does this mean for the future of eliciting witness testimony? One positive change is a shift in some jurisdictions from confession-based interrogation methods such as the Reid Technique (Inbau, Reid, Buckley, & Jayne, 2013) to evidence-gathering investigative interviewing methods such as PEACE and the CI (see Meissner, Redlich, Bhatt, & Brandon, 2012). Increasingly, the terms interrogation and interview are being recognised as *not* synonymous or interchangeable (see Chapter 8, this volume).

Given significant interest by researchers, police and legal stakeholders with respect to improving the efficacy and efficiency of investigative interviewing, there are significant opportunities for future collaboration in the pursuit of evidence-based policing. The forward thinking police organisation should view this as an ideal opportunity to both assist the researcher in achieving their goals of conducting high quality applied research, while facilitating the police service to benefit from the end product of research efforts. In the same vein, academics working in the area of applied memory research should ensure their work has real life application for the practitioner. This practitioner/academic collaborative approach has already led to the formation of strong links between academics and police departments to great effect. Future efforts should continue to endorse a joint academic and practitioner approach to resolve real world problems with research-based practices.

References

Anderson, J. R. (1983). A spreading activation theory of memory. *Journal of Verbal Learning and Verbal Behavior*, 22, 261–295.

Begg, I., & Wickelgren, W. (1974). Retention functions for syntactic and lexical versus semantic information in recognition memory. *Memory and Cognition*, 2, 353–359.

Cathcart, B. (2001). *Jill Dando: Her Life and Death*. London: Penguin.

Chrobak, Q. , & Zaragoza, M. S. (2013). The misinformation effect: An experimental paradigm for studying eyewitness suggestibility. In A. M. Ridley, F. Gabbert, & D. J. La Rooy (eds), *Suggestibility in Legal Contexts: Psychological Research and Forensic Implications* (pp. 63–84). London: Wiley-Blackwell.

Columb, C., & Ginet, M. (2012). The cognitive interview for use with adults: An empirical test of an alternative mnemonic and of a partial protocol. *Applied Cognitive Psychology*, 26, 35–47.

Coroners and Justice Act (2009). Accessed 13 November 2016, http://www.legislation.gov.uk/ukpga/2009/25/contents

Dalrymple-Alford, E. C., & Aamiry, A. (1969). Language and category clustering in bilingual free recall. *Journal of Verbal Learning and Verbal Behavior*, 8, 762–768.

Dando, C. J., Wilcock, R., & Milne, R. (2008). Victims and witnesses of crime: Police officers' perceptions of interviewing practices. *Legal & Criminological Psychology*, 13, 59–70.

Dando, C. J., Wilcock, R., & Milne, R. (2009). The Cognitive Interview: The efficacy of a modified mental reinstatement of context procedure for frontline police investigators. *Applied Cognitive Psychology*, 23, 138–147.

Dando, C. J., Wilcock, R., Behnkle, C., & Milne, R. (2011). Modifying the cognitive interview: Countenancing forensic application by enhancing practicability. *Psychology, Crime, & Law*, 17, 491–511.

Deffenbacher, K. A., Bornstein, B. H., Penrod, S. D., & McGorty, E. K. (2004). A meta-analytic review of the effects of high stress on eyewitness memory. *Law and Human Behavior*, 28, 687–706.

Deffenbacher, K. A., Bornstein, B. H., McGorty, K., & Penrod, S. D. (2008). Forgetting the once-seen face: Estimating the strength of an eyewitness's memory representation. *Journal of Experimental Psychology: Applied*, 14, 139–150.

De Quervain, D. J., Roozendaal, B., Nitsch, R. M., McGaugh, J. L., & Hock, C. (2000). Acute cortisone administration impairs retrieval of long-term declarative memory in humans. *Nature Neuroscience*, 3, 313–314.

Ebbinghaus, H. (1913). *Memory: A Contribution to Experimental Psychology*. New York: Teachers College, Columbia University. (Original work published 1885).

Fawcett, J. M., Russell, E. J., Peace, K. A., & Christie, J. (2013). Of guns and geese: A meta analytic review of the 'weapon focus' literature. *Psychology, Crime and Law*, 19, 35–66.

FinsterwaldC., & AlberiniC. M. (2014). Stress and glucocorticoid receptor-dependent mechanisms in long-term memory: From adaptive responses to psychopathologies. *Neurobiology of Learning and Memory*, 112, 17–29.

Fisher, R. P., & Geiselman, R. E. (1992). *Memory-enhancing Techniques for Investigating Interviewing: The Cognitive Interview*. Springfield, IL: Charles C. Thomas.

Fisher, R. P. (1996). Implications of output-bound measures for laboratory and field research in memory. *The Behavioral and Brain Sciences*, 19, 197.

Fisher, R. P., Schreiber, N.Compo, N., Rivard, J., & Hirn, D. (2014). Interviewing witnesses. In T. Perfect & S. Lindsay (eds), *Handbook of Applied Memory* (pp. 559–578). Los Angeles, CA: SAGE Press.

Frenda, S. J., Nichols, R. M., & Loftus, E. F. (2011). Current issues and advances in misinformation research. *Current Directions in Psychological Science*, 20, 20–23.

Gabbert, F., & Hope, L. (2013). Suggestibility and memory conformity. In A. M. Ridley, F. Gabbert, & D. J. La Rooy (eds), *Suggestibility in Legal Contexts: Psychological Research and Forensic Implications* (pp. 63–84). London: Wiley-Blackwell.

Gabbert, F., Memon, A., & Wright, D. B. (2006). Memory conformity: Disentangling the steps toward influence during a discussion. *Psychonomic Bulletin & Review*, 13, 480–485.

Gabbert, F., Hope, L., & Fisher, R. P. (2009). Protecting eyewitness evidence: Examining the efficacy of a self-administered interview tool. *Law and Human Behavior*, 33(4), 298–307.

Gabbert, F., Hope, L., Fisher, R. P., & Jamieson, K. (2012). Protecting against susceptibility to misinformation with the use of a Self-Administered Interview. *Applied Cognitive Psychology*, 26, 568–575.

Gabbert, F., Hope, L., La Rooy, D., McGregor, A., Ellis, T., & Milne, R. (June, 2016). Introducing a PEACE-compliant 'Structured Interview Protocol' to enhance the quality of investigative interviews. Paper presented at the 9th Annual Conference of the International Investigative Interviewing Research Group (iIIRG), London, UK.

Goldsmith, M., Koriat, A., & Pansky, A. (2005). Strategic regulation of grain size in memory reporting over time. *Journal of Memory and Language*, 52, 505–525.

Griffiths, A., Milne, R., & Cherryman, J. (2011). A question of control? The formulation of suspect and witness interview question strategies by advanced interviewers. *International Journal of Police Science and Management*, 13(3), 255–267.

Hewitt, M. (2001). *Nine Force Attrition Study*. London: The Association of Chief Police Officers of England, Wales, and Northern Ireland.

Hope, L., Ost, J., Gabbert, F., Healey, S., & Lenton, E. (2008). "With a little help from my friends ...": The role of co-witness relationship in susceptibility to misinformation. *Acta Psychologica*, 127, 476–484.

Hope, L., Lewinski, W., Dixon, J., Blocksidge, D., & Gabbert, F. (2012). Witnesses in action: The effect of physical exertion on recall and recognition. *Psychological Science*, 23, 386–390.

Hope, L. (2016). Evaluating the effects of stress and fatigue on police officer response and recall: A challenge for research, training, practice and policy. *Journal of Applied Research in Memory and Cognition*, 5, 239–245.

Hope, L., Gabbert, F., Kinninger, M.Hanger, A., & Bracey, A. (2016). Who said what in the plot? Using a multi-modal timeline technique to elicit details of group conversations. Paper presented at the 9th Annual Conference of the International Investigative Interviewing Research Group, London, 22–24 June 2016.

Hope, L., Gabbert, F., Fisher, R. P., & Jamieson, K. (2014). Protecting and enhancing eyewitness memory: The impact of an initial recall attempt on Performance in an Investigative Interview. *Applied Cognitive Psychology*, 28, 304–313.

Hope, L., Mullis, R., & Gabbert, F. (2013). Who? What? When? Using a timeline technique to facilitate recall of a complex event. *Journal of Applied Research in Memory and Cognition*, 2, 20–24.

Howard, M. W., & Kahana, M. J. (1999). Contextual variability and serial position effects in free recall. *Journal of Experimental Psychology: Learning, Memory & Cognition*, 25, 923–941.

Hulse, L. M., & Memon, A. (2006). Fatal impact? The effects of emotional arousal and weapon presence on police officers' memories for a simulated crime. *Legal and Criminological Psychology*, 11, 313–325.

Inbau, F., Reid, J., Buckley, J., & Jayne, B. (2013). *Criminal Interrogation and Confessions* (5th ed.). Burlington, MA: Jones & Bartlett.

Kahana, M. J. (1996). Associative retrieval processes in free recall. *Memory & Cognition*, 24, 103–109.

Kahana, M. J., Howard, M. W., & Polyn, S. M. (2008). Associative retrieval processes in episodic memory. In H. L.RoedigerIII (ed.), *Cognitive Psychology of Memory*. Vol. 2 of *Learning and Memory: A Comprehensive Reference*. Oxford: Elsevier.

Kebbell, M. R., & Wagstaff, G. F. (1999). The cognitive interview: An analysis of its forensic effectiveness. In D. V. Canter (ed.), *Interviewing and Deception*. Aldershot, UK: Dartmouth.

Köhnken, G., Milne, R., Memon, A., & Bull, R. (1999). The cognitive interview: A meta analysis. *Psychology, Crime, & Law*, 5, 3–27.

Kontogianni, F., Hope, L., Taylor, P., Vrij, A., & Gabbert, F. (in submission). Introducing a new mnemonic to the Timeline Technique: The use of self-generated cues. Poster presented at SARMAC XII Conference, Sydney, 2017.

Koriat, A., Levy-Sadot, R., Edry, E., & De Marcas, G. (2003). What do we know about what we cannot remember? Accessing the semantic attributes of words that cannot be recalled. *Journal of Experimental Psychology: Learning, Memory and Cognition*, 29, 1095–1105.

Kuhlmann, S., Piel, M., & Wolf, O. T. (2005). Impaired memory retrieval after psychosocial stress in healthy young men. *Journal of Neuroscience*, 25, 2977–2982.

La Rooy, D., Lamb, M. E., & Memon, A. (2011). Forensic interviews with children in Scotland: A survey of interview practice among police. *Journal of Police and Criminal Psychology*, 26, 26–34.

Leveson, B. (2015, January 23). *Review of Efficiency in Criminal Proceedings Final Report.* Retrieved from https://www.judiciary.gov.uk/publications/review-of-efficiency-in-criminal-proceedings-final-report/

Levett, L. M. (2013). Co-witness information influences whether a witness is likely to choose from a lineup. *Legal and Criminological Psychology*, 18, 168–180.

Loftus, E. F. (1979). *Eyewitness Testimony.* Cambridge, MA: Harvard University Press.

Loftus, E. (2005). Planting misinformation in the human mind: A 30-year investigation of the malleability of memory. *Learning & Memory*, 12, 361–366.

Loftus, E. F., Levidow, B., & Duensing, S. (1992). Who remembers best? Individual difference in memory for events that occurred in a science museum. *Applied Cognitive Psychology*, 6, 93–107.

Manning, J. R., & Kahana, M. J. (2012). Interpreting semantic clustering effects in free recall. *Memory*, 20, 511–517.

Meissner, C. A., Redlich, A. D., Bhatt, S., & Brandon, S. (2012). Interview and interrogation methods and their effects on true and false confessions. *Campbell Systematic Reviews*, 8, 1–49.

Memon, A., Meissner, C. A., & Fraser, J. (2010). The Cognitive Interview: A meta-analytic review and study space analysis of the past 25 years. *Psychology, Public Policy, and Law*, 16, 340–372.

Ministry of Justice (2013). *Code of Practice for Victims of Crime.* Accessed 13 November 2016, https://www.gov.uk/government/publications/the-code-of-practice-for-victims-of-crime

Ministry of Justice (2011). *Achieving Best Evidence: Guidance on Interviewing Victims and Witnesses and Guidance on Using Special Measures.* London: Ministry of Justice. Accessed 13 November 2016, https://www.cps.gov.uk/publications/prosecution/victims.html

Ministry of Justice (2013). *The Witness Charter: Standards of Care for Witnesses in the Criminal Justice System.* Accessed 13 November 2016, https://www.gov.uk/government/publications/the-witness-charter-standards-of-care-for-witnesses-in-the-criminal-justice-system

Ministry of Justice (2016). *Process Evaluation of Pre-recorded Cross-examination Pilot (Section 28).* Accessed 11 April 2016, https://www.gov.uk/government/publications/process-evaluation-of-pre-recorded-cross-examination-pilot-section-28

Miranda v. Arizona, 384 U.S. 436 (1966).

MorganIII, C. A., Southwick, S., Steffian, G., Hazlett, G. A., & Loftus, E. F. (2013). Misinformation can influence memory for recently experienced, highly stressful events. *International Journal of Law and Psychiatry*, 36, 11–17.

MorganIII, C. A., Hazlett, G. A., DoranA., Garrett, S., Hoyt, G., Thomas, P. et al. (2004). Accuracy of eyewitness memory for persons encountered during exposure to highly intense stress. *International Journal of Law and Psychiatry*, 27, 265–279.

Nairne, J. S. (2002). The myth of the encoding-retrieval match. *Memory*, 10, 389–395.

National Police Chief's Council (2015). *Advice on the Structure of Visually Recorded Witness Interviews.* Accessed 13 November 2016, http://www.app.college.police.uk/app-content/investigations/linked-reference-material/

Oxburgh, G. E., Myklebust, T., & Grant, T. D. (2010). The question of question types in police interviews: A review of the literature from a psychological and linguistic perspective. *International Journal of Speech, Language and the Law*, 17, 45–66.

Paterson, H. M., & Kemp, R. I. (2006). Co-witnesses talk: A survey of eyewitness discussion. *Psychology Crime and Law*, 12, 181–191.

Paulo, R. M., Albuquerque, P. B., & Bull, R. (2016). Improving the enhanced Cognitive Interview with a new interview strategy: Category Clustering Recall. *Applied Cognitive Psychology*, 30, 775–784.

Penrod, S. D., Loftus, E. F., & Winkler, J. (1982). The reliability of eyewitness testimony: A psychological perspective. In N. L. Kerr & R. M. Bray (eds), *The Psychology of the Courtroom* (pp. 119–168). Orlando, FL: Academic Press.

Perfect, T. J., Andrade, J., & Eagan, I. (2011). Eye closure reduces the cross-modal memory impairment caused by auditory distraction. *Journal of Experimental Psychology – Learning Memory and Cognition*, 37, 1008–1013.

Police and Criminal Evidence Act (1984). Accessed 13 November 2016, www.legislation.gov.uk/ukpga/1984/60/data.pdf

Powell, M. (2013). An overview of current initiatives to improve child witness interviews about sexual abuse. *Current Issues in Criminal Justice*, 25, 711–720.

R v Christopher Halliwell (2012).

R v Turnbull (1977). QB 224.

Reyna, V. F., & Kiernan, B. (1994). The development of gist versus verbatim memory in sentence recognition: Effects of lexical familiarity, semantic content, encoding instruction and retention interval. *Developmental Psychology*, 30, 178–191.

Ridley, A. M., Gabbert, F., & La Rooy, D. J. (eds) (2013). *Suggestibility in Legal Contexts: Psychological Research and Forensic Implications*. London: Wiley-Blackwell.

Robinson, J. A. (1966). Category clustering in free recall. *The Journal of Psychology: Interdisciplinary and Applied*, 62, 279–286.

Rubin, D. C., & Wenzel, A. E. (1996). One hundred years of forgetting: A quantitative description of retention. *Psychological Review*, 103, 734–760.

Salehi, B., Cordero, M. I., & Sandi, C. (2010). Learning under stress: The inverted-u-shape function revisited. *Cold Spring Harbor Laboratory Press*, 17, 522–530.

Scoboria, A., & Fisico, S. (2013). Encouraging and clarifying "don't know" responses enhances interview quality. *Journal of Experimental Psychology: Applied*, 19, 72–82.

Shepherd, E., & Griffiths, A. (2013). *Investigative Interviewing: The Conversation Management Approach* (2nd edition). London: Oxford University Press.

St-Yves, M. (2015). *Investigative Interviewing: The Essential Handbook of Best Practices*. Canada: Carswell.

Stanny, C. J., & Johnson, T. C. (2000). Effects of stress induced by a simulated shooting on recall by police and citizen witnesses. *American Journal of Psychology*, 113, 359–386.

Taverniers, J., Taylor, M. K., & Smeets, T. (2013). Delayed memory effects after intense stress in Special Forces candidates: Exploring path processes between cortisol secretion and memory recall. *Stress*, 16, 311–320.

Tuckey, M. R., & Brewer, N. (2003). The influence of schemas, stimulus ambiguity, and interview schedule on eyewitness memory over time. *Journal of Experimental Psychology: Applied*, 9, 101–118.

Tulving, E., & Thomson, D. M. (1973). Encoding specificity and retrieval processes in episodic memory. *Psychological Review*, 80, 352–373.

Unsworth, N. (2008). Exploring the retrieval dynamics of delayed and final free recall: Further evidence for temporal–contextual search. *Journal of Memory and Language*, 59, 223–236.

Valentine, T., Pickering, A., & Darling, S. (2003). Characteristics of eyewitness identification that predict the outcome of real lineups. *Applied Cognitive Psychology*, 17, 969–993.

Vredeveldt, A., & Perfect, T. (2014). Reduction of environmental distraction to facilitate cognitive performance. *Frontiers in Psychology*, 5, 860.

Vredeveldt, A., Tredoux, C. G., Nortje, A., Kempen, K., Puljevic, C., & Labuschagne, G. N. (2015). A field evaluation of the Eye-Closure Interview with witnesses of serious crimes. *Law and Human Behavior*, 39, 189–197.

Wells, G. L. (1978). Applied eyewitness-testimony research: System variables and estimator variables. *Journal of Personality and Social Psychology*, 36, 1546–1557.

Wetmore, S. A., Neuschatz, J. S., Gronlund, S. D., Wooten, A., Goodsell, C. A., & Carlson, C. A. (2015). Effect of retention interval on showup and lineup performance. *Journal of Applied Research in Memory and Cognition*, 4, 8–14.

Wheeler, R. L., & Gabbert, F. (2017). Using self-generated cues to facilitate recall: A narrative review. *Frontiers in Psychology*, section Theoretical and Philosophical Psychology. doi:10.3389/fpsyg.2017.01830

Wixted, J., & Ebbesen, E. B. (1991). On the form of forgetting. *Psychological Science*, 2, 409–415.

Wixted, J., & Ebbesen, E. B. (1997). Genuine power curves in forgetting: Quantitative analysis of individual subject forgetting functions. *Memory & Cognition*, 23, 731–739.

Wright, A. M., & Holliday, R. E. (2005). Police officers' perceptions of older eyewitnesses. *Legal and Criminological Psychology*, 10, 211–223.

Wright, D. B, & McDaid, A. T. (1996). Comparing system and estimator variables using data from real line-ups. *Applied Cognitive Psychology*, 10, 75–84.

Youth Justice and Criminal Evidence Act (1999). Accessed 13 November 2016, http://www.legislation.gov.uk/ukpga/1999/23/contents

Chapter 7

Identification evidence

Graham Pike and Clifford Clark

Introduction

Working out who committed the crime is perhaps the most important element in any criminal investigation. If you are familiar with fictional crime drama you would be forgiven for thinking that most perpetrators are identified through some form of forensic analysis, but in reality forensic evidence is *not* a routine part of most criminal investigations. Using a prospective analysis of official US record data, Peterson et al. (2010) concluded that "Very few reported crime incidents had forensic evidence that linked a suspect to the crime scene and/or victim (~2% of all cases, 6% of cases with crime scene evidence, and 12% of cases with examined evidence)" (Peterson et al., 2010, p. 9). Instead, it is identification by an eyewitness that tends to be the method more commonly used by police to determine the identity of a perpetrator.

Eyewitness identification evidence can be obtained by means of a number of methods, which vary depending on the medium used (e.g. 'live' appearance or images presented through photographs or video) and the number of people seen in the procedure. As a result there is considerable variability around the world as to the specific methods employed. For example, in the US and New Zealand photospreads are the most common form of identification procedure, whereas in the UK video parades are the standard. There is also variation in the terminology used, and in this chapter the term 'lineup' will be used to refer to identification procedures generically, with more specific terms being employed when a distinction between methods is required.

Perhaps the most straightforward, but also most problematic, method is to simply present the suspect to the eyewitness and ask them if that is the person they saw commit the crime. Known as a 'show-up' in the US and a 'confrontation' in the UK, research has shown this method to be particularly prone to misidentifications (Lindsay et al., 1997). Instead, lineups are commonly used that consist of the suspect and a number of other people, known as 'foils', who resemble the description of the perpetrator provided by the witness (Wells & Olson, 2002). When determining the outcome of a lineup it is usual for the police to record a positive identification if the witness selects the suspect, with all other outcomes being classified as a negative identification (Pike, Brace & Kynan, 2002). In contrast, researchers employ four possible outcomes, based on the application of signal detection theory (Tanner & Swets, 1954).

Box 1 Signal detection and the design of eyewitness identification research

Developed to assist in improving the accuracy of radar operators, the theory describes four possible outcomes depending on whether a signal is present or absent, and whether the operator judges a signal to be present or absent (see Figure 7.1). For example, if the operator thinks a signal is present but one is not then the outcome would be a 'false alarm'.

		Operator judges the signal to be:	
		Present	Absent
The signal is actually:	Present	Hit	Miss
	Absent	False Alarm	Correct Rejection

Figure 7.1 The possible outcomes of a decision in signal detection theory

When applied to eyewitness identification the 'signal' becomes the perpetrator, which leads to a complication because it is possible for the suspect being investigated to be innocent of the crime (i.e. the suspect is not actually the perpetrator), in which case if the witness selects them then they will be making a 'false alarm' rather than a 'hit'. This also means there are two types of false alarm; one in which the witness selects a foil and one in which they select an innocent suspect. This complication is the reason why eyewitness identification research routinely employs two conditions, one in which the perpetrator (usually referred to as the 'target') is present and one in which they are absent (thus known as target present and target absent or culprit present and culprit absent conditions). This mimics scenarios where the suspect being investigated by the police is actually the perpetrator and where the suspect is innocent. It is also the reason why experimental research that replicates eyewitness identification can be more powerful and useful than research utilising real investigations, as in the latter there is often no way of determining whether the suspect in the lineup is guilty or innocent (Horry et al., 2014).

One important lesson to learn from signal detection theory is that human operators are not capable of performing with 100 per cent accuracy and that any attempt to increase the incidence of one particular outcome will also increase the incidence of another. For example, trying to maximise hits would entail operators increasing the number of times they judge a signal to be present, but this would have the consequence of also increasing the number of false alarms. Likewise, making fewer judgements that the signal is present in order to minimise false alarms would also increase the number of misses. With regards to identification evidence, this means that trying to increase the number of guilty suspects identified is likely to also lead to an increase in the number of innocent suspects identified. As we shall discuss later, the difference between maximising hits and avoiding false alarms is an important distinction between the aims of many practitioners and researchers.

Another difference between research and practice is that research has tended to classify variables that might affect the outcome of the lineup as either estimator or system variables (Wells, 2014; see also Chapters 1 and 6, this volume, for more on estimator and system variables). A system variable is any factor that is under the control of the criminal justice system, such as the method used to obtain the identification evidence, and an estimator variable is one that is not, such as how far away the witness was from the perpetrator. In practice, some factors are not easy to classify in this way. For example, the length of time between the crime and lineup is partly, but not entirely, under the control of the justice system. In addition, the criminal justice system is not a single institution or represented by any one person, and officers responsible for obtaining identification evidence may not see themselves as having control over many system variables beyond ensuring that relevant guidelines are adhered to (Pike, Havard & Ness, 2014).

Miscarriages of justice were discussed in Chapter 1 of this book and it is clear that misidentification by an eyewitness has been, and indeed continues to be, a prominent factor in causing such miscarriages. For example, eyewitness misidentification featured in 235 (72 per cent) of the first 325 exonerations secured by The Innocence Project (Innocence Project, 2016).

Box 2 The Ronald Cotton case

The wrongful conviction of Ronald Cotton is one of the cases in which The Innocence Project secured an exoneration and that received a great deal of attention in the media, in part because of the willingness of those involved (the falsely accused, the eyewitness and law enforcement personnel) to talk openly about the case (e.g. the BBC series, 'Eyewitness' – Pike & Fletcher-Hill, 2010).

In July 1984 Jennifer Thompson-Cannino (a 22 year old student) was sexually assaulted by a man who broke into her apartment. She stated later that she studied her assailant so that she would later be able to help the police catch him. In January 1985, Ronald Cotton was convicted of rape and burglary, and in a second trial two years later (which added additional rape and burglary charges) he was sentenced to life in prison plus 54 years. The conviction was on the basis of a flashlight found in his home that resembled the one used by the assailant, the fact that the rubber on his shoes was consistent with rubber traces found at the crime scene and two identifications made by Thompson-Cannino; one in a photo lineup and a later one in a live lineup. She was 100 per cent confident that she was identifying the perpetrator.

In July 1995, after serving more than 10 years in prison, Cotton was released following the results of DNA analysis which not only showed physical evidence from the crime scene was not his, but that it was a match for a convict named Bobby Poole, who had previously confessed to a fellow inmate. The Ronald Cotton case has several components that occur again and again in exonerations; namely, that the key evidence comes from an eyewitness who was very confident in their decision and that the other evidence available was not sufficient to establish the identity of the perpetrator. It therefore serves as an example of just how inaccurate eyewitness identification evidence can be and how misidentifications can lead to major miscarriages of justice.

Although many of the original investigations that have featured in prominent miscarriages of justice happened decades ago and pre-date many advances in criminal investigation and relevant legislation, contemporary practice still includes many of the components that research has shown can lead to misidentifications, and moreover the number of lineups being conducted has increased greatly over the last 30–40 years. Valentine (2009) estimated that whilst about 2000 identification procedures were held per year in the UK in 1976, the figure is closer to 100,000 lineups in the modern era. Although some improvements to practice have been made, the number of misidentifications made will still be proportionate to the number of procedures that are conducted (Valentine, 2009). This means that even if the ratio of legitimate identifications to misidentifications has increased (and it is certainly debateable whether it has), the overall number of misidentifications may well have gone up, simply because more lineups are being conducted. The potential for miscarriages of justice occurring because of identification evidence is, therefore, still an issue of vital importance today.

Research, practice and costs

It should be clear that there is evidence of significant problems with identification evidence and a great deal of research has been devoted to improving its accuracy. Because it addresses an issue of significance to society, eyewitness identification has also proven to be an attractive research topic as it allows the application of knowledge gained from more theoretical studies of face recognition and memory, and is based on procedures that are relatively straightforward to replicate in a laboratory setting. As a result, a review of approximately three decades of policing psychology research conducted by Snook et al. (2009) found that of articles focusing on operational policing issues, 27 per cent were about eyewitness memory and 16 per cent on lineups compared with 13 per cent on interviewing and 10 per cent on profiling.

So, have investigative practices now changed in light of this research? Unfortunately, the answer to this question is that although some changes have been implemented, the methods used to obtain identification evidence in police investigations are still fundamentally different to those that would be recommended on the basis of research results. For example, recommendations have been made by academic and research organisations in many countries, perhaps most notably by the American Psychology/Law Society (AP/LS), which suggested four rules regarding: who conducts the lineup (primarily the use of 'double-blind' procedures in which the person conducting the lineup should not be aware of the identity of the suspect); the instructions given to the eyewitness prior to viewing the lineup (including explicitly informing them that the perpetrator may not be present); the structure of the lineup (to ensure that the suspect does not stand out); and that confidence statements should be taken at the time of the identification (Wells et al., 1998). The subcommittee of the AP/LS responsible for drafting the recommendations also recognised two additional recommendations: that the members/images in a lineup be presented sequentially rather than simultaneously; and that the lineup procedure be recorded on video. These two recommendations were not included as 'core' recommendations due to a variety of issues, including potential additional costs, that they may require significant deviation from current practice and that their utility may not be self-evident to the legal system.

More recently the US National Research Council (2014) endorsed the scientific evidence underpinning these recommendations, going on to establish recommendations for best practice for the law enforcement community and to strengthen the value of eyewitness evidence in court. With regards to investigative procedures, best practice was seen to be: training all officers in eyewitness identification; implementing double-blind procedures; the use of standardised witness instructions (including that the perpetrator may or may not be present); documenting witness confidence judgements; and videotaping the identification process.

In the US, at the time of writing, five states (New Jersey, Wisconsin, North Carolina, Ohio and West Virginia) and a number of local jurisdictions have adopted relevant legislation or guidelines concerning eyewitness identification (Clark, 2012). In addition, the double-blind, sequential procedure was trialled successfully in the two Minnesota counties of Hennepin and Ramsey in 2006 (Gaertner & Harrington, 2009), with Ramsey County concluding that, "it is confident that this change represents an improvement over prior practice. The Ramsey County experience unequivocally demonstrates that this model can work in a law enforcement setting" (Gaertner & Harrington, 2009).

However, despite some significant inroads, to date it is still the case that procedures for obtaining identification evidence do not adhere to all of the above recommendations. Importantly, the use of double-blind procedures remains very scarcely implemented indeed. We will explore the research behind this and the other recommendations later, and instead now consider some of the reasons why practice does not better reflect evidence from research.

The problems of implementing the results of research and of evidence-based practice are well documented generally (Mullen & Streiner, 2006) and within specific domains such as the criminal justice system (Sherman, 2013). Rather than review the more generic problems, here we will concentrate on those that are specific to identification evidence; although the broader problems in establishing evidence-based practice (particularly in policing practice) should not be underestimated and almost certainly are a strong influence in the case of identification evidence.

Pike, Havard and Ness (2014) explored potential reasons why the results of relevant research were not influencing eyewitness identification procedures in England and Northern Ireland by surveying policing personnel who routinely worked with identification evidence. The results showed that 86 per cent of respondents believed that current identification practice either worked well or didn't need much improvement and well over half indicated they had either no, or vague, knowledge about existing research-based recommendations. Critically, the large majority (84 per cent) thought that any changes introduced should attempt to increase positive identifications, with more than half of these respondents believing this should even be at the cost of also increasing misidentifications. There are several possible explanations for this, including that the respondents didn't think that misidentifications presently occurred. However, respondents' mean estimate of the percentage of lineups in which the witness made a positive identification was 40.56 per cent, which is a good match for research estimates based on analysis of real lineup procedures in the UK (Pike, Brace & Kynan, 2002). Moreover, the respondents' mean estimate of the percentage of lineups which feature an innocent suspect (20.76 per cent) was also very similar to estimates made in research; for example, about 20 per cent according to Clark and Godfrey (2009).

This means that the policing staff surveyed tended to have a good idea regarding the outcome of lineup procedures and the incidence of misidentifications and *yet still* the majority thought that increasing the number of positive identifications should be the priority. Clearly this suggests that misidentifications were not a concern for these officers, or at least that they were far less of a concern than was obtaining positive identifications. This issue was explored further through focus groups, where it became apparent that staff were driven by quantitative performance measures to do with completing specific tasks which taken together would amount to successful arrests and prosecutions. Thus, the pressure was to obtain positive identifications, with misidentifications often being seen as errors for others to resolve, particularly through subsequent court hearings. This situation is likely to have arisen in part from performance cultures, but also from the adversarial justice system which can cast investigative and prosecutorial teams in the role of finding evidence of guilt, whilst proving innocence is left to the defence – indeed many of the free text responses in the

Pike, Havard and Ness survey were officers commenting on the need to constrain the influence of defence lawyers.

The picture that emerges from Pike et al. (2014) is of an eyewitness identification practitioner body that does not think significant changes are needed, is unfamiliar with research recommendations, has a good idea regarding the rates of positive and misidentifications and believes that any changes should be aimed at increasing positive identifications. Such a picture helps explain why the results of identification research, which often focuses on reducing misidentifications, have not been put into practice more widely.

The sensitivity of policing personnel to a potential drop in the rate of positive identifications has been a component of eyewitness research, and subsequent recommendations, for some time. For example, when outlining the recommendations of the American Psychology/Law Society, Wells et al. (1998) stated,

> We are mindful of the problems with making recommendations for which there are significant financial or other costs to the legal system. Accordingly, we think it important that the four recommendations that we have made are largely without financial cost to the justice system … . We have taken great care to recommend procedures that do not serve to reduce the changes that the guilty party will be identified.
>
> (Wells et al., 1998, pp. 28–9)

Researchers have also been careful to point out that a misidentification not only results in an innocent person potentially being sent to prison, but also means the guilty party remains free *and* that the state incurs the cost of an expensive investigation and trial (Clark et al., 2015).

More recently there has been debate about whether the AP/LS recommendations really do involve 'no cost', which has concentrated on the negative impact they may have on positive identifications (see Clark, 2012). Regardless of the extent of any drop in positive identifications, there is a significant difference between research demonstrating how to reduce the rate of misidentifications whilst (arguably) having a negligent effect on positive identifications, and the development of techniques that actively improve positive identifications; which is what many practitioners seem to be interested in.

Likewise, there is a difference between recommendations that will not cost the criminal justice system more money, and the development of techniques that could actually *save* money. In many countries and organisations there tends to be an emphasis on procedural changes that reduce expenditure; a situation that has been significantly augmented by the implementation of austerity measures in public sectors around the world. This can mean that proposed changes that do not cut expenditure, even if they do not actually increase it either, may not be seen as a priority by practitioner organisations. In terms of identification evidence, this could mean placing more emphasis on calculating the costs of proceeding with investigations and trials that later fail to gain a conviction because of misidentifications, or of developing new recommendations or techniques that are also cheaper to administer. For example, automating identification processes using computers could help to standardise the characteristics of the images, the construction of the lineup and the instructions given to the eyewitness, and also provide a means of double-blind testing whilst also potentially reducing expenditure.

A similar approach was used in England and Wales in the development of video identification parade systems, which research showed to be fairer (i.e. more of the foils were a reasonable match to the witness' description of the perpetrator) than existing 'live' parades (Valentine & Heaton, 1999) and also much cheaper to administer as they did not require such extensive facilities and personnel (Pike, Brace & Kynan, 2002). Pike et al. (2002) also drew attention to an aspect of identification evidence that is often overlooked, which is that many lineups do not produce identification evidence because the witness, suspect or required legal personnel do not turn up. Such cancellations represent considerable expenditure for no outcome, an element that makes video (and photo) parades attractive as they do not require all parties to be present at the same time, making them less likely to be cancelled. In addition, if a new procedure or technique can be shown to reduce cancelled procedures, then it can also be used to show that it is likely to lead to an overall increase in the number, if not rate, of positive identifications. These economic considerations and potential improvements to positive identifications proved to be vital to changing practice in England and Wales in 2003 to a system based on video identification parades rather than live lineups, despite the original research being aimed at making fairer lineups that would result in fewer misidentifications.

The focus group study conducted by Pike, Havard and Ness (2014) revealed another barrier, as policing staff reported feeling unable to make any changes to practice as national legislation and guidelines dictated what must happen. Thus one downside of being successful in gaining guidelines and legislation, even if they offer a significant short term fix of existing problems, is that they can make any future changes to practice much harder to achieve. It also serves as a reminder for researchers that neither the criminal justice system nor the police are a single entity and that change is hard to secure by lobbying one particular element.

One possibility for communicating the dangers of misidentifications might be to adapt existing frameworks for evaluating harm, such as the multicriteria decision analysis procedure (e.g. Nutt, King & Phillips, 2010), which would allow the quantification of misidentifications in a broader context of the cost to individuals, families and to society in general. Such frameworks are useful in providing an objective and broad picture of the harm caused by various phenomena – for example, that smoking cigarettes is particularly harmful not just because of the impact on individual health, but because half of all the world's fires are caused by cigarettes (Nutt, 2015) – and could potentially be a persuasive approach to securing relevant changes to policies governing identification evidence by estimating the true harm and cost of misidentifications.

Constructing and conducting lineups

As was stated previously, lineups consisting of just a single person tend to lead to a high rate of misidentifications (Lindsay et al., 1997). One problem with such procedures is that it is impossible for a witness to make a selection that is incorrect (i.e. not the suspect). The same would be true of any size of lineup where all the members were also suspects, and research has shown that single suspect lineups lead to significantly fewer misidentifications than do all-suspect procedures (Wells & Turtle, 1986). Wells, Cutler and Hasel (2009) note an extreme example of this in which the witness in the 2006 Duke University rape case, involving multiple suspects from the lacrosse team, was shown a lineup consisting of the entire team of 46 players. In this case, making *any* selection would mean picking a suspect as at that point all 46 players were under suspicion and no foils had been included. As the witness could not make an incorrect selection as would be the case if foils had been used, the lineup was not diagnostic of their ability to identify the perpetrator. As Steblay (2015) points out, throwing a dart at the lineup would also have yielded a suspect hit.

It follows that having only a single suspect and increasing the size of the lineup by adding foils will also decrease the probability that the witness will select the suspect by chance alone. Selecting a foil is counted by the police as a 'negative identification', so there is no risk of a true misidentification occurring unless the witness selects an innocent suspect. However, it is obvious that simply adding any foils is insufficient, but instead the foils must resemble the suspect; a point that has led researchers to distinguish between 'actual' and 'functional' lineup size (Wells, Leippe & Ostrom, 1979; Valentine & Heaton, 1999). To reduce the chance that a lineup will result in a misidentification, it is important that is has high functional size (Lindsay & Wells, 1980) as this will reduce the chances of a witness selecting the suspect for any other reason than that they recognise them as the person seen committing the crime. To ensure the lineup has high functional size, foils need to be selected that match the description of the perpetrator that was provided by the witness (Wells et al., 1998). Selecting foils that directly resemble the suspect may appear to be a more logical approach, but this can rely too heavily on the subjective judgement of the lineup administrator and could also lead to a lineup where the members are *too* similar to one another and make it very difficult for the witness to make a positive identification (Tredoux, 2002). However, match to description lineups may be problematic if the witness provides an inaccurate or even vague description that allows the selection of foils who do not particularly resemble the suspect (Meissner, Sporer & Schooler, 2007), thus requiring some caution be exercised in their use.

One aspect of lineups that has received a great deal of attention from researchers is whether the members of the parade should be presented simultaneously or sequentially one at a time (Brewer & Palmer, 2010). It has been suggested that seeing all the members of the lineup simultaneously allows a witness to compare the faces in the lineup directly and arrive at a 'relative judgement' about who is most like their memory of the perpetrator (Wells, 1984). The problem with such decisions is that the witness may be drawn into selecting the most similar face even if it is not that of the perpetrator. By presenting the lineup members sequentially, witnesses are forced to make an absolute judgement about whether each face is that of the perpetrator, which reduces the likelihood of their being able to simply choose the best match (Wells, 1984). Alternatively, Palmer and Brewer (2012) have argued that rather than the use of absolute judgements *per se*, the reduction in misidentifications when using a sequential lineup is a result of participants adopting a more conservative decision process in which they are less likely to make a selection at all.

Whatever the cause may be, a great deal of research has shown that sequential presentation reduces the incidence of misidentifications when the lineup contains an innocent suspect. This includes meta-analyses conducted in 2001 (Steblay et al., 2001) and in 2011 (Steblay, Dysart & Wells, 2011, which analysed data from 13,143 participant witnesses), both of which showed that sequential lineups resulted in 22 per cent fewer errors than their simultaneous counterparts. However, more recently research employing a different type of statistical analysis (receiver operating characteristic analysis) has suggested that simultaneous lineups may allow innocent and guilty suspects to be discriminated more reliably than when using sequential lineups (e.g. Seale-Carlisle & Mickes, 2016).

There is also debate regarding whether sequential parades lead to a significant reduction in the rate of correct identifications. In the two meta-analyses the sequential lineups produced fewer correct identifications than did the simultaneous lineups. The current consensus seems to be that rather than have no impact on positive identifications in target present lineups, as was claimed in the AP/LS recommendations (Wells et al., 1998), sequential presentation *does* result in a reduction in positive identifications compared with simultaneously presented lineups, though this is smaller than the reduction in misidentifications that occur in target absent lineups (Lindsay et al., 2009). Clark (2012) suggests that the reductions are more likely to be comparable and points out the problems of presenting 'no cost' recommendations to practitioners, who may hold differing views regarding the relative importance of correct identifications and misidentifications than do researchers. The survey of identification police staff conducted by Pike, Havard and Ness (2014) provides evidence that practitioners are unlikely to want to adopt a technique that results in *any* reduction in identifications, suggesting that sequential lineups could be a hard-sell to many law enforcement officers.

Another element that can make truly sequential lineups unattractive to the police is the notion that the procedure might end once the witness has made an identification. This is because if the witness selects a foil before seeing the suspect then they will not get to see them, and the witness not viewing the suspect seems to run contradictory to the demands of the investigation. It is common in the UK to use video parades, which use a sequential presentation. However, the Codes of Practice of the Police and Criminal Evidence Act (PACE), which govern identification evidence in England and Wales, state that "The witness must also be told they should not make any decision about whether the person they saw is on the identification parade until they have looked at each member at least twice" (PACE, 1984, Code D, Annex C, Section 16). Although this means that the witness will definitely see the suspect (at least twice), it also affects the witness's decision criteria and ability to make comparisons between lineup members.

The instructions given to the witness prior to the lineup are also critical, and research has shown that simply informing the witness that the perpetrator 'may or may not be present' can dramatically reduce the chance of a misidentification being made. For example, using a meta-analysis of 16 experimental studies, Steblay (2013) demonstrated that including the 'may or may not' instruction resulted in a significant reduction of identification errors from 70 per cent to 43 per cent in target absent lineups. The importance of the 'may or may not be present' instruction was further demonstrated by Rose, Bull and Vrij (2005), who found that participants who did not remember this instruction when making an identification were less accurate than those who did, and that older participants were more likely to forget the instruction than were younger participants.

In England and Wales, the PACE Codes of Conduct state that the witness be instructed that "the person they saw on a specified earlier occasion may, or may not, be present and if they cannot make a positive identification, they should say so" (PACE, 1984). It is likely that this has helped reduce the incidence of mistaken identification compared with countries that do not have a similar guideline.

It is also important that the person conducting the lineup refrains from giving the witness any additional instructions or cues, whether verbal or non-verbal, as these could provide the witness with clues as to the identity of the suspect. It is hard to underestimate the impact that even inadvertent or unconscious verbal and non-verbal cues can have and medical researchers have found that these can even result in a change in health outcome (De Craen et al., 1999). As a result it is necessary to use a 'double-blind' procedure in medical trials in which neither the patient nor the person administering the treatment knows whether the actual treatment or a placebo is being used (Hulley et al., 2013). Research has shown that similar biasing effects can occur in lineups (e.g. Fanselow & Buckhout, 1976) and researchers therefore advocate that lineups should be administered using a double-blind procedure, such that neither the witness nor person administering the lineup knows the location of the suspect (Wells et al., 1998). Not only can using a double-blind procedure guard against the witness making a selection because of cues from an officer, but it can also help ensure that witnesses do not inflate the confidence expressed in their decision when given feedback after the lineup, even when the feedback was not specifically about the identification made (Dysart, Lawson & Rainey, 2012).

One of the recommendations from both the AP/LS (Wells et al., 1998) and the US National Research Council (2014) is that the confidence of the eyewitness in their decision be taken immediately following the lineup. This is based on research that has found that if confidence can be recorded *immediately* after identification is made and before the witness is provided with any feedback on their decision, then it can be a useful indicator as long as the witness selected someone from the lineup (Sauerland & Sporer, 2009). Research has shown that although not *always* correct, very confident eyewitnesses are associated with relatively high degrees of accuracy whilst unconfident witnesses are not (Brewer & Palmer, 2010). In other words, a witness recording a very high degree of confidence immediately after selecting the suspect from the lineup can be a good indicator to the police that the suspect is worth investigating further, whilst an unconfident decision suggests that they may be wise to investigate other suspects.

Problems faced by eyewitnesses

There are many hurdles that stand in the way of a witness attempting to provide an accurate identification. Moreover, the high error rates associated with eyewitness identification contradict our usual experience of being able to recognise faces very accurately, over long periods of time and despite significant changes in appearance. The reason for this is that our everyday experience is of recognising faces that are *familiar* (e.g. family and friends), a task that we perform very well. However, we perform far less accurately when a task requires us to recognise an *unfamiliar* face (Hancock, Bruce & Burton, 2000), as is the case when providing eyewitness identification evidence.

Other factors that have been shown to negatively impact identification evidence include the presence of a weapon, which can have a detrimental effect on eyewitness memory of the event, and a small to moderately negative effect on identification accuracy (Fawcett et al., 2013). The practical elements of how the perpetrator was viewed are also important. Both distance from the perpetrator and the ambient illumination can have a profound effect on identification accuracy (Wagenaar & Van Der Schrier, 1996), and Memon, Hope and Bull (2003) showed that witnesses who saw the perpetrator for a longer duration tended to make more accurate identifications than was the case for a shorter duration (45 s and 12 s in this study).

The accuracy of identification evidence can also be affected by information seen or heard by the witness between witnessing the crime and attending the lineup procedure. This can include information gained from talking to another witness, referred to as the co-witnessing effect by researchers. A survey of officers and witnesses conducted by Paterson (2010) revealed that discussion amongst witnesses is a common phenomenon, but if witnesses share their memory of what happened then they are also very likely to alter their own memory in line with what others say, even to the extent of remembering aspects of the event that they didn't see (Paterson & Kemp, 2006). Further, Levett (2013) found that participant-witnesses who received information that a co-witness had made a selection from a lineup were more likely to make a selection themselves.

Alternatively, witnesses can sometimes be shown information as part of the investigation. If the police need to generate potential suspects, this can include showing the witness an album of mug-shots, which research has demonstrated can then have a negative impact on identification accuracy when the same witness is shown a lineup. A meta-analysis conducted by Deffenbacher, Bornstein and Penrod (2006) showed that exposure to mug-shots decreased accuracy at a subsequent lineup both in terms of decreasing correct identifications (and correct rejections) and resulted in an even bigger effect in terms of increasing the number of misidentifications made. In the case where a witness selects a suspect in a lineup because they had seen them previously in a mug-shot album, their memory of the mug-shot face has been *transferred* into their memory of the actual perpetrator. As this is not done intentionally and the witness is unaware that it has happened, it is referred to as the 'unconscious transference' effect (Read et al., 1990). Such transference can also occur for innocent bystanders seen at the crime scene, and even for an innocent person seen a week later (Read et al., 1990). There also appears to be a 'commitment effect', whereby most witnesses who select someone from a mug-shot will also pick that person again if they see them in the lineup, even though they were not the perpetrator (Dysart et al., 2001).

An alternative method of generating potential suspects is for the witness to generate a likeness of the perpetrator. This can be done through an artist's impression or by using specialist software that creates a facial composite image (e.g. E-FIT, EFIT-V, EvoFIT, FACES or Photofit). Research has also explored whether facial composites can reduce lineup identification accuracy in the same way that mug-shots do, though results have been far more mixed, with some studies reporting a detrimental effect on lineup accuracy (e.g. Topp-Manriquez, McQuiston & Malpass, 2016), some no effect (e.g. Davis, Thorniley, Gibson & Solomon, 2016) and others that creating a composite can actually improve the accuracy of later identifications (e.g. Davis, Gibson & Solomon, 2014).

Differences between the witness and perpetrator can also lead to problems with regards to identification accuracy. One of the most significant, and worrying given the likely relative ethnic make-up of typical suspects and witnesses in some countries, is 'own-race bias', whereby witnesses tend to be better at identifying perpetrators of their own ethnicities. In a meta-analytic review of own-race bias, Meissner and Brigham (2001) found a 'mirror effect' in which other-race faces yielded a higher proportion of misidentifications and a lower rate of positive identifications than did own-race faces. As well as identification accuracy, ethnicity can also affect the construction of lineups, as both black and white lineup administrators tend to adopt looser criteria, resulting in a tendency to see faces as being more similar to one another, when constructing lineups for a suspect of a different race from their own (Brigham & Ready, 1985).

In a similar fashion to ethnicity, own-age bias can also affect the accuracy of identification evidence, although research on this topic does not produce such clear-cut results as that on own-race bias. For example, Havard et al. (2012) found that children aged 6–8 years were more accurate at correctly recognising a perpetrator of their own age group from a target-present lineup, but that adults showed a reversed own-age bias and were actually more accurate when the target was a child than if they were an adult. As well as own-age bias creating problems for obtaining eyewitness identification from children, there are many other factors to bear in mind, which will be explored in the next section.

Children as eyewitnesses

In many jurisdictions around the world witnesses under 18 years old are treated very differently from adults. For example, in the UK they are classified as 'vulnerable' (see Chapter 5, this volume) and the use of specialist interviewing procedures is advocated. Indeed, younger children may be excluded from an investigation altogether because of a perception that the evidence they provide is far less reliable than that of an adult. There are several reasons for this: that a child's cognitive processes are not yet fully developed and so may be more prone to error; that a child may not understand complex situations involving 'right' and 'wrong' and so may misinterpret acts and scenarios; and that children tend to be far more susceptible to suggestion than are adults. In addition, there may be the perception that they will make bad witnesses when in court. Of course, the cognition, understanding and suggestibility of adults is not assessed before they give evidence, and as you read in the previous two chapters, a common theme in the research in this area is to find great variability amongst both children and adults in terms of the accuracy of the testimony they provide.

In terms of identification evidence, and as with adult witnesses, the key question is whether a child can select a person from an identification procedure because they saw that person previously committing the crime. This question can usefully be divided into two elements: Are the face recognition abilities of the child sufficiently developed that they can accurately recognise a face seen at some point in the past; and are they able to make a decision based solely on their memory of the perpetrator's appearance rather than what they might perceive to be the answer wanted by the investigators.

As with most cognitive processes, there is a developmental trend such that the speed, accuracy and capacity to recognise a face increases until the mid-teens. It has been suggested that as well as a quantitative improvement, there is also a qualitative change such that younger children tend to encode faces in a piecemeal fashion (e.g. feature by feature) whilst older children and adults encode faces more holistically using the configuration of the features (Diamond & Carey, 1986). One pertinent conclusion to arise from the more theoretical study of face recognition in children is that it is vital to use testing techniques that have been appropriately designed for use with children, and that simply using the same technique as used with adults is likely to lead to poorer accuracy (Brace et al., 2001). Two key components of developing child-oriented techniques are to explain the task in a way that the child will understand and to bear in mind that children tend to be suggestible and thus any questions need to be posed very carefully.

Child-oriented research techniques have provided valuable theoretical knowledge (e.g. Karmiloff-Smith et al., 2004) and have also been applied successfully in forensic settings. For example, Paine, Pike, Brace and Westcott (2008) developed a set of visual cues that are used to obtain information about facial appearance rather than ask verbal questions. The cues are used in conjunction with the E-FIT facial composite system, and have the advantage both that they help the child provide more accurate information whilst also avoiding potentially leading questions.

Although focusing on facial composite construction rather than identification evidence per se, Paine et al. (2008) draw attention to the fact that younger children can feel obliged to provide an answer when asked a question and may find it difficult to tell an adult, authority figure that they 'don't know' or 'are uncertain'. When being interviewed more generally, this tendency can be minimised by using appropriate questioning techniques that avoid placing the child in a position where they feel compelled to provide an answer. In the case of identifying someone from a lineup, however, the witness has to provide a specific answer. To compensate for this, Paine et al. included a '?' in their visual cues (see Figure 7.2), so that the children could indicate that they didn't know or were uncertain of the appearance of a particular facial feature in the same way that they would indicate what they thought that feature looked like – in this instance by pointing to the appropriate image. The idea behind this was to avoid the child thinking that a 'don't know' response was undesirable, incorrect or not wanted by the researcher.

Using a similar technique to Paine et al. (2008), Havard and Memon (2013) created a black silhouette of a face covered by a white question mark that could be placed in a video lineup to allow children to indicate they could not make an identification (see Figure 7.3). Use of this 'mystery man' procedure resulted in children making fewer misidentifications in target-absent lineups compared with lineups in which they had to verbally indicate that they couldn't make an identification.

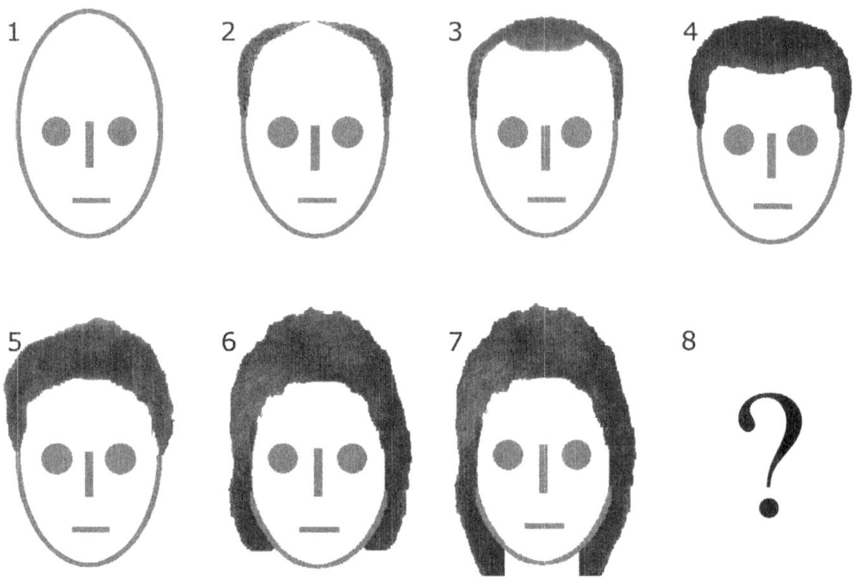

Figure 7.2 An example of the visual cues used by Paine et al. (2008)

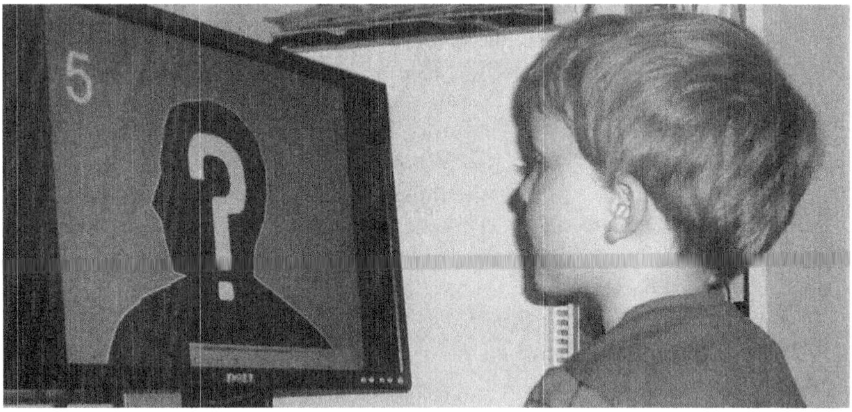

Figure 7.3 The mystery man silhouette developed by Havard and Memon (2013)

Conclusion

Hopefully this chapter has made clear that the accuracy of eyewitness identification evidence is an important issue, and that it is likely that current ID procedures could be improved further to reduce misidentifications. It should also be apparent that a great deal of research has been conducted into identification evidence and that as a result we now know a great deal about the causes of misidentifications and also have some good ideas about how to reduce the number that occur. Unfortunately, it is unlikely that misidentifications can be eradicated entirely as long as human witnesses are relied upon to produce identification evidence.

Although there are some good examples of researchers and practitioners working together to improve eyewitness identification procedures, there is also still a very long way to go. If significant changes to practice are to be made, it is critical that researchers and practitioners find effective methods of communicating and collaborating. The authors (one researcher and one practitioner) would suggest that this should not be through a model of researchers informing practitioners about research results, but instead that a collaborative model be adopted whereby practitioners can input throughout the research process, including in the generation of research questions.

Note

The authors would like to thank Dr Nicky Brace for her invaluable feedback and input.

References

Brace, N. A., Hole, G. J., Kemp, R. I., Pike, G. E., Van Duuren, M., & Norgate, L. (2001). Developmental changes in the effect of inversion: Using a picture book to investigate face recognition. *Perception*, 30, 85–94.

Brewer, N., & Palmer, M. A. (2010). Eyewitness identification tests. *Legal and Criminological Psychology*, 15(1), 77–96.

Brigham, J. C., & Ready, D. J. (1985). Own-race bias in lineup construction. *Law and Human Behavior*, 9(4), 415–424.

Clark, S. E. (2012). Costs and benefits of eyewitness identification reform: Psychological science and public policy. *Perspectives on Psychological Science*, 7(3), 238–259.

Clark, S. E., Benjamin, A. S., Wixted, J. T., Mickes, L., & Gronlund, S. D. (2015). Eyewitness identification and the accuracy of the criminal justice system. *Policy Insights from the Behavioral and Brain Sciences*, 2(1), 175–186.

Clark, S. E., & Godfrey, R. D. (2009). Eyewitness identification evidence and innocence risk. *Psychonomic Bulletin & Review*, 16(1), 22–42.

Davis, J. P., Gibson, S., & Solomon, C. (2014). The positive influence of creating a holistic facial composite on video line-up identification. *Applied Cognitive Psychology*, 28(5), 634–639.

Davis, J. P., Thorniley, S., Gibson, S., & Solomon, C. (2015). Holistic facial composite construction and subsequent lineup identification accuracy: Comparing adults and children. *The Journal of Psychology*, 150(1), 1–20.

De Craen, A. J., Kaptchuk, T. J., Tijssen, J. G., & Kleijnen, J. (1999). Placebos and placebo effects in medicine: Historical overview. *Journal of the Royal Society of Medicine*, 92(10), 511–515.

Deffenbacher, K. A., Bornstein, B. H., & Penrod, S. D. (2006). Mugshot exposure effects: Retroactive interference, mugshot commitment, source confusion, and unconscious transference. *Law and Human Behavior*, 30(3), 287–307.

Diamond, R., & Carey, S. (1986). Why faces are and are not special: An effect of expertise. *Journal of Experimental Psychology: General*, 115, 107–117.

Dysart, J. E., Lawson, V. Z., & Rainey, A. (2012). Blind lineup administration as a prophylactic against the postidentification feedback effect. *Law and Human Behavior*, 36(4), 312–319.

Dysart, J. E., Lindsay, R. C. L., Hammond, R., & Dupuis, P. (2001). Mug shot exposure prior to lineup identification: Interference, transference, and commitment effects. *Journal of Applied Psychology*, 86(6), 1280–1284.

Fanselow, M. S., & Buckhout, R. F. (1976). *Nonverbal cueing as a source of biasing information in eyewitness identification testing*. Center for Responsive Psychology Monograph No. CR-26. New York: Brooklyn College CUNY.

Fawcett, J. M., Russell, E. J., Peace, K. A., & Christie, J. (2013). Of guns and geese: A meta-analytic review of the 'weapon focus' literature. *Psychology, Crime & Law*, 19(1), 35–66.

Gaertner, S., & Harrington, J. (2009). Successful eyewitness identification reform: Ramsey County's blind sequential lineup protocol. *The Police Chief*, LXXVI(4), April 2009; http://www.policechiefmagazine.org/magazine/index.cfm?fuseaction=display&article_id=1776&issue_id=42009

Hancock, P. J., Bruce, V., & Burton, A. M. (2000). Recognition of unfamiliar faces. *Trends in Cognitive Sciences*, 4(9), 330–337.

Havard, C., & Memon, A. (2013). The mystery man can help reduce false identification for child witnesses: Evidence from video line-ups. *Applied Cognitive Psychology*, 27(1), 50–59.

Havard, C., Memon, A., Laybourn, P., & Cunningham, C. (2012). Own-age bias in video lineups: A comparison between children and adults. *Psychology, Crime & Law*, 18(10), 929–944.

Horry, R., Halford, P., Brewer, N., Milne, R., & Bull, R. (2014). Archival analyses of eyewitness identification test outcomes: What can they tell us about eyewitness memory? *Law and Human Behavior*, 38(1), 94–108.

Hulley, S. B., Cummings, S. R., Browner, W. S., Grady, D. G., & Newman, T. B. (2013). *Designing clinical research* (4th edn). Philadelphia, PA: Lippincott Williams & Wilkins.

Innocence Project (2016). Innocence Project Case Profiles. Retrieved January 21, 2016 from: http://www.innocenceproject.org/

Karmiloff-Smith, A., Thomas, M., Annaz, D., Humphreys, K., Ewing, S., Brace, N., Van Duuren, M., Pike, G., Grice, S., & Campbell, R. (2004). Exploring the Williams syndrome face-processing debate: The importance of building developmental trajectories. *Journal of Child Psychology and Psychiatry*, 45(7), 1258–1274.

Levett, L. M. (2013). Co-witness information influences whether a witness is likely to choose from a lineup. *Legal and Criminological Psychology*, 18(1), 168–180.

Lindsay, R. C., Mansour, J. K., Beaudry, J. L., Leach, A. M., & Bertrand, M. I. (2009). Sequential lineup presentation: Patterns and policy. *Legal and Criminological Psychology*, 14(1), 13–24.

Lindsay, R. C., Pozzulo, J. D., Craig, W., Lee, K., & Corber, S. (1997). Simultaneous lineups, sequential lineups, and showups: Eyewitness identification decisions of adults and children. *Law and Human Behavior*, 21(4), 391–404.

Lindsay, R. C., & Wells, G. L. (1980). What price justice? *Law and Human Behavior*, 4(4), 303–313.

Meissner, C. A., & Brigham, J. C. (2001). Thirty years of investigating the own-race bias in memory for faces: A meta-analytic review. *Psychology, Public Policy, and Law*, 7(1), 3–35.

Meissner, C. A., Sporer, S. L., & Schooler, J. W. (2007). Person descriptions as eyewitness evidence. In R. C. L. Lindsay, D. F. Ross, J. D. Read, & M. P. Toglia (eds), *Handbook of eyewitness psychology: Memory for people* (pp. 1–34). Mahwah, NJ: Erlbaum.

Memon, A., Hope, L., & Bull, R. (2003). Exposure duration: Effects on eyewitness accuracy and confidence. *British Journal of Psychology*, 94(3), 339–354.

Mullen, E. J., & Streiner, D. L. (2006). The evidence for and against evidence-based practice. In A. R. Roberts & K. Yeager (eds), *Foundations of evidence-based social work practice* (pp. 21–34). New York: Oxford University Press.

National Research Council (2014). *Identifying the culprit: Assessing eyewitness identification.* Report from the Committee on Scientific Approaches to Understanding and Maximizing the Validity and Reliability of Eyewitness Identification in Law Enforcement and the Courts; Committee on Science, Technology, and Law; Policy and Global Affairs; Committee on Law and Justice; Division of Behavioral and Social Sciences and Education; National Research Council. National Academies Press. http://www.nap.edu/catalog/18891/identifying-the-culprit-assessing-eyewitness-identification

Nutt, D. J., King, L. A., & Phillips, L. D. (2010). Drug harms in the UK: A multicriteria decision analysis. *The Lancet*, 376(9752), 1558–1565.

Nutt, D. (2015). When evidence and politics collide: The David Nutt affair. Presentation at the Centre for Crime and Justice Studies, September, London.

Paine, C. B., Pike, G. E., Brace, N. A., & Westcott, H. L. (2008). Children making faces: The effect of age and prompts on children's facial composites of unfamiliar faces. *Applied Cognitive Psychology*, 22(4), 455–474.

Palmer, M. A., & Brewer, N. (2012). Sequential lineup presentation promotes less-biased criterion setting but does not improve discriminability. *Law and Human Behavior*, 36(3), 247–255.

Paterson, H. (2010). *Co-witnesses talk: The effects of discussion on eyewitness memory.* USA and UK: VDM Verlag Dr Muller.

Paterson, H. M., & Kemp, R. I. (2006). Comparing methods of encountering post-event information: The power of co-witness suggestion. *Applied Cognitive Psychology*, 20(8), 1083–1099.

Peterson, J., Sommers, I., Baskin, D., & Johnson, D. (2010). *The role and impact of forensic evidence in the criminal justice process.* Revised final report. Washington, DC: National Institute of Justice.

Pike, G., Brace, N., & Kynan, S. (2002). *The visual identification of suspects: Procedures and practice.* A Publication of the Policing and Reducing Crime Unit, Home Office Research, Development and Statistics Directorate, Briefing Note 2(02). London: Home Office.

Pike, G. (Writer/Academic consultant), & Fletcher-Hill, T. (Director). (2010, April 17). Episode 1 (Television series episode). In Fletcher-Hill, T. (Executive Producer) and Shiers, K. (Producer), *Eyewitness.* London, UK: British Broadcasting Company.

Pike, G., Havard, C., & Ness, H. (2014). Putting research evidence into practice using the Mystery Face Procedure. *Report to the College of Policing*, April 2014.

Police and Criminal Evidence Act 1984 (s.60(1)(a)) Code of Practice (D) on identification of persons. Section 2: Identification by witnesses (2005). London: Home Office Communication Directorate.

Read, J. D., Tollestrup, P., Hammersley, R., McFadzen, E., & Christensen, A. (1990). The unconscious transference effect: Are innocent bystanders ever misidentified? *Applied Cognitive Psychology*, 4(1), 3–31.

Rose, R. A., Bull, R., & Vrij, A. (2005). Non-biased lineup instructions do matter – a problem for older witnesses. *Psychology, Crime & Law*, 11(2), 147–159.

Sauerland, M., & Sporer, S. L. (2009). Fast and confident: Postdicting eyewitness identification accuracy in a field study. *Journal of Experimental Psychology: Applied*, 15(1), 46–62.

Seale-Carlisle, T. M., & Mickes, L. (2016). US line-ups outperform UK line-ups. *Open Science*, 3(9); doi:00A0;10.1098/rsos.160300.

Sherman, L. W. (2013). The rise of evidence-based policing: Targeting, testing, and tracking. *Crime and Justice*, 42(1), 377–451.

Snook, B., Doan, B., Cullen, R. M., Kavanagh, J. M., & Eastwood, J. (2009). Publication and research trends in police psychology: A review of five forensic psychology journals. *Journal of Police and Criminal Psychology*, 24(1), 45–50.

Steblay, N. K. (2013). Lineup instructions. In B. L. Cutler (ed.), *Reform of eyewitness identification procedures* (pp. 68–72). Washington, DC: American Psychological Association.

Steblay, N. K. (2015). Scientific advances in eyewitness identification evidence. *William Mitchell Law Review*, 41(3), 101–137.

Steblay, N., Dysart, J., Fulero, S., & Lindsay, R. C. (2001). Eyewitness accuracy rates in sequential and simultaneous lineup presentations: A meta-analytic comparison. *Law and Human Behavior*, 25(5), 459–473.

Steblay, N. K., Dysart, J. E., & Wells, G. L. (2011). Seventy-two tests of the sequential lineup superiority effect: A meta-analysis and policy discussion. *Psychology, Public Policy, and Law*, 17(1), 99–139.

TannerJr, W. P., & Swets, J. A. (1954). A decision-making theory of visual detection. *Psychological Review*, 61(6), 401–409.

Topp-Manriquez, L. D., McQuiston, D., & Malpass, R. S. (2016). Facial composites and the misinformation effect: How composites distort memory. *Legal and Criminological Psychology*, 21(2), 372–389.

Tredoux, C. (2002). A direct measure of facial similarity and its relation to human similarity perceptions. *Journal of Experimental Psychology: Applied*, 8(3), 180–193.

Valentine, T. (2009). Quoted in 'Wrongful conviction throws spotlight on unreliability of eyewitness evidence', *The Guardian*, 18 August 2009. See: http://www.theguardian.com/uk/2009/aug/18/eyewitness-evidence-wrongful-conviction

Valentine, T., & Heaton, P. (1999). An evaluation of the fairness of police line-ups and video identifications. *Applied Cognitive Psychology*, 13(1), S59–S72.

Wagenaar, W. A., & Van Der Schrier, J. H. (1996). Face recognition as a function of distance and illumination: A practical tool for use in the courtroom. *Psychology, Crime and Law*, 2(4), 321–332.

Wells, G. L. (1984). The psychology of lineup identifications. *Journal of Applied Social Psychology*, 14, 89–103.

Wells, G. L. (2014). Eyewitness identification probative value, criterion shifts, and policy regarding the sequential lineup. *Current Directions in Psychological Science*, 23(1), 11–16.

Wells, G. L., Cutler, B. L., & Hasel, L. E. (2009). The Duke-lacrosse rape investigation: How not to do eyewitness identification procedures. In M. Seigel (ed.), *Race to*

injustice: Lessons learned from the Duke University lacrosse rape case (pp. 307–321). Durham, NC: Carolina Academic Press.
Wells, G. L., Leippe, M. R., & Ostrom, T. M. (1979). Guidelines for empirically assessing the fairness of a lineup. *Law and Human Behavior*, 3(4), 285–293.
Wells, G. L., & Olson, E. A. (2002). Eyewitness identification: Information gain from incriminating and exonerating behaviors. *Journal of Experimental Psychology: Applied*, 8(3), 155–167.
Wells, G. L., Small, M., Penrod, S. J., Malpass, R. S., Fulero, S. M., & Brimacombe, C. A. E. (1998). Eyewitness identification procedures: Recommendations for lineups and photospreads. *Law and Human Behavior*, 22, 603–647.
Wells, G. L., & Turtle, J. W. (1986). Eyewitness identification: The importance of lineup models. *Psychological Bulletin*, 99(3), 320–329.

Chapter 8

From interrogation to investigative interviewing

The application of psychology

Andy Griffiths and Asbjørn Rachlew

Introduction

The significance of confessions within the investigation and trial process is historically established through the perceived association between confession and redemption within religious trials, which assumed all confessions sincere and reliable (Trainum, 2016). However, at the start of the twentieth century, Munsterburg (1908), a pioneering criminal psychologist, highlighted the potential unreliability of confessions and ignited a debate over the reliability of suspect testimony that continues to the current day (e.g. Gudjonsson, 2003; Leo, 2008; Meissner et al., 2012). This debate, about the most effective way in which to obtain reliable information when questioning a criminal suspect, has produced a body of research literature which acknowledges that, globally, thousands of miscarriages of justice have been caused by coercive, oppressive or inept police behaviour when questioning suspects; a situation exacerbated by certain suspects' vulnerability (see Chapter 1, this volume). Consequently, the questioning of suspects by law enforcement is now considered one of the most controversial subjects in the whole investigative process (Softley, 1980; Leo, 2008).

Despite the recent acknowledgement that the relevant psychological research has provided "decades of data" and a "significant amount of knowledge on what works" (HIG, 2016a), there is still no universally agreed approach on how police best conduct this most important task. Where psychological theory is identified within ethical law enforcement techniques it is important to distinguish whether this is due to conscious incorporation within properly designed training programmes or simply by chance, through heuristic evolution (see Chapters 2 and 12, this volume), or the natural communication skills of individual officers (Baldwin, 1993; Leo, 1996a). Furthermore, quasi-psychological techniques are also used within guilt presumptive approaches (e.g. the Reid technique) as a way of gaining an admission (Inbau, Reid, Buckley, & Jayne, 2011). It appears, therefore, that across the world as a whole, the range of techniques utilised is generally governed not by empirically based psychological theory but by the culture, politics and legislation of individual countries (Walsh et al., 2016), which influence the overall mindset and approach of both individual officers and the justice systems of those countries. Therefore, in discussing how much psychological theory has been incorporated into the questioning of suspects this chapter will also explore these important contextual variables.

The chapter discusses three country specific case studies in exploring the level of psychological theory used in practise. The first of these is the United Kingdom, which led the world in attempting to operationalise the presumption of innocence within a legal framework that controlled the behaviour of officers questioning suspects (Police and Criminal Evidence Act, 1984). The second is the Norway, who followed the UK's 'turn-around' operation, from interrogation *to* investigative interviewing. With great relevance to the concept of this book, it was Norwegian police officer practitioners who undertook psychological study that evolved the original PEACE approach into the KREATIV (Fahsing & Rachlew, 2009) philosophy through critical thinking and subsequent inclusion of further psychological concepts.[1] The third case study will examine the USA, which has not seen the same legal, policy or widespread practice changes as either the UK or Scandinavia (Meissner et al., 2017), despite academic literature highlighting the flaws within their system (e.g. Kassin, 1997; Leo, 2008; Kassin et al., 2010; Garrett, 2015) and regular miscarriages linked to coercive police interrogation (www.innocenceproject.org). In fact, it is only since 2009 that a government led body called the High Value Detainee Interrogation Group (HIG) has been conducting research on the subject; even though motivated by a desire to identify an alternative method of interrogation for terrorists as part of a response to the 9/11 attacks. Following this case study analysis, the chapter will broaden its focus by discussing the fundamental issue of the influence of mindset on both developing psychological theory and interview practice before presenting our conclusions.

Interrogation and investigative interviewing

It is important to address the distinction between the terms *interrogation* and *investigative interviewing* prior to any discussion on the subject, as the terms are often casually and incorrectly interchanged. The historic literature around *interrogation* refers to a heuristic approach, including coercive and/or manipulative techniques designed to obtain a confession. *Investigative interviewing* is an evidence based approach designed to gather and test accurate and reliable information from suspects of crime, balancing the need for accurate information from suspects with respect for individual human rights and the rule of law (Williamson, 1993). To confuse matters, the recent HIG initiative in the USA has retained the term interrogation in its terminology, while simultaneously promulgating a research driven approach that is closer to investigative interviewing in its philosophy and techniques. For the purpose of this chapter, we will use the term investigative interviewing to describe the process of questioning a criminal suspect while preserving the presumption of innocence.

In contrast, we see torture, psychological coercion and manipulative confession oriented interrogation techniques as (different) means to the same end; all used by law enforcement to confirm a belief of guilt. Although manipulative techniques are less brutal than more obviously coercive means, the mindset of interrogating detectives is identical in that they are trying to solve their (sometimes complex) tasks with a methodology designed to confirm their presumption of guilt. This is because dominant thinking styles produce this behaviour (see Chapter 3) and also because some justice systems still value confessions as the queen of evidence; hence upholding the widespread myth that torture and other coercive interrogation tactics represent an efficient way of inducing information and solving crime (Bybee, 2002; Inbau et al., 2011).

The UK 'turn-round' operation

In the UK, the sequence of events that moved the police away from a confession-focused culture to a less coercive, and more professional approach was triggered 40 years ago by the Confait case (Gudjonsson, 2003). After the Court of Appeal quashed the convictions of Colin Lattimore (aged 18 with learning difficulties), Ronnie Leighton (14 and illiterate) and Ahmed Salih (15 and of Turkish origin), who had had allegedly confessed to murder and arson, a subsequent official enquiry (Fisher, 1977) recommended a review of criminal justice procedures (Royal Commission on Criminal Procedure (RCCP), 1981). In turn, this led to the Police and Criminal Evidence Act (PACE) 1984, which regulated police questioning of suspects, and introduced the requirement for the electronic (tape) recording of questioning in the police station. A decade after the RCCP, a landmark event occurred with the creation of a national investigative interview model known as PEACE (Central Planning and Training Unit (CPTU), 1992a, 1992b; see also Chapter 11). However, in discussing the influence of psychological theory on these developments, it is noteworthy that at the outset its contribution was not universally welcomed. Indeed, Fisher rejected the expert opinion of a psychologist, Barrie Irving, that the confessions in the Confait case were coerced. It is also the case that contextual factors, namely organisational culture and the autonomous nature of police forces, were also major influences.

The RCCP (1981) commissioned several research studies to examine the way that police questioned suspects in custody. In Study 1 – *'The Psychological Approach'* – Irving and Hilgendorf (1980) reviewed the literature on interrogation, then wholly American. They described interrogation skills training in the San Francisco police department, noting that British police forces offered nothing similar. In Study 2 Irving (1980) conducted an observational study of interrogation practice, examining 60 interrogations in one English police station, to establish whether that within the American literature occurred in Britain. In 47 out of 60 interrogations Irving identified distinct patterns: authoritative and dominating (23/47), business like and professional (16/47) and overtly friendly (8/47). He also reported how detectives attempted to obtain confessions by manipulating suspects' self esteem, social identity and relationships, bluffing over evidence, and offering deals (Gudjonsson, 2003). He concluded that the officers were using the same techniques identified as those taught to American officers. In Study 4 Softley (1980) observed 245 interviews across four different police areas. He found officers used a variety of tactics such as pointing out contradictions in the suspect's account, or between that account and other evidence (22 per cent), stressing the overwhelming evidence (13 per cent) and employing friendly conversation (11 per cent).There were relatively few breaches of the rules of evidence obtaining at the time.

Research by a serving detective (Walkley, 1982) conducted contemporaneously to the RCCP studies casts doubt on their ecological validity. Walkley surveyed detectives regarding their preferred interrogation tactics. Forty-three per cent of respondents agreed that "It is sometimes helpful to slap a suspect across the face", and 40 per cent agreed that "With some suspects the only way of getting their respect is by using some form of physical force". Detectives responding to another detective were uninhibited: physical force was a commonplace interrogation technique.

PACE (1984) defined an interview with a suspect, as "The questioning of a person about their involvement, or suspected involvement, in a criminal offence" (Code C.11 PACE, 1984). It also significantly addressed the fundamental issues of reliability and the admissibility of confession evidence obtained through oppression (s.76), and also unfairness (s. 78). A series of judgements in the Court of Appeal, many informed by psychologists' expert testimony concerning reliability, further defined the common law on oppression (Gudjonsson, 2003). Thus psychologists and their research when assisting the RCCP and when giving evidence in court contributed to shaping the law and therefore police practice. In effect providing the "rulebook" specifying what was *not* permissible. It is nonetheless true that until the universal installation of recording equipment, which took several years, behaviours disclosed in Walkley's research (1982) continued being evidenced sporadically in cases in the Appeal courts.

Two years prior to the enactment of PACE the Metropolitan Police in London introduced Human Awareness Training (HAT) as a means of combatting serious problems in police management of encounters with the public and prejudice identified within the workforce (Cridland, 1984). HAT sought to train officers in "handling people, finding out facts and applying the law" (Shepherd, 1984, p. 290) by progressively developing officers' interpersonal skills: communication, then conversation, and then "purposive encounters" (p. 292) with the public, including interviews about criminal offences. The programme incorporated material on underlying ethics and psychology of, as well as through video-recorded practical exercises developing skill in, communication and conversation. Shepherd identified the core requirement for conversation management and investigative interviewing – in contrast to interrogation. In 1983 Shepherd developed a simple framework for conversation: GEMAC – an acronym for Greeting, Explanation, Mutual Activity, Closure (Shepherd, 1986a). This framework defines interviewing as a task of joint orientation that involves mutual respect, and a commitment to empathy as the cornerstone of effective police interviewing. From 1985 onwards, one British police force, Merseyside, delivered investigative interviewing founded on conversation management to detectives, and to trainers from approximately one third of the police forces in England and Wales through an Interview Development Unit (Shepherd, 1986b; Shepherd & Kite, 1988, 1989). Other forces continued to train detectives in confession-focused interrogation using strategies (Mortimer & Shepherd, 1999) advocated by Walkley (1987) or the Reid Technique (Inbau et al., 2011). However, as electronic recording equipment became widespread the manipulative tactics observed in Irving's RCCP research decreased (Irving & McKenzie, 1989). The initial post-PACE situation in England and Wales was therefore one of co-existence between the conversation management philosophy and strategies philosophy (Shepherd & Kite, 1988). This was the case until pressure for change built through a series of successful appeals in high profile cases, in which confessions were coerced (e.g. Guildford Four terrorist case, see Gudjonsson, 2003). In late 1990 the Home Office directed that there would be a single, national approach to questioning suspects – investigative interviewing – that was not confession oriented (Shepherd, 1991).

Following upon this directive a working group was formed to develop a national model. Comprising police officer, lawyers and psychologists it incorporated materials from Merseyside Police on the philosophy and practice of conversation management. An early challenge was to tackle the historical police belief that interrogating suspects was *real detective work* and a skill – whereas interviewing victims and witnesses was neither (Shepherd & Griffiths, 2013). The eventual model – PEACE (Central Planning and Training Unit (CPTU), 1992a, 1992b) – placed professional questioning of suspects, victims and witnesses on a par: founded on the same psychological and ethical foundations, and demanding the same conversation management skills (Bull, 2014).

To support the implementation of the model, the Home Office (Association of Chief Police Officers (ACPO), 1992) issued a circular to all forces. It introduced the term *investigative interviewing to the whole service*, clearly stating that the term *interrogation* was incompatible with the new ethos. The first three principles emphasise this change in practitioner mindset.

1 The role of investigative interviewing is to obtain accurate and reliable information from suspects, victims and witnesses, in order to discover the truth about matters under investigation.
2 Investigative interviewing should be approached with an open mind. Information obtained from the person who is being interviewed should always be tested against what the interviewing officer already knows or what can be established.
3 When questioning anyone a police officer must act fairly in the circumstances of each individual case.

(ACPO, 1992)

The design of a model, and a publication of principles provided no guarantee that real life practice would change. An evaluation of the pilot course was favourable (McGurk, Carr, & McGurk, 1993). However, it was delivered by trainers close to the design team, and the students were volunteers, mainly young in service without the hardened cynicism of older detectives (Griffiths, 2008). To change the mindset of 140,000 officers in England and Wales was an immense task. The training programme was "cascaded" to 43 separate forces. While psychological theory and knowledge within the model certainly were a large part of the UK turn-around operation, cultural and ethical issues also dominated much of the pioneering work. Shepherd (1991) drew the analogy between an officer's use of words and a weapon, arguing that unethical interviewing by a police officer is akin to using a loaded gun "Malevolently, to coerce the person opposite to submit to the officers view of the world. Language will always be a loaded weapon. The only difference between the firearms and interviewing context is that in the latter every officer is armed" (p. 54).[2]

To inculcate a different mindset within investigators necessitated an "anti-coercion bias" within the original PEACE training. This had the practical effect of rendering skills development secondary. Alison (1998) observed, "The general theme is ... defensive in its tone and whilst it [PEACE] alerts officers to the dangers outlined here, it provides little positive guidance or assistance in formulating strategies to improve information retrieval from suspects" (p. 133). This view was confirmed by a Home Office sponsored national evaluation conducted by a police officer and psychologist (Clarke & Milne, 2001) Few examples of oppressive behaviour were observed, but skill levels were variable.

The turn-round operation required a second wave, that focused equally on skills development, to evolve the PEACE methodology (Griffiths & Milne, 2006). This second wave had the commitment of practitioner pioneers who crucially realised that: Officers dealing with more complex crime needed more sophisticated and in-depth training; not all officers possessed the potential to reach the required standard; and the "one size fits all" ethos behind the original PEACE model was more effective in preventing miscarriages than raising the skill levels of officers (Griffiths & Milne, 2006). Supported by the results and recommendations of the earlier Home Office evaluation (Clarke & Milne, 2001), the evolved strategy became known as the tiered approach (Griffiths & Milne, 2006) and was underwritten by a national agreement from all police forces in the country, demonstrating the interdependency of research and policy.

Since the RCCP (1981), three decades of research in the UK by cognitive and social psychologists on how the police interview suspects has produced a significant body of evidence on (i) common flaws, (ii) what police officers think of their own techniques, and (iii) what techniques are most effective. To that end *investigative interviewing*, as defined by Home Office in the UK in 1992, developed and refined by pioneering scholars in close cooperation with British police, has influenced police training outside the UK and extended to various regions of the world (Williamson, Milne, & Savage, 2009). The British experience shows an evolution in the contribution of psychologists to the development of interviewing practice: fulfilling initially the role of external dispassionate, sometimes ignored observer, then one of harsh critic, often as an expert witness in cases involving coercion and false confessions, then as advisors in training, law and policy development, before finally becoming respected compatriots as co-trainers, mentors and operationally deployed within the police itself. An interesting feature in the latest stage is the merging of the two fields, with police officers (and increasingly so) undertaking graduate and post-graduate studies in forensic psychology.

The Scandinavian 'second-jumpers'

The influence of police pracademics[3] was even stronger in our second case study. The initial catalyst for change in Scandinavia was provided by a disputed confession case where the expert witness evidence of two UK forensic psychologists whose analysis resulted in the acquittal of a young defendant (Fahsing & Rachlew, 2009). The fundamental problem with the interviews was the extreme use of isolation, combined with an instrumental-like, therapeutic rapport building, solely designed to obtain a confession from someone presumed, in the eyes of the interviewing officer, to be guilty (Gudjonsson, 2003, pp. 590–614). The case also revealed that Norwegian police officers had little or no formal training in how to question suspects, and utilised secret interrogation techniques (Rachlew, 1999), where the most[4] experienced and highly regarded detectives personally passed on their 'tricks of the trade' (Fahsing & Rachlew, 2009). The heuristic approach included various manipulative techniques designed to get the suspect to confess. This informal 'training' was supplemented by informal written advice. For example:

> Use your influence to 'soften him up' from the very beginning. Your goal is to become the only one providing him with comfort and support in his difficult situation. You control who he is allowed to have contact with, and in that way prevent him receiving psychological support from others.

The case shocked the Norwegian justice system, and led to Norway's own turn-round operation; initiated by two senior officers who had previously attended UK conferences in investigative psychology and gained an understanding of academic, critical thinking.[5] Two detectives were sponsored to complete UK forensic psychology MSc courses, and initiate, upon their return, a national, investigative interviewing training course (KREATIV). The project was commissioned by the National University Police College in 2002, based on a pilot training programme in Oslo. The training was heavily influenced by the British PEACE course, including the use of UK experts to educate Norwegian trainers, and was made mandatory for all detectives seeking further specialisation.

Norway had the advantage of being the 'second jumper' in following the UK, as pointed out by Rachlew (1999):

> The P.E.A.C.E. course stands out as a solid foundation, suitable for Norwegian interviewers .... A training program in Norway can avoid the same

mistakes and take advantage of the development Investigative Interviewing has undergone in Britain during the last 15 years.

The evolution of positive psychological influence on investigative interviewing in Norway mirrored the experience of the UK; but progress was much quicker and achieved in three years what took two decades in the UK (from 'harsh critics' to 'advisors within'). Apart from the obvious privilege of being a 'second jumper' (with relevant knowledge at hand), and allowing for the relative size of each country, it is our contention that swifter progress was achieved because: (1) the change came from within the police force; (2) the new methodology (and thinking style) was embraced and launched by a National University Police College; (3) it was supported by other stakeholders, including the General Prosecutor's Office and a Supreme Court ruling; and, finally, (4) it was operated by police officers with post-graduate studies in forensic psychology.

The last point is crucial, particularly in the refinement process. With knowledge of critical studies and 10 years' experience with PEACE training in the UK, the Norwegian approach addressed theoretical, practical, pedagogical and cultural issues. For instance, concerns had been raised that UK officers were somewhat reluctant to apply cognitive interview techniques due to limited understanding of the theories underpinning the techniques (Clarke & Milne, 2001; Dando, Wilcox, & Milne, 2008). Consequently, time and resources were invested in the creation of training materials on human memory. To prevent what had happened in the UK, where the PEACE training had drifted from its original 'package' with local interpretations (Clarke & Milne, 2001), the Norwegian training materials could not be altered without approval from the Norwegian University Police College. Furthermore, trainers, accredited only after successfully completing courses in pedagogy (three weeks) and 'Investigative Interviewing' (three weeks), also attend annual refresher seminars covering new theory, case law and practical issues. The complete training package is currently undergoing its fourth major revision. Also, in Norway senior officers were amongst the first students, stimulating a deeper, organisational and cultural understanding of the new philosophy and addressing[6] Shepherd's (1991) assessment that training individual officers will achieve nothing if the organisation does not develop a matching appropriate moral infrastructure.

Disclosure of evidence: the key development?

The most significant enhancement in the process of converting the PEACE course from UK to Norway draws upon evidential studies carried out by the legal scholar Christian Diesen (1994), [7] who examined how members of the Swedish Supreme Court evaluated evidence presented to them. For Norwegian detectives returning from the UK with degrees in forensic and investigative psychology, Diesen's pragmatic model for the testing of evidence formed a possible solution to the 'missing link' in the psychological literature on investigative interviewing in general, and the PEACE model in particular (Fahsing & Rachlew, 2009).

In short, Diesen's model (1994) "Alternative hypothesis: A pragmatic model for the testing of evidence" can briefly be described as the opposite of the rationale behind confession oriented interrogation techniques in which detectives peruse information, confirming their view of the world. Instead, Diesen encouraged all legal factfinders (police, prosecution, defence lawyers and judges) to identify alternative hypotheses, i.e. to look for reasonable, alternative explanations for the evidence pointing towards the suspect, and actively test them by perusing information liable to challenge or support the alternative (plausible) explanations. If the suspicion is not weakened through the testing of the alternative hypotheses, the thesis of guilt is strengthened. As we will explain in more detail below, a tactical element was added to these ideas; namely, to delay disclosure of evidence in suspect interviews until the alternative hypotheses are explored in detail.

The necessity of a strategy on what, when, why and how to disclose evidence was emphasised in the *Practical Guide to Investigative Interviewing* (National Crime Faculty, 1998, p. 77). However, the instructions to employ a disclosure strategy were not accompanied by positive guidance, models or logical reasoning. The guidelines failed to inform officers of what the objectives of such a strategy were within the ethos of investigative interviewing. Without a clear objective, it became difficult (impossible) to explain or articulate best practice. Consequently, strategic disclosure was not embedded into the PEACE module. The call for a strategy, without articulating what it would look like in practical terms, left an important part of information retrieval from suspects unresolved – a situation still not resolved, we would argue, in the latest version of the national guidelines on investigative interviewing in the UK (College of Policing, 2013). As pointed out by Sukumar, Hodgson and Wade (2016) "Some police are completely forthcoming with evidence, disclosing extensive detail of the case matter to lawyers, while others reveal no evidence at all prior to the suspect interview".

Throughout the Norwegian refinement of the PEACE model, it has been argued that investigative interviewing necessitates strategic disclosure of evidence for a variety of reasons. As described in more detail below, one of them is the suspect's right to be presumed innocent. The fact that detectives need a strategy stimulating both open mindedness and the retrieval of verifiable information is another.

In combination with Diesen's pragmatic model, KREATIV provided Norwegian detectives with clear and positive instructions on how, when and – all importantly – *why* they should delay disclosure until all plausible, alternative explanations had been tested through (P) systematic preparation, (E) empathic rapport building, (A) the use of open-ended questions, active listening and strategic probing, (C) professional closure and (E) systematic evaluation (analysis) of the information obtained. As later explained by Fahsing and Rachlew (2009, p. 54):

> Prior to the introduction of the tactical interview model, Norwegian police officers (including the authors) had a hard time explaining exactly what characterises a successful interview strategy. We could not describe what essential components, or constituent parts, would separate a well-conducted interview from a well-conducted tactical interview.

The model was introduced through the National Police University College in 2001 (Rachlew, 2002), launched as a "tactical interviewing technique" in line with the ethos of investigative interviewing and immediately embraced by police detectives (Fahsing & Rachlew, 2006). Forensic psychologists from Sweden were also inspired by Diesen's ideas (Hartwig et al., 2005). Hartwig's work has been further developed and tested; predominantly by psychologists as a strategy to assist lie-detection, today globally known as the SUE-technique (Hartwig, Granhag, & Luke, 2014), discussed further below. In the Norwegian process of change, however, Diesen's original model formed the basis for a methodology designed to change the mindset of Norwegian detectives (Rachlew & Fahsing, 2015). Norwegian detectives were encouraged to generate and test alternative hypotheses by actively searching for information indicating innocence; hence – as acknowledged by the UN special rapporteur on torture in a report to the UN General Assembly – "helping to ensure that the presumption of innocence is respected while strengthening the case against a guilty suspect" (Mendez, 2016, art 54).

The US: lagging behind or deliberately different?

The US first addressed concerns over the actions of police officers when questioning suspects before either the UK or Scandinavia when the 1931 Wickersham Commission outlawed the physical abuse of suspects, known as the 'third degree' (Trainum, 2016). The US Supreme Court has also reinforced the right to silence for suspects (*Miranda v Arizona*, 384 U.S. 436, 1966). However, the federal structure of government, decentralised nature of policing and dominant political ideology have precluded nationwide government intervention and therefore national legislative change on this subject, despite a growing number of publicised miscarriages, many featuring false confessions.

The end of physical abuse, and the parallel rise of forensic science in areas such as ballistics, saw US law enforcement adopt quasi-psychological interrogation methods, the best known of which is the Reid technique (see Trainum, 2016 for a detailed description of this period, and Chapter 11 this volume for a more detailed description of the Reid technique). Empirical research into a core part of the technique known as The Behavioural Analysis Interview (Inbau, Reid, Buckley, & Jayne, 2011), which claims that certain non-verbal behaviours are diagnostic of guilt, has undermined the myth that there are reliable and consistent physiological indicators of guilt (Vrij, 2008).

Given the quasi-psychological basis of the Reid technique, and its widespread use by US law enforcement (Leo, 2008; Kelly & Meissner, 2016), it is surprising that no empirical studies on real-life interrogation were conducted in the US between 1960 and 1996 – a period spanning the lead up to and three decades after the *Miranda* ruling on self-incrimination (Leo, 1996b). Hence, Leo's (1996a) observational study of the tactics used in 500 police interrogations is an important piece of research on a par with research conducted for the RCCP (1981) or Baldwin's (1993) study in the UK. Leo found a link between incriminating admissions and (a) the number of different tactics used and (b) the length of the interrogation, concluding there was a correlation between the effort of the interrogator and 'success'. The single most successful tactic was *appealing to the suspect's conscience*, utilised in 97 per cent of the 64 per cent of interviews deemed successful across the sample. The other three most successful tactics were *identifying contradictions in the suspect's account* (91 per cent), *the use of praise or flattery* (91 per cent) and *offering moral justification or excuses* (90 per cent). A wider range of tactics were associated with a lack of success, with the most frequent being *touching the suspect* (88 per cent), *invoking guilt* (87 per cent), and *behavioural analysis questions, appealing for co-operation*, and *appeal to detective's authority* (all 84 per cent). Leo concluded, in a hindsight diagnosis, that "in the three decades since Miranda American interrogation techniques have become entirely psychological in nature" (1996b, p. 669). In the absence of observational research, US academics have resorted to survey data in attempting to establish what happens in police interrogations (see Kelly & Meissner, 2016, pp. 257–259 for a summary of these results). These data also show the domination of psychologically manipulative and accusatorial tactics (Kelly & Meissner, 2016). This approach to interrogation has to be viewed as a major contributory cause in the numbers of confession-fuelled miscarriages of justice recorded in the same period (Scheck, Neufeld, & Dwyer, 2000; Garrett, 2010). However, neither the rising numbers of false confessions nor authoritative texts describing the problem have produced any reaction from legislators and policy makers within US federal government.

In fact, the next stage of the evolution of US interrogation and interview practice was influenced not by any concern over miscarriages of justice or dubious techniques, but by the aftermath of the 9/11 terrorist attacks (see Chapter 9 this volume). The High Value Detainee Interrogation Group (HIG) was formed in the name of national security to obtain better intelligence from captured terrorists, and as an alternative to the Army Interrogation Manual (US Army, 2006), although its scope does include acting as a focus for the 'best' interrogation techniques on behalf of the federal government (HIG, 2016a, 2016b). Leo (2008, p. 7) highlights the difference between US police interrogation designed to gather incriminating evidence from a suspect and US military interrogation designed to save lives, and it is important to consider this point in detail. Questioning a suspect as part of an investigation, where the focus is an individual's culpability for a criminal act, is different in many respects from questioning for intelligence where the goal is to build an accurate information picture from various sources for further action or a response (see Chapter 11 for more on intelligence interviewing). In a criminal investigation a suspect's answers (or silence in some cases) will be used as part of a decision making process that may result in conviction and punishment. In addition the fear of terrorism invokes strong feelings, and a more lenient attitude to coercive practice, including torture (Houck, Conway, & Repke, 2014; Ames & Lee, 2015), that skews the debate on permissible tactics and limits the applicability of research on terrorism to the investigation of crimes such as rape, assault and murder, that are not politically motivated.

Nevertheless, following a 7-year research programme the HIG has placed before government a ratified body of scientific knowledge (2016b), and recommended certain practices, which are broadly:

- Careful planning and management of first impressions
- Use of models to build and gauge rapport
- Employment of strategies to encourage conversation and to cover specific objectives
- Strategic use of evidence [SUE]
- Use of memory enhancing techniques to discover additional information
- Primary reliance on verbal cues to detect deception
- Close down each interrogation with an intentional planned strategy.

(HIG, 2016a)

In relation to the empirical body of psychological knowledge the HIG (2016a) research concurs with the positive impact of behaviours such as *building rapport, demonstrating empathy, active listening, funnel questioning* encompassed within conversation management (Shepherd & Griffiths, 2013) and KREATIV (Fahsing & Rachlew, 2009; CTI, 2017) and strengthens the evidence base with regard to effective tactics. Likewise, the HIG emphasises that non-verbal cues to deception are not reliable. Therefore, in both positive and negative dimensions, the HIG research supports many of the same behaviours recommended by information gathering interview models. In relation to their work HIG describes a circle where research informs training, training informs practice, which leads to more research (2016a). However, crucially this circle omits any mention of legislation or policy. The HIG has no direct link to the Department of Justice (DoJ) and so lacks an ability to influence policy, law and training providers for law enforcement at local levels within the US; a situation that will limit psychology's influence on investigative practice. In order to maximise the influence of psychological theory the HIG research should be targeted at judges and DoJ policy in order to produce real change. The adversarial system only responds to judicial case law. This is shown, in a legal sense by the period before the eventual *Miranda* ruling (see Leo, 1996b, 2008 for a fuller discussion). Therefore, the HIG's ability to leverage the significant research evidence it has amassed into investigative practice will remain limited unless there is a sea change in the leadership approach.

Evidence from other countries covered in this chapter indicates that the environment is critical to the level of influence empirical evidence is capable of exerting. If one compares the current situation in the US to the phases of the UK turn-around operation (external critic to compatriot), then psychology is in a position somewhere between harsh critic and collaborator in the US. The collaboration is on a unilateral basis, and with 18,000 law enforcement agencies will take a long time to implement unless there is a national policy change.

The involvement of psychologists in the HIG initiative is a progressive and important step. However, it will never reach its potential without a mandate from DoJ to operationalise their work. This is crucial because there is strong evidence of a need for change provided by the Innocence Project database of miscarriages of justice and work conducted by Conviction Integrity Units across the nation. In short, the US DoJ does not seem to embrace the concept of evidence based change.

There are, unfortunately, several reasons for pessimism in this area. First, the DoJ seems notably impervious to the ability of science to inform or influence the rules governing the admissibility of evidence and therefore investigations. This was seen in the recent independent review of forensic comparison techniques, where despite very strong evidence of the admission on sub-standard evidence into a high number of cases from an eminent panel of scientists (PCAST, 2016), the Attorney General refused to implement any of the recommendations (Weedn, 2017). Secondly, the US approach to evidence produced from the questioning of suspects is not codified into law the same way that it is elsewhere, allowing legislators the opportunity to strengthen the rules under which police operate. The admissibility of a suspect's testimony is governed by three constitutional rights (Leo, 2008), These include the right not to self-incriminate, like the UK and unlike the UK, a right not to be questioned. However, should a suspect waive their *Miranda* right not to be questioned, the test of that interrogation is whether any subsequent confession was voluntary. It is recognised that there is a low likelihood of a confession being excluded once obtained (Kassin et al., 2010) but separately, from an investigative point, it is not in the officers' interest to gather information and allow the remainder of the evidence to test the validity of that account at trial. Pre-trial examination of the product of any such interrogation only focuses on two matters; firstly, was the *Miranda* waiver sincere and, secondly, was the subsequent confession voluntary. Furthermore, the USA does not have national legislation mandating the audio or video recording of police questioning of suspects, and this is unlikely to ever change. Federal agencies are directed as a matter of policy to record all interrogations (Cole, 2014) but there is no formal technical specification or audited storage of recordings. Therefore, as a practical consideration there is less data available for evaluation and researchers are dependent on survey data or potentially unrepresentative data samples when attempting to present empirical evidence of appropriate or inappropriate techniques. This situation hampers the construction of a broad evidence base to drive national change. In the absence of these drivers any change is likely to be localised, which will inevitably take longer. As Leo said, "American police in the modern era have succeeded in eliciting confessions by developing interrogation methods that rely on fraud, persuasion, and impression management" (2008, p. 6). In the last few years US funded empirical research prompted by other events has produced a strong evidence base for change (HIG, 2016a, 2016b); however, it appears that government is unwilling to drive change. Overall, US interrogation practice is at crossroads (Kelly & Meissner, 2016; Trainum, 2016). Significant change in real-life interview practice amongst law enforcement across the US now requires strong leadership of the type shown by the UK Home Office's *Principles of Investigative Interviewing* (1992; Schollum, 2017) or the self-generated initiative of the Norwegian police in their own turn-round operation, coupled with open and enthusiastic co-operation with psychologists already conducting laboratory based research which could assist.

Investigative interviewing, human rights and the presumption of innocence

The specific country case studies used within this chapter confirm our initial assertion that there is no universally agreed and applied method of questioning suspects. However, the research evidence referenced demonstrates that there is consensus on the psychological principles that underpin investigative interviewing. Therefore, the 'theory–practice gap' is measured not in fundamental differences in what the research literature shows, but in the strength of other country specific influences such as culture, policy and legislation, which together form a prevailing mindset in relation to human rights and the presumption of innocence that dictates real-life practice. The influence of these factors is particularly apparent when undertaking a thematic examination of a subject common to every interrogation or investigative interview in any country; that is, the way in which police or law enforcement use evidence when questioning suspects. Variants of strategic disclosure of evidence appear to have been a favoured interview strategy by police officers for many decades, perhaps centuries, whether as part of the craft or science approach (Doyle, 1892; King, 2002; van Beek & Hoekendijk, 2015). Different models, theories and principles for strategic disclosure of evidence have emerged from the legal and psychological literature regarding interrogations and investigative interviewing of suspects, particularly so in the last decade (Hartwig, Granhag, Strömwall, & Vrij, 2005; Sellers & Kebbell, 2009; Granhag & Vrij, 2010; Dando & Bull, 2011; Shepherd & Griffiths, 2013; van Beek & Hoekendijk, 2015; HIG, 2016a; Sukumar, Hodgson, & Wade, 2016).

Although strategic disclosure of evidence (SUE) clearly has potential to strengthen fair trial principles and the gathering of accurate and reliable information, it has predominantly been advocated, and hence understood, as a lie-detecting exercise (Sukumar, Hodgson, & Wade, 2016). The SUE technique (Hartwig et al., 2005) has gradually and successfully diverted the longstanding myths of lie detection through emotional responses ('body language') toward a framework more interested in cognitive differences between liars and truth tellers (Granhag & Vrij, 2010). This is a significant contribution as the alleged ability to 'read' a suspect's body-language was – and still is – an essential element of manipulative confession orientated interrogation techniques. However, by exploring Diesen's (1994) model as a lie-detection methodology, instead of the principles underpinning it, we argue that its potential to alter traditional 'lie-catchers' interrogative mindset is reduced. The focus on lie-catching diverts focus away from the core principles of investigative interviewing. The nourishing of the traditional 'lie-catching' paradigm may also explain why human rights lawyers and others concerned with the fairness of police interviews, have misunderstood the logic – and ethos – underpinning the original idea. As pointed out by Rachlew and Fahsing (2015), a typical misconception is that the technique is designed with an objective to exclude or 'rule out' the alternative hypotheses. Perceptions along that singular line do not bring about a new mindset. Neither do strategies to 'pin down', 'encircle', 'enclose' or 'corner' suspects by delaying disclosure. It hampers the much-needed shift away from a confession oriented (confirmative) mindset and constitutes a violation of the abductive logic (see Chapter 3, this volume). The merger of investigative interviewing principles, Diesen's pragmatic model for the testing of evidence and strategic disclosure, shaped an applicable interviewing technique in which training to detect deception during suspect interviews no longer encompassed the objective of the exercise. One of the founders of investigative interviewing, the late Tom Williamson was eager to underline the connection between human rights and investigative interviewing (2006); however, the merging of psychology and human rights has not inspired mainstream, forensic psychology research into this area, and may explain why legal scholars concerned with human rights have expressed concerns related to recent developments in investigative interviewing.

In relation to psychological theory, although the presumption of innocence is a cornerstone of criminal procedures, and clearly incites a number of fundamental psychological questions, the subject is not high profile within the discipline (Cohrs, Maes, Moschener, & Kleinman, 2007; Hulsizer & Woolf, 2012). This is unfortunate because, although a number of legal and political initiatives within the European Community have been promoted to strengthen its member states' ability to apply the presumption of innocence, including a EU directive *on the strengthening of certain aspects of the presumption of innocence*, none of these legal texts addresses the fundamental problem related to human cognition, such as confirmation bias and group think (EU Directive 2016/343). In contrast, when applied as a procedure to operationalise the presumption of innocence, as part of investigative interviewing, strategic disclosure of evidence, guided by abductive logic, includes clear and positive instructions on how, when and – all importantly – why detectives should delay disclosure of the potential evidence forming the suspicion (and/or the case) against the suspect.

From a human rights perspective, all suspects are entitled to enjoy a procedure in which they are provided with an opportunity to demonstrate their innocence under optimal conditions during police interviews (Migacheva, 2015). Investigators with no clear strategy on how to operate the presumption of innocence and fair trial principles may disclose potential evidence at the outskirts of the interview and hence strip an innocent suspect's opportunity to prove their innocence. By disclosing case-related information too early, the police are potentially creating a situation that opens up accusations against an innocent suspect; that he or she may have fabricated the statement, based on the knowledge provided by the police.

Psychologists have demonstrated that one of the reasons why police, prosecutors and judges sometimes fail to distinguish genuine from false confessions, is that false confessions often appear true because they contain content cues associated with truthfulness (Kassin et al., 2010). In his detailed studies of the first 40 documented false confessions uncovered through The Innocence Project in the United States, Garrett (2010) demonstrated that the innocent must have received unique information "that only the perpetrator could have known" in 95 per cent of the cases (38 of 40), and that the crucial information was disclosed by the police. Subsequent analysis revealed a similar pattern (Garrett, 2015). Hence, the testing of alternative explanations in combination with strategic disclosure of evidence is an important step to prevent false confessors appearing credible

The most important feature of the Norwegian development of the PEACE model is that it reduces the risk of premature cognitive closure and confirmation bias (Ask & Granhag, 2005). From a human rights perspective, the model assists fact-finders to operationalise the presumption of innocence in a sustainable way (Mendez, 2016). Sustainable because the collection of information necessarily to test the alternative explanations (hypotheses) will reduce the guilty suspect's opportunity to advance plausible defence strategies at any given stage of the criminal process (Hartwig et al., 2005). Detectives operating the model have already identified and tested the alternatives in their investigation in general, and in the interview of the suspect in particular.

In contrast, the consequence of a guilt-oriented mindset indicated by a preoccupation with lie detection is that, at the investigation level, while many law enforcement officers demonstrate elements of investigative interviewing in their initial questioning, they progress to accusation and persuasion based on subjective and unreliable cues interpreted as guilt. Our understanding of the ethical principles, values and critical thinking communicated by the pioneering creators behind investigative interviewing, suggests that training courses offering such 'combo-packages' have missed the essential point, that to commence with 'investigative interviewing' and then move on to interrogation at the end has been a common, manipulative technique in confession oriented interrogations for decades. The manipulation tactic has been played out in numerous combinations, sometimes with two interviewers; one interviewer (the good guy), one interrogator (the bad guy), alternating the social exchange within the interrogation. In Norwegian training manuals from the late 1990s, detectives were advised to portray themselves as the suspect's best friend – presumably making it more difficult for the suspect to deny the charges to his new 'friend'. In the US similar, manipulative thinking was referred to as "the feather approach" (Napier & Adams, 1998). A related tactic, based on the same logic, has been to divide the interrogation in two distinct parts: An 'informal' part, followed by an official part. The informal approach was particularly popular amongst serious crime detectives who often had their suspect remanded in custody, providing the detectives with plenty of time to manipulate the situation and the suspect (Fahsing & Rachlew, 2009).

The introduction of new terminology in contemporary training packages advocating strategies as outlined above might be offering a new soup, but the dinner remains the same. The fundamental problem identified by scholars in their analysis of suspect interviews across nations is not addressed. Crucially, the 'combo-package' does not facilitate the necessary change of mindset required to move from interrogation to investigative interviewing (Shepherd, 1991). Training, methodology and guidelines encouraging detectives to solve their (sometimes) complex problems by searching for confirmations are not only ignoring knowledge derived from research on human reasoning and decision-making in which good thinking is promoted as a thorough search for an alternative, without favouring the one already on mind (Canter & Alison, 1999); they are in contravention of the mindset required to operationalise the values and principles imbedded in the presumption of innocence, one of the paramount characteristics of fair trials (ECHR art. 6).

The difference between interrogations and investigative interviewing is fundamental and distinct and cannot, as we understand the terms and concepts, be mixed up. As pointed out by the European Committee for the Prevention of Torture (CPT, 2002) in their standard for suspect interviews (art. 34):

> The questioning of criminal suspects is a specialist task, which calls for specific training if it is to be performed in a satisfactory manner. First and foremost, the precise aim of such questioning must be made crystal clear: that aim should be to obtain accurate and reliable information in order to discover the truth about matters under investigation, not to obtain a confession from someone already presumed, in the eyes of the interviewing officers, to be guilty.

We acknowledge that all interpersonal communication, including ordinary conversation, often involves rhetorical devices that are (more or less conscious) attempts to persuade others (Alison, 1998). But psychological research, designed to persuade suspects to cooperate with the state, wave their fundamental human right to remain silent or to create (false) feelings of being 'liked', 'admired' or 'respected' remains, in our view, disingenuous, unethical and potentially dangerous. Vulnerable people – and people in vulnerable situations – may feel compelled to give something back.

When the police arrest and interview a suspect, the balance of power is disproportionate by its very nature (Shepherd, 1991). Instead of an honest attempt to minimise the inherited imbalance, interrogators seeking confessions or "cooperation" through means of coercion, manipulation and/or instrumental persuasion strategies, increase problems associated with *asymmetric communication*, which in turn threatens the reliability of the information provided by the manipulated subject.

In his book, *Reliability of Evidence: Methods for Analyzing and Assessing Witness Statements*, Trankel (1972, p. 27) alerts the reader of the potentially dangerous, and mutually influential, interpersonal dynamics that asymmetric communication all too easily may lead into – even without psychological tactics designed to manipulate or persuade the suspect. More recent knowledge, derived from scientific studies of human cognition and decision making, confirms Trankel's early warning: Detectives seeking confirmation are – like any other fact finder – in a vulnerable situation, unconsciously influenced by cognitive biases that increase the risk of (1) looking (only) for information that confirms their position, (2) interpreting neutral information as confirmation and (3) ignoring or explaining away information pointing in another direction (Ask & Alison, 2010; Fahsing, 2016).

Professional investigative interviewers seek to establish trust and rapport through professional, empathic behaviour. From our point of view, it is counterproductive to train detectives to employ instrumental 'liking' and other influencing strategies because they lack sincerity, and hence run the risk of backfire (HIG, 2016a, 2016b). It is also unnecessary because the essential elements within most of them – the ones that stimulates ethical, interpersonal communication – are already embedded in the ethos of investigative interviewing (Milne & Bull, 1999; Schollum, 2005; Shepherd & Griffiths, 2013). The essential components (conversational management) within the ethos of investigative interviewing will increase detectives' ability to gather and test accurate and reliable information and hence increase the likelihood of solving the case at hand (Shepherd & Griffiths, 2013).

Conclusion

This chapter has established that there is a consensus of published research across all developed countries that points towards investigative interviewing as both effective and ethical (e.g. Leo, 1998; Milne & Bull, 1999; Gudjonsson, 2003; Meissner et al., 2012); a consensus strengthened by the recent government funded research programme in the USA (HIG, 2016a, 2016b), However, this chapter has also shown that this body of empirical research is in competition with cultural and ideological (Cohrs et al., 2007) factors in determining its influence on current real-life law enforcement practice when interviewing suspects. In reality this means that where the pre-dominant cultural influence is a guilt-oriented mindset then this will overpower research evidence because the majority of police forces in the world have not committed themselves to the fundamental principles and ethos underpinning the concept of investigative interviewing (Walsh et al., 2016) or to an evidence based philosophy (Sherman, 2013). The UK and Norway turn-round operations can both demonstrate that it takes all areas of the criminal justice system to be pulling in the same direction for transformational change to occur. The philosophy of these two movements, plus their integration within a professionalised investigation process (see Chapter 2, this volume), demonstrates that there is an effective and ethical alternative to confession focused interrogation as a core part of pre-trial investigation and delivery of justice.

The HIG (2016a) proposes a vision where research informs training, training informs practice, which leads to more research. However, we would contend that even this laudable proposal is vulnerable to culture as in the example of the strategic use of evidence (SUE) where its contribution to dispelling heuristic myths over lie detection has overshadowed its potential in other areas of investigative interviewing. We argue that, based on the evidence of the case studies presented, more research must be conducted into the influence of mindset on the adoption of more effective investigative interview practice, particularly to combat problems associated with confirmation bias and failure to consider the presumption of innocence.

It is also important that change is either driven from within police organisations or in collaboration with academics. The increasing number of police officers who have obtained degrees in forensic psychology in certain countries, has facilitated the evolution of psychology from external critic to integrated collaborator in those countries, enabling and accelerating the development and refinement of investigative interviewing techniques that embrace the ethos of investigative interviewing and knowledge from cognitive decision-making theory. The multidisciplinary merging of theoretical knowledge and practical experience is providing a promising model, developed, not only as a possible answer to the calls for positive strategies to improve information retrieval from suspects, but more fundamentally as a sustainable procedure for detectives left with the impossible task (from a psychological perspective) to remain 'objective' or 'neutral' following a decision to arrest a suspect.

In one of its latest legal directives the European Union (2016) attempts – as indicated from its title – to operationalise *certain aspects* of the presumption of innocence. The directive highlights various legal safeguards that have potential to strengthen a suspect's procedural rights when questioned by the police, either in isolation or when combined. However, these (and other) legal safeguards are nonetheless complementary measures to the most important safeguard against injustice during questioning, which is the interview methodology employed by the police. Therefore, it is our opinion that this or any similar directive does not solve or address the fundamental mindset problem that is generally accepted as the underlying cause to wrongful convictions, and which is interlinked to human cognition and decision-making.

Confirmation bias, primacy effect, group-think and heuristics, to name a few, are cognitive biases that the human mind cannot tackle in complex situations without strategies (methods) literally requiring detectives to generate and actively test alternative hypotheses in order to reduce the cognitive biases that activates from the moment we form our first opinion or perceived solution to the problem at hand (Kahneman, 2011). However, the altering of detectives' mindset required in the turn-around operation, *from* interrogation *to* investigative interviewing, will never reach its potential unless senior detectives, prosecutors and judges, legally responsible for the investigation, all understand and adopt the same logic. After all, investigative interviewing of suspects is not an isolated activity; it is just one part of the overall investigation but currently viewed as its most controversial component (Softley, 1980; Leo, 2008). This will not change until there is not only consensus on the research but on practice too.

Notes

1 KREATIV acronyms for the values and principles underpinning the training programme: **K(C)**ommunication, **R**ule of law, **E**thics and Empathy, **A**ctive awareness **T**rust through openness, **I**nformation, and **V**erified through science.
2 Not all police officers in the UK routinely carry a firearm.
3 Skilled police practitioners also with subject relevant Masters or PhD qualifications.
4 Their skill was based upon their own experience and advice from older colleagues. Police officers were left to the precarious processes of observational learning, i.e. watching others do it, doing it oneself in the absence of critical, constructive feedback from others, and 'surviving' (achieving a seemingly acceptable outcome most of the time) (Shepherd & Kite, 1988).
5 International conference of Investigative Psychology, University of Liverpool.
6 In hindsight, it has been noted both by the police- and the prosecution service that prosecutors, including State attorneys, should have been included in the KREATIV-programme to secure a better, more holistic process. Although prosecutors have participated throughout the years, training was never made mandatory. This is about to change: Following two national enquires (Norway and Sweden) into the infamous case against Sture Bergwall (previously known as Thomas Quick) who was wrongfully convicted for seven separate murders based on his false confessions, the Norwegian Attorney general office has promulgated that prosecutors need a mandatory training programme, based on KREATIV, designed for prosecutors (Riksadvokaten, 2017).
7 The ideas behind the model, namely to delay the presentation of evidence, were relayed to Norway by Royne Nilsson (former detective superintendent and lecturer at the Swedish Police Academy) who, in turn, had trained Swedish police officers in cooperation with Christian Diesen in the mid-1990s.

References

ACPO (1992). *Principles of Investigative Interviewing (HOC 22/1992)*. London: Home Office.

Alison, L. (1998). *Criminal Rhetoric and Investigative Manipulation*. Doctoral thesis, University of Liverpool, UK.

Ames, D.R. & Lee, A.J. (2015). Tortured beliefs: How and when prior support for torture skews the perceived value of coerced information. *Journal of Experimental Social Psychology*, 60, 86–92.

Ask, K. & Alison, L. (2010). Investigators' decision making. In P. A. Granhag (ed.), *Forensic Psychology in Context: Nordic and International Perspectives* (pp. 35–55). Cullompton, UK: Willan.

Ask, K. & Granhag, P.A. (2005). Motivational sources of confirmation bias in criminal investigations: The need for cognitive closure. *Journal of Investigative Psychology and Offender Profiling*, 2, 43–63.

Baldwin, J. (1993). Police interview techniques. *The British Journal of Criminology*, 33, 325–352.

Bull, R. (2014). Foreword. In R. Bull (ed.), *Investigative Interviewing*. New York: Springer.

Bybee, J.S. (2002). *Memorandum for Alberto R. Gonzales*. Counsel to the president. August 1.

Canter, D. & Alison, L.J. (eds) (1999). *Offender Profiling Series Vol I: Interviewing and Deception* (pp. 1–21). Aldershot, UK: Ashgate.

Canter, D.V. & Alison, L. (1999). Beyond profiling: Developments in investigative psychology. In D.V. Canter & L.J. Alison (eds), *Interviewing and Deception* (pp. 23–40). Aldershot, UK: Ashgate.

Central Planning and Training Unit (1992a). *A Guide to Interviewing*. Harrogate, CPTU.

Central Planning and Training Unit (1992b). *The Interviewer's Rule Book*. Harrogate, CPTU.

Clarke, C. & Milne, R. (2001). *National Evaluation of PEACE Investigative Interviewing (rep. No. PRAS/149)*. London: Police Research Award Scheme.

Cohrs, J.C., Maes, J., Moschener, B. & Kleinman, S. (2007). Determinants of human rights attitudes and behavior: A comparison and integration of psychological perspectives. *Political Psychology*, 28(4), 441–469.

Cole, J. (2014). *Policy Concerning Electronic Recording of Statements* [online]. Washington, DC: US Department of Justice. Available at http://www.fpd- ohn.org/cja/blog/doj-policy-concerning-electronic-recording-statements (accessed 12 May 2017).

College of Policing (2013). *Authorised Professional Practice: Investigative Interviewing* [online]. Available at https://www.app.college.police.uk/app-content/investigations/investigative-interviewing/ (accessed 1 June 2017).

Committee for the Prevention of Torture and Inhumane Treatment (CPT) (2002). *CPT Standards*. 12th General Report on the CPT's activities, CPT/Inf/E (2002) 1. Rev. 2013.

Cridland, W. (1984). Human Awareness Training for the police: Theory, practise and principles. *Police Journal*, 57, 36–39. https://doi.org/10.1177/0032258X8405700107 (accessed 14 March 2018).

CTI (2017). *Investigative Interviewing for Criminal Cases*. Convention against torture (CTI) training tools 1/2017. Prepared for the CTI by The Norwegian Centre for Human Rights, University of Oslo in cooperation with the Norwegian Police University College.

Dando, C.J. & Bull, R. (2011). Maximising opportunities to detect verbal deception: Training police officers to interview tactically. *Journal of Investigative Psychology and Offender Profiling*, 8, 189–202.

Dando, C., Wilcox, R. & Milne, R. (2008). The cognitive interview: Inexperienced police officers' perceptions of their witness interviewing behaviour. *Legal and Criminological Psychology*, 13, 59–70.

Diesen, C. (1994). *Bevisprövning i brottmål*. Stockholm: Norstedts Juridik.

Doyle, A.C. (1892). *The Adventures of Sherlock Holmes*. London, UK: The Strand Magazine.

European Union Directive (EU) 2016/343 of the European Parliament and of the Council of 9 March 2016 on the strengthening of certain aspects of the presumption of innocence and of the right to be present at the trial in criminal proceedings. http://eur-lex.europa.eu/legal-content/EN/TXT/PDF/?uri=CELEX:32016L0343&from=EN

Fahsing, I.A. (2016). *The Making of an Expert Detective*. PhD Thesis, University of Gothenburg, Gothenburg.

Fahsing, I.A. & Rachlew, A. (2006). Etiske og effektive avhør, *Politiforum*, juni/juli.

Fahsing, I. & Rachlew, A. (2009). Investigative interviewing – the Nordic region. In T. Williamson, R. Milne & S.P. Savage (eds), *International Developments in Investigative Interviewing* (pp. 39–65). Cullompton, UK: Willan.

Hon. Sir. Henry Fisher (1977). *The Confait Case. Report of an Enquiry into the Circumstances Leading to the Trial of Three Persons on Charges Arising from the Death of Maxwell Confait*. London: HMSO.

Garrett, B.L. (2010). The substance of false confessions. *Stanford Law Review*, 62(4), s. 1051–1119.

Garrett, B.L. (2015). Contaminated confessions revisited. *Virginia Law Review*. 101 Va. Rev. 395 Provided by: University of Virginia Law Library, pp. 395–454

Granhag, P.A. & Vrij, A. (2010). Interrogating suspects: Deception detection. In P.A. Granhag (ed.), *Forensic Psychology in Context: Nordic and International Approaches* (pp. 75–93). Cullompton, UK: Willan Publishing.

Griffiths, A. (2008). *An Examination into the Efficacy of Police Advanced Investigative Interview Training*. Unpublished Doctoral thesis, University of Portsmouth.

Griffiths, A. & Milne, R. (2006). Will it all end in tiers? In T. Williamson (ed.), *Investigative Interviewing; Rights, Research, Regulation* (pp. 167–189). Cullompton, UK: Willan.

Gudjonsson, G.J. (2003). *The Psychology of Interrogations and Confessions*. Chichester, UK: Wiley.

Hartwig, M., Granhag, P.A., Strömwall, L.A. & Vrij, A. (2005). Detecting deception via strategic disclosure of evidence. *Law and Human Behavior*, 29(4), 469–484.

Hartwig, M., Granhag, P.A. & Luke, T. (2014). Strategic use of evidence during investigative interviews: The state of the science. In D.C. Raskin, C.R. Honts & J.C. Kircher (eds), *Credibility Assessment: Scientific Research and Applications* (pp. 1–36). Waltham, MA: Academic Press.

HIG (2016a). *Interrogation Best Practises*. https://www.fbi.gov/file-repository/hig-report-august-2016.pdf/view. August. Accessed 4 August 2017.

HIG (2016b). *Interrogation: A Review of the Science*. https://www.fbi.gov/file-repository/hig-report-interrogation-a-review-of-the-science-september-2016.pdf/view. September. Accessed 4 August 2017.

Houck, S.C., Conway, L.G. & Repke, M. (2014), Personal closeness and perceived torture efficacy: If torture will save someone I'm close to, then it must work. *Peace and Conflict: Journal of Peace Psychology*, 20(4), 590–592. http://dx.doi.org/10.1037/pac0000058

Hulsizer, M.R. & Woolf, L.M. (2012). Enhancing the role of international human rights in the psychology curriculum. *Psychology Learning & Teaching*, 11(3), 382–387. http://dx.doi.org/10.2304/plat.2012.11.3.382

Inbau, F.E., Reid, J.E., Buckley, J.P. & Jayne, B. (2011). *Criminal Interrogations and Confessions*. Burlington, MA: Jones & Bartlett Learning.

Irving, B. (1980). *Police Interrogation: A Case Study of Current Practice. Research Study No. 2*. London: HMSO.

Irving, B. & Hilgendorf, L. (1980). *Police Interrogation: The Psychological Approach*. Research Study No. 1. London: HMSO.

Irving, B. & McKenzie, I.K. (1989). *Police Interrogation: The Effects of the Police and Criminal Evidence Act*. London: Police Foundation of Great Britain.

Kahneman, D. (2011). *Thinking, Fast and Slow*. New York: Penguin.

Kassin, S., Drizin, S., Grisso, T., Gudjonsson, G., Leo, R. & Redlich, A. (2010). Police-induced confessions: Risk factors and recommendations. *Law and Human Behaviour*, 34(1), 3–38. doi:10.1007/s10979–10009–9188–9186

Kassin, S. (1997). The psychology of confession evidence. *American Psychologist*, 52, 222–233.

Kelly, C. & Meissner, C. (2016). Interrogation and investigative interviewing in the United States: Research and practice. In D. Walsh, G. Oxburgh, A. Redlich & T. Mykelbust (eds), *International Developments and Practices in Investigative Interviewing and Interrogation* (pp. 255–266). London: Routledge.

King, P.J. (2002). *Negotiated Disclosure: An Examination of Strategic Information Management by the Police at Custodial Interrogation*. Unpublished PhD thesis, University of Warwick, School of Law. Available at http://wrap.warwick.ac.uk/4049/

Leo, R.A. (2008). *Police Interrogation and American Justice*. Cambridge, MA: Harvard University Press.

Leo, R.A. (1996a). Inside the interrogation room. *Journal of Criminal Law and Criminology*, 86(2). https://scholarlycommons.law.northwestern.edu/jclc/vol86/iss2/2

Leo, R.A. (1996b). The impact of Miranda revisited. *Journal of Criminal Law and Criminology*, 86. Available at SSRN: https://ssrn.com/abstract=1134047

McGurk, B.J., Carr, M.J. & McGurk, D. (1993). *Investigative Interviewing Courses for Police Officers: An Evaluation*. Report No. 4. London: Police Research Group, The Home Office.

Meissner, C.A., Redlich, A.D., Bhatt, S. & Brandon, S. (2012). Interview and interrogation methods and their effects on true and false confessions. *Campbell Systematic Reviews*, 13.

Meissner, C.A., Surmon-Bohr, F., Oleswkwiecz, S. & Alison, L. (2017). Developing an evidence-based perspective on interrogation: A review of the U.S. government's High-Value Detainee Interrogation Group research program. *Psychology, Public Policy, and Law*, 23(4), 438–457. doi:10.1037/law0000136

Mendez, J.E. (2016). *Interim Report to the General Assembly (A/71/298)*. Submitted by the Special Rapporteur on torture and other cruel, inhuman or degrading treatment or punishment, Juan E. Méndez, in accordance with Assembly resolution 70/146. Geneva: United Nations. https://digitallibrary.un.org/record/839995/files/A_71_298-EN.pdf (accessed on 1 July 2017).

Migacheva, K. (2015). Searching for puzzle pieces: How (social) psychology can help inform human rights policy. *Peace and Conflict: Journal of Peace Psychology*, 21(1), 142–149. http://dx.doi.org/10.1037/pac0000089

Milne, R. & Bull, R. (1999). *Investigative Interviewing. Psychology and Practice*. Chichester, UK: Wiley.

Mortimer, A. & Shepherd, E. (1999). Frames of mind: Schemata guiding cognition and conduct in the interviewing of suspected offenders. In A. Memon & R. Bull (e), *Handbook of the Psychology of Interviewing*. Chichester, UK: Wiley.

Munsterburg, H. (1908). *On the Witness Stand: Essays on Psychology and Crime*. New York: McClure.

Napier, M.R. & Adams, S. (1998). Magic words to obtain confessions. *FBI Law Enforcement Bulletin*, 67(10), 1–6.

National Crime Faculty (1998). *A Practical Guide to Investigative Interviewing*. Bramshill, UK: National Police Training College.

PCAST (2016). *Forensic Science in Criminal Courts: Ensuring Scientific Validity of Feature-Comparison Methods*. September. https://obamawhitehouse.archives.gov/sites/default/files/microsites/ostp/PCAST/ pcast_forensic_science_report_final.pdf (accessed 1 June 2017).

Rachlew, A. (1999). *An Evaluation of Norwegian Police Officers' Perception of Investigative Interviewing; Implications for Training*. Unpublished thesis (MSc), University of Liverpool.

Rachlew, A. (2002). Interview strategy. Presentation at the 7th International Conference on Investigative Psychology, University of Liverpool, 13 June 2002.

Rachlew, A. (2009). *Justisfeil ved politiets etterforskning – noen eksempler og forskningsbaserte mottiltak, doktoravhandling* (Errors of justice in police investigations, a few examples and research based countermeasures), University of Oslo.

Rachlew, A. (2017). From interrogating to interviewing suspects of terror: Towards a new mindset. Expert blog. Penal Reform International. Available at https://www.penalreform.org/blog/interrogating-interviewing-suspects-terror-towards-new-mindset/

Rachlew, A. & Fahsing, I. (2015). Politiavhøret (Investigative Interviewing). In R. Aarli, M. Hedlund & S.E. Jebens (eds), *Bevis i straffesaker* (Evidence in criminal cases). Oslo: Gyldendal Akademiske.

Riksadvokaten (2016). *Riksadvokatens rundskriv 2/2016*. Directive no 2/2016 from the Norwegian Director of Public Prosecutions.

Royal Commission on Criminal Procedure Report (1981). Cmnd 8092. London: HMSO.

Scheck, B., Neufeld, P. & Dwyer, J. (2000). *Actual Innocence. Five Days to Execution and Other Dispatches From the Wrongly Convicted*. New York: Doubleday.

Schollum, M. (2005). *Investigative Interviewing: The Literature*. Wellington: New Zealand Police.

Schollum, M. (2017). Bringing PEACE to the United States: A framework for investigative interviews. *International Association of Chiefs of Police Journal*, November, 30–37.

Sellers, S. & Kebbell, M. (2009). The role of evidence in interviewing of suspects: An analysis of Australian police transcripts. *The British Journal of Forensic Practice*, 13(2), 84–94. doi:10.1108/14636641111134323.

Shepherd, E. (1991). Ethical interviewing. *Policing*, 7, 42–60.

Shepherd, E. (1988). Developing interviewing skills: A career span perspective. In P. Southgate (ed.), *New Directions in Police Training*, London: HMSO. Chapter 13.

Shepherd, E. (1986a) Conversational Core of Policing. *Policing*, 2, 294–303.

Shepherd, E. (1986b) Interviewing Development: Facing up to Reality. *Police Journal*, 59, 35–44.

Shepherd, E. (1984). Values into practice: The implementation and implications of human awareness training. *Police Journal*, 57, 286–300.
Shepherd, E. & Griffiths, A. (2013). *Investigative Interviewing: The Conversation Management Approach*. Oxford: Oxford University Press.
Shepherd, E. & Kite, F. (1989). Teach 'em to talk. *Policing*, 5, 33–47.
Shepherd, E. & Kite, F. (1988). Training to interview. *Policing*, 4, 264–280.
Sherman, L. (2013). *The Rise of Evidence Based Policing: Targeting, Testing and Tracking*. Available at http://cebcp.org/wp-content/evidence-based-policing/Sherman-TripleT.pdf. May 20. Accessed 1 June 2017.
Softley, P. (1980) with assistance from D. Brown, B. Forde, G. Mair & D. Moxon. *Police Interrogation: An Observational Study in Four Police Stations*. London: HMSO.
Sukumar, D., Hodgson, J. & Wade, K. (2016). Behind closed doors: Live observations of current police station disclosure practices and lawyer-client consultations. *Criminal Law Review*, 12, Dec 1. SSRN: https://ssrn.com/abstract=2980310
Trainum, J.L. (2016). *How the Police Generate False Confessions: An Inside Look at the Interrogation Room*. New York: Rowman & Littlefield.
Trankel, A. (1972). *Reliability of Evidence: Methods for Analyzing and Assessing Witness Statements*. Stockholm: Beckman.
US Army (2006). *Human Intelligence Collector Operations* (FM 2–22.3; FM34–52), Washington. Available at www.us.army.mil (accessed 19 October 2017).
van Beek, M.L.J. & Hoekendijk, J. (2015). The investigative interviewing of suspects in the Netherlands: Current practices and historical developments. In D. Walsh, G.E. Oxburgh, A.D. Redlich & T. Myklebust (eds), *International Developments and Practices in Investigative Interviewing* (pp. 157–170). London: Routledge.
Vrij, A. (2008). *Detecting Lies and Deceit: Pitfalls and Opportunities* (2nd edn). New York: Wiley.
Walkley, J. (1987). *Police Interrogation: A Handbook for Investigators*. London: Police Review.
Walkley, J. (1982). *Police Interrogation: A Study of the Psychology, Theory and Practice of Police Interrogation and the Implications for Police Training*. MSc Thesis. Cranfield Institute of Technology, Department of Social Policy.
Walsh, D., Oxburgh, G.E., Redlich, A.D. & Myklebust, T. (2016). *International Developments and Practices in Investigative Interviewing and Interrogation: Volume 2: Suspects*. Routledge Frontiers of Criminal Justice. London: Routledge.
Weedn, V. (2017). Recent developments in the forensic sciences. *United States Attorneys' Bulletins [online], Forensic Science and Forensic Evidence*. January 1. Available at https://www.justice.gov/usao/resources/united-states-attorneys-bulletins (accessed on 1 September 2017).
Williamson, T. (1993). From interrogation to investigative interviewing: Strategic trends in police questioning. *Journal of Community and Applied Psychology*, 3, 89–99.
Williamson, T. (2006). Towards greater professionalism: Minimising miscarriages of justice. In T. Williamson (ed.), *Investigative Interviewing: Rights, Research, Regulation* (pp. 147–166). Cullompton, UK: Willan.
Williamson, T., Milne, R. & Savage, S.P. (2009). Foreword. In T. Williamson, R. Milne & S.P. Savage (eds), *International Developments in Investigative Interviewing*. Cullompton, UK: Willan.

Chapter 9

Detecting deceit via verbal cues

Towards a context sensitive research agenda

Pär Anders Granhag, Mark Fallon, Zarah Vernham and Erik Mac Giolla

A table with some nice white lilies, a bottle of Prosecco and four glasses. Three researchers from the field of legal psychology and one experienced interviewer. The practitioner was glad to accept the invitation as the promise was to discuss research on 'how to interview and how to detect deception'. The first researcher presents herself "I do research on how to detect deception". The second is quick to add "My research is on how to elicit intelligence from human sources", and finally the third researcher explains "I study how to obtain admissions and confessions, and to avoid false confessions". The interviewer smiles and says: "Great stuff – I am interested in all of this. In fact, many times I have to do all of this – can you please tell me how to best achieve all this in the same interview?" The researchers look at each other.

Research on deception detection has exploded since the mid 1990s and it continues to be popular among students and an attractive topic for psycho-legal scholars. In an era of threat and terrorism, a premium is placed on research dealing with security, control and the collection of intelligence. We believe that research on deception detection has an important role to play in the fight for a safer society. However, in order for research to make a difference – to have an impact on the quality of interviews that aim to assess veracity – several tough challenges must be dealt with. First, it is necessary to debunk the 'fool-proof-way-to-detect deception' claims flourishing in pseudo-science and the media. Second, researchers need to take a critical look at their own activities. The time is more than ripe to move away from old-school deception detection studies, mapping people's detection performance by having them watch brief video-clips (Vrij & Granhag, 2012). Third, knowing what to move away from does not necessarily inform on where to go. In order to make a difference, researchers must; (a) learn more about the problems that practitioners face; (b) keep these problems in mind when setting up their research; and (c) frame the outcome of the research in an accessible and thoughtful manner. In brief, without increased involvement and interaction with practitioners as collaborative partners, the research will remain academic and assimilation challenges will continue within the very community that can benefit most from the science (Fallon,, 2014).

Verbal markers to deceit: a brief summary of past research

Over the years, verbal markers to deceit, such as the level of detail, have recurrently been examined (DePaulo et al., 2003; Vrij, 2008), which is predominantly due to verbal cues being deemed more diagnostic of deceit than nonverbal cues (Vrij, 2008). Whilst verbal markers can be measured individually, it is important to develop tools that specifically measure speech content and can assist with the accurate identification of deceit (Vrij, 2015a). Three verbal veracity assessment tools have been developed that are frequently used and discussed: Statement Validity Analysis (SVA) of which Criteria-Based Content Analysis (CBCA) is the core component; Reality Monitoring (RM) and Scientific Content Analysis (SCAN). Recently, a fourth approach has been proposed, the Verifiability approach (Nahari, Vrij & Fisher, 2014a). Below we will review each of these approaches.

Statement Validity Analysis (SVA) and Criteria-Based Content Analysis (CBCA)

SVA is the most frequently used tool for assessing credibility (Vrij, 2008). It originates from the 'Undeutsch Hypothesis', which states that memories of actual experienced events are different from subjective imagined events in terms of content and quality (Steller, 1989; Undeutsch, 1967). SVA was originally designed to determine the credibility of child witness statements of sexual abuse. SVA consists of four phases: (i) a case-file analysis to gain information about the case and formulate hypotheses about what may have happened; (ii) a semi-structured interview to obtain a statement from the victim (interviewee) in his/her own words; (iii) CBCA to systematically assess the credibility of the statement; and (iv) a validity checklist to evaluate the CBCA outcome through a use of standardised criteria (Köhnken, 2004; Steller & Boychuck, 1992). Although research has shown that SVA can help to discriminate between true and false statements (e.g., Lucas & McKenzie, 1999), the third phase, CBCA, will be the focus below for two reasons: (i) CBCA is most relevant to verbal cues of deceit and (ii) the majority of research has examined the use of CBCA for assessing statement credibility.

CBCA requires the statements provided by victims to be transcribed and coded. The use of transcripts, instead of actual interviews, removes the impact of nonverbal behaviours from influencing the decision of the CBCA examiner (Vrij, 2008). The transcripts are coded for the presence or absence of 19 criteria grouped into four subcategories (Steller & Köhnken, 1989): general characteristics (e.g., logical structure), specific contexts (e.g., unusual details), motivation-related contents (e.g., admitting lack of memory) and offence-specific elements (e.g., details characteristic of the offence). The criteria can either be judged as present or absent via dichotomous scales (Horowitz, 1998; Köhnken, 2004), or via a more objective frequency system whereby the number of times each criterion is present within the transcript is considered (Vrij, 2008). All CBCA criteria are indicative of truth; thus, they are more likely to be present in truthful statements than in deceptive statements. For a full list of the 19 CBCA criteria, see Vrij (2015a).

Research examining the utility of CBCA tends to obtain robust findings in support of the 'Undeutsch Hypothesis': Each of the CBCA criteria does emerge more frequently in truthful statements than in deceptive statements (Akehurst, Köhnken & Höfer, 2001; Akehurst, Manton & Quandte, 2011). Furthermore, whereas general deception detection studies frequently show that both lay people and practitioners obtain low accuracy rates, ranging from 45 per cent to 60 per cent (Vrij, 2000), laboratory studies using CBCA assessments frequently obtain accuracy rates of approximately 70 per cent (Akehurst et al., 2001; Vrij, 2008).

Reality Monitoring (RM)

RM is a verbal approach based on human memory and refers to the cognitive processes that are used to discriminate between perceived and imagined events (Johnson & Raye, 1981). Central to RM is that memories of actually experienced events differ in terms of quality compared with memories of imagined events. Many scholars (e.g., Johnson & Raye, 1981; Johnson, Hashtroudi & Lindsay, 1993) argue that memories of actually experienced events are obtained through perceptual processes (an external source) and so, in comparison with imagined events, they are more likely to contain (i) sensory information (e.g., visual, auditory and olfactory details); (ii) contextual information (e.g., spatial and temporal details); and (iii) affective information (e.g., details about thoughts and feelings). As a result, true memories appear more vivid and clear. In contrast, memories of imagined events are obtained through internal sources, containing more cognitive operations (e.g., thoughts and reasonings), which are vague and non-specific. Because of the robust theoretical underpinnings, RM is a popular tool among academics (Masip, Sporer, Garrido & Herrero, 2005), but is not currently used by practitioners.

RM has much empirical support with many studies demonstrating that, in accordance with RM theory, the qualities of memories do differ depending on whether they were actually experienced or imagined. People who report true experienced events tend to have clearer memories and to provide more qualitative details than those who report imagined events (Johnson, Foley, Suengas & Raye, 1988; Sporer & Sharman, 2006). In addition, research has shown that people can use RM to judge whether someone else's memory is an actual experienced event or an imagined event (referred to as interpersonal RM; Vrij, 2008; Vrij, Akehurst & Knight, 2006). On average, the RM tool achieves accuracy rates of approximately 70 per cent (similar to CBCA; Masip et al., 2005; Vrij, 2008). Despite the support for RM, there are limitations to using it as a verbal veracity tool (see e.g., Lindsay, 2002; Vrij et al., 2004) For example,

RM is not a standardised test; thus, different RM researchers use different criteria, making it difficult to compare across studies.

From a practitioner's perspective it can be argued that trying to judge truthful information from deceptive information by means of cognitive or motivational factors, tools like CBCA and RM, may be of limited utility to an interviewer. While the results of interviews and review of written content are factors used within the public safety community, they are only facets of broader investigative protocols. An investigator is responsible for placing information gathered during an interview into context with information that is known or suspected. The interview helps determine what still needs to be known by an investigator. Hence, tools like CBCA and RM have less relevance during the investigative phase, and more relevance in court.

Scientific Content Analysis (SCAN)

The underlying assumption of SCAN is that a statement derived from a memory of an actual experienced event will differ in content and quality from that of an imagined event. SCAN requires statements to be handwritten. During these statements interviewees are required to write about their activities during a critical period and to state in their own words what happened. There is no fixed number of criteria, but typically studies analyse statements using 12 criteria (e.g., denial of allegations, emotions, missing information; see Vrij, 2008 for a full list of the 12 SCAN criteria). The SCAN examiner will determine whether the statement includes each of the criteria in order to make a decision about the veracity status of the interviewee. Some SCAN criteria are more likely to occur in truthful statements and other SCAN criteria are more likely to occur in deceitful statements (Sapir, 1987, 2000, 2005).

There are many issues associated with SCAN, and compared with CBCA and RM, SCAN is the most problematic tool. First, there is very little empirical research (especially in comparison with the amount of research that explores CBCA and RM). Only one study favours the use of SCAN (Driscoll, 1994), but in this study ground truth could not be established. All other studies that explore SCAN show that it cannot accurately discriminate between truthful and lying statements, yet the same studies demonstrate that CBCA and RM criteria can significantly discriminate between truthful and lying statements (Bogaard, Meijer, Vrij & Merckelbach, 2016; Nahari et al., 2012). Second, there is a lack of standardisation, which makes SCAN very subjective: Different SCAN examiners use different criteria to assess the same statement and there is no consensus amongst SCAN examiners about which criteria are indicative of truth and which are indicative of deceit (Vrij, 2008). Third, unlike RM, SCAN has no theoretical rationale to explain why truth tellers and liars differ from each other in the way that SCAN assumes (Vrij, 2015a).

The use of SCAN by some public safety professionals is reflective of a community of practice that seeks methods to enhance their capabilities, but neither understands nor integrates with the scientific community studying related issues. Researchers have studied what they view might be beneficial to practitioners, without first seeking to understand what practitioners might view as useful. Practitioners often employ techniques that are not scientifically validated, in pursuit of an advantage. If our goal is to fight for a safer society, research must not only validate methods that are successful, we must also debunk the existing pseudo-science of deception and practices that may be ineffective and counterproductive.

The Verifiability approach

The Verifiability approach was developed by Nahari et al. (2014a), and it is based on two assumptions that result in a dilemma for liars. First, research frequently demonstrates that more detailed accounts signify truthfulness (Vrij, 2008) and as a result liars want to provide numerous details in order to make an honest impression (Nahari et al., 2012). Second, although liars want to provide many details to appear truthful, they are simultaneously motivated to avoid mentioning details that can be checked through fear that the investigator will uncover their lies (Nahari et al., 2012). This therefore leads liars to employ a strategy that minimises their chances of being caught: Liars provide many details, but focus on details that cannot be verified (e.g., "I felt very upset and cold as I was walking around the park"). Conversely, truth tellers focus on proving their innocence so provide details that can be verified (e.g., "I walked past CCTV located in the entrance to the park at approximately 2 pm"). Hence, liars report fewer verifiable details than truth tellers. To date, the studies that have been conducted using the Verifiability approach have found support for the approach and achieved accuracy rates similar to CBCA and RM (around 70 per cent accuracy; Nahari & Vrij, 2014; Nahari, Vrij & Fisher, 2014a, 2014b). However, the Verifiability approach still needs more extensive research and there are some limitations because it cannot be applied to all circumstances (e.g., non-recent cases, such as historical child sexual abuse, whereby there are rarely any details that can be verified).

Interviewing strategically to elicit cues to deceit: a shift in paradigm

During recent years researchers have introduced interview strategies that draw on the differing psychological states experienced by truth tellers and liars, with the aim of eliciting and magnifying the verbal cues to deception. These strategies include: 'asking unanticipated questions', 'imposing cognitive load', the 'strategic use of evidence' and 'collective interviewing'. Below we will review all these four approaches.

Asking unanticipated questions

The benefit of asking unanticipated questions during suspect interviews builds on the different counter-interrogation strategies that liars and truth tellers employ. Truth tellers' strategy, or lack thereof, primarily consists of 'telling it all' (Granhag, Hartwig, Mac Giolla & Clemens, 2015). That is, truth tellers are typically forthcoming, and tell everything from memory to the best of their ability. It is argued that this naïve strategy is driven by a belief in a 'just world' (Lerner, 1980) and that their honesty will shine through ('illusion of transparency'; Gilovich, Savitsky & Medvec, 1998). Liars, in contrast, do not take their credibility for granted. Liars are more systematic than truth tellers, and, when given the opportunity, will prepare for an interview (Hartwig, Granhag & Strömwall, 2007; Hines et al., 2010; Granhag, Andersson, Strömwall & Hartwig, 2004). Prepared lies reduce the cognitive demands typically associated with lying (Vrij et al., 2009) and accordingly produce fewer cues to deceit than spontaneous lies (DePaulo et al., 2003). The preparation of liars, however, depends on correctly anticipating what questions they will be asked. Hence, by asking questions that liars are less likely to have prepared for – by asking unanticipated questions – it should be possible to circumvent liars' preparations, ensuring that they have to fabricate answers on-the-spot. By carefully choosing the unanticipated questions, truth tellers should still be able to rely on their memory to answer them. Truth tellers' primary strategy of honest recall should therefore be unaffected when answering unanticipated questions, thereby resulting in comparable answers to anticipated questions.

Empirical research on asking unanticipated questions to truth tellers and liars supports this reasoning. In studies comparing anticipated with unanticipated questions, truth tellers and liars often provide comparable answers to the anticipated questions. However, when asked unanticipated questions truth tellers have been shown to provide longer (Mac Giolla & Granhag, 2015), more detailed (Sooniste, Granhag, Knieps & Vrij, 2013), more plausible (Vrij, Leal, Mann, Warmelink, Granhag & Fisher, 2010), and more consistent answers (Vrij, Leal, Granhag, Mann, Fisher, Hillman & Sperry, 2009) compared with liars (for a review see Vrij, 2014).

In its simplest form, unanticipated questions can be targeted at specific topics that liars are unlikely to prepare for. For example, Vrij et al. (2009) asked pairs who had eaten lunch together (truth tellers) and pairs who only claimed to have done so (liars), specific questions concerning spatial (*In relation to the front door and where you sat, where were the closest diners?*) and temporal details (*Who finished their lunch first?*) of the event. The statements of truth telling pairs showed a higher degree of overlap for these unanticipated questions, compared with liars. Another approach is to ask people to provide their answers to questions in an unanticipated response format. Here, the topic of the question can be anticipated, but the format of the answer should be unanticipated. Asking people to draw a scene (unanticipated response format), rather than verbally describe a scene (anticipated response format), is one such example. Researchers who have examined the use of drawings to distinguish between truth tellers and liars argue that drawings play on liars' verbal script-like preparations. This cognitive inflexibility makes it difficult for liars to translate their prepared answers to an unanticipated recall format. Truth tellers, in contrast, can simply rely on their memories to produce their drawings. In accordance, research has shown that truth tellers can provide more detailed and more consistent drawings than liars (e.g., Leins, Fisher, Vrij, Leal & Mann, 2011; Roos af Hjelmsäter, Öhman, Granhag & Vrij, 2014).

Imposing cognitive load

Lying is often more cognitively demanding than truth-telling (Vrij et al., 2008). This is because: (i) formulating a lie in itself is mentally taxing as the liar needs to make the lie coherent and plausible; (ii) liars are typically less likely than truth tellers to take their credibility for granted; (iii) liars monitor interviewers' reactions more carefully than truth tellers to check whether they are being believed; (iv) liars will constantly need to remind themselves that they are acting; (v) liars have to supress the truth whilst they are lying; (vi) lying is more intentional and deliberate compared with truth-telling which is more natural – thus, lying requires more mental effort than does truth-telling; and (vii) lying requires justification (e.g., for money or to protect oneself from being imprisoned), whereas truth-telling does not (Vrij, Granhag & Porter, 2010). However, lying is not always more cognitively demanding than truth-telling (McCornack, 1997). In fact, lying is only more cognitively demanding than truth-telling if the above seven principles apply, which require two key elements to occur: (i) the interviewee must be motivated to be believed and (ii) the interviewee must be able to retrieve, and have a clear image of, the truthful event. In forensic settings, it can be assumed that interviewees are motivated to be believed because in such settings there are high-stake consequences. Additionally, it can be assumed that the truthful event has been retrieved clearly if the interviewee is given enough time to prepare for the interview and is able to inform the interviewer when they feel ready to be interviewed (Vrij, 2015b).

An understanding of the cognitive difficulties associated with lying means that an investigator can exploit the differing levels of cognitive load that truth tellers and liars experience. The approach of imposing cognitive load requires the interviewer to make additional and mentally-taxing requests during the interview that are more difficult for liars, than for truth tellers, to cope with. In comparison with truth tellers, liars have fewer cognitive resources left to deal with these additional requests, making the liars more vulnerable to 'slipping up'. This elicits more cues to deceit and magnifies the differences between truth tellers and liars.

Numerous techniques have been suggested for imposing cognitive load. First, the investigator can ask unanticipated interview questions (see previous section). Second, the interviewer can ask the interviewee to answer the interview questions in reverse order. This increases cognitive load because it counteracts the normal flow and sequence of recalling information (Gilbert & Fisher, 2006) and disrupts the natural reconstructing of events from a schema (Geiselman & Callot, 1990). Studies have shown that asking an interviewee to answer questions in reverse order does elicit more cues to deceit, which can be recognised by observers to improve their ability at accurately differentiating between truth tellers and liars (Vrij et al., 2008; Vrij, Leal, Mann & Fisher, 2012). Third, the interviewer can ask the interviewee to maintain eye contact with the interviewer throughout the interview. This increases cognitive load because maintaining eye contact is distracting and reduces the interviewees' ability to concentrate only on telling their story (Doherty-Sneddon & Phelps, 2005). Research has shown that instructing interviewees to maintain eye contact elicits more cues to deceit and increases the ability of observers to accurately discriminate between truths and lies (Vrij, Mann, Leal & Fisher, 2010).

We argue that the use of unanticipated questions and the imposition of cognitive load have direct applicability for practitioners. Both approaches allow for on-the-spot assessments to be made by the interviewer, without transcript reviews or independent analysis. While liars maintain consistency in their statements, the 'tell it all' strategy of truth tellers indicates that although truth tellers may provide more information than liars, the information changes and is more inconsistent than liars. The research results are contrary to popular belief within the public, among practitioners, judges and jurors. Many within those communities focus on inconsistent statements as a sign of deception.

Strategic Use of Evidence (SUE)

Police officers will typically hold some evidence against a suspect who is to be interviewed. The importance of such evidence in a suspect interview is acknowledged by researchers (Bull, 2014), practitioners (Kelly et al., 2015) and offenders (Kebbell, Alison, Hurren & Mazerolle, 2010). Despite this acknowledgement, police officers receive little training on how best to use evidence in interviews (Smith & Bull, 2014) and interview manuals have often little to say on the topic (Hartwig, Granhag, Strömwall & Kronkvist, 2006). The Strategic Use of Evidence (SUE) technique (Hartwig, Granhag, Strömwall & Vrij, 2005; Hartwig, Granhag & Luke, 2014) marks one of the few attempts by researchers to fill this gap. The aim with the SUE-technique is to systematise how interviewers should best use evidence during suspect interviews in order to distinguish innocent from guilty suspects.

Like the unanticipated questions approach, the starting point for the SUE-technique is the differing counter-interrogation strategies that innocent and guilty suspects avail of to create a believable impression (Hartwig, Granhag & Luke, 2014). In brief, innocent suspects are expected to be more forthcoming than guilty suspects. This is because guilty suspects are actively working against the interviewer uncovering information indicative of their guilt, and hence must withhold critical pieces of information during the interview. In contrast, innocent suspects are expected to tell a great deal during interviews in order to ensure that the interviewer comes to know what they know (Granhag & Hartwig, 2008). Put differently, guilty suspects are expected to avoid critical information, whereas innocent suspects should be less likely to do so.

Early disclosure of evidence not only provides the suspect with indications and warnings about what the investigators know, such confrontational approaches tend to limit, rather than precipitate dialog between the investigator and suspect. Confrontational approaches, with early disclosure of evidence focus on obtaining a confession, based on what the interrogator believes may have happened, rather than the elicitation of information. This limits the acquisition of checkable facts to corroborate or refute the information provided, and may also produce false confessions and fabricated information (Gudjonsson, 2003; Bull, 2014).

Based on these counter-interrogation strategies, the SUE-technique advocates a late or gradual disclosure of evidence during suspect interviews (Granhag & Hartwig, 2015). This is because an early disclosure of evidence plays into the strategies of guilty suspects: By informing guilty suspects of what evidence is held, it is possible for them to create a story that is consistent with both the evidence and their claimed innocence (Sellers & Kebbell, 2009). In contrast, by encouraging suspects to give an account of events before the evidence is presented, it is likely that guilty suspects will employ withholding strategies and refrain from mentioning incriminating information in their statements. Truth tellers are expected to employ forthcoming strategies regardless of when the evidence is presented, and as such should be more likely to spontaneously mention information related to the evidence. Hence, late presentation of evidence should result in more statement-evidence inconsistencies for guilty suspects compared with innocent suspects (Granhag & Hartwig, 2015; for similar evidence focused interviewing techniques see e.g., Dando & Bull, 2011).

Empirical research has been conducted on the SUE-technique for over a decade (for a review see Granhag & Hartwig, 2015). The results consistently show that the late or gradual disclosure of evidence consistently results in a higher number of statement-evidence inconsistencies for guilty compared with innocent suspects. The most striking study to date involved trainee police officers (Hartwig, Granhag, Strömwall & Kronkvist, 2006). The officers interviewed guilty and innocent suspects. Half of the officers were instructed to use the SUE-technique and to base their judgements of guilt and innocence on statement–evidence inconsistencies. The other half received no training in the SUE-technique. These officers were instructed to interview the suspects in whatever manner they deemed most appropriate to ascertain guilt and innocence. Approximately 85 per cent of suspects were correctly identified as guilty or innocent by the officers using the SUE-technique. In sharp contrast, the untrained officers performed little better than chance, correctly classifying only 56 per cent of suspects.

The gradual and strategic use of evidence disclosure method also enables the interviewer to gauge the level of cooperation of the person being interviewed, without having to confront the person, or telegraphing to the suspect what is known or unknown. This can be a very useful tool during the recruitment process of a potential informant. The emphasis within the context of some real-world police interrogations needs to change from a confrontational confession-based methodology to a rapport-building information-gathering methodology (Meissner, Kelly & Woesterhoff, 2015). The strategic use of evidence enables an ongoing assessment of the information and increased dialog between the interviewer and interviewee (Vrij & Granhag 2012, 2014; Granhag et al., 2015; Vrij 2008). The strategic use of evidence disclosure throughout the course of an interrogation and the increased dialog established also promotes the building of a rapport between the suspect and interrogator. Regardless of the techniques or approaches interrogators are taught, experienced interrogators view rapport as one of the most important factors that contributes to successful interrogations (Russano, Narchet & Meissner, 2014). After the attacks of September 11th, the United States established a task force to bring terrorists to justice, conducting thousands of interrogations in Afghanistan, Iraq and Guantanamo Bay. Those terrorist investigators were directed to disregard any prior Reid training, which was viewed as totally ineffective, and exclusively focus on rapport-based information gathering techniques (Fallon, 2017).

Collective interviewing

Crimes commonly involve pairs or groups of individuals (McGloin & Piquero, 2009; Van Mastrigt & Farrington, 2009), yet group deceit has been, until recently, significantly neglected. Traditionally, regardless of the number of interviewees, police detectives separate individuals as soon as possible to reduce opportunity for planning of responses and to increase the interviewees' stress and anxiety (Kassin & Gudjonsson, 2004). As a result, deception research has focused on developing interview protocols that increase the discrepancies between truth tellers and liars interviewed individually (e.g., Granhag et al., 2003; Strömwall, Granhag & Jonsson, 2003; Vrij et al., 2009). Despite this, there are several settings whereby interviewing multiple interviewees together (known as collective interviewing) would be more timely and convenient. For example, when there are multiple suspects but only one interviewer available, such as during police stop and searches or at security checkpoints (e.g., airports). These settings tend to involve gathering intelligence to prevent harm rather than gathering evidence to charge someone for committing an offence. Additionally, there are many benefits to using a collective interviewing technique: (i) it captures deception at a social level as well as at an individual level, enabling the identification of cues to deceit that are present in groups, but which cannot be explored in individuals (e.g., cues stemming from interviewees communicating and interacting with one another); (ii) it automatically imposes cognitive load because individuals have to impression manage themselves as well as others; (iii) it has a strong theoretical foundation and coincides with memory theory, such as collective memory (Barnier & Sutton, 2008) and transactive memory (Wegner, 1987); and (iv) it is already part of some existing procedures. For example, in Canada, customs officers carry out collective interviews at airports because groups are deemed to have a 'similar agenda', so if only one person in the group is examined, this could result in a wasted effort or missed opportunity (A. Leach, Canadian former customs officer, personal communication, 12 November 2013) and in the UK immigration officers are often required to collectively interview couples seeking British Citizenship in order to uncover sham marriages (Home Office, 2013).

To date, seven empirical collective interviewing studies have been conducted (see Vernham & Vrij, 2015 for an overview) and these studies demonstrate that a collective interviewing approach can elicit novel cues to deceit associated with how the group members interact and communicate with one another. For example, when groups of truth tellers are asked to recall a shared event together, they collectively recall the information, which results in truth-telling groups exhibiting significantly more interactions and communications than lying groups (e.g., posing questions to one another, looking at one another, correcting one another, adding information to each other's accounts, and finishing each other's sentences; e.g., Driskell, Salas & Driskell, 2012; Vernham, Vrij, Leal, Mann & Hillman, 2014; Vrij, Jundi, et al., 2012). Additionally, when further techniques that impose cognitive load are applied to collective interviewing, such as a forced turn-taking technique, then additional cues to deceit emerge (e.g., continuations, repetitions and waiting; Vernham, Vrij, Mann, Leal & Hillman, 2014) Such a technique has been found to considerably improve observer's ability to accurately detect deceit (73.3 per cent for truths and 80 per cent for lies; Vernham, Vrij, Mann et al., 2014) with the accuracy rates obtained being amongst the highest found in verbal lie detection research.

Whilst the findings of the collective studies to date are positive, collective interviewing should not replace individual interviewing. Instead, it should be employed as an additional approach. For example, the collective interview could be used in isolation whereby if the group raises suspicion in a collective interview, investigators take the required actions they would normally take after interviewing individuals who raise suspicion (e.g., calling for assistance, collecting further evidence), or collective interviewing could act as an initial screening process to determine whether interviewees then need to be interviewed individually.

Nevertheless, there is clear potential for the use of a collective interviewing approach within investigative contexts. Collective interviewing may have potential applications in witness interviews in mass casualty investigations or crisis situations that require numerous witnesses to be quickly interviewed to assess an incident. Of course, issues of the possible cross-contamination of information would have to be considered. Collective interviews might be useful in the identification and prioritisation of witnesses for more structured individual interviews. Such an approach does elicit novel and unique cues to deception and intelligence collection that can only emerge when groups are interviewed together. The accuracy rates are very promising, but we also argue that more research is required.

True and false intentions: a new strand of research

From security operations to border controls, from insurance salesmen to judges at parole hearings, an ability to distinguish between statements of true and false intent is crucial in many situations. Despite this applied value, the topic has largely been ignored by deception researchers. It is only in the last half-decade or so that researchers have turned their attention to the topic of true and false intentions (Granhag, 2010). In brief, a statement of true intent refers to a future action a speaker genuinely intends to carry out. A statement of false intent refers to a future action a speaker claims, but does not in fact intend to carry out. Research on true and false intentions focuses on how one can discriminate between these forms of statements. To date, researchers have approached the topic of true and false intentions in two different ways. First, researchers have sought to extend more established deception detection techniques to intent situations. Second, researchers have sought to develop unique, intention-specific deception detection approaches (see Granhag & Mac Giolla, 2014 for a review).

With regard to the first approach, a number of more traditional deception detection methods have been successfully extended to situations of intent. These include physiological measures such as the Concealed Information Test (Meijer, Smulders & Merckelbach, 2010; Meijer, Verschuere & Merckelbach, 2010; Meixner & Rosenfeld, 2011; Noordraven & Verschuere, 2013), and reaction time measures such as the autobiographical Implicit Association Test (Agosta, Castiello, Rigoni, Lionetti & Sartori, 2011) and the Sheffield Lie-Test (Suchotzki, Verschuere, Crombez & De Houwer, 2013). A number of strategic interviewing approaches have also been extended to intent situations, such as the unanticipated questions approach (Sooniste, Granhag, Strömwall & Vrij, 2015) and the SUE-technique (Clemens, Granhag & Strömwall, 2011). For example, in the study by Sooniste et al. (2015), half of the participants had planned to conduct an innocuous future task (truth tellers), whereas the other half had planned to conduct a mock-crime (liars). In addition, liars had been told to prepare a cover story to be used if they were questioned about their intentions. The theme of the cover story was the truth tellers' innocuous task. During subsequent interviews about their intentions, participants were asked unanticipated questions about the planning that went into their stated intentions. It was assumed that liars would have difficulty answering these questions since their preparations were expected to focus on their cover stories, rather than the planning required to perform the task described in their cover stories. In contrast, truth tellers were expected to have engaged in concrete planning activities, as is typical of many intentions (Malle & Knobe, 1997). Since truth tellers could rely on their memories they provided richer descriptions of their planning activities than liars. Furthermore, since truth tellers, but not liars, had a genuine memory of the planning phase, memory enhancing techniques derived from the cognitive interview further increased differences between the two groups.

With regard to the second approach of developing unique intention-specific lie detection techniques, Granhag (2010) explains that it is only possible to recognise a false intention once it is known what demarcates a true intention. Hence, the first task for researchers is to identify the typical behaviour of people stating a true intention. Basic psychological research on intentions (Malle & Knobe, 1997) and related fields such as goal-directed behaviour (Martin & Tesser, 2009) and planning (Mumford, Schultz & Van Doorn, 2001) goes a long way to answering this question. For example, intentions are often accompanied by concrete plans to perform the intention. Plans are in turn often accompanied by episodic future thoughts (EFT; mental images of the future task to be performed; Szpunar, 2010). EFTs are functional: By allowing people to mentally pre-experience a future event, EFTs aid preparations and help people carry out their intentions (Schacter, Addis & Buckner, 2008). However, liars do not aim to carry out their stated intentions; hence the functional properties of EFTs are lost on liars. For this reason it is expected that liars will experience EFTs to a lesser extent than truth tellers. This idea has received support in a series of studies (Knieps, Granhag & Vrij, 2013a, 2013b, 2014). In brief, the studies show that those stating a true intention experience clearer and more EFTs related to their stated intention compared with those stating false intentions. EFTs, however, are just one example of expected consequences of a true intention. The ongoing research on intention-specific approaches to deception aims to uncover other consequences of the formation of true intentions that are expected to be weaker for those forming false intentions (see Granhag & Mac Giolla, 2014; Mac Giolla, Granhag & Vrij, 2015, for reviews). The eventual goal of this line of research is to identify unique intention-specific cues to truth-telling and deceit, which can guide interviewers when questioning people about their intended future actions.

Deception detection in context

Most researchers who conduct research on deception detection have an ambition to produce knowledge that can be useful for legal practitioners. This may be knowledge on which criteria to use when assessing the veracity of an already produced statement or it may be knowledge on how to interview to elicit cues that reliably discriminate between truth tellers and liars. In this section, three interrelated problems that we believe characterise past and present research will be acknowledged. In our view, these problems are roadblocks impacting the ability of deception detection research to make a difference in practice.

The first problem has to do with how most of the past research has been set up. In short, researchers have mapped people's ability to detect truthfulness and deceit by having their 'observers' watch brief video-clips, and after each clip assessing the veracity of the person just seen. That is, the lie-catchers under examination have not had access to any background information about the persons shown on tape, or have they had the opportunity to ask questions. The message sent from these studies is clear: Under such circumstances people are poor at discriminating between truth tellers and liars. A person naïve to the paradigmatic way of conducting deception detection research, and who comes across the often broadcasted message that "40 years of research shows that people are poor at detecting deceit", might think that people's performance has been tested under a number of different circumstances reflecting real-life situations. However, this is in fact not the case. Hence, the outcome of past research should be summarised: "People are poor at detecting deceit when they, passively and without any background information, watch brief video-clips". In real-life settings the investigating officer usually conducts the interrogation of the suspects they are investigating. They are generally thought to have the prerequisite background information and knowledge of the case, enabling them to differentiate between fact and fiction. It is that knowledge that guides their judgments about whether the person interviewed is being deceptive, based on existing evidence, or what might seem plausible based on both the case and their practical experience level. In brief, we have a difficult time finding real-life situations that are structurally similar to this old-school way of mapping people's lie-catching performance.

The second problem is the prevalent output measure of much past and current research: Detection accuracy framed in a percentage score. In fairness, there are advantages with this outcome measure. For example, it is straightforward and allows for easy-to-grasp comparisons within and between studies. However, we believe that there are problems with 'accuracy-driven' deception detection research. First, for many studies little or no information is provided with respect to why the examined lie-catchers arrived at a particular accuracy level (often a modest one). In short, ignoring the processes that explain the accuracy rates will not push the research field forward. Second, we believe it is possible to question the judicial value of the accuracy score. It is true that if an interviewer, during the investigative phase, is able to correctly detect deceit in a suspect's statement, this may result in a more effective allocation of the resources at hand (e.g., to investigate certain circumstances further). However, in a broader sense an interviewer's assessment of a suspect's veracity is of no evidentiary value. That is, such an assessment has no relevance for the prosecutor's case-construction. In contrast, a suspect interview, which, by means of strategic interviewing, results in blatant statement-evidence inconsistencies, might add to the prosecutor's construction of the case. That is, the prosecutor can make these statement-evidence inconsistencies clear to the triers of fact. Critically, it is the elicited cues to deceit that matter, not the interviewer's own assessment. For investigators, a lie during an interrogation can be as useful as an admission, especially if the evidence establishes the suspect's deception. An investigator might seek to lock the suspect into a deceptive position, establishing them as a liar to discredit them. Once the suspect provides a statement, it is the investigation that is used as the lie-catcher, rather than the visible observations much of research focuses on.

The third problem relates back to the opening paragraph; the three researchers planned to have some Prosecco with the experienced police interviewer. Researchers tend to study one topic at a time, and to some extent this makes sense. To put too many factors into play will make it difficult, or even impossible, to assess what is responsible for any observed effects. However, we believe that to move the field forward researchers must be more sensitive to what is taking place in real suspect interviews. It is rare for an interviewer to have 'detecting deceit' as his or her single objective. Researchers often fail to realise that when investigators interview a suspect, they are not only seeking confessions, but also admissions to elements of the offenses investigated and intelligence. Differently put, many interviews have multiple objectives. While sometimes seemingly innocuous, those elements of offenses, which may not individually be criminal in nature, are necessary thresholds that need to be established in judicial proceedings. Like a mosaic, investigators arrange the pieces of information and evidence collected into discernible patterns to form a clearer understanding of specific events. The process is dynamic and investigators use information gathered to prioritise resources and focus efforts rapidly while an investigation is underway.

In fact, for the large majority of cases the interviewer's objective is (or should be) to gather information; information that can be used to infer whether the suspect is related to the crime under investigation or to generate additional leads. Obviously, the interviewer will assess the veracity of the information that he or she collects. In brief, as the interviewer aims to both *collect* and *assess* information, it is not enough with techniques limited to aid in discriminating between truthful and fabricated statements. To make a difference, researchers need to guide the interviewer on how to, within the same interview, effectively collect new information and assess the reliability of the information collected. In a recent line of research, Serra Tekin and her colleagues (2015, in press) have taken on this challenge. In essence, they have provided empirical support to the idea that rests on the following train of thoughts: (a) strategically playing the evidence (critical background information) when speaking to a suspect's guilt, will (b) result in statement–evidence inconsistencies (due to the suspect's aversive counter-interrogation strategies), which, in turn, (c) will result in the suspect changing his or her initial, and proven ineffective, strategies to more forthcoming counter-interrogation strategies ("I am better off telling what they already know"), (d) resulting in an increased amount of admissions (information previously unknown to the interviewer). In essence, for this line of research cues to deceit are not an end in itself (which is the case for most previous research); instead, the cues to deceit are means to an end. The cues to deceit are used to collect more information (admissions).

Enhanced interrogation methods: some reflections

There are countless fictional accounts of what those in the entertainment industry depict as occurring in an interrogation. They seek to maximise the drama for a reader or viewer. These scenes of an interrogation, depending on the context, can be brutal and sometimes depict torture as a method to obtain accurate and reliable information. Those accounts have little basis in reality. To the uninformed and misinformed, those fictional accounts can help shape, and be used to justify preconceived notions of what might be effective during a real-world interrogation. They also fail to account for the effects of the brain under stress and how harsh practices impact memory negatively (O'Mara, 2015).

Following the attacks of September 11th 2001, both the United States Central Intelligence Agency (CIA) and Department of Defence (DOD) adopted brutal techniques that they purported were effective. The techniques employed were not created by interrogation professionals, but by psychologists lacking any relevant real-world interrogation experience (see U.S. Senate Armed Service Committee Report: Inquiry into the Treatment of Detainees in U.S. Custody, 2008). These psychologists were involved in DOD Survival, Evasion, Resistance and Escape (SERE) training. The SERE programme is designed to harden the resistance of U.S. military personnel by simulating the physical and psychological pressures they might be exposed to if captured by an enemy that did not observe the Geneva Conventions, such as North Korea. SERE simulations are based largely on a study conducted of how the Chinese Communist methods used by North Korean interrogators were able to elicit false confessions from U.S. Air Force Prisoners of War (Biderman, 1957). These techniques included stripping, stress positions, hooding, dietary manipulation, exposure to temperature extremes, disruption of sleep pattern, and total degradation. The U.S. Navy included waterboarding as part of their SERE training. When these techniques were adapted for use by the CIA, they called them "Enhanced Interrogation Techniques".

The SERE based techniques that were utilised by both the CIA and DOD were intended to create a condition known as learned helplessness (Seligman, 1972). The use of the SERE based tactics was opposed by experienced interrogation professionals (Fallon, 2017) and those SERE tactics were not only ineffective, they were counterproductive (see U.S. Senate Intelligence Committee Study on CIA Detention and Interrogation Program, 2014). During the timeframe the SERE tactics were being employed in interrogations, the lack of evidence-based research on interrogations allowed those involved to utilise untested techniques (Fallon, 2014).

Truly enhanced interrogation methods are those that are informed by science. The research reflected in this chapter offers scientifically validated insights that practitioners can employ to enhance the rapport based methods that are the hallmark of the most effective interrogators (Fallon, 2017). The research promotes lawful and human rights compliant practices that can aid in the detection of deception, gathering as much information as possible, eliciting intelligence and avoiding false confessions.

Final words

In this chapter we have summarised past research on verbal markers to deceit and truthfulness, for example what we currently know about tools such as CBCA, RM and SCAN. We have also acknowledged a new line of research that fits under the umbrella term 'strategic interviewing to detect deceit'. This line is about interviewing in ways which elicit or enhance cues to deceit and truthfulness (Vrij & Granhag, 2012). Specifically, we reviewed four such strategic interviewing methods: (1) asking unanticipated questions, (2) imposing cognitive load, (3) Strategic Use of Evidence (SUE) and (4) collective interviewing. Our ambition stretched beyond summarising the outcome of past and current research, in that we made an attempt to place deception detection research in context. Differently put, throughout the chapter we offered reflections on the applicability of existing research, and we discuss to what extent the paradigmatic designs used within the field mirror the situations and the problems that practitioners face. In brief, we suggest that researchers (a) move away from 'old school' research mapping people's ability to detect deceit when passively observing short video-clips, (b) cease to be blinded by numbers (accuracy rates) and (c) acknowledge that 'detecting deceit' rarely takes place in isolation.

True, there are indications of a shift in paradigm (Vrij & Granhag, 2012), but perhaps the bottle of Prosecco should remain uncorked until we can see even clearer signs that researchers start to acknowledge that detecting deceit demands active and strategic interviewing, until researchers pay more attention to the judicial meaning and relevance of the outcome of their research and until there is more research reflecting the fact most real-life interviews come with multiple objectives. To have practitioners accepting invitations to discuss research is a necessary first step. The second step is to move from reflections and discussions to carefully constructing the problems identified. The third and most challenging step is to chisel out research designs which reflect the problems that practitioners face. But not only should researchers collaborate more with experienced practitioners, they also need to collaborate more with each other. Back to the experienced interviewer around the table, impressed by the experts in detecting deceit, eliciting intelligence and obtaining admissions. Recall the question asked: *Can you please tell me how to best achieve all this in the same interview?* The journey has just begun.

References

Agosta, S., Castiello, U., Rigoni, D., Lionetti, S., & Sartori, G. (2011). The detection and the neural correlates of behavioral (prior) intentions. *Journal of Cognitive Neuroscience*, 23, 3888–3902. doi:10.1162/jocn_a_00039.

Akehurst, L., Köhnken, G., & Höfer, E. (2001). Content credibility of accounts derived from live and video presentations. *Legal and Criminological Psychology, 6*, 65–83. doi:10.1348/135532501168208.

Akehurst, L., Köhnken, G., Vrij, A., & Bull, R. (1996). Lay persons' and police officers' beliefs regarding deceptive behaviour. *Applied Cognitive Psychology, 10*, 461–471. doi:10.1002/(SICI)1099–0720(199612)10:6<461:AID-ACP413>3.0.CO;2–2.

Akehurst, L., Manton, S., & Quandte, S. (2011). Careful calculation or a leap of faith? A field study of the translation of CBCA ratings to final credibility judgements. *Applied Cognitive Psychology*, 25, 236–243. doi:10.1002/acp.1669.

Barnier, A.J., & Sutton, J. (2008). From individual to collective memory: Theoretical and empirical perspectives. *Memory, 16*, 177–182. doi:10.1080/09541440701828274.

Biderman, A.D. (1957). Communist attempts to elicit false confessions from air force prisoners of war. *Bulletin of the New York Academy of Medicine*, 33, 616–626. Retrieved from: http://www.ncbi.nlm.nih.gov/pmc/articles/PMC1806204/pdf/bullnyacadmed00378-0046.pdf.

Bogaard, G., Meijer, E., Vrij, A., & Merckelbach, H. (2016). Scientific Content Analysis (SCAN) cannot distinguish between truthful and fabricated accounts of a negative event. *Frontiers in Psychology*, 7. doi:10.3389/fpsyg.2016.00243.

Bull, R. (2014). When in interviews to disclose information to suspects and to challenge them? In R. Bull (ed.), *Investigative interviewing* (pp. 167–181). New York: Springer-Verlag.

Clemens, F., Granhag, P.A., & Strömwall, L.A. (2011). Eliciting cues to false intent. *Law and Human Behavior*, 35, 512–522. doi:10.1007/s10979–10010–9258–9259.

Dando, C.J., & Bull, R. (2011). Maximising opportunities to detect verbal deception: Training police officers to interview tactically. *Journal of Investigative Psychology and Offender Profiling*, 8, 189–202. doi:10.1002/jip.145.

DePaulo, B.M., Lindsay, J.J., Malone, B.E., Muhlenbruck, L., Charlton, K., & Cooper, H. (2003). Cues to deception. *Psychological Bulletin, 129*, 74–118. doi:10.1037/0033–2909.129.1.74.

Doherty-Sneddon, G., & Phelps, F.G. (2005). Gaze aversion: A response to cognitive or social difficulty? *Memory and Cognition*, 33, 727–733.

Driscoll, L. (1994). A validity assessment of written statements from suspects in criminal investigations using the SCAN technique. *Police Studies*, 4, 77–88.

Driskell, J.E., Salas, E., & Driskell, T. (2012). Social indicators of deception. *Human Factors: The Journal of the Human Factors and Ergonomics Society, 54*, 577–588. doi:10.1177/0018720812446338.

Fallon, M. (2014). Collaboration between practice and science will enhance interrogations. *Applied Cognitive Psychology*, 28, 949–950. doi:00A0;10.1002/acp.3091.

Fallon, M. (2017). *Unjustifiable means: The inside story of how the CIA, Pentagon, and US Government conspired to torture*. New York: Simon & Schuster, Regan Arts.

Geiselman, R.E., & Callot, R. (1990). Reverse versus forward recall of script-based texts. *Applied Cognitive Psychology*, 4, 141–144. doi:10.1002/acp.2350040206.

Gilbert, J.A.E., & Fisher, R.P. (2006). The effects of varied retrieval cues on reminiscence in eyewitness memory. *Applied Cognitive Psychology*, 20, 723–739. doi:10.1002/acp.1232.

Gilovich, T., Savitsky, K., & Medvec, V.H. (1998). The illusion of transparency: Biased assessments of others' ability to read one's emotional states. *Journal of Personality and Social Psychology, 75*, 332–346. doi:10.1016/S0022–1031(03)00056–00058.

Granhag, P.A. (2010). On the psycho-legal study of true and false intentions: Dangerous waters and some stepping stones. *The Open Criminology Journal, 3*, 37–43. doi:10.2174/1874917801003010037.

Granhag, P.A., Andersson, L.O., Strömwall, L.A., & Hartwig, M. (2004). Imprisoned knowledge: Criminals' beliefs about deception. *Legal and Criminological Psychology*, 9, 103–119. doi:00A0;10.1348/135532504322776889.

Granhag, P.A., & Hartwig, M. (2008). A new theoretical perspective on deception detection: On the psychology of instrumental mind-reading. *Psychology, Crime & Law*, 14, 189–200. doi:10.1080/10683160701645181.

Granhag, P.A., & Hartwig, M. (2015). The strategic use of evidence (SUE) technique: A conceptual overview. In P. Granhag, A. Vrij, & B. Verschuere (eds), *Deception detection: New challenges and cognitive approaches* (pp. 231–251). Chichester, UK: John Wiley & Sons.

Granhag, P.A., Hartwig, M., Mac Giolla, E., & Clemens, F. (2015). Suspects' verbal counter-interrogation strategies: Towards an integrative model. In P.A. Granhag, A. Vrij, & B. Verschuere (eds), *Detecting deception: Current challenges and cognitive approaches* (pp. 293–314). Chichester, UK: John Wiley & Sons.

Granhag, P.A., & Mac Giolla, E. (2014). Preventing future crimes: Identifying markers of true and false intent. *European Psychologist, 19*, 195–206. doi:10.1027/1016–9040/a000202.

Granhag, P.A., Strömwall, L.A., & Jonsson, A.C. (2003). Partners in crime: How liars in collusion betray themselves. *Journal of Applied Social Psychology*, 33, 848–868. doi:10.1111/j.1559–1816.2003.tb01928.x.

Gudjonsson, G. (2003). *The psychology of interrogations and confessions: A handbook*. Chichester, UK: John Wiley & Sons.

Hartwig, M., Granhag, P.A., & Luke, T.J. (2014). Strategic use of evidence during investigative interviews: The state of the science. In D.C. Raskin, C.R. Honts, & J.C. Kircher (eds), *Credibility assessment: Scientific research and applications* (pp. 1–36). Amsterdam: Elsevier.

Hartwig, M., Granhag, P.A., & Strömwall, L.A. (2007). Guilty and innocent suspects' strategies during police interrogations. *Psychology, Crime & Law*, 13, 213–227. doi:10.1080/10683160600750264.

Hartwig, M., Granhag, P.A., Strömwall, L.A., & Kronkvist, O. (2006). Strategic use of evidence during police interviews: When training to detect deception works. *Law and Human Behavior*, 30, 603–619. doi:10.1007/s10979-006-9053-9.

Hartwig, M., Granhag, P.A., Strömwall, L.A., & Vrij, A. (2005). Detecting deception via strategic disclosure of evidence. *Law and Human Behavior*, 29, 469–484. doi:10.1007/s10979-005-5521-x.

Home Office. (2013). *Sham marriages and civil partnerships: Background information and proposed referral and investigation scheme*. Retrieved from: https://www.gov.uk/government/uploads/system/uploads/attachment_data/file/256257/Sham_Marriage_and_Civil_Partnerships.pdf.

Horowitz, S.W. (1998). Reliability of criteria-based content analysis of child witness statements: Response to Tully. *Legal and Criminological Psychology*, 3, 189–193. doi:10.1111/j.2044–8333.1998.tb00359.x.

Johnson, M.K., Foley, M.A., Suengas, A.G., & Raye, C.L. (1988). Phenomenal characteristics of memories for perceived and imagined autobiographical events. *Journal of Experimental Psychology: General*, 117, 371–376. doi:10.1037/0096–3445.117.4.371.

Johnson, M.K., Hashtroudi, S., & Lindsay, D.S. (1993). Source monitoring. *Psychological Bulletin*, 114, 3–28. Retrieved from: http://memlab.yale.edu/sites/default/files/files/1993_Johnson_Hashtroudi_Lindsay_PsychBull.pdf.

Johnson, M.K., & Raye, C.L. (1981). Reality monitoring. *Psychological Review*, 88, 67–85. doi:10.1037/0033–295X.88.1.67.

Kassin, S.M., & Gudjonsson, G.H. (2004). The psychology of confessions: A review of the literature and issues. *Psychological Science in the Public Interest*, 5, 33–44. doi:10.1111/j.1529–1006.2004.00016.x.

Kebbell, M., Alison, L., Hurren, E., & Mazerolle, P. (2010). How do sex offenders think the police should interview to elicit confessions from sex offenders? *Psychology, Crime & Law*, 16, 567–584. doi:10.1080/10683160902971055.

Kelly, C.E., Abdel-Salam, S., Miller, J.C., & Redlich, A.D. (2015). Social identity and the perceived effectiveness of interrogation methods. *Investigative Interviewing: Research and Practice*, 7, 24–42. Retrieved from: https://www.researchgate.net/publication/291343954_Social_Identity_and_the_Perceived_Effectiveness_of_Interrogation_Methods.

Knieps, M., Granhag, P.A., & Vrij, A. (2013a). Back to the future: Asking about mental images to discriminate between true and false intentions. *The Journal of Psychology*, 147, 619–640. doi:10.1080/00223980.2012.728542.

Knieps, M., Granhag, P.A., & Vrij, A. (2013b). Repeated visits to the future: Asking about mental images to discriminate between true and false intentions. *International Journal of Advances in Psychology*, 2, 93–102.

Knieps, M., Granhag, P.A., & Vrij, A. (2014). Been there before? Examining "familiarity" as a moderator for discriminating between true and false intentions. [Original Research]. *Frontiers in Psychology*, 5, 1–9. doi:10.3389/fpsyg.2014.00677.

Köhnken, G. (2004). Statement validity analysis and the 'detection of the truth'. In P.A. Granhag & L.A. Strömwall (eds), *Deception detection in forensic contexts* (pp. 41–63). Cambridge, UK: Cambridge University Press.

Leins, D.A., Fisher, R.P., Vrij, A., Leal, S., & Mann, S. (2011). Using sketch drawing to induce inconsistency in liars. *Legal and Criminological Psychology*, 16, 253–265. doi:10.1348/135532510x501775.

Lerner, M.J. (1980). *The belief in a just world*. New York, NY: Plenum Press.

Lindsay, D.S. (2002). Children's source monitoring. In H.L. Westcott, G.M. Davies, & R.H.C. Bull (eds), *Children's testimony: A handbook of psychological research and forensic practice* (pp. 83–98). Chichester, UK: John Wiley & Sons.

Lucas, R., & McKenzie, I.K. (1999). The detection of dissimulation: Lies. Damned lies and SVA. *International Journal of Police Science & Management*, 1, 347–359. doi:10.1177/146135579900100403.

Mac Giolla, E., & Granhag, P.A. (2015). Detecting false intent amongst small cells of suspects: Single versus Repeated interviews. *Journal of Investigative Psychology and Offender Profiling*, 12, 142–157. doi:00A0;10.1002/jip.1419.

Mac Giolla, E., Granhag, P.A., & Vrij, A. (2015). Discriminating between true and false intentions. In P.A. Granhag, A. Vrij, & B. Verschuere (eds), *Deception detection: Current challenges and new approaches* (pp. 155–173). Chichester, UK: John Wiley.

Malle, B.F., & Knobe, J. (1997). The folk concept of intentionality. *Journal of Experimental Social Psychology*, 33, 101–121. doi:10.1006/jesp.1996.1314.

Martin, L.L., & Tesser, A. (2009). Five markers of motivated behavior. In G. B. Moskowitz & H. Grant (eds), *Psychology of goals*. London: The Guilford Press.

Masip, J., Sporer, S.L., Garrido, E., & Herrero, C. (2005). The detection of deception with the reality monitoring approach: A review of the empirical evidence. *Psychology, Crime & Law*, 11, 99–122. doi:10.1080/10683160410001726356.

McCornack, S.A. (1997). The generation of deceptive messages: Laying the groundwork for a viable theory of interpersonal deception. In J.O. Greene (ed.), *Message production: Advances in communication theory* (pp. 91–126). Mahwah, NJ: Lawrence Erlbaum.

McGloin, J.M., & Piquero, A.R. (2009). 'I wasn't alone': Collective behaviour and violent delinquency. *Australian & New Zealand Journal of Criminology*, 42, 336–353. doi:10.1375/acri.42.3.336.

Meijer, E.H., Smulders, F.T.Y., & Merckelbach, H.L.G.J. (2010). Extracting concealed information from groups. *Journal of Forensic Sciences*, 55, 1607–1609. doi:10.1111/j.1556–4029.2010.01474.x.

Meijer, E.H., Verschuere, B., & Merckelbach, H. (2010). Detecting criminal intent with the concealed information test. *Open Criminology Journal*, 3, 44–47doi:10.2174/1874917801003020044.

Meissner, C.A., Kelly, C.E., & Woestehoff, S.A. (2015). Improving the effectiveness of suspect interrogations. *Annual Review of Law and Social Science*, 11, 211–233. doi:10.1146/annurev-lawsocsci-120814-121657.

Meixner, J.B., & Rosenfeld, J.P. (2011). A mock terrorism application of the P300-based concealed information test. *Psychophysiology*, 48, 149–154. doi:10.1111/j.1469–8986.2010.01050.x.

Mumford, M.D., Schultz, R.A., & Van Doorn, J.R. (2001). Performance in planning: Processes, requirements, and errors. *Review of General Psychology*, 5, 213–240. doi:10.1037/1089–2680.5.3.213.

Nahari, G., & Vrij, A. (2014). Can I borrow your alibi? The applicability of the verifiability approach to the case of an alibi witness. *Journal of Applied Research in Memory and Cognition*, 3, 89–94. doi:10.1016/j.jarmac.2014.04.005.

Nahari, G., Vrij, A., & Fisher, R.P. (2012). Does the truth come out in the writing? SCAN as a lie detection tool. *Law and Human Behavior*, 36, 68–76doi:10.1037/h0093965.

Nahari, G., Vrij, A., & Fisher, R.P. (2014a). Exploiting liars' verbal strategies by examining the verifiability of details. *Legal and Criminological Psychology*, 19, 227–239. doi:10.1111/j.2044–8333.2012.02069.x.

Nahari, G., Vrij, A., & Fisher, R.P. (2014b). The verifiability approach: Countermeasures facilitate its ability to discriminate between truths and lies. *Applied Cognitive Psychology*, 28, 122–128. doi:10.1002/acp.2974.

Noordraven, E., & Verschuere, B. (2013). Predicting the sensitivity of the Reaction Time-based Concealed Information Test. *Applied Cognitive Psychology*, 27, 328–335. doi:10.1002/acp.2910.

O'Mara, S. (2015). *Why torture doesn't work: The neuroscience of interrogation*. Cambridge, MA: Harvard University Press.

Roos af Hjelmsäter, E., Öhman, L., Granhag, P.A., & Vrij, A. (2014). 'Mapping' deception in adolescents: Eliciting cues to deceit through an unanticipated spatial drawing task. *Legal and Criminological Psychology*, 19, 179–188. doi:10.1111/j.2044-8333.2012.02068.x.

Russano, M.B., Narchet, F.M., Kleinman, S.M., & Meissner, C.A. (2014). Structured interviews of experienced HUMINT interrogators. *Applied Cognitive Psychology*, 28, 847–859. doi:00A0;10.1002/acp.3069.

Sapir, A. (1987, 2000, 2005). *The LSI course on scientific content analysis (SCAN)*. Phoenix, AZ: Laboratory for Scientific Interrogation.

Schacter, D.L., Addis, D.R., & Buckner, R.L. (2008). Episodic simulation of future events. *Annals of the New York Academy of Sciences*, 1124, 39–60. doi:10.1196/annals.1440.001.

Seligman, M.E.P. (1972). Learned helplessness. *Annual Review of Medicine*, 23, 407–412. doi:00A0;10.1146/annurev.me.23.020172.002203.

Sellers, S., & Kebbell, M.R. (2009). When should evidence be disclosed in an interview with a suspect? An experiment with mock-suspects. *Journal of Investigative Psychology and Offender Profiling*, 6, 151–160. doi:10.1002/jip.95.

Smith, L.L., & Bull, R. (2014). Exploring the disclosure of forensic evidence in police interviews with suspects. *Journal of Police and Criminal Psychology*, 29, 81–86. doi:10.1007/s11896-013-9131-0.

Sooniste, T., Granhag, P. A., Knieps, M., & Vrij, A. (2013). True and false intentions: Asking about the past to detect lies about the future. *Psychology, Crime & Law*, 19, 673–685. doi:10.1080/1068316x.2013.793333.

Sooniste, T., Granhag, P.A., Strömwall, L.A., & Vrij, A. (2015). Statements about true and false intentions: Using the Cognitive Interview to magnify the differences. *Scandinavian Journal of Psychology*, 56, 371–378. doi:10.1111/sjop.12216.

Sporer, S.L., & Sharman, S.J. (2006). Should I believe this? Reality monitoring of accounts of self-experienced and invented recent and distant autobiographical events. *Applied Cognitive Psychology*, 20, 837–854. doi:10.1002/acp.1234.

Steller, M. (1989). Recent developments in statement analysis. In J.C. Yuille (1989), *Credibility assessment* (pp. 135–154). Deventer, The Netherlands: Kluwer.

Steller, M., & Boychuk, T. (1992). Children as witnesses in sexual abuse cases: Investigative interview and assessment techniques. In H. Dent & R. Flin (eds), *Children as witnesses* (pp. 47–73). New York, NY: John Wiley & Sons.

Steller, M., & Köhnken, G. (1989). Criteria-based content analysis. In D.C. Raskin (ed.), *Psychological methods in criminal investigation and evidence* (pp. 217–245). New York: Springer-Verlag.

Strömwall, L.A., Granhag, P.A., & Jonsson, A.C. (2003). Deception among pairs: "Let's say we had lunch and hope they will swallow it!" *Psychology, Crime & Law, 9*, 109–124. doi:10.1080/1068316031000116238.

Suchotzki, K., Verschuere, B., Crombez, G., & De Houwer, J. (2013). Reaction time measures in deception research: Comparing the effects of irrelevant and relevant stimulus–response compatibility. *Acta Psychologica, 144*, 224–231. http://dx.doi.org/10.1016/j.actpsy.2013.06.014

Szpunar, K.K. (2010). Episodic future thought an emerging concept. *Perspectives on Psychological Science, 5*, 142–162. doi:10.1177/1745691610362350.

Undeutsch, U. (1967). Beurteitlung der glaubhaftigkeit von aussagen [Veracity assessment of statements]. In U. Undeutsch (ed.), *Handbuch der psychologie. Vol. II: Forensische psychologie* (pp. 26–181). Göttingen, Germany: Hogrefe.

Van Mastrigt, S.B., & Farrington, D.P. (2009). Co-offending, age, gender and crime type: Implications for criminal justice policy. *British Journal of Criminology*, 49, 552–573. doi:10.1093/bjc/azp021.

Vernham, Z., & Vrij, A. (2015). A review of the collective interviewing approach to detecting deception in pairs. *Crime Psychology Review*, *1*, 43–58. doi:10.1080/23744006.2015.1051756.

Vernham, Z., Vrij, A., Leal, S., Mann, S., & Hillman, J. (2014). Collective interviewing: A transactive memory approach towards identifying signs of truthfulness. *Journal of Applied Research in Memory and Cognition*, 3, 12–20doi:10.1016/j.jarmac.2014.01.001.

Vernham, Z., Vrij, A., Mann, S., Leal, S., & Hillman, J. (2014). Collective interviewing: Eliciting cues to deceit using a turn-taking approach. *Psychology, Public Policy and Law*, 20, 309–324. doi:10.1037/law0000015.

Vrij, A. (2000). *Detecting lies and deceit: The psychology of lying and its implications for professional practice*. Chichester, UK: John Wiley & Sons.

Vrij, A. (2008). *Detecting lies and deceit: Pitfalls and opportunities* (2nd edn). Chichester, UK: John Wiley & Sons.

Vrij, A. (2015a). Verbal lie detection tools: Statement validity analysis, reality monitoring and scientific content analysis. In P.A. Granhag, A. Vrij, & B. Verschuere (eds), *Detecting deception: Current challenges and cognitive approaches* (pp. 3–35). Chichester, UK: John Wiley & Sons.

Vrij, A. (2015b). A cognitive approach to lie detection. In P.A. Granhag, A. Vrij, & B. Verschuere (eds), *Detecting deception: Current challenges and cognitive approaches* (pp. 205–229). Chichester, UK: John Wiley & Sons.

Vrij, A., Akehurst, L., & Knight, S. (2006). Police officers', social workers', teachers' and the general public's beliefs about deception in children, adolescents and adults. *Legal and Criminological Psychology*, 11, 297–312. doi:10.1348/135532505X60816.

Vrij, A., Akehurst, L., Soukara, S., & Bull, R. (2004). Detecting deceit via analyses of verbal and nonverbal behavior in children and adults. *Human Communication Research*, 30, 8–41. doi:10.1111/j.1468-2958.2004.tb00723.x.

Vrij, A., Fisher, R., Mann, S., & Leal, S. (2008). A cognitive load approach to lie detection. *Journal of Investigative Psychology and Offender Profiling*, 5, 39–43. doi:10.1002/jip.82.

Vrij, A., & Granhag, P.A. (2012). Eliciting cues to deception and truth: What matters are the questions asked. *Journal of Applied Research in Memory and Cognition*, 1, 110–117. doi:10.1016/j.jarmac.2012.02.004.

Vrij, A., & Granhag, P.A. (2014). Eliciting information and detecting lies in intelligence interviewing: An overview of recent research. *Applied Cognitive Psychology*, 28, 936–944. doi:10.1002/acp.3071.

Vrij, A., Granhag, P.A., & Porter, S. (2010). Pitfalls and opportunities in nonverbal and verbal lie detection. *Psychological Science in the Public Interest*, 11, 89–121.doi:10.1177/1529100610390861.

Vrij, A., Leal, S., Mann, S., Warmelink, L., Granhag, P.A., & Fisher, R.P. (2010). Drawings as an innovative and successful lie detection tool. *Applied Cognitive Psychology*, 24, 587–594. doi:10.1002/acp.1627.

Vrij, A., Jundi, S., Hope, L., Hillman, J., Gahr, E., Leal, S., Warmelink, L., Mann, S., Vernham, Z., & Granhag, P.A. (2012). Collective interviewing of suspects. *Journal of Applied Research in Memory and Cognition*, 1, 41–44. doi:10.1016/j.jarmac.2011.12.002.

Vrij, A., Leal, S., Granhag, P.A., Mann, S., Fisher, R.P., Hillman, J., & Sperry, K. (2009). Outsmarting the liars: The benefit of asking unanticipated questions. *Law and Human Behavior*, 33, 159–166. doi:10.1007/s10979–10008–9143-y.

Vrij, A., Leal, S., Mann, S., & Fisher, R. (2012). Imposing cognitive load to elicit cues to deceit: Inducing the reverse order technique naturally. *Psychology, Crime & Law*, 18, 579–594. doi:10.1080/1068316X.2010.515987.

Vrij, A., Mann, S., Leal, S., & Fisher, R. (2010). Look Into My Eyes: Can an instruction to maintain eye contact facilitate lie detection? *Psychology, Crime, & Law*, 16, 327–348. doi:10.1080/10683160902740633.

Vrij, A., Mann, S., Leal, S., & Granhag, P.A. (2010). Getting into the minds of pairs of liars and truth-tellers: An examination of their strategies. *The Open Criminology Journal*, 3, 17–22. doi:10.2174/1874917801003010017.

Wegner, D. M. (1987). Transactive memory: A contemporary analysis of the group mind. In B. Mullen & G.R. Goethals (eds), *Theories of group behaviour* (pp. 185–208). New York, NY: Springer-Verlag.

Weldon, M.S., & Bellinger, K.D. (1997). Collective memory: Collaborative and individual processes in remembering. *Journal of Experimental Psychology: Learning, Memory, and Cognition*, 23, 1160–1175. doi:10.1037/0278–7393.23.5.1160.

Zuckerman, M., DePaulo, B.M., & Rosenthal, R. (1981). Verbal and nonverbal communication of deception. In L. Berkowitz (ed.), *Advances in experimental social psychology* (Vol. 14, pp. 1–59). New York: Academic Press.

Chapter 10

Behavioural investigative advice

A contemporary commentary on offender profiling activity

Michael Davis, Lee Rainbow, Kate Fritzon, Adrian West and Nathan Brooks

Introduction

The term "profiling" (as in "offender profiling", "criminal profiling", or "psychological profiling") was first regularly used by members of the Federal Bureau of Investigation's (FBI) Behavioral Science Unit who defined it as the process of drawing inferences about a suspect's characteristics from details of his or her actions exhibited during the commission of a crime (Douglas & Burgess, 1986; Teten, 1989). Much discussion has subsequently been focussed on whether such activity represents art or science, with the discipline being subject to considerable scrutiny by both practitioners and academics alike (Cook & Hinman, 1999). Whilst many practitioners have been strident in advocating the relative merits of their specific methodological approach over that of their "competitors", of greater concern is the recent proliferation within the academic literature of rather uninformed commentaries and perceptions of the contemporary role of the "profiler", which are at best outdated, and at worst based upon misconceptions served up by crime writers, Hollywood producers, and the misconstructions of the media (Rainbow & Gregory, 2011).

The role of the contemporary "profiler" has undergone significant evolution in recent times. Beginning in the United Kingdom, the emergence of Behavioural Investigative Advice (BIA) as a distinct profession best exemplifies this shift in focus from the traditional, narrow view of "offender profiling" to a discipline which now encompasses a broad range of scientifically based yet pragmatic activities related to supporting police investigations (Rainbow et al., 2014).

Contemporary BIAs are no longer isolated experts restricted to generating inferences about offenders in an investigative void. Rather they have become a more professional group of individuals with a vast experience of serious crime and how best to integrate their behavioural advice into the modern day major investigation. BIAs can offer Senior Investigating Officers (SIOs) an additional perspective and decision support throughout a serious crime investigation through the pragmatic application of behavioural science theory, research, and experience. Although all the products and services available offer tactical or strategic solutions in their own right, all are underpinned by a broader philosophy of adding value to the decision making of the SIO through an enhanced understanding of the offence and offender from a perspective different from that routinely employed within major crime investigation teams. Such differences in perspective can be broadly characterised as evidence (SIO) versus understanding (BIA), although both are directed at supporting the single goal of case resolution. It is this additional perspective and associated expertise which should be recognised as the critical success factor of contemporary BIA.

Although the emergence of BIA should be recognised as a qualitatively distinct profession (rather than a variation of technique), its foundations are built firmly upon the historical precursor influences of criminal investigative analysis, clinical diagnostic evaluations, and investigative psychology. As such, a brief description of these approaches will be presented to provide both a historical context and to begin to illustrate the redundancy of such rigid historical approaches when assessing the contemporary distinctions within BIA/profiling methodologies.

Traditional "approaches" to offender profiling

The clinical approach

The first group of professionals to provide offender profiling advice to police investigations were clinical practitioners of medicine, psychiatry, and psychology. Indeed, while there are arguably some rudimentary precursors to profiling as far back as biblical times (Canter & Youngs, 2009), the first published offender profile to bear similarity to modern practice is described in the "Jack the Ripper" case in 1888. A Police Surgeon named Dr Thomas Bond performed a post-mortem examination of the fifth victim and reviewed documentation in the four previous murders. Dr Bond's report included a number of inferences as to crime scene behaviour, suggested that the offender may have been suffering from satyriasis (i.e., hyper-sexuality), hypothesised as to his lack of occupation, and made some investigative suggestions that included offering a financial incentive to those who may know the offender (Rumbelow, 1987; see also http://www.casebook.org/witnesses/thomas-bond.html).

During World War II mental health professionals were tasked with providing "profiles" of Adolf Hitler for the United States government (e.g., Langer, 1972; Murray, 1943). These reports drew heavily upon the dominant psychoanalytic theories of the time in providing an assessment of the German leader without benefit of direct examination. They included hypotheses regarding personality structure, predictions as to future behaviour, and suggestions as to how to deal with Hitler and the German people. While the parallels with offender profiling are clear, this type of activity differs in both scope and focus as the subject of the analysis is known. In contemporary criminal investigative contexts such an analysis, in order to assist investigative strategy, is known as an *indirect personality assessment* (Ault, 2010; Ault & Hazelwood, 1995). The indirect analysis of political leaders for government purposes has since resulted in the field and profession of *political psychology* (Post, 2002).

The ad-hoc use of clinicians as consultants in criminal investigations continued after World War II. The most well-known practitioner, and arguably the father of modern offender profiling, was Dr James Brussel, a psychiatrist who served as the Assistant Director of Mental Hygiene for the State of New York. He commenced assisting police in 1956 during the case of the "Mad Bomber". Dr Brussel's ultimate description of the offender was quite accurate. Amongst other things, he had described the bomber as single, aged 40–50 years, resentful of criticism, and an introverted paranoiac who felt superior to others. He was hypothesised to be moral, honest, cunning, and a skilled mechanic who was neat with tools. Dr Brussel also suggested that the offender would be of Slavic origin, symmetrically built, and suffering from a chronic illness. The profiling advice included some investigative suggestions involving the use of the media (Brussel, 1968).

It is perhaps a shame that Dr Brussel's initial offender profile is most remembered for his prediction as to the bomber's likely attire when he was eventually arrested. In his memoir, Brussel (1968) noted that he told investigators "when you catch him – and I have no doubt you will – he'll be wearing a double-breasted suit … And it will be buttoned" (p. 46). When police ultimately visited the home of the offender during the evening, he was dressed in pyjamas. However, when asked to get dressed, he returned with "his hair combed in a neat pompadour, and his shoes were freshly shined. He wore a blue pin-striped double-breasted suit. It was buttoned" (p. 69).[1]

While it is easy to view the pioneering work of Brussel as being of historical interest only, a close examination of his memoir provides insights into his methods of profile construction that suggests similarities with current BIA practice. In a somewhat glib introductory comment, Brussel (1968) noted that:

> Generally, a psychiatrist can study a man and make a few reasonable predictions about what the man may do in the future – how he will react to such-and-such a stimulus, how he will behave in such-and-such a situation. What I have done is reverse the terms of the prophecy. By studying a man's deeds, I have deduced what kind of man he might be … . The technique has no magic in it, as I hope I can show. It was simply my own way of applying what I had learned about people in years of studying and wondering – and my way of taking a step on the road toward unraveling the great mystery of human behavior.
>
> (p. 4)

Similar to the work of modern day BIAs, Brussel's (1968) descriptions of his profiling activity include explanations for his varying inferences. What is clear is that these hypotheses drew upon the empirical and theoretical knowledge base of the day. For example, the bomber's letters suggested the diagnosis of paranoia, along with some psychoanalytic inferences as to sexual functioning. Several inferences flowed from the hypothesis that the offender was paranoid (e.g., age). Even the likely physical characteristics of the offender were based on Kretschmer's (1925) since debunked morphological theory of physique and character. The interplay between nomothetic empirical and theoretical knowledge with the idiographic aspects of the individual case was also clear. Brussel (1968) noted that:

> I always start such a deduction with a solid basis of science, but somewhere along the way intuition and imagination begin to take over. When you think about an unknown criminal long enough, when you've assembled all the known facts about him and poked at them and stirred them about in your mind, you begin to *see* the man.
>
> (p. 80)

Interestingly, Brussel was aware of the probabilistic nature of profiling activity and readily admitted that his use of the extant literature sometimes produced erroneous results in the individual case. For example, he stated that:

> There were times when I made mistakes. There were times when I lacked enough information to build an image of the criminal. There were times when the law of averages let me down: I'd diagnose a man as a paranoiac and imagine him as having a well-proportioned physique, and then he'd turn out to be among the 15 percent of paranoiacs who are not so built.
>
> (p. 74)

It should be noted that Brussel was not the only clinician involved in providing behavioural investigative advice during this period. However, the reliability of such advice is open to question. Indeed, during the Boston Strangler investigation in 1964 the Assistant Attorney General of Massachusetts assembled a "Medical-Psychiatric Committee" to provide advice. This consisted of four psychiatrists, including Brussel, and a psychologist, medical examiner, anthropologist, and sociologist. The committee disagreed on many aspects of the murders, including whether they were committed by the same individual. Importantly, Kenefick (1968), who was the coordinator of the committee, suggested that the approach most consistent with the task would be to "set down what is known of various types of murderers, attempt to describe what if any obvious differentiating behavior such persons might show, and try to set these out as clearly as possible" (p. 92). However, Kenefick also lamented the state of the empirical evidence base:

> The thought that such knowledge was already at the fingertips of psychiatrists was shaken by a review of the literature. With few exceptions, the contributions of psychiatrists were anecdotal – interesting but plausible

> only for those whose faith does not need the vulgarity of demonstration. If my faith was shaken by the literature, it was also kept in gentle oscillation by the committee. While the conversations were interesting and occasionally insightful, none of the contributions seemed very useful. It became fairly obvious that modern psychiatry did not know very much about multiple sexual murderers, or at least that we did not.
>
> (p. 92)

A more recent description of offender profiling by clinical practitioners in the UK was described by Copson, Badcock, Boon, and Britton (1997). This described the commonalities in the profiling practices of three individuals who were then providing advice to police investigations (one psychiatrist and two psychologists), some of which mirror the earlier work noted above. The various common steps included a reconstruction of events as to what occurred, how it occurred, and to whom it occurred. This was followed by the inference of motive and the "importation of factors from relevant literature" (p. 15), along with the development of psychological constructs based on the literature and the crime reconstruction (e.g., personality disorders). Hypotheses as to demographic and social factors were also provided "with probability markers as appropriate" (p. 16). Importantly, it was also posited that "the clinical profiler must be prepared to explain his/her constructs and reasoning, and sometimes to enlighten the officer in aspects of psychological and criminological learning ..." (p. 16).[2]

Despite some commonalities, the profiling work of clinical practitioners can hardly be seen as a unified "approach" to offender profiling and behavioural investigative advice. Indeed, some clinicians have successfully provided useful advice to police investigations, whereas others have not. Though there are likely to be considerable differences in the way that individual clinicians approach the BIA tasks, descriptions of their contributions in the non-clinical academic literature are often overly simplistic or downright dismissive. For example, Wilson, Lincoln, and Kocsis (1997) gave clinical profiling the label of "diagnostic evaluations" and argued that "the construction of profiles is achieved by diagnosing the probable psychopathology and/or personality type likely to have committed the crime" (p. 3). Even more simplistically, Vettor, Woodhams, and Beech (2013) stated that "this approach is primarily based on the individual clinician's experience and knowledge gained through working with individual clients, and the application of this to drawing conclusions or inferences from crime scene information" (p. 371). Such opinions seem to ignore the fact that clinical practice itself is built on an extensive literature base, rather than simply learning on the job, as well as the fact that clinicians involved in profiling since the 1950s have explicitly described drawing upon the extant literature. Nonetheless, the extent to which clinicians anchor their opinions in the formal knowledge base of the discipline likely varies substantially from practitioner to practitioner.

Criminal investigative analysis

The very use of the term "profiling" is almost synonymous with the work of the FBI's Behavioral Science Unit and its successor units (there are currently five Behavioral Analysis Units within the FBI's National Center for the Analysis of Violent Crime; NCAVC). The pioneer of profiling at the FBI was Howard Teten, a criminologist and former police officer (Depue, 2014). Interestingly, Teten reportedly sought some instruction from Dr. James Brussel when developing the initial FBI profiling approach (DeNevi & Campbell, 2004). Offender profiling and the various other behavioural investigative techniques subsequently became known under the umbrella term "Criminal Investigative Analysis" (CIA). This emphasised the fact that while the practitioners of CIA may have had qualifications in the behavioural sciences, they were law enforcement officers, and as such, the term "was coined to differentiate the procedure from that used by mental health professionals" (Hazelwood, Ressler, Depue, & Douglas, 1995, p. 115). As such, research and other scholarly activity emanating from the NCAVC has always had a strong criminal investigative focus (Depue, 2014).

CIA is the dominant approach to offender profiling in North America and Australia. While the FBI NCAVC is well known, the methods that emanated from the FBI Academy have also found widespread use via the International Criminal Investigative Analysis Fellowship (ICIAF). This grew out of the FBI's Police Fellowship Program that ran from 1984 to 1991, whereby police officers spent one year with the NCAVC and received training in CIA that they could then use in their home police agency (Hazelwood, 1986). When the Program ended, the fellows developed an understudy programme to replicate their training. The ICIAF continues to provide FBI-approved training to police officers around the world (Depue, 2014; see also http://www.iciaf.org). In recognition of the multidisciplinary nature of this field, the ICIAF also allows for non-police professionals (e.g., mental health professionals) to be elected to membership in recognition of their contribution to cases and assistance to members of the fellowship (Davis & Bennett, 2006).

The criminal investigative analysis process in regard to offender profiling has been described in varying degrees of detail in different publications through the years (e.g., Douglas, Ressler, Burgess, & Hartman, 1986; Hazelwood, 1987). One particularly useful overview was described by Dietz (1985), who has been the forensic psychiatrist consultant to the FBI NCAVC for several decades. He described five stages in the offender profiling process. The first was *Data Assimilation*, whereby the various materials are analysed. Dietz noted that:

> the profiler inevitably begins to formulate hypotheses and to test them against the facts as they unfold. In this process, some ideas are discarded as disconfirmatory evidence is encountered, while others are strengthened by confirmatory evidence .... Often an otherwise attractive set of hypotheses has to be discarded when a piece of evidence is recalled or newly

> discovered that does not fit, and when this occurs the profiler returns to the data base and repeats the process.
>
> (p. 210)

The second stage is *Behavioral Reconstruction*. As the name suggests, this involves establishing the sequence of events before, during, and after the offence. Dietz noted that:

> as the profiler reconstructs the events, he checks tentative formulations against the data base, revising and rearranging until he finds a reasonable sequence that fits all the known facts. Here, as at each subsequent stage, there is a risk of becoming overly committed to a formulation that leaves some pieces of evidence unexplained or that is only one of several formulations that fit the facts equally well.
>
> (p. 211)

The third stage involves the formulation of *Motivational Hypotheses* that account for the behavioural reconstruction. Some profilers have described motivation as "the primary psychological evidence" (Ault & Reese, 1980, p. 25). Nonetheless, Dietz (1985) noted that "it should be understood that such motivational hypotheses are psychological fictions used as one step in solving a problem" (pp. 211–212) and suggested that they were analogous to the fictions of other fields such as "the dummy variables of the statistician, the rational man of the economist, or the free will of the jurist. Like motives, these fictions are useful in helping us feel as if we have explained some set of observed relationships" (p. 212). It was noted that:

> there is no way to measure the validity of motivational hypotheses. They can be judged only by the degree to which they appear to make sense of the factual evidence and the behavioural reconstruction and by their usefulness in moving on to the fourth stage.
>
> (p. 213)

The fourth stage involves the development of *Typological Hypotheses*. The degree of organisation or disorganisation in an offence (see below) is one such typological consideration, but there are a number of offender typologies, some of which explicitly rely on the inference of motive and some of which do not. Dietz (1985) noted that:

> in profiling, of course, much more is desired than the assignment of the offender to a category. It is desirable that he be assigned to one category in each of a number of typologies. Theoretically, the more typological 'dimensions' on which he is located, the more specific one should be able to be in formulating attributional hypotheses in the fifth stage.
>
> (p. 215)

The final stage is the development of *Attributional Hypotheses* in which "the profiler uses the case-specific data, behavior, motivational hypotheses, and typological hypotheses to deduce the particular attributes expected to characterize the individual" (p. 215). Dietz (1985) noted that some such hypotheses derive directly from typologies, while interactions between multiple attributional hypotheses can provide greater specificity.

It is particularly interesting to note that Dietz's conceptual model of the profiling process is very similar to the clinical profiling model described by Copson and colleagues (1997) in the UK 12 years later. Both describe a reconstruction stage, and a central stage in which motivational hypotheses are inferred. Indeed, both conceptual models require such hypotheses in order to progress with the construction of an offender profile.

In regard to the knowledge base for CIA, the FBI NCAVC has developed a number of offence typologies and conducted research on topics such as sexual homicide (Burgess & Ressler, 1985; Ressler, Burgess, & Douglas, 1988), elderly sexual homicide (Safarik, Jarvis, & Nussbaum, 2002), rape (Hazelwood & Burgess, 1987; Hazelwood, Reboussin, & Warren, 1989), arson (Icove & Estepp, 1987; Sapp, Huff, Gary, Icove, & Horbert, 1996), and stalking (Wright, Burgess, Burgess, Laszlo, McCrary, & Douglas, 1996). In addition, members of the NCAVC developed the *Crime Classification Manual* (CCM) in 1992 (Douglas, Burgess, Burgess, & Ressler, 1992), which is now in its third edition (Douglas et al., 2013). The CCM includes a number of rationally-derived typologies in regard to homicide, arson and bombing, sexual offending, non-lethal crimes, and computer crimes, to assist in crime classification and investigation. The manual also provides descriptions of CIA concepts such as the difference between modus operandi and personation (i.e., ritualistic offence behaviour).

While offender profiling is frequently misunderstood in the literature (often by those not actually involved in this area of practice), the work of the FBI NCAVC is particularly misunderstood. One overwhelmingly misinterpreted aspect is that of the organised-disorganised concept in sexual homicide. This was initially described by Hazelwood and Douglas (1980) who posited that there were two broad groupings of sexual homicide offenders. The organised nonsocial were described as self-centred and indifferent to others and left largely organised crime scenes. The disorganised asocial were thought to be socially averse and commit more frenzied offences. Davis (2016) described how this simple concept, which has also been found or suggested by a range of authors using different terminology (e.g., Beauregard, Proulx, & St-Yves, 2007; Gerard, Mormont, & Kocsis, 2007; Meloy, 2000; Revitch & Schelsinger, 1978, 1981, 1989; Trojan & Salfati, 2011) was subsequently misinterpreted in two baffling ways by those contributing to the profiling literature. First, the concept was considered to be a rigid dichotomy whereby all offenders could be considered either organised or disorganised. Indeed, a myth began to circulate in the literature that a "mixed" category had to be developed when the CCM was published in 1992 (e.g., Canter, Alison, Alison, & Wentink, 2004; Vettor et al., 2013).

However, the earliest empirical explorations of this construct indicated that it was always viewed as a continuum. Indeed, the first study by Burgess and Ressler (1985) considered offences on a five-point ordinal scale of: very organised, organised, mixed, disorganised, and very disorganised.

The second way in which the organised–disorganised concept was misinterpreted was in many ways an extension of the initial error. Once the concept was viewed as a strict dichotomy, a number of critical authors formed the view that the profiling of sexual homicide offences by CIA practitioners was a simple exercise in which there was an organised profile and a disorganised profile (e.g., Devery, 2010; Kocsis, 2009; Turvey, 2012). This was clearly erroneous. In fact, as can be readily appreciated from the above discussion, creating an offender profile is a far more involved process than simply deciding which of two boilerplate descriptions is appropriate to the individual case. Moreover, Douglas et al. (1986) indicated that the degree of organisation or disorganisation at the crime scene is just one of several considerations that may contribute to the final profile opinion.

Investigative psychology

Investigative psychology was developed in the UK by Professor David Canter. This grew out of his serendipitous work on the "Railway Rapist" case in 1985 in which he developed an offender profile based on social psychological principles that was ultimately accurate, and more importantly, useful to investigating police. Canter (1994) explained that this initial success motivated him to develop a scientific evidence base for such advice. He termed this new discipline investigative psychology. Taking a more social psychological perspective than had hitherto been the norm when considering offender profiling, Canter devised models illustrating consistency in both an offender's behaviour and their patterns of crime scene behaviour. These models were invariably developed using multivariate statistical analyses from the facet theory approach to research (Canter, 1985; Guttman, 1954a, 1954b; Guttman & Greenbaum, 1998). However, despite the advanced statistical modelling, this was not simple atheoretical number-crunching. Rather, in line with the facet theory approach, the multivariate analyses were used to develop models with a strong theoretical component.

Canter's work in regard to offender profiling has centred around two key models, the victim role model and the actions systems model (Canter, 1994, 2010; Shye, 1985). As the name suggests, the victim role model posited that offence behaviours could be considered through the role which the offender assigns their victim during their interaction. In this way, the victim is viewed as an object, vehicle, or person. The theory that the role of a victim was of importance in homicide cases was addressed by Wolfgang (1958) in his book, *Patterns in Criminal Homicide*. Wolfgang reported that violent homicides were often multifaceted interactions between offender characteristics, victim characteristics, and the environmental context. The victim role provides a fundamental structure that is diverse and flexible, capable of accommodating different contexts and offender presentations (Canter & Youngs, 2009; see also Canter & Youngs, 2012).

According to Canter's (1994) model, offences in which the victim is an object involve limited feelings being associated with the victim. Canter and Youngs (2009) believed that in cases where the victim is an object, the offender has a focus on control and competent mastery of the crime (victim) or event. In the victim as vehicle context, the victim is assigned some meaningful role to the offender and therefore a specific victim type is targeted. The victim in this role is likely to form an outlet for the offender's vindictive and angry desires. Finally, in the victim as person case, the victim is often known to the offender and the offender may recognise the humanity of the victim, and engage in a style of attack that may be less violent in nature. In these cases the offender may seek a distorted form of intimacy with the victim to address their sense of emptiness (Canter & Youngs, 2009).

Fritzon and Ridgway (2001) applied the victim role model to a sample of 93 attempted homicide cases. The study utilised smallest space analysis (SSA) to analyse offender behaviour in relation to victim resistance. Results of the study supported the three themes of victim–offender role proposed by Canter (1994). Within the victim as person theme the level of violence used in the attack was minimal and weapon choice primarily pertained to a blunt object. In the victim as a vehicle theme, the offender was more likely to be opportunistic, consumed alcohol, and used a weapon at the scene. The act of violence was a singular act resulting in a singular wound, while other associated acts included binding, gagging, and theft. The victim as object theme involved the offender having limited recognition that the victim was a human being. The victim had many severe wounds to multiple body parts and it was evident from the crime that the offender used excessive violence. The study demonstrated that the application of Canter's (1994) victim role can provide a structured and systematic method for classifying homicide behaviour. Notably, one implication of this study was that cases analysed pertained to attempted murder and as such the role of the victim in the offence was more paramount (due to the survival of the victim).

The actions system model was originally devised by Shye (1985) as method of modelling quality of life concerns, which were proposed as deriving from internal or external sources. The differentiation of behaviour was also believed to be impacted by whether the desired locus of effect was either an internal or external target (Fritzon, 2012). The actions system proposed that four modes of functioning (action systems) existed; these were expressive, integrative, adaptive, and conservative.

The adaptive mode occurs when external events become the source of interaction or conflict, whereby the individual attempts to change the external circumstance. The expressive mode pertains to the individual demonstrating internal psychological aspects to their external world (Neville, Miller, &

Fritzon, 2007). The integrative mode concerns adjustments that take place within the system itself. Specifically, this refers to the source of conflict being internal and the individual reacting in an attempt to change this internal state. Finally, in the conservative mode the source of conflict is external and the individual reacts and attempts to change their internal psychological state. Since first being applied to analyse criminal behaviour by Fritzon, Canter, and Wilton (2001), the model has been demonstrated to successfully distinguish different modes of action, criminal behaviours, and explanations for crime (Almond, Duggan, Shine, Canter, 2005; Canter & Youngs, 2009). The first study that applied this model to analyse criminal behaviour involved a sample of 230 individuals convicted of arson and 41 incidents of terrorist hostage taking (Fritzon et al., 2001). Results of this study have since been replicated using the same model for different and varying samples, including a female population with mental illness (Miller & Fritzon, 2007), and an incarcerated population (Almond et al., 2005).

The contribution of investigative psychology to the empirical and theoretical evidence base of offender profiling cannot be underestimated. Over more than three decades, Canter and his colleagues and students have published a wealth of studies that can inform those involved in the provision of behavioural investigative advice (see Canter & Youngs, 2009, for an overview). However, while there was some initial suggestion that investigative psychology constituted an "approach" to offender profiling (e.g., Alison & Salfati, 1998), more recent literature by those who have completed doctoral level study in investigative psychology has questioned whether this actually constitutes an approach to BIA work. For example, Snook, Eastwood, Gendreau, and Bennell (2010) stated that "frankly, we are not even clear what an 'investigative psychology approach to criminal profiling' is, given that people who have studied IP appear to advocate different profiling methods" (p. 219). Indeed, while many of those engaged in the practice of behavioural investigative advice within the UK have received training in investigative psychology, BIA itself is now a profession in its own right, one that has been influenced by all of its historical precursors.

What are the differences between contemporary profilers?

As can be readily appreciated from the preceding material, there is considerable overlap between the various movements that have contributed to offender profiling. As such, the idea that someone is using one "method" in opposition to another is more of an academic myth than reality. Some literature has suggested that profilers can be differentiated based on whether they use a clinical or statistical approach (Copson, 1995), whether their inferences are inductive or deductive (Turvey, 1999), or somewhat bizarrely, whether they write their profiles or provide them verbally (Turvey & Esparza, 2016). However, we disagree that such crude distinctions have any real validity. The authors of this chapter have worked with profiler practitioners in the UK, North America,

Australia, and several countries in Europe and Asia. Though there have undoubtedly been interesting differences observed, we have become convinced that these are primarily in regard to emphasis rather than distinctive methods. As one would expect in any area of applied behavioural science, we have observed differing emphases in the use of formal knowledge (empirical evidence) and tacit knowledge (knowledge derived from individual or collective experience; see Collins, 2010). Moreover, we have ascertained that most differences in BIA practice arise from differing emphasis on the use of deductive, inductive, and abductive reasoning (Davis, 2011), which in turn often vary between individual practitioners dependent upon the specific task at hand.

Deductive reasoning

An argument is deductively valid (see Chapter 3, Ask and Fahsing) if its premises logically imply its final conclusion. For example, the *modus ponens* is a deductive argument of the form: If A then B; A; therefore B. Similarly, the *modus tollens* is a deductive argument of the form: If A then B; not-B; therefore, not-A. Accordingly, if all of the premises in a deductively valid argument are true, the conclusion must also be true (Curd & Cover, 1998).

Because of this, Turvey (1999) argued that a deductive approach to offender profiling is to be preferred (although, in his defence, Turvey did not claim that the approach outlined in his publications was entirely deductive; it is not). It is an admittedly enticing proposition on its surface. However, Davis (2011) has noted that the use of deductive reasoning with valid premises requires universal laws. These are extremely rare in the behavioural sciences. This is far from a new argument. Indeed, in regard to making clinical predictions about individuals, Meehl (1954) argued that

> the facts of the psychometrics, the history, and the interview are not related by direct causal laws to the events we wish to predict . . . There is, because of our lack of specific information (and our lack of knowledge of laws) merely a crude and fragmentary relationship between the predictive data and our hypothesis concerning the inner state or structure of the person at hand.
>
> (p. 45)

Given the lack of universal laws in the behavioural sciences, attempts at making deductive arguments in profiling, especially those that refer to psychological constructs, are rarely going to be based on true premises. The exception would be inferences based on purely physical aspects of an offence, such as knife wounds indicating that a sharp weapon was used or tyre tracks indicating that a vehicle was present. In fact, Davis (2011) performed a content analysis of a report that was prepared using a claimed "deductive" profiling method. As one would expect, most of the inferences actually involved abductive or inductive reasoning. Deductive reasoning was primarily present in regard to physical aspects of the crime scene. These are arguably the aspects of an offence in which investigators are less likely to require the assistance of a behavioural analyst, or indeed where behavioural competence represents relevant domain specific expertise.

Inductive reasoning

In contrast to deduction, inductive reasoning is inherently probabilistic. Broad (1952, as cited in Lipton, 1998) described induction as "'the glory of science' but 'the scandal of philosophy'" (p. 497). Indeed, all empirical inference is formally invalid (Meehl, 1961). Induction is the form of reasoning we apply when making inferences about an individual from group data. For example, a profiler analysing a rape offence may note that the offender broke into the victim's home, took precautions not to leave fingerprints, stole from the victim, used a weapon to intimidate them, and had been drinking alcohol. The profiler might consider that when this combination of offence behaviours co-occurred in a sample of 210 British rapists (Davies, 1997), the probability that the offender had a prior conviction for burglary was between 0.93 and 1.00. Thus, the practitioner may conclude that this is a likely demographic characteristic of the offender, even though this was not a universal finding. However, if the rapist used a weapon to intimidate the victim without the other four behaviours, the probability of a prior burglary conviction was between 0.08 and 0.31 (Davies, 1997). Therefore, the profiler may not make the same conclusion, even though this would be true for some individual offenders.

Abductive reasoning (see also Chapter 3 this volume for more on abductive reasoning)

The third type of reasoning is abduction (also known as hypothesis, retroduction, or inference to the best explanation).[3] It was promoted by C. S. Pierce in the nineteenth century but dates back to Aristotle's concept of *apagoge* (Brogaard, 1999; Niinuluoto, 1999). Pierce (1898, as cited in Niiniluoti, 1999) stated that induction involves probable reasoning in the third figure of the syllogism, whereas abduction involves "probable reasoning in the second figure" (p. s438). Niiniluoto (1999) cited the following as Pierce's general form for an abductive argument:

> The surprising fact C is observed;
> But if A were true, C would be a matter of course,
> Hence, there is reason to suspect that A is true.
>
> (p. s439)

It is perhaps unremarkable that decisions in offender profiling, and for that matter all of forensic-clinical psychology, involve a great deal of abductive reasoning. The above syllogism also strongly indicates that profilers should take time to argue against their opinions and consider alternate hypotheses. Such an activity is familiar to clinicians as the practice of differential diagnosis, and forms of the cornerstone of crime scene assessment and hypotheses generation and prioritisation as practised by UK BIAs (Rainbow & Gregory, 2011).

Modern offender profiling

As noted above, it is our opinion that all modern offender profiling practitioners use a pragmatic combination of inductive, deductive, and abductive reasoning. Differences between practitioners will generally be found in regard to the emphasis placed on these three modes of reasoning. The various forms of evidence that may be relied upon are described in Figure 10.1.

It can be seen in Figure 10.1 that those providing offender profiling opinions potentially have a range of empirical and theoretical considerations upon which to base their inferences. Ideally, one would initially anchor their opinion in the available empirical literature. However, it is important for professional judgment to also play a role. Empirical links between offence actions and offender characteristics are weak for some forms of offending. Moreover, the links that have been found may be compromised by situational influences, such as the

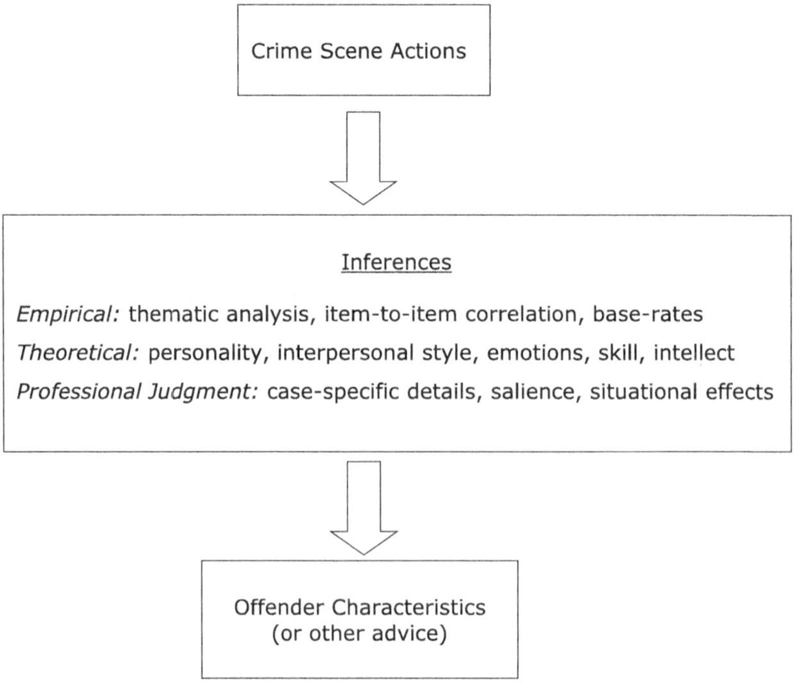

Figure 10.1 Conceptual model of the offender profiling inferential process

victim's reaction, so that the offender's intended behaviour does not match their actual behaviour. Solid abductive reasoning should be used to individualise the nomothetic empirical information where possible. This combination of formal and tacit knowledge, combining a nomothetic empirical anchor with case-specific idiographic consideration, has been described as *pragmatism* (Alison, 2005; Alison, Goodwill, Almond, van den Heuvel, & Winter, 2010; Alison, West, & Goodwill, 2004) and *structured professional judgment* (Davis, 2003, 2012; Davis & Bennett, 2016) after the decision-making process used in assessing risk for violence. It arguably provides a flexible and defensible framework for constructing offender profiles (Davis & Bennett, 2016).

Illustrative case example

The following vignette taken from the case notes of an experienced profiler has been presented to contextualise the argument regarding the inferential process with regard to one aspect of a profiling report. Any commentary or evaluation of the profiler's contribution is deliberately absent, with the reader invited to assess the relative presence, absence and merits of *formal* and *tacit* knowledge and *deductive, inductive*, and *abductive* reasoning in inference generation and support.

Case overview

The case involved a female victim who was discovered clothed and had sustained multiple sharp injuries to her neck and upper chest. There were no forensic findings to indicate sexual activity, although the murder occurred at a location associated with sex workers and an unused condom was recovered at the scene. Pathological and forensic analyses suggested an initial sharp injury to the victim's throat when she was standing, followed by a sequence of wounds inflicted as she was lying on her back after she had been moved a short distance from the initial attack site. No weapon had been recovered.

Investigating officers accepted that the victim's vulnerability to assault and sexually related assault by a stranger was significantly increased because of her involvement in street prostitution. However, because of her chaotic lifestyle, history of substance misuse, and related drug debts, they also questioned whether the presence of the condom indicated an element of staging in an effort to conceal other more personally directed motives by a person or persons known to her.

Inferential process

Since conventional evidence of the crime's sexual nature was absent at the crime scene, the possibility of a sexual motivation for this murder was not readily apparent. However, the force and focus of the injuries even at first impression seemed incongruous with some of the preliminary hypotheses formulated by the investigation, namely; had the victim been killed secondary to a street robbery or to prevent disclosure of drug supply information to the police? Although it is acknowledged that such punishment type murders do occur and are usually understood locally to represent a form of warning, it was soon clear that there was no local intelligence to support these lines of enquiry.

The investigation also questioned whether the victim had been murdered by a partner or ex-partner. Such circumstances, with close parallels to domestic murder, are often preceded by a history of threats to harm, assault, and attempts to separate from the abusive partner against a background of possessiveness, control, and prior involvement with agencies such as the police and the courts (Websdale, 1999). Again, local intelligence from the victim's associates and other sex workers did not support the involvement of a significant partner or previous client who might have developed some kind of obsessive interest in her.

Reference to the academic literature suggests that unprovoked lethal assaults against strangers can arise as a result of acute mental illness, particularly during a first episode – that is, in the earlier stages before the development of disabling negative symptoms. Whilst family members or close associates are more frequently the victims of homicide committed during psychotic illness (stabbing is a common method), unprovoked assaults against strangers also occur. It is well established that drug use increases the risk of violence by people with psychotic illness (Nielssen et al., 2007). In this instance, given the victim's involvement with substance misuse services and the backgrounds of many of her associates, contact with local mental health services was encouraged.

Consideration of the force and number of sharp injuries inflicted on the victim prompted review of the relevant research. Megargee (1966) identified that over-controlled personality types appear with greater frequency among extremely assaultive groups than among moderate assaultives. He suggested that the over-controlled murderer experiences powerful inhibitions against expressing aggression, such that he does not learn to displace aggression, or to release it in small amounts. Consequently, he engages in much less violence and aggression overall than others, but on the infrequent occasions when inhibitions are overcome, he erupts in a display of uncontrolled aggression that is very extreme and violent (Ogle et al., 1995). Prior experience in clinical assessments of mentally disordered offenders had already provided confirmation of the model boy who having released all of his supressed aggression in a violent catastrophic act, then becomes a model boy again.

Blackburn (1968a; 1968b; 1971) also reported that extremely assaultive criminals appeared to be more repressed and over-controlled than moderately assaultive criminals. Furthermore, the extremely assaultive criminals were not on the whole persistently assaultive, but were more likely to be depressed, inhibited, and socially withdrawn. Alongside this hypothesised implicit personality, the place of the victim as a vehicle for the expression of the perpetrator's own inner conflicts gained more resonance in the context of the sexual setting in which the murder occurred leading to the hypothesis that this was a sexual homicide committed by a stranger; that is, someone with whom the victim had no previous association (Meloy, 2000; Schlesinger, 2007). Awareness of other patients and research prompted review of Grubin's (1994) research in which he compared a group of 21 sexual murderers with a group of 121 men who had raped but not killed, and found that a history of social and personal isolation was a critical differentiating variable: Many of the murderers lived alone, and many had little in the way of social contacts or social interaction; even as children many were not part of their peer groups. In addition, most of the murderers had few if any intimate relationships with women, and the relationships they did form tended to be emotionally limited, with little sharing or confiding. Social and emotional isolation, although not emphasised, are also characteristics that appear consistently in the published work on sexual murderers (Brittain, 1970; Burgess et al., 1986; Ressler et al., 1988).

Some time later a local man with a schizoid personality disorder was apprehended, having been identified through forensic DNA analyses.

Conclusions and reflections

The aim of this chapter was to illuminate the contemporary practice of offender profiling/behavioural investigative advice, and to describe the range of psychological ideas, theories, and constructs that have informed the development of the field to its current form. Though historically divergent methods existed, and for some the focus was less on psychological theory and more on behavioural sciences processes and methods, the modern approaches used throughout Europe, North America, and Australia are now both integrated and informed by psychology and criminology research and practice. It is our thesis that behavioural science oriented advice to major crime investigations should be continually evolving through a pragmatic "horses for courses" philosophy, whereby practitioners apply a hybrid methodology, skilfully adapting various but complementary approaches dependent upon the available data, research, and experience, tailored to the needs of each specific enquiry. It is our strongly held view that such practice represents the most effective way forward and should be adopted as contemporary best practice. It is further hoped that a shared appreciation of a multidisciplinary and mixed methodological approach will contribute to the much needed reframing of the profiling agenda from distasteful competition to constructive collaboration. To this end, we have been impressed by the willingness and enthusiasm of our practitioner colleagues around the world to engage in multidisciplinary discussion and collaboration and hope to see this extend to the often caustic scholarly literature.

Notes

1 We consider the focus on this piece of information to be a shame for several reasons. First, the investigative relevance and utility of a buttoned double-breasted suit is

questionable. Indeed, how are police to use such information to further their investigation? Furthermore, and admittedly with the benefit of hindsight, we do not believe that this was such a miraculous inference. Rather, it is arguably a case of simple base rates. After making the inference that the offender was likely a neat man aged 40–50 years, the most likely attire for such a man in 1950s New York would have been a double-breasted suit. Few individuals would wear such a suit unbuttoned. Moreover, Brussel (1968) also indicated some initial reticence in providing this final feature to his profile. He noted that as investigators were leaving his office "I decided there was no use in doing things halfway. If I was going to be wrong, I might as well be like the Bomber – 100 percent wrong. 'Inspector.' The three men turned toward me. 'Doctor?' 'One more thing.' I closed my eyes because I didn't want to see their reaction. I saw the Bomber: impeccably neat, absolutely proper. A man who would avoid the newer styles of clothing until long custom had made them conservative. I saw him clearly – much more clearly than the facts really warranted. I knew I was letting my imagination get the better of me, but I couldn't help it" (p. 46).

2 While a thorough description of the clinical profiling literature is beyond the scope of this chapter, it should be noted that various authors have described particular emphases within their profiling practice, such as personality theories (Boon, 1997, 1998) and psychoanalytic theory integrated with neurological data (Liebert, 1985; Turco, 1990).

3 Curd and Cover (1998) noted that some philosophers treat abduction as distinct from inference to the best explanation based on abduction suggesting a single theory and the latter involving a comparison of several theories. However, they note that the majority of philosophers use the terms interchangeably.

References

Alison, L. (2005). *The forensic psychologist's casebook: Psychological profiling and criminal investigation*. Devon, UK: Willan.

Alison, L. A., West, A., & Goodwill, A. (2004). The academic and the practitioner: Pragmatists' views of offender profiling. *Psychology, Public Policy and Law*, 10(1/2), 71–101.

Alison, L. A., Goodwill, A., Almond, L., van den Heuvel, C., & Winter, J. (2010). Pragmatic solutions to offender profiling and behavioural investigative advice. *Legal and Criminological Psychology*, 15(1), 115–132.

Alison, L., and Salfati, G. (1998). Der ermittlungspsychologische Ansatz. In Bundeskriminalamt (Hg.): Methoden der Fallanalyse. Ein internationales Symposium. (BKA – Forschungsreihe Bd. 38.1). Wiesbaden 1998.

Almond, L., Duggan, L., Shine, J., & Canter, D. (2005). Test of the arson action system model in an incarcerated population. *Psychology, Crime & Law*, 11(1), 1–15. http://dx.doi.org/10.1080/10683160310009634287.

Ault, R. L. (2010). Indirect personality assessment. In M. R. Napier (ed.), *Behavior, truth and deception: Applying profiling and analysis to the interview process* (pp. 63–75). Boca Raton, FL: CRC Press.

Ault, R. L., & Hazelwood, R. R. (1995). Indirect personality assessment. In R. R. Hazelwood & A. W. Burgess (eds), *Practical aspects of rape investigation: A multidisciplinary approach* (2nd edn; pp. 205–218). Boca Raton, FL: CRC Press.

Ault, R. L., & Reese, J. T. (1980, March). A psychological assessment of crime: Profiling. *FBI Law Enforcement Bulletin*, 49(3), 22–25.

Beauregard, E., Proulx, J., St-Yves, M. (2007). Angry or sadistic: Two types of sexual murderers. In J. Proulx, E. Beauregard, M. Cusson, & A. Nicole (eds), *Sexual murderers: A comparative analysis and new perspectives* (pp. 123–141). Chichester, UK: John Wiley.

Blackburn, R. (1968a). Personality in relation to extreme aggression in psychiatric offenders. *British Journal of Psychiatry*, 114, 821–828.

Blackburn, R. (1968b). Emotionality, extroversion and aggression in paranoid and nonparanoid schizophrenic offenders. *British Journal of Psychiatry*, 114, 1301–1302.

Blackburn, R. (1971). Personality types among abnormal homicides. *British Journal of Criminology*, 11(1),14–31.

Brittain, R. (1970). The sadistic murderer. *Medical Science and the Law*, 10, 198–207.

Brogaard, B. (1999). A Piercean theory of decision. *Synthese*, 118, 383–401.

Brussel, J. A. (1968). *Casebook of a crime psychiatrist.* London, UK: New English Library.

Burgess, A. W., & Ressler, R. K. (1985, May). *Sexual homicide crime scenes and patterns of criminal behavior.* Final report to the National Institute of Justice.

Burgess, A. W., Hartman, C. R., Ressler, R. K., Douglas, J. E., & McCormack, A. (1986). Sexual homicide: A motivational model. *Journal of Interpersonal Violence*, 1, 251–272.

Canter, D. (1994). *Criminal shadows.* London: HarperCollins.

Canter, D. (ed.). (1985). *Facet theory: Approaches to social research.* New York: Springer.

Canter, D. V. (2010). Offender profiling. In *The Cambridge Handbook of Forensic Psychology.* Cambridge Handbooks in Psychology (pp. 236–241). Cambridge, UK: Cambridge University Press.

Canter, D., & Youngs, D. (2012). Sexual and violent offenders' victim role assignments: A general model of offending style. *Journal of Forensic Psychiatry & Psychology*, 23(3), 297–326.

Canter, D., & Youngs, D. (2009). *Investigative psychology: Offender profiling and the analysis of criminal action.* Chichester, UK: John Wiley & Sons.

Canter, D. V., Alison, L. J., Alison, E. K., & Wentink, N. (2004). The organized / disorganized typology of serial murder: Myth or model? *Psychology, Public Policy and Law*, 10(3), 293–320.

Collins, H. (2010). *Tacit and explicit knowledge.* Chicago, IL: University of Chicago Press.

Cook, P. E., & Hinman, D. L. (1999). Criminal profiling: Science and art. *Journal of Contemporary Criminal Justice*, 15, 230–241.

Copson, G. (1995). *Coals to Newcastle? Part 1: A study of offender profiling.* Police Research Special Interest Series, Paper 7. London: Home Office.

Copson, G., Badcock, R., Boon, J., & Britton, P. (1997). Articulating a systematic approach to clinical crime profiling. *Criminal Behavior and Mental Health*, 7, 13–17.

Curd, M., & Cover, J. (1998). Glossary. In M. Curd & J. A. Cover (eds), *Philosophy of science: The central issues* (pp. 1291–1310). New York, NY: W. W. Norton & Company.

Davies, A. (1997). Specific profile analysis: A data based approach to offender profiling. In J. Jackson & D. Bekerian (eds), *Offender profiling: Theory, research and practice.* New York: John Wiley.

Davies, A., Wittebrood, K., & Jackson, J. L. (1997). Predicting the criminal antecedents of a stranger rapist from his offence behaviour. *Science and Justice*, 37, 161–170.

Davis, M. R. (2003, July). A structured professional judgment approach to offender profiling: Bridging the gap between research and practice. Paper presented at the 2nd International Psychology and Law conference (joint EAP&L/AP-LS/ANZAPPL conference), Edinburgh, Scotland, United Kingdom.

Davis, M. R. (2011, April). Unravelling the inductive-deductive debate in offender profiling. Paper presented at the 12th International Investigative Psychology conference, Amsterdam, The Netherlands.

Davis, M. R. (2012, September). Of straw men and empirical relationships: What can we glean from the profiling literature? Two-hour address presented at the training conference of the International Criminal Investigative Analysis Fellowship (ICIAF), Forsyth, Georgia, USA.

Davis, M. R. (2016, May). Another look at the organised-disorganised concept in sexual homicide: Myth, straw-man, or useful construct? Paper presented at the 17th International Investigative Psychology conference, New York, USA.

Davis, M. R., & Bennett, D. (2006, October). Criminal investigative analysis in the Australian context. *Psych: The Bulletin of the Australian Psychological Society*, 28(5), 17–19.

Davis, M. R., & Bennett, D. (2016). Future directions for criminal behaviour analysis of deliberately set fire events. In R. Doley, G. Dickens, & T. Gannon (eds), *The psychology of arson: A practical guide to understanding and managing deliberate firesetters* (pp. 131–146). Oxon, UK: Routledge.

DeNevi, D., & Campbell, J. H. (2004). *Into the minds of madmen: How the FBI's Behavioral Science Unit revolutionized crime investigation*. Amherst, NY: Prometheus Books.

Depue, R. L. (2014). Criminal investigative analysis. In G. J. N. Bruinsma & D. L. Weisburd (eds), *Encyclopedia of criminology and criminal justice* (pp. 828–838). New York: Springer.

Devery, C. (2010). Criminal profiling and criminal investigation. *Journal of Contemporary Criminal Justice*, 26, 393–409. doi:10.1177/1043986210377108

Dietz, P. E. (1985). Sex offender profiling by the FBI: A preliminary conceptual model. In M. H. Ben-Aron, S. J. Hucker, & C. D. Webster (eds), *Clinical criminology: The assessment and treatment of criminal behaviour* (pp. 207–219). Toronto: M & M Graphics Ltd.

Douglas, J. E., & Burgess, A. E. (1986, December). Criminal profiling: A viable investigative tool against violent crime. *FBI Law Enforcement Bulletin*, 55(12), 1–5.

Douglas, J. E., Ressler, R. K., Burgess, A. W., Hartman, C. R. (1986). Criminal profiling from crime scene analysis. *Behavioral Sciences and the Law*, 4, 401–421.

Douglas, J. E., Burgess, A. W., Burgess, A. G., & Ressler, R. K. (1992). *Crime classification manual: A standard system for investigating and classifying violent crime*. New York, NY: Simon and Schuster.

Douglas, J., Burgess, A. W., Burgess, A. G., & Ressler, R. K. (2013). *Crime classification manual: A standard system for investigating and classifying violent crime* (3rd edn). Hoboken, NJ: John Wiley & Sons.

Fahsing, I., & Ask, K. (2013). Decision making and decisional tipping points in homicide investigations: An interview study of British and Norwegian detectives. *Journal of Investigative Psychology and Offender Profiling*, 10, 155–165. doi:10.1002/jip.1384

Fritzon, K. (2012). Theories on arson: The action systems model. In G.L. Dickens, P.A. Sugarman, & T.A. Gannon (eds), *Firesetting and mental health* (pp. 28–47). London: Royal College of Psychiatrists.

Fritzon, K., & Ridgway, J. (2001). Near-death experience: The role of victim reaction in attempted homicide. *Journal of Interpersonal Violence*, 16(7), 679–696.

Fritzon, K., Canter, D., & Wilton, Z. (2001). The application of an action system model to destructive behaviour: The examples of arson and terrorism. *Behavioral Sciences & the Law*, 19(5–6), 657–690.

Gerard, F., Mormont, C., & Kocsis, R. N. (2007). Offender profiles and crime scene patterns in Belgian sexual murders. In R. N. Kocsis (ed.), *Criminal profiling: International Theory, Research and Practice* (pp. 27–47). Totowa, NJ: Humana Press.

Grubin, D. (1994). Sexual murder. *British Journal of Psychiatry*, 165, 624–629.

Guttman, L. (1954). A new approach to factor analysis: The radex. In P.F. Lazarsfeld (ed.), *Mathematical thinking in the social sciences* (pp. 258–348). New York: Free Press.

Guttman, L. (1954). An outline of some new methodology for social research. *Public Opinion Quarterly*, 18, 395–404.

Guttman, R., & Greenbaum, C. W. (1998). Facet theory: Its development and current status. *European Psychologist*, 3(1), 13–36. doi:10.1027/1016-9040.3.1.13.

Hazelwood, R. R. (1986, December). The NCAVC training program: A commitment to law enforcement. *FBI Law Enforcement Bulletin*, 55(12), 23–26.

Hazelwood, R. R. (1987). Analyzing the rape and profiling the offender. In R. R. Hazelwood & A. W. Burgess (eds), *Practical aspects of rape investigation: A multidisciplinary approach* (pp. 169–199). New York, NY: Elsevier Science.

Hazelwood, R. R., & Burgess, A. W. (1987, September). An introduction to the serial rapist: Research by the FBI. *FBI Law Enforcement Bulletin*, 56(9), 16–24.

Hazelwood, R. R., & Douglas, J. E. (1980, April). The lust murderer. *FBI Law Enforcement Bulletin*, 49(4), 18–22.

Hazelwood, R. R., Reboussin, R., & Warren, J. I. (1989). Serial rape correlates of increased aggression and the relationship of offender pleasure to victim resistance. *Journal of Interpersonal Violence*, 4, 65–78.

Hazelwood, R. R., Ressler, R. K., Depue, R. L., & Douglas, J. C. (1995). Criminal investigative analysis: An overview. In R. R. Hazelwood & A. W. Burgess (eds), *Practical aspects of rape investigation: A multidisciplinary approach* (2nd edn; pp. 115–126). Boca Raton, FL: CRC Press.

Icove, D. J., & Estepp, M. H. (1987, April). Motive-based offender profiles of arson and fire-related crimes. *FBI Law Enforcement Bulletin*, 56(4), 17–23.

Kenefick, D. P. (1968). The social psychiatry of public consultation. In A. L. McGarry, W. J. Curran, & D. P. Kenefick (Chairs), Problems of consultation in medicolegal matters: A symposium. *American Journal of Psychiatry*, 125, 42–97.

Kocsis, R. N. (2009). Criminal profiling. In R. N. Kocsis (ed.), *Applied criminal psychology: A guide to forensic behavioural sciences* (pp. 213–234). Springfield, IL: Charles C Thomas Publisher Ltd.

Kretschmer, E. (1925). *Physique and character: An investigation of the nature of constitution and of the theory of temperament.* London: Kegan, Paul, Trench, Trubner & Co, Ltd.

Langer, W. C. (1972). *The mind of Adolf Hitler: The secret wartime report.* New York: Basic Books.

Lipton, P. (1998). Commentary: Lipton on the problem of induction. In M. Curd & J. A. Cover (eds), *Philosophy of science: The central issues* (pp. 495–505). New York, NY: W. W. Norton & Company.

Meehl, P. E. (1961). Logic for the clinician [Review of the book *Clinical inference and cognitive theory* by T. R. Sarbin, R. Taft, & D. E. Bailey]. *Contemporary Psychology*, 6, 389–391.

Meehl, P. E. (1954). *Clinical versus statistical prediction: A theoretical analysis and a review of the evidence.* Minneapolis, MN: University of Minnesota Press.

Megargee, E. I. (1966). Undercontrolled and overcontrolled personality types in extreme antisocial aggression. *Psychology Monograph*, 80(3), no. 611.

Meloy, J. R. (2000). The nature and dynamics of sexual homicide: An integrated review. *Aggression and Violent Behavior*, 5, 1–22. doi:1359–1789/00

Miller, S., & Fritzon, K. (2007). Functional consistency across two behavioural modalities: Fire-setting and self-harm in female special hospital patients. *Criminal Behaviour and Mental Health*, 17(1), 31–44.

Murray, H. A. (1943). *Thematic apperception test*. Cambridge, MA: Harvard University Press.

Neville, L., Miller, S., & Fritzon, K. (2007). Understanding change in a therapeutic community: An action systems approach. *The Journal of Forensic Psychiatry & Psychology*, 18(2), 181–203.

Nielssen, O. B., Westmore, B. D., Large, M. M. B., & Hayes, R. A. (2007). Homicide during psychotic illness in New South Wales between 1993–2002. *Medical Journal of Australia* 186(6), 301–304

Niiniluoto, I. (1999). Defending abduction. *Philosophy of Science*, 66, s436–s451.

Ogle, R. S., Maier-Katkin, D., & Bernard, T. J. (1995). A theory of homicidal behavior among women. *Criminology*, 33(2), 173–192.

Post, J. M. (2002). Ethical considerations in psychiatric profiling of political figures. *Psychiatric Clinics of North America*, 25, 635–646. doi:0193–0953X/02

Rainbow, L., & Gregory, A. (2011). What behavioural investigative advisers actually do. In L. Rainbow & A. Gregory, *Professionalizing offender profiling: Forensic and investigative psychology in practice* (pp. 18–34). New York: Routledge.

Rainbow, L., Gregory, A., & Alison, L. (2014). Behavioral investigative advice. In G. J. N. Bruinsma & D. L. Weisburd (eds), *Encyclopedia of criminology and criminal justice* (pp. 125–134). New York: Springer.

Ressler, R. K., Burgess, A. W., & Douglas, J. E. (1988). *Sexual Homicide: Patterns and Motives*. Massachusetts: Lexington Books.

Revitch, E., & Schlesinger, L. B. (1989). *Sex murder and sex aggression: Phenomenology, psychopathology, psychodynamics, and prognosis*. Springfield, IL: Charles C Thomas.

Revitch, E., & Schlesinger, L. B. (1981). *Psychopathology of homicide*. Springfield, IL: Charles C Thomas.

Revitch, E., & Schlesinger, L. B. (1978). Murder: evaluation, classification, and prediction. *Violence: perspectives on murder and aggression*. San Francisco, CA: Jossey-Bass.

Rumbelow, D. (1987). *The complete Jack the Ripper*. London: Penguin.

Safarik, M. E., Jarvis, J. P., Nussbaum, K. E. (2002). Sexual homicide of elderly females: Linking offender characteristics to victim and crime scene attributes. *Journal of Interpersonal Violence*, 17, 500–525.

Sapp, A. D., Huff, T. G., Gary, G. P., Icove, D. J., & Horbert, P. (1996). *Essential findings from a study of serial arsonists*. Quantico, VA: U.S. Department of Justice, Federal Bureau of Investigation, National Center for the Analysis of Violent Crime.

Schlesinger, L. B. (2007). Sexual homicide: Differentiating catathymic and compulsive murderers. *Aggression and Violent Behaviour*, 12(2), 242–256.

Shye, S. (1985) Nonmetric multivariate models for behavioural action systems. In D. Canter (ed.), *Facet Theory approaches to social research* (pp. 97–148). Springer Series in Social Psychology. New York: Springer Verlag.

Snook, B., Eastwood, J., Gendreau, P., & Bennell, C. (2010). The importance of knowledge cumulation and the search for hidden agendas: A reply to Kocsis, Middledorp, and Karpin (2008). *Journal of Forensic Psychology Practice*, 10(3), 214–223.

Teten, H. D. (1989). Offender profiling. In W.G. Bailey (ed.), *The encyclopedia of police science* (pp. 365–367). New York, NY: Garland Publishing.

Trojan, C., & Salfati, C. G. (2011). Linking criminal history to crime scene behavior in single-victim and serial homicide: Implications for offender profiling research. *Homicide Studies*, 15(1), 3–31.

Turvey, B. E. (2012). *Criminal Profiling. An Introduction to Behavioral Evidence Analysis* (4th edn). San Diego, CA: Academic Press..

Turvey, B. E. (1999). The deductive method of criminal profiling. In B. Turvey (ed.), *Criminal Profiling* (pp.25–32). San Diego, CA: Academic Press.

Turvey, B. E., & Esparza, M. A. (eds). (2016). *Behavioral evidence analysis: International forensic practice and protocols*. Amsterdam, The Netherlands: Academic Press.

Vettor, S., Woodhams, J., & Beech, A. R. (2013). Offender profiling: A review and critique of the approaches and major assumptions. *Journal of Current Issues in Crime, Law & Law Enforcement*, 6(4), 354–387.

Websdale, N. (1999). *Understanding Domestic Homicide*. Boston, MA: Northeastern University Press.

Wilson, P., Lincoln, R., & Kocsis, R. (1997). Validity, utility and ethics of profiling for serial violent and sexual offenders. *Psychiatry, Psychology and Law*, 4(1), 1–12.

Wolfgang, M. E. (1958). *Patterns in criminal homicide*. Oxford: University of Pennsylvania Press.

Wright, J. A., Burgess, A. G., Burgess, A. W., Laszlo, A. T., McCrary, G. O., & Douglas, J. E. (1996). A typology of interpersonal stalking. *Journal of Interpersonal Violence*, 11(4), 487–502.

Chapter 11

Reframing intelligence interviews

The applicability of psychological research to HUMINT elicitation

Ian Stanier and Jordan Nunan

Introduction

Effective discovery and subsequent threat mitigation is predicated on accurate, timely and detailed actionable information. Information, an important element within intelligence and investigation ensures appropriate judicial disposal in Law Enforcement Agency's (LEA) efforts to bring offenders to justice. The value of information to delivering community safety is reflected in associated policy, practice, and process. Effective interviewing, in both its formal and informal interactive states, offers a significant opportunity to elicit critical strategic and tactical information that both informs and drives LEA activity. It is unexpected then, that within the context of information collection, not only are human interactions between LEA and members of the public under-exploited but also, when the intention is to collect information, how unsatisfactorily it is approached and executed. It is apparent that the required elicitation skills, including rapport building and the identification of source motivation, are not sufficiently taught, and the governing policy is overly cautious with a negligible evidence base. Whilst this chapter focuses on the psychological aspects of techniques available for gathering information, and in particular intelligence collection, the underlying psychological principles of conducting an effective interview are relevant to a wider audience.

Definitional clarity

The broad discipline of interviewing has attracted extensive academic attention although, perhaps understandably, there is no agreement as to what is meant by *intelligence interviewing*. At its most general level, and for the purpose of this chapter, *interviewing* is used to describe the interaction between a LEA official (the *interviewer*) and any person who may hold information of interest (the *interviewee*). In this context, interview interaction will include both the *formal* interview often undertaken as a *search for truth* as part of a criminal investigation (for example, underpinned in the UK by the provisions of the *Police and Criminal Evidence Act 1984* and its accompanying *Codes of Practice*) and the *informal* interview. The *informal* interview includes all interaction between a LEA official and a person who may hold information of interest to LEA, but this information is not formally disclosed as part of an investigative interview process. In practitioner terms, this will include intelligence interviews undertaken as part of deliberately planned operational activities. These may include approaches to prisoners in Police Prisoner Custody suites, meetings with Covert Human Intelligence Sources (CHIS), or LEA visits to people held in prison establishments. Alternatively, the information may fall out of ad hoc LEA–public interactions arising from routine policing duties including a community or patrol officer meeting a member of the public in the street where information is disclosed.

The *Regulation of Investigatory Powers Act 2000* now covers aspects of LEA (and other public authorities) interaction with members of the public. In particular circumstances, the interaction may fall under legislative qualification. The popular terms *informants* or *confidential sources* now take on a defined legal specification. However, for the purposes of this chapter, the use of the term *informant* will be used to refer to both the person attracting formal CHIS status and any other person who imparts information during an interaction with LEA, formally or informally, either purposely or unwittingly. The overall elicitation process will be referred to as HUMINT, an abbreviation for human intelligence.

What is meant by *intelligence* is, perhaps, the most important element in determining the success of elicitation techniques. Interpreting and measuring the effectiveness of these techniques requires common agreement on what actually constitutes *information* and *intelligence*. Grasping what each LEA understands by intelligence is important, as this will determine the direction of the interaction, what is elicited, recorded, and subsequently made available for sharing.

Lowenthal (2009, p. 1) holds "information is anything that can be known, regardless of how it's discovered. Intelligence refers to information that meets the stated or understood needs of policy makers and has been collected, processed, and narrowed to meet those needs". He describes intelligence as a sub-set of information, but stated that while "all intelligence is information; not all information is intelligence" (Lowenthal, 2009, p. 1). His definition is useful in acknowledging that potentially all information may, depending on the context, become intelligence. A telephone book may be information, but if it contains the address of a wanted person then the telephone entry under that person's name may become intelligence. This does not mean, though, that the whole telephone book becomes intelligence. An ad hoc *intelligence* conversation between a LEA official in the street with a known criminal about their social network may be become evidence where co-conspirators are outstanding suspects who are subsequently sought. The majority of interactions with interviewees provide some degree of valuable information, be it personal characteristics, habits, interests, potential indicators of future criminal intent, cooperative states, social and criminal history, or indicators for opportunistic rapport building.

There is an expectation that what happens to the received information determines its intelligence value. In this, "intelligence is information designed for action" (Grieve, 2004, p. 25) and for the purpose of this chapter, the adopted working definition, developed from Brown (2007, p. 340), is that intelligence is "all information which is significant, or potentially significant, for a police activity, or potential action". In effect, this definition holds that intelligence is simply information – it is the use to which it is subsequently put that determines its significance. How this is best obtained in LEA interviews, both formal and informal, relies on a better understanding and application of psychological based research.

Evidence based research and intelligence

For elicitation interactions to be optimised, the policy and practice supporting deployment must be anchored in research evidence. An Evidence-Based Policing (EBP) research approach can systematically identify *what works* or *what does not work* and then be applied as best practice in LEA. The adoption of an evidence based approach, and subsequent underpinning of LEA policy and practice development, is still relatively embryonic despite the energetic determination of the Society of Evidence-Based Policing (Sherman & Murray, 2015). EBP's application within intelligence and covert-policing practice is negligible. Wider adoption of intelligence related EBP is confronted by numerous challenges; namely, legal constraints, a failure to recognise that current methods are neither effective or efficient, difficulties in securing access to sensitive data sets, difficulty in comparing datasets due to disparate intelligence data systems, insufficient *security cleared* or *developed vetted* researchers, a dearth of pro-active senior manager level EBP champions across intelligence, minimal United Kingdom's (UK) College of Policing commissioned research, and an absence of specialist policing EBP networks.

There is a requirement to secure strategic LEA commitment to ensuring the evidence is applied to practice even when it challenges long held policy assumptions. This will require leaders to defend the application of the findings when inevitably faced with powerful but flawed anecdotal justification and intuitive decision-making. The possibilities for future evidence based research in this area are endless. It has the potential to better inform or increase the probability of a successful interview, to maximise the probability of a successful CHIS recruitment approach by LEA. It may offer a better understanding of the dynamics behind CHIS motivation, or support the development of rapid rapport building techniques to assist with CHIS recruitment. Research could help practitioners better understand recruitment methodology, to identify what works most effectively, when, where, and against whom it is deployed. It may help inform the use of new technology in a way that reduces costs and enhances communication while still maintaining security and welfare commitments.

Notwithstanding these new research opportunities, existing evidence-based policing, including applied psychology findings associated with interviewing, is yet to be routinely applied in an intelligence elicitation context. As a result, professional practice development is still primarily informed by both anecdotal experience and defensive drafting in response to public, media, and judicial criticism.

The elicitation of intelligence: existing psychological research

The diverse circumstances leading to HUMINT related encounters each bring differing social and psychological conditions. The subsequent interaction will comprise of not one but rather a concoction of challenges, including an interviewer's inability to effectively communicate in the interviewee's native or preferred language, internal and external pressures that may impact on an interviewee's memory, and the motivations of an informant to disclose information that may be true or false (Evans, Meissner, Brandon, Russano, & Kleinman, 2010; Hartwig, Meissner, & Semel, 2014). In general terms, we note three main elements to the process of eliciting intelligence. First, is the securing of an interviewee's compliance and cooperation through the interviewers' application of rapport building techniques. By doing so the interviewer may be able to critically identify the motivation for the interviewee's collaboration; an element critical to maintaining longevity of elicitation relationships. Second, with cooperation secured, LEA officers are focused on drawing out from the interviewee, the pertinent information in a way that maximises the quality and quantity of memory recall, via appropriate interviewing techniques. Third, once the information is elicited, the next stage is to understand, not only how the information should be actioned but also whether it should be. This stage involves the information going through a process of corroboration, validation, and assurance, all of which will be used to understand the integrity of the information. The application of psychological science can provide and promote tools and techniques that support LEA through these three core HUMINT stages. Accordingly, this chapter will introduce what is known and where the research deficits remain.

Rapport: "Getting them to stop and talk"

Successful generation of potential new sources primarily relies on the effective application of rapport building techniques. The deployment circumstances differ, and some rapport techniques need to be utilised against a collapsing time frame. In LEA there are a number of occasions where rapid rapport building application would be helpful. The first example may be by way of *exploratory prison debriefing* where rapport needs to be established and information needs to be gained from a prisoner during the 45 minutes a prison legal visit offers. Second, as a consequence of a Port Stop of a passenger disembarking off aircraft and ships arriving into the UK where the circumstances of the transit may only offer a short operational window in which to deploy rapid rapport building techniques during the period between disembarking, passing through passport control, and collecting baggage. Third, external physical or telephone cold call pitching as a consequence of an opportunity identified through pattern of life analysis; i.e., the LEA official making an unexpected approach during the person of interest's route to work. Fourth, an area commonplace for initial interactions is the police custody block during a detained prisoner's detention. In the UK, the prisoner's detention is regulated by the *Police and Criminal Evidence Act 1984* and consequently only a short window for an approach is often available, often falling between the point after criminal charge and the release from the police custody block or the remanding of the prisoner to appear before a court.

Police approaches to prisoners detained in custody suites offer fertile ground for intelligence exploitation. However, who undertakes this activity will determine the success or otherwise of the collection effort. Research undertaken in an urban police station examined 146 prisoner approaches held in police custody after an arrest for an array of different offences (Stanier, Wadie, & Nunan, 2018). The two cohorts examined were dedicated Detectives and Intelligence Officers. Both had been briefed prior to the approach to consider making an attempt to encourage the detainee to disclose intelligence. There was a significant difference between the role (Intelligence Officer or Detective) when conducting the interview and whether an Intelligence report and CHIS referral was generated. Overall, the Intelligence Officers conducted fewer interviews (n = 60) than Detectives (n = 86), but generated more Intelligence reports (52 per cent compared with 14 per cent) and more CHIS referrals for the Dedicated Source Unit (18 per cent compared with 1 per cent) (Stanier et al., 2018).

It is worth noting that neither the UK Police Force region subject to the research project or the UK's College of Policing's Intelligence Officers course provide any input on cell approaches on intelligence courses. Detective training (Initial Investigators-PIP1 and Crime Investigators ICIDP – PIP2 levels in the UK) has negligible input on the identification and recruitment of informants or intelligence concepts nor does the UK's Authorised Professional Practice for Investigations.

Another research study examined the circumstances of those detained prisoners who accepted referrals to a Dedicated Source Unit (Cooper, 2011). The findings identified that the primary disclosed motivation of those at the initial interaction was money. However, when their status was revisited four weeks later, many of those who agreed to be prospective informants did not progress into authorised CHIS. The exception were those prisoners whose initial motivation appeared to be based on ideology / moral grounds (i.e., a dislike of drugs). This category of prisoner appears also to have, in contrast, a degree of longevity to their CHIS status. The learning here for the practitioner is to consider developing initial rapport building approach strategies around ideological hooks.

Importance of source motivation

For LEA to both elicit and judge the value of the information, an awareness of the interviewees' current motivation for disclosure of the specific detail may be useful. Understanding the motivation of an interviewee can provide an insight into future effective management of this source of intelligence. It can introduce a cautionary element when determining the provenance, veracity, and the actionability of elicited information.

It is important not to conflate incorrect information with interviewees' deception. While it is accepted an interviewee who is unwilling or uncooperative is likely to make a deliberately incorrect or misleading disclosure, cooperative sources can also be unwittingly wrong or disclose incorrect detail where it is not clear that the interviewee is making a supposition, rather than disclosing objective *hard facts* or is simply passing on information in good faith but the original source is actually incorrect. More provenance based questioning may offer a partial safeguard.

Motivations are diverse, changeable, and nuanced. Motivations vary considerably; payment, revenge, self-protection, damage to a competitor, secure esteem of the officer, and personal satisfaction (Deininger, 1977). These traits are found to be consistent across different jurisdictions (Dunnighan, 1992; Lee, 1993). Motivation to elicit information may change depending on the question asked by the interviewer. A more systematic analysis revealed that the core six reasons given by a CHIS to start informing were (in order of frequency): (i) financial, (ii) dislike of a crime, (iii) reduced sentence, (iv) revenge, (v) being on the right side of the law, and (vi) looking for a favour (Billingsley, 2001). However, Billingsley evidenced that motivation changes throughout the Source–Handler relationship, and that the reasons given for this change (in order of frequency) were identified as: (i) change for their own benefit, (ii) change due to a social conscience, (iii) change so as to help LEA, and (iv) change to remove opposition (Billingsley, 2001).

The rapport literature

The importance of rapport to elicitation success is rarely challenged by practitioners (Semel, 2012). Rapport facilitates the establishment of effective professional alliances between a Source Handler and informant or between an investigative interviewer and the interviewee. It can assist with personalising the interview, and in turn aid recall by reducing anxiety on the part of the interviewee (Lipton, 1977). It helps exercise "social influence, and educing information from a source" (Abbe & Brandon, 2013, p. 237), and can enhance accuracy of witness reports and "diagnosticity of evidence obtained from suspects"

(Vallano, Evans, Schreiber Compo, & Kieckhaefer, 2015, p. 369). When successfully applied within the first few minutes, rapport can positively inform the interviewee's first impressions (Zunin & Zunin, 1972).

It is important to firstly acknowledge the underlying principles of rapport that can be applied universally. Tickle-Degnen and Rosenthal (1990) critically discuss rapport as a dynamic structure consisting of three interconnecting elements: *mutual attentiveness, positivity*, and *coordination*. They place an emphasis on *positivity* and *mutual attentiveness* in early interactions, with *coordination* and *mutual attentiveness* considered more important in later interactions. Their discussion, which stresses the importance of building as well as maintaining rapport (Tickle-Degnen & Rosenthal, 1990), has significant application to the collection of intelligence from human sources. As our discussion develops, it will be evident that from the rapport literature, terminology changes depending on the interview context.

In relation to gathering human intelligence, rapport can be defined as developing and maintaining a working relationship with a human source, by managing their motivations and welfare, whilst ensuring they understand the purpose of the relationship in order to secure reliable intelligence. The term *operational accord* incorporates but goes beyond rapport, providing an additional explanation of the interviewer–source relationship, by exploring their mutual affinity and level of source conformity (Evans et al., 2010). The relationship is benefited when the intentions, concerns, and desired outcomes of the interaction are appreciated (Kelman, 2006).

Securing disclosure from subjects of significant interest or those considered *high value detainees* is critical to disrupting terrorist planning and identifying emerging threats. Research has examined four types of coercive and non-coercive interview strategies (legalistic, physical, cognitive, and social) used to elicit disclosure by high value detainees (Goodman-Delahunty, Martschuk, & Dhami, 2014). The findings revealed that where social strategies were adopted, detainees were more likely to disclose meaningful information and earlier in the interview when rapport building techniques were applied. The research also revealed that interviewees were less likely to cooperate when confronted with evidence. Disclosures were more complete in response to noncoercive strategies, especially rapport building and procedural fairness elements of respect and voice (Goodman-Delahunty et al., 2014).

The use of rapport building is also considered significant in securing successful disclosure of information from terrorists in an operational setting (see ORBIT; Alison, Alison, Noone, Elntib, & Christiansen, 2013). Research has suggested that rapport building improves the quality of both child and adult witness recall, by decreasing the amount of inaccurate and misinformation reported, particularly in response to open-ended questions (Vallano & Compo, 2011). A group of experienced military and intelligence interrogators placed an emphasis on rapport and relationship-building techniques as fundamental to successful elicitation of intelligence (Russano, Narchet, Kleinman, & Meissner,

2014). An additional study, this time examining the frequency of use and perceived effectiveness of interrogation techniques of U.S. military and federal-level interrogators, focused on the who (objective and subjective interrogator characteristics), the what (situational and detainee characteristics), and the why (intended goal of interrogation) (Redlich, Kelly, & Miller, 2014). The findings indicated that rapport and relationship-building techniques were employed most often and perceived as the most effective regardless of context and intended outcome, particularly in comparison with confrontational techniques (Redlich et al., 2014).

Further, LEA interviewers reported building rapport with adult witnesses and suspects in a similar manner, often by using verbal techniques (e.g., discussing common interests via small talk) and nonverbal techniques (e.g., displaying understanding via empathy and sympathy) (Vallano et al., 2015). It has long been known that effective rapport requires empathy, especially where the information is highly personal (Rogers, 1942). Research suggests that overly formal and officious introductions (i.e. warning about lying and an absence of rapport) generate unfavourable perceptions from witnesses (or in this context Covert Human Intelligence Sources) (MacDonald, Keeping, Snook, & Luther, 2016). The formality of the interview further impacts upon rapport, especially when an interviewee chooses to have legal advice. In this situation, interviewees are four times less likely to provide an admission or confession in comparison with those without such advice (Pearse, Gudjonsson, Clare, & Rutter, 1998). Moreover, functional pre-determined questions, overly formalised and delivered, further undermine rapport building (Milne & Bull, 1999).

Environmental factors can influence the success or otherwise of elicitation interviews. Research on implicit cognition demonstrates that priming can influence processes such as cooperation and goal pursuit (Fitzsimons & Bargh, 2003). Priming is referred to as a nonconscious process of memory, recalling or recognising a stimulus previously exposed to. This may consist of the physical layout and/or items contained within the interview room or psychological states of the interviewee, which may promote the interviewer's goals (Dawson, Hartwig, & Brimbal, 2015). With regards to the environment (physical priming), the conventional size of a small interviewing room is questioned by Dawson, Hartwig, Brimbal, and Denisenkov (2017), reporting that larger rooms can influence a person's tendency to be open about information (Okken, van Rompay, & Pruyn, 2013). Furthermore, participants were found to report more accurate information than those in an abrupt condition, where a desk served as a barrier between the interviewer and witness (Collins, Lincoln, & Frank, 2002), though other variables such as voice intonation and body language were also at play. Further research is warranted regarding changes to the environment and its impact on interviewees.

However, within policing, the environment is not always controllable. Within custody areas, LEA officers are usually able to prepare an interview room, positioning tables and chairs and controlling access. Other environments may be more challenging, for example prison legal visit areas where the importance of security considerations often outweighs intelligence collection. Seats can be allocated to prisoners, chairs and tables made immovable, and interruptions likely by patrolling/monitoring prison officers. Therefore, within uncontrollable environments, the impact of physical priming is diminished. Hence, research on priming the psychological state may be of use. Although this research is in its infancy, interviewees primed with a psychological state of attachment security (characterised by empathy and compassion) resulted in interviewees reporting significantly more information than those not primed (Dawson et al., 2015).

Concerns arise regarding the introduction of a third individual and their impact on rapport during an interview, especially when this third individual is an interpreter. Interviewers have conflicting views regarding the use of interpreters, with some believing that an interpreter's presence negatively impacts on rapport (Driskell, Blickensderfer, & Salas, 2013; Soufan, 2011). However, the limited research that has examined the effect of interpreters on rapport, reported no significant differences between interviews with and without an interpreter present (Ewens et al., 2014). Furthermore, this finding is supported by some interviewers and most interpreters reporting that interpreters provide an insight into the culture of the interviewee, which in turn aids rapport (Russano et al., 2014). This insight is invaluable, especially when the culture of both the interviewee and interviewer has been found to impact on the effectiveness of interviewing techniques (Beune, Giebels, & Taylor, 2010).

Limited research addresses how rapport benefits educing interviewee memories, especially in relation to human sources. However, simply having a positive and encouraging interviewer was found to elicit more detail from a witness without increasing errors, compared with a neutral or abrupt interviewer (Collins et al., 2002). Furthermore, some research suggests that the effects of rapport are more beneficial than cognitive retrieval mnemonics when using cognitive interviewing techniques (Memon, Wark, Holley, Bull, & Koehnken, 1997), though the benefits of specific mnemonics have been demonstrated (Leins, Fisher, Pludwinski, Rivard, & Robertson, 2014; Memon, Meissner, & Fraser, 2010; Milne, 2016). Rapport may advantage memory recall due to its motivational stance. Interviewees may try harder and use multiple attempts to recall in order to cooperate. Moreover, rapport advocates transferring the control of the recall process to the interviewee (Memon et al., 1997).

Memory retrieval and interviewing models/techniques: "Securing vital intelligence"

It is important to acknowledge that human memory is not a video recording (see Chapter 6, this volume). Therefore, interviewers tasked with collecting accurate and detailed intelligence from an interviewee require some understanding of the key principles of memory.

Developments within psychology have provided significant contributions to the mechanisms of human memory, as well as establishing numerous tools and techniques that can minimise disruption and enhance memory retrieval (see Chapter 6 this volume). Due to the vast array of memory research and to align with the scope of this chapter, a focus will be placed on memory recall and current retrieval techniques that can be applied to the intelligence interview.

An interviewer's understanding of the fundamental principles of memory and the powerful influence they can have as an interviewer on retrieval, provides a foundation of knowledge from which successful interviewing can take place (Milne & Bull, 1999). However, an understanding of memory alone is not sufficient, as the next phase comprises of actually conducting the interview, which incorporates strategic planning, effective implementation of interviewing techniques, and disseminating the gathering of information post-interview. Therefore, the following will contain a synthesis of a number of models and techniques relevant to the collection of HUMINT.

The PEACE model

PEACE (Central Planning and Training Unit, 1992) provides suspect and witness interview training for LEA officers, within a tiered approach (Clarke & Milne, 2001; Griffiths & Milne, 2006), underpinned by psychological theory and research, highlighting memory fallibility, interviewee vulnerability, and the consequences of unethical interviewing procedures (Loftus, 1979; Nunan & Milne, 2016). The PEACE model exemplifies the information gathering approach, whereby this non-accusatory model focuses on open-mindedness, rapport building, an understanding of memory, and information gathering. As will be discussed, each stage comes together to create a model, rather than what is commonly misunderstood as PEACE being an interview technique. Therefore, this model is flexible, often encouraging the use of Cognitive Interview (CI) or Conversation Management (CM) techniques within the *Account* stage. This section will discuss the PEACE model's application when interviewing for HUMINT.

The first stage of PEACE requires interviewers to *Plan and Prepare* for the interaction. This may include accessing information already held on the interviewee or where appropriate through proactive means (i.e. through pattern of life surveillance and analysis). Prior knowledge of the interviewee enhances interviewer understanding of questioning strategies and techniques including building rapport. The second stage encourages interviewers to actively *Engage and Explain* with the interviewee, by building rapport while outlining the interview process. This stage allows the interviewer to determine the interviewee's possible motivations for cooperation (or not) and reinforce the desired outcomes of the current interview, secure and then organise subsequent meetings. The third stage permits the interviewee to provide their *Account*, requiring the interviewer to actively listen and question the interviewee. This stage incorporates the use of the CI or CM techniques. The *Closure* of the interview is vital to summarise, clarify, and if appropriate challenge the interviewee's account. Finally, an *Evaluation* of all previous stages is conducted together with a critical reflection from the interviewer (Milne & Bull, 1999). One obvious difference between an investigative interview and an intelligence interview is that the former is generally undertaken within the context of a collapsing detention time frame, known as the *PACE* clock associated with *relevant time* (see *Police and Criminal Evidence Act 1984*). The circumstances associated with intelligence interviews vary, some requiring the application of rapid rapport building, while other circumstances can afford a more patient and long term approach to rapport building i.e. a sentenced prisoner or an existing CHIS (informant) relationship. Although the PEACE model is situated within the domain of investigative interviewing, its application to interviewing for intelligence is possible due to the model's flexible design and emphasis on rapport.

An evaluation of PEACE's application in the field will determine its impact on LEA interviewing practices. Since the introduction of PEACE, the general standard of investigative interviewing has considerably improved, as confession-gathering techniques have been replaced with ethical and open-minded interviews, with an information gathering focus (Milne & Bull, 2016). Clarke and Milne (2001) established evidence for improved planning and preparation in comparison with Baldwin's (1992) research, which reported a need for training developments which go beyond improving training courses. However, this improvement appeared to concern procedural and legal aspects rather than the more complex skills of communication (Clarke, Milne, & Bull, 2011), information linking, and challenging accounts (Griffiths & Milne, 2006). These more elusive and complex aspects of interviewing remain a demanding task for interviewers to maintain after training. Thus, empathising the importance of continuous professional development and intrusive supervision of LEA officers' ongoing application of learnt interviewing techniques and associated methodology.

The National Prison Debriefing Model

The process of eliciting intelligence from remanded and sentenced prisoners across the English and Welsh prison estate requires a systematic approach, emphasising the application of rapport building before the interview moves to elicitation strategies. The *National Prison Debriefing Model* (NPDM), has five stages to its planning and implementation. The NPDM is not about securing evidence as part of a traditional PACE 1984 interview. It is about exploiting the prisoner community knowledge of criminality to close intelligence gaps, to corroborate existing intelligence, and to identify emerging trends in criminality. The first two stages relate to the identification and prioritising of suitable prisoners for approach but the third stage, the *Exploratory Initial Interview*, is the focus of rapid rapport building between the interviewer and interviewee. The fourth and fifth stage relate to the development of intelligence opportunities provided by the prisoner.

The effectiveness of the NPDM was examined by Jeffrey (2011). This research examined debriefing of 243 prisoners held in English and Welsh prison establishments. While the overall figure showed high levels of prisoner cooperation (57 per cent), the findings revealed a significant correlation between age and cooperation, with older prisoner debriefs deemed more effective. In terms of sentences served, the highest degree of cooperation (73 per cent of approaches) was those serving indeterminate sentences, and those serving 4 years or more. The lowest cooperation came from mandatory lifers (only 50 per cent cooperated) and those held for immigration sentences (36 per cent), whereas debriefed drug offenders (79 per cent) were the most cooperative. Interestingly, the reality is that Authorising Officers and Controllers are reluctant to support drug offenders as CHIS, even when the proportionality case is justified.

There was also a significant correlation between interviewee gender, where 61 per cent of successful debriefs were with male interviewees, although this dropped to 45 per cent if one or both interviewers were female. Where the study scrutinised the success of female debriefers, the sample subject to analysis was heavily based on debriefs of male Muslim prisoners (Iraqi and Algerian males). Accordingly, it may be that there was a negative impact based on the influence of faith and cultural norms. This raises the issues of ensuring diversity is a consideration at the operational planning stage for any intelligence approach.

Cognitive Interview techniques

To date, memory research within forensic psychology has predominantly focused on the retrieval stage of the three-part memory process (see Chapter 6, this volume for more on this subject). Simply addressing the question, what techniques enhance the quality and quantity of interviewee recall? Within this wealth of research, the CI has by far received most attention, by empirically testing the CI in numerous contexts (see Memon et al., 2010). However, a lack of research has applied the CI to the context of gathering intelligence. Nonetheless, the evidence so far still applies, because regardless of how HUMINT is defined, it is quite simply units of information collected from an interviewee by which the CI could be used to assist.

The CI, originally developed by Geiselman and Fisher during the 1980s, aims to elicit accurate and reliable accounts from witnesses. The original CI techniques (context reinstatement, report everything, change order, and change perspective) were designed to assist the interviewee's retrieval process. *Context reinstatement* instructs the interviewee to mentally recreate the physical environment (e.g., the location, people present, and encouraging use of the human senses) and psychological environment (e.g., the interviewee's feelings while the event took place), as context can support memory retrieval for the to-be-remembered (TBR) event (Godden & Baddeley, 1975).

The *report everything* instruction encourages interviewees to actively engage with the interviewer, reporting all information regardless of how partially remembered or trivial it seems, and not to confabulate. This technique is popular among LEA due to its effectiveness and simplicity (Kebbell, Milne, & Wagstaff, 1999). The *change order* instruction is designed to increase recall after the interviewee has provided their account in their desired order. This is to avoid recalling expectations or probabilities of what typically happens, commonly known as memory *scripts*, and places a focus on recalling what happened at the particular TBR event (Milne & Bull, 1999). The *change perspective* instruction asks the interviewee to recall from the perspective of another witness/victim. However, there are concerns that the change perspective instruction may confuse the interviewee and lead to fabricated accounts (Memon et al., 2010). Hence, contemporary use refers to a *spotlight* technique, whereby the interviewee is instead instructed to focus on one individual from the event and report all they can about the actions of that individual (Milne, 2016; Milne & Bull, 2016).

To incorporate the CI techniques into practice, a review conducted by Fisher and Geiselman (1992) introduced a framework that fused the social psychology of communication theory together with the techniques of the original CI, thus developing the Enhanced Cognitive Interview (ECI). The ECI provided the interview with a structure (introduction, explain the aims of the interview, initiate a free report, questioning, varied and extensive retrieval, important investigative questions, summary, closure, and evaluation), introducing the significant elements of rapport building, appropriate questioning, and transfer of control to the interviewee (Milne & Bull, 2016). Over 100 empirical studies have tested the effectiveness of the CI and ECI, with the majority providing evidence that they elicit more correct information than a comparison interview (Memon et al., 2010).

In cases where the interviewee is required to recall specific details from a series of events, (e.g., serious organised crime networks, human trafficking victims, informants attending numerous meetings), cognitive interviewing techniques may help. Cognitive mnemonics (based on the CI) can be used by the interviewee, for example, a timeline (see Hope, Mullis, & Gabbert, 2013, and Chapter 6 this volume, for a timeline technique) and self-generated cues (see Leins et al., 2014). It was found that the use of self-generated cues within a set of mnemonics helped interviewees recall more than twice as many person, conversation, action, and setting details (Leins et al., 2014). Furthermore, the CI has been found to elicit significantly more event related information in comparison with the five-step model (standard training offered at Federal Law Enforcement Training Centre), in regards to specific details of recurring events (Rivard, Fisher, Robertson, & Hirn Mueller, 2014). Skilled and professional interview trainers who understand the psychological theory are key to providing an interview training programme, which educates and transfers the skills learnt into practice (Milne & Bull, 2016). However, the application of the CI/ECI to the forensic field has encountered numerous practitioner barriers (see Chapter 6, this volume).

Regardless of the interview context, whether that be an investigative or intelligence interview, the aim is to elicit information that is accurate and detailed from the interviewee. Although the CI has predominantly been tested and applied to witnesses, the underlying psychological principles of human sources are equivalent. This overlap between interview aims and the underlying psychological principles, provides a strong foundation for the implementation of the CI instructions into HUMINT practices.

The Scharff technique

The Scharff technique is a HUMINT collection technique that was established for detained individuals who were not fully cooperative (Scharff, 1950). Its origins can be traced back to a World War II German Luftwaffe interrogator Hanns Joachim Scharff. In stark contrast to his colleagues' approach at the time, Scharff's success incorporated a friendly, noncoercive, and conversational approach to eliciting intelligence (Scharff, 1950). His genuine ability to take an interest in the prisoners, as well as treat them humanely may have caught some individuals by surprise. However, behind his *innocent* depiction, Scharff's goal was that of *information elicitation*; a technique used to gain information in a way that the source remains oblivious to the collector's real goal.

In order to maintain the effectiveness of this technique, Scharff adopted the prisoner's perspective and was therefore able to understand, effectively converse with the prisoner, and counteract counter-interrogation strategies. *Perspective taking* is considered a skilful ability, which requires the cognitive capacity to understand the past, present, and future situation from another's viewpoint, thereby anticipating their reactions and behaviour. This skill is considered beneficial for implementing an effective interviewing strategy (see Risan, Binder, & Milne, 2016 for emotional intelligence). By using perspective taking, Scharff identified three counter-interrogation strategies employed by Allied airmen:

1 "I will not tell very much during the interrogation."
2 "I will try to figure out what they are after, and then make sure not to give them what they want."
3 "It is meaningless to withhold or deny what they already know."

(Granhag, Kleinman, & Oleszkiewicz, 2016, p. 136)

It was from identifying these counter-interrogation strategies that the following tactics were established. Granhag et al. (2016) outline five interrelated tactics that make up the Scharff technique:

1 *A friendly approach.* This comprises of a humanistic style of interviewing, by making the interviewee feel comfortable and at ease. This may be demonstrated by the interviewer displaying elements of perspective taking and accepting the interviewee.

2 *Not pressing for information.* The interviewer will provide the interviewee with opportunities to confirm or disconfirm claims, instead of being asked specific questions. This tactic requires the interviewer to acknowledge the interviewee's motivations and autonomy.
3 *The illusion of knowing-it-all.* The interviewer will begin the interaction by discussing known information to the interviewee, displaying some degree of reliable knowledge about the topic of interest. First, this tactic requires the interviewee to provide information that was not provided by the interviewer to be perceived as cooperative. Second, the interviewee might assume that the interviewer holds additional information to what was discussed. Therefore, if the interviewee misperceives the interviewer's knowledge on the topic of interest, as well as aiming to provide information already known (a common counter-interrogation strategy), the interviewee could unknowingly provide new information.
4 *Confirmation/disconfirmation of claims.* The interviewer will provide the interviewee with a series of claims that requires the source to confirm or disconfirm. The purpose of this tactic is to encourage the interviewee to cooperate in a less formal or active manner as perceived by answering direct questions.
5 *Ignore new information.* This tactic requires the interviewer to downplay the importance or state that new information provided by the interviewee was already known. This may encourage the interviewee to share additional information (on top of the already provided new information) in order to feel they have cooperated.

The Scharff technique has been tested against the Direct Approach, which is commonly used by U.S. interrogators stated within the U.S. Army Field Manual (2006). It has been consistently established that the Scharff technique elicits more new information than the Direct Approach, is better at disguising the objectives of the interview, interviewees underestimate the amount of new information they reveal during the Scharff technique and overestimate when faced with the Direct Approach, and those interviewed by the Scharff technique believe the interviewer held more information than what was portrayed (Granhag et al., 2016; Granhag, Oleszkiewicz, Strömwall, & Kleinman, 2015). Echoing earlier research findings, using the Scharff technique in a series of interviews resulted in a greater amount of information elicited in comparison to the Direct Approach (Oleszkiewicz, Granhag, & Kleinman, 2017a). A strong evidence base exists in favour of the Scharff technique, but can it be trained to practitioners?

Despite limited research addressing this question, handlers who experienced Scharff training embellished *the illusion of knowing-it-all* tactic, used claims to elicit conformations/disconfirmations, and used comparatively less (if any) explicit questions to the topic of interest. In comparison, untrained handlers relied on the interviewees' motivations to elicit information and used an abundance of explicit questions (Oleszkiewicz, Granhag, & Kleinman, 2017b). Not only does it seem possible to train the Scharff technique, Scharff-trained handlers elicited more new information in a less eager manner than those untrained in the technique. The Scharff technique provides a subtle, yet effective way of gathering human intelligence.

The Scharff technique does have its limitations. As it is designed for detained individuals, its effectiveness in some HUMINT interactions requires further research. *The illusion of knowing-it-all* should not comprise of particularly sensitive or detailed information when the interviewee is not in custody. Disclosing such information may well be detrimental if the interviewee's motivation is to share what is known by LEA and is free to leave after the interaction (Granhag et al., 2015). However, this illusion can be established with general background information if carefully and skilfully portrayed. Nonetheless, interviewers may only hold little (if any) information in the first place, thereby rendering the illusion tactic impractical. The *confirmation/disconfirmation of claims* tactic did not produce any issues within the laboratory research, though this tactic should be used with caution, as there is the possibility that false intelligence could be generated by the interviewee disconfirming correct claims or providing false positive claims (Oleszkiewicz et al., 2017b). Finally, the previous treatment of detainees before meeting Scharff, such as experiencing accusatory methods of interrogation, may have positively impacted on Scharff's techniques. This variable may be of importance to further establishing the capabilities of the Scharff technique. However, this will require a strong imagination on behalf of researchers to truly test this whilst achieving ethical approval.

The Reid Technique

The Reid Technique of interviewing and interrogation consists of a nine-step process (see Inbau, Reid, Buckley, & Jayne, 2013 for a detailed outline of each step). Within this process, the early steps instruct LEA to conduct a Behaviour Analysis Interview (BAI) to determine signs of guilty knowledge. If these signs are identified, the interaction becomes accusatory in nature, whereby the interviewing officer employs a range of persuasive tactics to overcome objections, denials, and gain a confession (see also Chapter 8 this volume).

The Reid Technique is often used to illustrate the accusatory approach of interviewing and interrogation. Some examples of the techniques used within the accusatory approach consist of repetitive questioning, intimidation, isolation, and the use of fabricating evidence against the interviewee (Kelly, Miller, Redlich, & Kleinman, 2013). The use of psychological coercion is promoted by the accusatorial approach, which usually contains three phases (Kassin & Gudjonsson, 2004):

1 Interviewee anxiety, uncertainty, and insecurity is created by manipulating the environment, such as leaving the interviewee in a small room;

2 Maximisation: The interviewee is accused/confronted (sometimes falsely), prevented from denying their involvement, and warned about the major consequences of their actions and/or involvement; and
3 Minimisation: An interrogator now provides a sympathetic approach by offering justifications for their involvement and aims to gain their trust by providing alternative and more lenient consequences should the interviewee comply.

Though the Reid Technique proposes the need to establish rapport, the use of psychological coercion overpowers any opportunity to effectively build and maintain rapport. This is because the interviewer creates a situation whereby it is psychologically and emotionally appealing to confess in order to escape the interrogation (Borum, Gelles, & Kleinman, 2009). Moreover, in contrast to the previously discussed interviewing models and techniques, the Reid interrogator *does all the talking*; how is information elicited if the interviewee is not talking? These methods used within the accusatory approach, especially The Reid Technique, contradict the optimum conditions required to build and maintain rapport and promote memory recall, detrimentally impacting on the collection of reliable and detailed information.

The Reid Technique is often viewed as the most commonly used *gold standard* of LEA interviewing across the United States (Gudjonsson & Pearse, 2011). However, the training application of this technique is not well understood, with limited research exploring its use (Cleary & Warner, 2016). While interrogators speak (from experience) that the accusatory approach is a successful technique for gaining a confession/information, scientific evaluations note that accusatorial methods increase the possibility of both true and false information (see Meissner et al., 2014). Thus, these methods lead to a confirmatory information gathering approach that is in fact detrimental to the collection of HUMINT. It is of no surprise that the Reid Technique has received an array of criticism throughout the academic literature (Gudjonsson & Pearse, 2011; Meissner et al., 2014).

Concluding remarks

Information is the lifeblood of LEA. It informs strategies that seek to deliver community safety through effective crime prevention and reduction programmes. It provides operational insight for decision-makers. It determines the prioritisation and allocation of finite resource prioritisation. The aim of this chapter was to highlight whether psychological based research could both support and enhance elicitation of information. The available extensive empirical and theoretical literature on rapport, memory, models and techniques of interviewing, all proffer powerful and compelling evidence of the benefits of psychological research and what it offers to enhance intelligence generation.

An understanding of the fundamental principles of memory provides a foundation of knowledge from which the appropriate selection and application of interviewing models and techniques can take place. This chapter does not advocate which interviewing model or technique is *superior* for elicitation, but rather promotes a tool belt approach, whereby models and techniques will be more or less appropriate depending on the context. A *one size fits all* approach to interviewing demonstrates an interviewer's lack of versatility and understanding of the interview's context they currently face. Furthermore, interviewing is not just a cognitive process, but a social one too. With all models and techniques, the golden thread of rapport flows throughout, establishing a platform for interviewers to maximise the likelihood of securing vital intelligence.

Interestingly, even with strong indications that rapport building may be a significant component of successful elicitation strategies, there is very little empirical research that has examined this area systematically in a covert LEA or intelligence setting (Abbe & Brandon, 2013). Nor does the research attempt to define what is meant by rapport, how it is built and then maintained in a LEA context (Vallano et al., 2015). A better understanding of how rapport develops in these contexts and its impact on interview outcomes would enhance awareness of the interpersonal dynamics in these situations, and the effectiveness of interviewing in general. This and subsequent research holds opportunities for LEA training and practice. By synthesising the existing psychological literature, identifying areas for future research, and acknowledging the potential that research can have on informing intelligence gathering practices, the underlying purpose of this chapter is to act as a force for change.

Public reaction to the extent of electronic surveillance highlighted through the Edward Snowden revelations and increasing encryption technology available on publicly accessible communication devices has meant that the landscape of intelligence collection is *going dark*. This now places an importance on HUMINT collection and requires the adoption of effective elicitation techniques based on scientific research.

Recommendations

To address these issues, a national response is required, one where research is viewed as a key component of developing and enhancing current policy and practice associated with elicitation techniques. The authors recommend six areas for change:

1 Law Enforcement learning and development leads should continue to support evidence based research but place a priority on intelligence elicitation techniques and wider intelligence based research.
2 Law Enforcement learning and development leads should produce guidance that is of sufficient depth to enable law enforcement agencies to provide effective training on intelligence elicitation to all staff involved in investigation and intelligence processes.

3 Law Enforcement learning and development leads should commission bespoke intelligence elicitation courses to be made available to law enforcement practitioners.
4 Law Enforcement learning and development leads should review existing investigative and intelligence (covert and overt) courses to ensure current practice is underpinned by available evidence based research.
5 An international adoption of the UK's *What Works Centre for Crime Reduction* model should strengthen the links between law enforcement, academia, and industry through enhanced collaboration and partnership on elicitation research and techniques.
6 Evidence based policing ethos should be embedded within policy development methodology. Findings should be shared with policy makers, investigators, and intelligence professionals.

References

Abbe, A., & Brandon, S. E. (2013). The role of rapport in investigative interviewing: A review. *Journal of Investigative Psychology and Offender Profiling*, 10(3), 237–249. doi:10.1002/jip.1386

Alison, L. J., Alison, E., Noone, G., Elntib, S., & Christiansen, P. (2013). Why tough tactics fail and rapport gets results: Observing Rapport-Based Interpersonal Techniques (ORBIT) to generate useful information from terrorists. *Psychology, Public Policy, and Law*, 19(4), 411–431. doi:10.1037/a0034564

Baldwin, J. (1992). *Video taping police interviews with suspects: An evaluation*. London: Home Office Police Department.

Beune, K., Giebels, E., & Taylor, P. J. (2010). Patterns of interaction in police interviews: The role of cultural dependency. *Criminal Justice and Behavior*, 37(8), 904–925. doi:10.1177/0093854810369623

Billingsley, R. (2001). Informers' careers: Motivations and change. In R. Billingsley, T. Nemitz, & P. Bean (eds), *Informers: Policing, policy, practice* (pp. 81–97). London: Routledge.

Borum, R., Gelles, M. G., & Kleinman, S. M. (2009). Interview and interrogation: A perspective and update from the USA. In T. Williamson, B. Milne, & S. Savage (eds), *International developments in investigative interviewing* (pp. 111–128). London: Routledge.

Brown, S. D. (2007). The meaning of criminal intelligence. *International Journal of Police Science & Management*, 9(4), 336–340. doi:10.1350/ijps.2007.9.4.336

Central Planning and Training Unit. (1992). *Investigativei interviewing: A guide to interviewing*. London: Home Office.

Clarke, C., & Milne, R. (2001). *National evaluation of the PEACE investigative interviewing course*. Police Research Award Scheme. London: Home Office.

Clarke, C., Milne, R., & Bull, R. (2011). Interviewing suspects of crime: The impact of PEACE training, supervision and the presence of a legal advisor. *Journal of Investigative Psychology and Offender Profiling*, 8(2), 149–162. doi:10.1002/jip.144

Cleary, H., & Warner, T. C. (2016). Police training in interviewing and interrogation methods: A comparison of techniques used with adult and juvenile suspects. *Law and Human Behavior*, 40(3), 270–284. doi:10.1037/lhb0000175

Collins, R., Lincoln, R., & Frank, M. G. (2002). The effect of rapport in forensic interviewing. *Psychiatry, Psychology and Law*, 9(1), 69–78. doi:10.1375/pplt.2002.9.1.69

Cooper, R. (2011). A captive audience – recruiting informants within police custody blocks. Paper presented at Cambridge Executive Programme, 4th international EBP conference. Retrieved from http://www.crim.cam.ac.uk/events/conferences/ebp/2011/

Dawson, E., Hartwig, M., & Brimbal, L. (2015). Interviewing to elicit information: Using priming to promote disclosure. *Law and Human Behavior*, 39(5), 443–450. doi:10.1037/lhb0000136

Dawson, E., Hartwig, M., Brimbal, L., & Denisenkov, P. (2017). A room with a view: Setting influences information disclosure in investigative interviews. *Law and Human Behavior*, 41(4), 333–343. doi:10.1037/lhb0000244

Deininger, R. (1977). Using informants and co-operative witnesses. *Law and Order*, July, 64–70.

Driskell, T., Blickensderfer, E. L., & Salas, E. (2013). Is three a crowd? Examining rapport in investigative interviews. *Group Dynamics: Theory, Research, and Practice*, 17(1), 1–13. doi:10.1037/a0029686

Dunnighan, C. (1992). Reliable sources. *Police Review*, 14, 1496–1497.

Evans, J. R., Meissner, C. A., Brandon, S. E., Russano, M. B., & Kleinman, S. M. (2010). Criminal versus HUMINT interrogations: The importance of psychological science to improving interrogative practice. *The Journal of Psychiatry & Law*, 38(1–2), 215–249. doi:10.1177/009318531003800110

Ewens, S., Vrij, A., Leal, S., Mann, S., Jo, E., & Fisher, R. P. (2014). The effect of interpreters on eliciting information, cues to deceit and rapport. *Legal and Criminological Psychology*, 21(2), 286–304. doi:10.1111/lcrp.12067

Fisher, R. P., & Geiselman, R. E. (1992). *Memory-enhancing techniques for investigative interviewing: The cognitive interview*. Springfield: Charles C Thomas Publisher.

Fitzsimons, G. M., & Bargh, J. A. (2003). Thinking of you: Nonconscious pursuit of interpersonal goals associated with relationship partners. *Journal of Personality and Social Psychology*, 84(1), 148–164. doi:10.1037/0022-3514.84.1.148

Godden, D. R., & Baddeley, A. D. (1975). Context-dependent memory in two natural environments: On land and underwater. *British Journal of Psychology*, 66(3), 325–331. doi:10.1111/j.2044-8295.1975.tb01468.x

Goodman-Delahunty, J., Martschuk, N., & Dhami, M. K. (2014). Interviewing high value detainees: Securing cooperation and disclosures. *Applied Cognitive Psychology*, 28(6), 883–897. doi:10.1002/acp.3087

Granhag, P. A., Kleinman, S. M., & Oleszkiewicz, S. (2016). The Scharff technique: On how to effectively elicit intelligence from human sources. *International Journal of Intelligence and CounterIntelligence*, 29(1), 132–150. doi:10.1080/08850607.2015.1083341

Granhag, P. A., Oleszkiewicz, S., Strömwall, L. A., & Kleinman, S. M. (2015). Eliciting intelligence with the Scharff technique: Interviewing more and less cooperative and capable sources. *Psychology, Public Policy, and Law*, 21(1), 100–110. doi:10.1037/law0000030

Grieve, J. G. D. (2004). Developments in UK criminal intelligence. In J. H. Ratcliffe (ed.), *Strategic thinking in criminal intelligence* (pp. 25–36). Sydney: The Federation Press.

Griffiths, A., & Milne, R. (2006). Will it all end in tiers: Police interviews with suspects in Britain. In T. Williamson (ed.), *Investigative interviewing rights, research, regulation* (pp. 167–189). Cullompton, UK: Willan.

Gudjonsson, G. H., & Pearse, J. (2011). Suspect interviews and false confessions. *Current Directions in Psychological Science*, 20(1), 33–37. doi:10.1177/0963721410396824

Hartwig, M., Meissner, C., & Semel, M. (2014). Human intelligence interviewing and interrogation: Assessing the challenges of developing an ethical, evidence-based approach. In R. Bull (ed.), *Investigative interviewing* (pp. 209–228). New York: Springer.

Hope, L., Mullis, R., & Gabbert, F. (2013). Who? What? When? Using a timeline technique to facilitate recall of a complex event. *Journal of Applied Research in Memory and Cognition*, 2(1), 20–24. doi:10.1016/j.jarmac.2013.01.002

Inbau, F. E., Reid, J. E., Buckley, J. P., & Jayne, B. C. (2013). *Criminal interrogation and confessions* (5th ed.). Burlington, MA: Jones & Bartlett Learning.

Jeffrey, A. (2011). Prisoner debriefing: An evidence based approach. Paper presented at Cambridge executive Programme, 4th international EBP conference. Retrieved from http://www.crim.cam.ac.uk/events/conferences/ebp/2011/

Kassin, S. M., & Gudjonsson, G. H. (2004). The psychology of confessions: A review of the literature and issues. *Psychological Science in the Public Interest*, 5(2), 33–67. doi:10.1111/j.1529-1006.2004.00016.x

Kebbell, M. R., Milne, R., & Wagstaff, G. F. (1999). The cognitive interview: A survey of its forensic effectiveness. *Psychology, Crime and Law*, 5(1–2), 101–115. doi:10.1080/10683169908414996

Kelly, C. E., Miller, J. C., Redlich, A. D., & Kleinman, S. M. (2013). A taxonomy of interrogation methods. *Psychology, Public Policy, and Law*, 19(2), 165–178. doi:10.1037/a0030310

Kelman, H. C. (2006). Interests, relationships, identities: Three central issues for individuals and groups in negotiating their social environment. *Annual Review of Psychology*, 57, 1–26. doi:10.1146/annurev.psych.57.102904.190156

Lee, G. D. (1993). Drug informants: Motives, methods, and management. *FBI Law Enforcement Bulletin*, 62, 10–15.

Leins, D. A., Fisher, R. P., Pludwinski, L., Rivard, J., & Robertson, B. (2014). Interview protocols to facilitate human intelligence sources' recollections of meetings. *Applied Cognitive Psychology*, 28(6), 926–935. doi:10.1002/acp.3041

Lipton, J. P. (1977). On the psychology of eyewitness testimony. *Journal of Applied Psychology*, 62(1), 90–93. doi:10.1037/0021-9010.62.1.90

Loftus, E. F. (1979). The malleability of human memory: Information introduced after we view an incident can transform memory. *American Scientist*, 67(3), 312–320. Retrieved from http://www.jstor.org/stable/27849223

Lowenthal, M. M. (2009). *Intelligence: From secrets to policy* (4th edn). Washington DC: CQ Press.

MacDonald, S., Keeping, Z., Snook, B., & Luther, K. (2016). Do not lie to me, or else: The effect of a turncoat warning and rapport building on perceptions of police interviewers. *Journal of Police and Criminal Psychology*, 1–15. doi:10.1007/s11896-016-9219-4

Meissner, C. A., Redlich, A. D., Michael, S. W., Evans, J. R., Camilletti, C. R., Bhatt, S., & Brandon, S. (2014). Accusatorial and information-gathering interrogation methods and their effects on true and false confessions: A meta-analytic review. *Journal of Experimental Criminology*, 10(4), 459–486. doi:10.1007/s11292-014-9207-6

Memon, A., Meissner, C. A., & Fraser, J. (2010). The Cognitive Interview: A meta-analytic review and study space analysis of the past 25 years. *Psychology, Public Policy, and Law*, 16 (4), 340–372. doi:10.1037/a0020518

Memon, A., Wark, L., Holley, A., Bull, R., & Koehnken, G. (1997). Eyewitness performance in cognitive and structured interviews. *Memory*, 5(5), 639–656. doi:10.1080/741941481

Milne, R. (2016). *CREST guide: The Cognitive Interview*. Retrieved from https://crestresearch.ac.uk/resources/crest-guide-cognitive-interview/

Milne, R., & Bull, R. (1999). *Investigative interviewing: Psychology and practice*. Chichester, UK: Wiley.

Milne, R. J., & Bull, R. (2016). Witness interviews and crime investigation. In D. Groome & M. Eysenck (eds), *An introduction to applied cognitive psychology* (2nd edn). Abingdon, UK: Routledge.

Nunan, J., & Milne, R. (2016). Turning research into practice in investigative interviewing. *Crest Security Review*, 1(1), 22–23.

Okken, V., van Rompay, T., & Pruyn, A. (2013). Room to move: On spatial constraints and self-disclosure during intimate conversations. *Environment and Behavior*, 45(6), 737–760. doi:10.1177/0013916512444780

Oleszkiewicz, S., Granhag, P. A., & Kleinman, S. M. (2017a). Gathering human intelligence via repeated interviewing: Further empirical tests of the Scharff technique. *Psychology, Crime & Law*, 1–16. doi:10.1080/1068316X.2017.1296150

Oleszkiewicz, S., Granhag, P. A., & Kleinman, S. M. (2017b). Eliciting information from human sources: Training handlers in the Scharff technique. *Legal and Criminological Psychology*, 1–20. doi:10.1111/lcrp.12108

Pearse, J., Gudjonsson, G. H., Clare, I. C. H., & Rutter, S. (1998). Police interviewing and psychological vulnerabilities: Predicting the likelihood of a confession. *Journal of Community & Applied Social Psychology*, 8(1), 1–21. doi:10.1002/(SICI)1099-1298(199801/02)8:1-1:AID-CASP435-3.0.CO;2-D

Redlich, A. D., Kelly, C. E., & Miller, J. C. (2014). The who, what, and why of human intelligence gathering: Self-reported measures of interrogation methods. *Applied Cognitive Psychology*, 28(6), 817–828. doi:10.1002/acp.3040

Risan, P., Binder, P. E., & Milne, R. J. (2016). Emotional Intelligence in police interviews – approach, training and the usefulness of the concept. *Journal of Forensic Psychology Practice*, 16(5), 410–424. doi:10.1080/15228932.2016.1234143

Rivard, J. R., Fisher, R. P., Robertson, B., & Hirn Mueller, D. (2014). Testing the Cognitive Interview with professional interviewers: Enhancing recall of specific details of recurring events. *Applied Cognitive Psychology*, 28(6), 917–925. doi:10.1002/acp.3026

Rogers, C. R. (1942). *Counseling and psychotherapy; newer concepts in practice*. Oxford, UK: Houghton Mifflin.

Russano, M. B., Narchet, F. M., Kleinman, S. M., & Meissner, C. A. (2014). Structured interviews of experienced HUMINT interrogators. *Applied Cognitive Psychology*, 28(6), 847–859. doi:10.1002/acp.3069

Scharff, H. J. (1950). Without torture. *Argosy*, 39, 87–91.

Semel, M. D. (2012). *Military interrogations: Best practices & beliefs*. New York, NY: City University of New York.

Sherman, L. W., & Murray, A. (2015). Evidence-based policing: From academics to professionals. *International Criminal Justice Review*, 25(1), 7–10. doi:10.1177/1057567715576174

Soufan, A. H. (2011). *The Black Banners: Inside the hunt for Al Qaeda*. London, UK: Allen Lane.

Stanier, I., Wadie, F., & Nunan, J. (2018). *Intelligence interview approaches*. Manuscript in preparation.

Tickle-Degnen, L., & Rosenthal, R. (1990). The nature of rapport and its nonverbal correlates. *Psychological Inquiry, 1*(4), 285–293. doi:10.1207/s15327965pli0104_1

U.S. Army Field Manual. (2006). *FM 2–22.3 Human Intelligence Collector Operations*. Washington, DC: Headquarters, Department of the Army.

Vallano, J. P., & Compo, N. S. (2011). A comfortable witness is a good witness: Rapport-building and susceptibility to misinformation in an investigative mock-crime interview. *Applied Cognitive Psychology*, 25(6), 960–970. doi:10.1002/acp.1789

Vallano, J. P., Evans, J. R., Schreiber Compo, N., & Kieckhaefer, J. M. (2015). Rapport-building during witness and suspect interviews: A survey of law enforcement. *Applied Cognitive Psychology*, 29(3), 369–380. doi:10.1002/acp.3115

Zunin, L., & Zunin, N. (1972), *Contact: The first four minutes*. New York, NY: Ballantine.

Chapter 12

Evidence based police training

The bedrock of effective criminal investigation?

Martin O'Neill and Dean Jones

Introduction

This chapter discusses the issue of investigative training in the context of the evidence based policing paradigm within the UK, USA and Canada. These jurisdictions are at different developmental points, although arguably the UK has made significant advances within the last few years. Put simply, evidence based policing (EBP) is the principle whereby policing policy and practice is determined by consideration of academic research and 'what works?' (Lum & Koper, 2017). This by its very nature includes the context of psychological research and its utilisation as evidence to support investigative training and practice. Any shift toward EBP will inevitably take time to gain a foothold, not only in terms of police leadership buy-in but also in relation to cultural acceptance (Sherman, 2015). Police are notoriously sceptical of academics and their research, as well as being conservative, cynical and wary of change. This chapter asks the question *to what extent does evidence based police training inculcate crime investigators with the appropriate knowledge skills and understanding to be able to carry out their role effectively?* Crime investigators are taken to include not only detectives but also patrol officers, who have consistently been shown by research to be central to clearing crime (Greenwood et al., 1977). The title of this chapter contains some assumptions; most notably that Evidence Based Police Training (EBPT) is a fundamental part of police training at the current time; that it leads to the production of effective investigators; that police science is advanced enough to understand what it is to be effective, and finally there is an assumption that training is assessed sufficiently to ensure that delivery, translation and increased effectiveness are consequences of any investigative training. EBPT is different from evidence based policing (EBP), although it is inextricably linked to it. It connotes the 'what works' agenda in relation to police policy and practice. The paradigm encourages a new approach by organisations to ensure that 'what works' is at the centre of policing activity. Rather than seeing police as a craft (see Chapter 2 for more on this), the engagement with science in this way can be seen as a merging of both craft and science so that any police activity has access to, and knowledge of, current research in order to make appropriately informed decisions (Willis, 2013; Willis & Mastrofski, 2018). EBPT has a central role to play in ensuring practitioners are aware of existing evidence in their field and they are able to independently research and assess whether there is any relevant evidence appropriate to given situations. EBPT can also connote training that in and of itself is evidence based, in the sense that learning is enabled utilising the most appropriate educational methods and strategies.

The UK

Evidence based policing

There is a new era in terms of the professionalisation agenda; not just in relation to investigations but policing in general and also concern that the road to professionalisation within the police is bound to be a controversial and difficult one (Sklansky, 2011). EBP represents a paradigm shift toward encompassing more empirical evidence into policing. Neyroud (2011) suggested that modern policing needed to grasp the nettle and own the science of policing in order to bring policing into the modern era. He observed that the service needed to embrace research and find the science behind the profession. Fraught with its own controversies, the arrival of EBP needs acceptance in order to be effective. There is an ongoing debate about what constitutes evidence in this new era; the priority areas to be dealt with first, and the position of the craft of investigation in the whole process (Stanko & Dawson, 2016). The definitional aspects of EBP have already been discussed in Chapter 2.

One of the promising developments of the EBP paradigm and the new Policing Education Qualifications Framework (PEQF) is the potential for stronger links between practitioners and academia in that many more practitioners may take academic routes where they will be able to explore problems they have encountered in their professional careers, thereby informing practice. Rather than there being a perceived divide between practitioners and academia, many practitioners of the future will also represent academia. The Society for Evidence Based Policing (SEBP) in the UK, the College of Policing research map and links forged with the academic community around the country, are evidence of a sea change. Sherman (2015) notes that UK policing has been quick to utilise evidence.

Evidence based investigator training

White (2006) noted the absence of theory and empirical research in police training, a finding echoed, for example, in relation to the policing of crowds (Hoggett & Stott, 2010). There appears to be a paucity of evidence around what works in relation to criminal investigation (Brodeur, 2010). Criminal investigation in the UK is undertaken by investigators at all levels of the police service, including uniformed constables and detectives (Burrows & Tarling, 1987). Detectives in the modern era investigate smaller numbers of crimes than their uniformed counterparts, as they are most likely to deal with crimes of such seriousness and complexity that they demand the skills of an appropriately trained investigator (Burrows et al., 2005). Under the auspices of the Professionalising Investigations Programme in the UK (PIP level one) uniformed officers and call handlers deal with the majority of reported volume crime investigations, and easier to solve cases are screened for investigation whilst others are 'filed' with little further investigation. Screening of reported crimes allows for resources to be focussed on areas where it is considered they will make the most impact (Harfield, 2008). PIP level two relates to serious and complex crime, whereas PIP levels three and four are reserved for the most serious crimes such as homicide, kidnap and terrorism, where the skills of an appropriately trained lead senior investigator are required (Stelfox, 2007, 2009). The so-called professionalisation of investigations entails the progression of officers within the PIP framework. Programmes were designed at each level to ensure that investigators had the appropriate knowledge and understanding required to investigate crimes, and to ensure that there was common understanding of both the practice and theory of investigation at each level (McGrory & Treacy, 2012; Tong et al., 2009; Stelfox, 2009). There is some tentative support for the PIP process in recent research (see Chapter 3). Yet James and Mills (2011) highlight in their small study of one police force, the lack of independent research of PIP and its effectiveness.

Many developments in police investigative training have their seeds in either research, miscarriages of justice or failed investigations (Bull, 2014). Previous studies have criticised police training for being too law centred (Irving & McKenzie, 1989; Morgan, 1990; Irving & Dunnighan, 1993), and for being too focussed upon achieving a confession (Baldwin, 1993). Consequently, changes were made. Various Public Inquiries suggested that the police needed further training in diversity matters (Scarman, 1981; MacPherson, 1999). As a result, training regimes were instigated to ensure officers were aware of diversity issues (Home Affairs Committee, 2009). By far the biggest changes, however, have come in the field of investigative interviewing, where the police had been criticised for use of oppressive tactics, poor quality investigative techniques and an overemphasis on securing confessions in suspect interviews.[1] Moreover, interviews of witnesses were criticised for providing a synthesis of the prevailing police account rather than an unvarnished account taken from a witness or victim (Bull, 2014).

The resulting model of police interviews is known as 'Investigative Interviewing' (see Chapter 8 for more on the UK turn-round operation). The effectiveness of the PEACE model has been researched extensively, the results of which have informed the very nature of investigative practice. The UK system of investigative interviewing, aligned as it is to the PIP process, is unrecognisable from the often unprofessional and questionable practices of the past. The developments in this area have been remarkable. Academics, police leaders, practitioners, public and government all appeared to agree that things needed to change, a powerful alliance that is always difficult to ignore. Researchers observed practice, interviewed practitioners, examined failed cases and miscarriages of justice, and considered the psychological literature (Williamson, 2007; Bull, 2014). As a result, a new emphasis was effectively imposed and a more professional practice emerged. Additionally, changes to practice were structured and supported through a national interview steering group made up of police leaders, academics and specialist practitioners. The creation of the tiers of interviewing also enabled training to be aligned with case seriousness (Griffiths & Milne, 2006). Moreover, other tiers focussed upon management and supervision of interviews, and a capacity to advise and coordinate interviews (Shawyer, Milne & Bull, 2009).

Further research informing investigative training relates to investigator bias. Rossmo (2006) describes a number of strategies to reduce the influence of bias affecting decision making, which includes the importance of study-based training. This is supported by Fahsing and Ask (2013) who identified that experience and training were the single most important safeguards against biasing influences. The effect of bias was identified in a study of decision making at the scenes of sudden and unexpected death where the vulnerability of deceased persons skewed thinking away from suspicion towards natural causes (Jones, 2016). It is interesting to note that little or no training is given to police officers attending the scenes of sudden death and there is an emphasis on national training products to concentrate on leadership and management competencies and therefore the system of delivery may be flawed (White, 2006; Peace, 2006). In police training, emphasis on cultural change and ethical standards leads the political agenda since the Neyroud report in 2011 triggered the government to setting up the College of Policing (Neyroud, 2011). The practical application of skills 'on the ground' appears to some to have taken second place.

One of the most significant reasons cited for poor scene investigations was the lack of training given to front line officers who are the most likely to be deployed to sudden and unexpected deaths (Jones, 2016). It was found that in some pockets of the country training was non-existent and in others at best patchy. It is fair to say therefore that as a whole, training was reported as insufficient to equip front line officers to deal with the scene and make reasoned and informed decisions. Training therefore needs to be developed and given to all front line and supervisory police officers. This training needs to be standardised and consistent (Home Affairs Committee, 2016) in order that the quality of scene investigation as well as other aspects of front line delivery is the same across England and Wales. Before a training package or learning descriptors can be developed, they must be based upon a standard and agreed evidenced based national policy and also a standard operating procedure (SOP). A benefit of a SOP or 'checklist' is that it is shown to improve performance in many professions (Gawande, 2010; Kahneman, 2011; Meehl, 1954, 1986).

The inexperience and training of police supervisors were similar to that of first attending officers (Jones, 2016). In the context of critical incident management, Eyre and Alison (2007) found that less experienced managers do not possess a complex memory structure that contains a broad repertoire of typical situations from which to generate first and best options and are more likely to be prone to error. Saunders (2001, p. 226) also found that police officers did not rely on a formal decision making process, but instead responded in ways that they had done in previous similar situations (see Chapter 3, this volume, for more on decision making). The shortfall of this experiential learning model is that when dealing with a relatively rare event such as a homicide, the repertoire of responses is likely to be more limited (Adhami, Browne & Laycock, 1996). In respect of the supervision of first attending officers, Dror (2013) discussed the effect of 'base rate' on the cognitive mechanism whereby the human brain gets used to base rate regularities which adjust cognitive attention and processing. A supervisor can fail to properly scrutinise a junior officer's decision making by failing to objectively assess first decisions in favour of that presented on face value. The supervisor can easily take on the hypothesis presented and through a process of confirmation bias find evidence which supports that hypothesis to the exclusion of information that challenges that hypothesis (Brandl, 2014; Fahsing, 2016).

As a final example, police in the UK have also tried to utilise research data to assist in the search for missing people (Gibb & Woolnough, 2007; Fyfe, Stevenson & Woolnough, 2015), although, as Fyfe et al. note, the College of Policing recently adopted a more risk based approach to initial responses to missing person reports, based upon research (Bayliss & Quinton, 2013; ACPO, 2013; Fyfe et al., 2015).

Evidence based police training

PIP level one encompasses officers undertaking training in their probationary period. The probationer training regime has undergone change since 1973. Prior to that it had remained fairly constant in its content and delivery style (HMIC, 1999, 2002; Heslop, 2006). Like detective training, it has been heavily criticised for concentrating upon law and procedure to the detriment of skills such as communication, and a greater understanding of areas such as diversity (Morgan, 1990). Whilst law and procedure is a component of the present probationer curriculum, a more varied approach is signalled, with community placements, tutor constable regimes and workplace competencies also the norm before an officer can be said to be 'qualified' to undertake criminal investigations at the basic level. Various incarnations of probationer training have attempted to move the training forward in terms of delivery; from a purely pedagogic to a more student centred andragogic approach. The curriculum for new recruit's attempts to produce a more rounded officer capable of dealing with twenty-first century problems in a more appropriate fashion (MacDonald, 1987; HMIC, 1999, 2002; Heslop, 2006). Detective training too has undergone similar changes with an accent in the modern PIP process upon a mixture of law and procedural knowledge aligned to skills as an investigator (MacDonald et al., 1987; Moore & Rubin, 2014).

The change of investigative interview practice coincided with changes to the way it was trained in some police forces. When the PEACE model was introduced in the early 1990s, the five-day training course involved some instruction, followed by practice interviews observed by peers, in conditions reflecting real life interviews (Clarke & Milne, 2001). This was often achieved via live television links between classrooms so that peers could observe the interviews and make notes as they progressed. Feedback was provided to interviewers immediately by both peers and trainers. In theory learning was achieved by practice and feedback in a realistic setting. In reality this relied upon the trainer being able to secure staff to perform the roles of solicitor and interviewee. Often, the roles were undertaken by other trainers, with the members of the course acting as interviewees for their peers, with the reality sometimes lost. The emergence of the use of interview practicals allowed practitioners to learn from peers, trainers and the practical realities of the situation, all within a safe learning environment. There is however evidence of inconsistent training throughout the country in relation to the PEACE process (Clarke & Milne, 2001). Research has consistently lauded the benefits of feedback in interview training, allowing students to develop (Smets & Rispens, 2014).

Elements of educational theory suggests that people learn more from doing rather than being passive receivers of information (Kolb, 1984; Schank, Berman & Macpherson, 1999). Whilst this is context specific and its utility open to question (Levitt & March, 1988), there is some attraction to the contention that learning by experience followed by instant feedback in circumstances that reflect reality is appropriate in circumstances such as investigative interviewing (Clarke & Milne, 2001). As Clarke and Milne (2001) suggested in their national evaluation of PEACE, that training can be nullified without appropriate supervision in the workplace, and workplace support. The development of effective supervision protocols, leadership buy-in, acceptance of the new practice and provision of appropriate refresher training are crucial to effective development of any training initiative.

The investigative field has also seen the rise in the use of simulation-based training such as the now well tested 'Hydra' system designed to enhance decision-making skills in a variety of settings (Alison et al., 2013). The system involves creating a realistic environment where students must make decisions in the context of situations likely to occur in real life. The principle of immersion suggests that students will learn from the realistic environment. Like the investigative interview courses, the more realistic the scenario, the more likely it is that the students will engage with the task in hand and the more benefit can be derived from feedback and group discussion. Moreover, observation of the decision-making process within such training is likely to be the best reflection of reality short of real life observation, which is almost impossible to achieve in the training context (Alison et al., 2013). The Hydra process is now a consistent presence within investigative training from the level of detective constable through to senior investigating officer (SIO).

Like other jurisdictions, UK policing has embraced technology in the learning context, and provides numerous e-learning courses for serving officers through the National Centre for Applied Learning Technologies (NCALT). Although there are benefits to this technology, such as cost savings, accessibility and flexibility for officers (Benson & Powell, 2015), a recent study suggests that products are little valued by practitioners and seen as a tool to prove disciplinary infractions (Honess, 2017). Moreover, HMIC (2014) noted the somewhat narrow approach to police e-learning packages, with the unimaginative use of material followed by multiple-choice questions. They urged face-to-face training, reflection and discussion for domestic abuse training, suggesting that some areas are not amenable to e-learning processes.

Whilst there is evidence that face to face UK investigative training has moved towards a more student centred andragogic methodology, Heslop (2006) cautions that training in the UK, though aspiring to andragogy, cannot truly reflect such an approach due to the dominance of organisational structures, rather than the primacy of student centred learning. That said, the UK system of investigative training has undergone a significant change both before and after the turn of the century. Since 2005, investigator development has been under the auspices of PIP. There is little empirical evidence relating to the effectiveness of PIP, but a suggestion that any system betters what had previously been in place. New initiatives in the EBP paradigm would need to be cognisant of existing research about what works in training.

USA

Evidence based policing

In the USA, EBP has been the mantra for longer than in the UK (Sherman, 2015). Sherman traces it back to 1975 in the USA, spanning 'hot spot' policing initiatives, Community Orientated Policing (COP); Problem Orientated Policing (POP); COMPSTAT[2] (Willis, Mastrofski & Weisburd, 2004); domestic abuse arrests (Sherman, 2013) and many others. However, Sherman (2013) observes that police practice does not always embrace existing research, even if it sometimes claims to. In relation to domestic abuse responses, for instance, there is a body of research suggesting in certain circumstances that arrest of the perpetrator can exacerbate problems rather than solve them. That said, police organisations tend to utilise policies that insist upon perpetrator arrest, despite the evidence (a situation similar to the UK). This type of issue accentuates the future problems that EBP and EBPT may have, where political, strategic and even cultural issues militate against prevailing research. Sometimes it may be better to be seen doing something rather than nothing, particularly if politicians and police leaders want to appear as though something is being done. In Canada and the USA police organisations have a legal duty of care to ensure effective training – a huge issue that police training in the UK does not have to contend with at present (Huey, Cyr & Ricciardelli, 2016).

In relation to investigative interviewing, the USA has lagged behind countries such as the UK, Norway, Australia and New Zealand (Bull, 2014) in turning their backs on persuasive interviewing (see Chapter 8), although Cleary and Warner (2016 do note a new training curriculum issued by the International Association of Chiefs of Police (IACP) in relation to the questioning of youths.

Lum and Koper (2017) suggest that professional development of officers is a good way to embed evidence-based practices, and this can take a number of different forms. Rather than just teaching the research about what works. Lum and Koper (2017) suggest teaching evidence based strategies without necessarily teaching the research that underpins them, as well as in appropriate circumstances teaching how to find relevant research and how to apply tools to ensure that research is operationalised. As Sherman (2013) points out, some evidence exists already, but police use of it is wanting. Where for instance there is what he describes as 'useful evidence' in relation to the screening of cases for investigation, use of the existing evidence is limited across continents. It is not just a question of actioning more research; it is also a question of utilising evidence already in existence in the most useful way. Whilst Martin and Mazerolle (2015) suggest that there is a willingness to embrace evidence based policing in the USA, White and Escobar (2008) observe that adopting new approaches to policing require something more than just a willingness to do so. Indeed, training has a significant role to play in embedding practice. As an example, White and Escobar (2008) discuss the concepts of both COP and POP. They demonstrate how COP received sporadic, limited and sometimes ineffective training, whereas POP appeared to have more support and better training and hence its perceived greater success and speedier implementation into policing (White & Escobar, 2008). Some of these problems may also stem from the lack of central oversight and ownership. For example, White and Escobar (2008) considered the implementation of Counter Terrorism training within US police departments following 9/11. The initiative was Federally led (Chappell, 2014), pervaded all police departments and became embedded into police training, demonstrating that where the will is present, centrally controlled and effectively promoted, initiatives can and do become part of the training process. Although it is not claimed that this initiative was evidence based, it does illustrate an important aspect of the police training milieu. If there is a political will to change then it will invariably take precedence whether there is evidence to support it being done that way or not. The formation of the American Society for Evidence Based Policing (ASEBP) in 2015 and the IACP partnership with the University of Cincinnati in forming the Centre of Police Research and Policy (CPRP) provide concrete evidence of a willingness to embrace change.

Evidence based investigator training

In terms of investigative training, the US system arguably suffers because of the fragmented and numerous police departments across the country (Lum & Koper, 2017). As Berlin (2014) points out, there is no national police department, and ownership thereby devolves to a more local level. In 2013 there were some 18,000 police and Sheriff's departments (Berlin, 2014) and more than 640 state and local training academies (Bureau of Justice Statistics, 2013). Carter and Phillips (2015) note the varied standards both within and between different jurisdictions, highlighting that new policing initiatives or Federal standards struggle to become embedded due to constraints on police departments, many of which have limited resources.

Lum and Koper (2017) provide examples of research evidence that could be utilised for criminal investigation training, such as more consideration of investigating places and problems rather than just individual criminals and crimes. This supports Sherman's (2015) contention that sometimes the evidence is there but it is not being used. Whilst the evidence base in relation to criminal investigation is still developing (Brodeur, 2010), there is research material available on certain aspects such as homicide investigations, place investigations and solvability factors. Though there is little room here to list all of the areas that require an evidence base to assist in training investigators, Gover, Paul and Dodge (2011) note the paucity of training and knowledge in relation to both sexual offences and domestic abuse. Considering these two areas are frequently highlighted as problematic in terms of police response and investigation, as Stanko and Dawson (2016) observe, there should be an assessment of priority areas that require urgent research.

Kingshott, Walsh and Meesig (2015) conducted a survey of larger law enforcement agencies in the USA in order to establish the extent of investigative training for both investigators and patrol officers. Previous research (Greenwood et al., 1977; Horvath, Meesig & Lee, 2001) had found that less than half of the agencies required formal investigator training at all. Horvath, Meesig and Lee (2001) reported that investigator training was often either too short or resource constraints led to inadequate provision. The 2015 study found some encouraging developments however. From less than half of agencies requiring investigator training in 2001, the 2015 study revealed that 69 per cent of agencies now require it. However, the authors noted that although the requirement rose, there was a minimal increase in investigative training for patrol officers. This is significant particularly in light of research highlighting the importance of patrol officers to investigations (Greenwood et al., 1977).

Agencies surveyed offered 147 investigator courses compared with 106 investigation courses for patrol officers (Kingshott, Walsh & Meesig, 2015). Worryingly, the content of courses, though seemingly covering issues such as crime types and investigative techniques, was shrouded in mystery. Many of the surveyed agencies declined to provide course content, citing commercial reasons. If the course content is not known, it is difficult to establish whether investigative training is consistent or utilising research evidence to support it. This makes it impossible for minimum standards to be set and assessed. In the UK, the College of Policing not only sets training objectives for all PIP accredited courses, they are also in the throes of agreeing content for Apprenticeship and Policing degrees with Higher Education Institutions (HEIs) where HEIs will utilise evidence based research to inform programmes. The conclusion by Kingshott, Walsh and Meesig (2015) is that investigator training has increased to the detriment of investigation training for patrol officers. However, there is a need for a national standard for investigator training at all levels. Whilst the PIP framework in the UK has its problems, it is an improvement on having no recognised structure for the mandatory development of investigators at every level.

Evidence based police training

There have been consistent calls for further research into 'what works' in relation to police training. Academics have noted the paucity of evidence in relation to what training enhances effective performance (Skogan & Frydl, 2004; Cordner & Shain, 2011). There is evidence that police training in the USA (and elsewhere) is still militaristic and pedagogic in nature (Birzer, 2003; Berlin, 2014). Efforts to move toward a more andragogic approach in the USA, together with more realistic scenario based approaches have been noted (White & Escobar 2008; Chappell, 2014). The advent of initiatives such as COP ensured that there was a move toward more andragogic practices, and it has been observed that there is also a move toward problem based learning, a strategy that puts the learner at the heart of the process (Werth, 2011). The President's Task Force on 21st Century Policing (2015) considered law enforcement training as an essential pillar of officer development. As part of its recommendations, the Task Force suggested federal involvement in promoting consistent, high quality training, ensuring the integration of current research into programmes, and the establishment of localised hubs to encourage training innovation (Presidents Task Force on 21st Century Policing, 2015, P4).

The Task Force also called for more use of technology to assist learners, particularly in the use of scenario based training. Whether the move to embrace e-learning reflects a genuine willingness to improve the learning of practitioners is questionable bearing in mind the consistent mantra internationally to try to decrease the expense of police training.

Canada

Evidence based policing

In Canada, EBP is only beginning to find a foothold. The Canadian Society for Evidence Based Policing (CAN-SEBP) was formed in 2015 as an offshoot of the SEBP in the UK (Huey & Ricciardelli, 2016). Huey and Ricciardelli (2016), like Martin and Mazerolle (2015) in the USA, identify that there is an increasing appetite amongst police officers for evidence based policing, and whilst it is not yet fully embedded, there is a suggestion that the transition could be rapid. The increased appetite amongst police organisations and individual officers for empirical evidence may stem from tight budgetary constraints and recognition that future police activity needs to be driven by efficiency and effectiveness. Public Safety Canada (2013) identified a dearth of empirical evidence in relation to 'what works'. They also identified that any evidence that did exist was often difficult to find and generally inaccessible. It was therefore not being utilised as much as it could have been. The House Standing Committee (2014) described the state of policing research in Canada as a 'barren landscape' for at least the preceding 30 years. The Council of Canadian Academies (2014) made similar overtones. Huey and Ricciardelli (2016) call for more localised research, as well as research that is useable by the police. They observe that research often fails to translate to the classroom. Future research outputs need to address this issue if research is to have utility, echoing Sherman (2015). That is not to say that evidence does not already exist; it may be that useful evidence is not being utilised at present (Slothower, Sherman & Neyroud, 2015).

Evidence based investigative training

Problems with the standard and consistency of police training in Canada were highlighted as recently as 2014 by the House Standing Committee (2014, p. 34), which found that police officer skills vary across jurisdictions. However, Wyatt and Bell (2014) consider that, despite Canada's large geographic size and mix of police organisations, the police training curriculum is standardised in relation to both investigation and patrol. A competency-based framework was developed by the Police Sector Council following a three-year research study.

In relation to empirical evidence concerning criminal investigation, Brodeur (2010) noted how the USA's National Research Council (2004) identified criminal investigation as one of the least studied areas (Skogan & Frydl, 2004). Although this does not mean that no research exists, the important point is that it has been under researched. As an example, Brodeur notes lack of research in the post charge aspect of detective work. There is little consideration of the case building function of investigators when they focus a case against a suspect. Investigative decision making is an aspect that has often been linked to associated miscarriages of justice, yet much research on investigative decision making has been descriptive rather than practical (Fahsing, 2016). Quinlan (2016) recently argued that more research was required into training provided to Canadian investigators, particularly in relation to assessing both the truth of victim accounts and the credibility of survivors in the investigation of sexual offences.

Though there are clear gaps to fill in investigative research, there is evidence that with the will to succeed and both academic and practitioner support, change is possible. For example, studies identified that witness interview practice in Canada was inadequate (Snook & Keating, 2011; Snook, Eastwood,Stinson, Tedeschini & House, 2010). Snook, House, MacDonald and Eastwood (2012) conducted a study of witness interview training in Canada and found that training was sometimes limited and sporadic, and often lacked any scientific basis in direct contrast to investigative training in the UK (this situation had been previously highlighted by Wright & Alison, 2004). There was found to be a lack of supervision and feedback following a training course, essential practice for the ongoing development of trained officers. Additionally, there were growing calls for the Canadian police to adopt the investigative interviewing principles favoured by UK and Australia, as opposed to the manipulative technique prominent in both USA and Canada at the time (Snook et al., 2010). The Royal Canadian Mounted Police adopted a 'phased interview' model for suspect interviewing (based on the UK PEACE model) in 2013, and it appears that strategic oversight is ensured through a mixture of both practitioners and academics.

Evidence based police training

There has been a proliferation of e-learning across Canada and, as with developments in the UK and USA, there has also been a rise in computer based simulation (Gibson & Goodwin, 2009; Mugford, Corey & Bennell, 2013) accompanied by a move to skills and scenario based training (White & Escobar, 2008). However, questions remain as to the amenability to standardisation, testing and clarification of scenario based training (Chappell, 2014). In 2010, it was estimated that some 8000 e-learning courses were available for police officers in Canada. Whilst the use of technology to harness e-learning is inevitable and sometimes useful if properly utilised, there is a danger that its excessive use without consideration of learning objectives can be a poor substitute to other forms of delivery. As an example, in the UK the HMIC criticised forces for using e-learning for issues such as domestic abuse. The HMIC, suggested that such training should be delivered face to face. Other studies situated in Canada observed the importance of activities and strategies *beyond* the training event. Snook et al. (2012) consider the importance of supervision and feedback in the workplace, whereas Ruff (2012) highlight the importance of ongoing training. Rather than seeing training as a one-off event therefore, Ruff notes the importance of ongoing training to ensure that learning is reinforced periodically. Ruff's study related to officer responses to domestic abuse following training.

Conclusion

Police organisations are now slowly embedding EBP into their training strategy. The jury is out as to whether the culture will fully embrace such a significant paradigm shift. Sherman (2015) has articulated the profound leadership qualities necessary to enable the transformation to occur. In terms of criminal investigation, in the UK, USA and Canada there is still a paucity of research evidence of 'what works'. As some commentators rightly suggest, research may have universal application, but other research needs to be contextual to the police organisation it serves. The area of investigative interviewing is perhaps the one that allows for comparison between jurisdictions discussed in this chapter. Canada has adopted a form of the PEACE model of interviewing after repeated criticisms of the REID technique relating to its manipulative and persuasive character and potential links to false confessions and miscarriages. The USA still clings to persuasive interview techniques as opposed to the more objective evidence gathering approach favoured in the UK and elsewhere. The adoption of the UK model was supported by psychological research, leadership and academic partnership, and most importantly widespread agreement that the time had come to change the face of interview practice. National standards were introduced, force champions identified and strategic oversight of the process put in place. In short, the will was there; evidence already existed, and attention was given to areas requiring further research. As a result significant changes were made. In Canada too, after lobbying from the academic community, changes were made. In the USA, persuasive interviewing persists; there are no national standards and a huge number of diverse police departments and academies with their own curricula. We have seen how little is known about the content of investigator courses in the USA and this seems astonishing in the modern era.

No single jurisdiction appears to have all of the answers. The UK and Canada seem to have embraced evidence based investigative interview practices quicker than the USA, and it is to be hoped that the USA too will follow suit and dispense with manipulative persuasive interviewing in favour of information gathering. The large geographical area together with the proliferation of law enforcement agencies throughout, make it difficult to make change without national oversight. It is not impossible though, with a willingness to accomplish real change, as the experience of Counter Terrorism training after 9/11 demonstrates. All jurisdictions are now turning toward evidence based practice, and the indications are that transformation is gathering apace and could be rapid, particularly in the UK (Sherman, 2015). All jurisdictions appear to share a willingness to engage with the 'what works' agenda, and this is important as a mechanism to fuel new training initiatives, particularly as it relates to investigative practice. A good deal of reflection is required to ensure that training delivery is based upon evidence. We have seen in this chapter examples where it is not being utilised, supporting the claims of Sherman and Lum and Koper that the existing evidence could be harnessed better. In a similar vein it is clear that the area of investigative training and training effectiveness needs further research and evidence based practice. The rise of technology to assist training is necessary in the modern era, yet caution is required to ensure that training initiatives are driven by the most appropriate methods, not just by the cheapest option. In the UK, HMIC (2014) have suggested that some training is not suitable for e-learning and that face to face training is required. The EBP paradigm promises much, and new training initiatives should be carefully planned, with existing educational research in mind. However, there must be a willingness to engage research to ensure that the new initiative is evidence based, both in terms of content and the educational strategies used to deliver it. Further consideration would need to be given to training effectiveness too, as all too often the transfer of skill to workplace is under researched. Psychological research has had and is continuing to have profound impact on areas of investigative practice, particularly in relation to investigative interviewing. Policing must continue to harness psychological research to ensure that investigations continue to be informed by the very best research in the field.

Notes

1 See for instance cases that cross the decades such as the investigation into the death of Maxwell Confait (1972); the Guildford Four and the Birmingham Six (from the 1980s) and the Cardiff Three and the case of George Heron (from the 1990s).
2 COMSTAT: Computer Statistics used to hold police commanders to account for poor performance.

References

ACPO (2013). *Interim guidance on the management, recording & investigation of missing persons 2013*. Wyboston, UK: College of Policing.

Adhami, E., Browne, D. P. & Laycock, G. K. (1996). *Major crime inquiries: Improving expert support for detectives*. London:Home Office, Police Research Group.

Alison, L., van den Heuvel, C., Waring, S., Power, N., Long, A., O'Hara, T. & Crego, J. (2013). Immersive simulated learning environments for researching critical incidents A knowledge synthesis of the literature and experiences of studying high-risk strategic decision making. *Journal of Cognitive Engineering and Decision Making*, 7(3), 255–272.

Baldwin, J. (1993). Police interview technique – establishing truth or proof? *British Journal of Criminology*, 33, 325–351.

Bayliss, A. & Quinton, P. (2013) *The initial police response to missing persons: An evaluation of a more risk-based approach*. London:College of Policing.

Benson, M. S. & Powell, M. B. (2015). Evaluation of a comprehensive interactive training system for investigative interviewers of children. *Psychology, Public Policy, and Law*, 21(3), 309–322.

Berlin, M. (2014). An overview of police training in the United States, historical development, current trends and critical issues: The evidence. In P. Stanislas (ed.),

International perspectives on police education and training. Abingdon, UK: Routledge, pp. 23–42.

Birzer, M. L. (2003). The theory of andragogy applied to police training. *Policing: An International Journal of Police Strategies & Management*, 26(1), 29–42.

Brandl, S. G. (2014). *Criminal investigation*. Thousand Oaks, CA: SAGE Publications.

Brodeur, J. P. (2010). *The policing web*. Oxford: Oxford University Press.

Bull, R. (2014). *Investigative interviewing*. New York: Springer

Bureau of Justice Statistics (2013). *Data collection: Census of law enforcement training academies*. Available at: https://www.bjs.gov/index.cfm?ty=dcdetail&iid=280

Burrows, J. & Tarling, R. (1987). The investigation of crime in England and Wales. *The British Journal of Criminology*, 27(3), 229–251.

Burrows, J., Hopkins, M., Hubbard, R., Robinson, A., Speed, M. & Tilley, N. (2005). *Understanding the attrition process in volume crime investigations*. Home Office Research Study, 295. London: Home Office.

Carter, J. G. & Phillips, S. W. (2015). Intelligence-led policing and forces of organisational change in the USA. *Policing and Society*, 25(4), 333–357, doi:10.1080/10439463.2013.865738

Clarke, C. & Milne, R. (2001). *A national evaluation of the PEACE Investigative Interviewing Course*. London: Home office.

Cleary, H. & Warner, T. C. (2016). Police training in interviewing and interrogation methods: A comparison of techniques used with adult and juvenile suspects. *Law and Human Behavior*, 40(3), 270–284.

Cordner, G. & Shain, C. (2011). The changing landscape of police education and training. *Police Practice and Research*, 12(4), 281–285

Council of Canadian Academies (2014). *Policing Canada in the 21st century: New policing for new challenges*. Ottawa: The Expert Panel on the Future of Canadian Policing Models, Council of Canadian Academies.

Dror, I. E. (2013). Practical solutions to cognitive and human factor challenges in forensic science. *Forensic Science Policy and Management: An International Journal*, 4(3–4), 105–113.

Eyre, M. & Alison, L. (2007). To decide or not to decide: Decision-making and decision avoidance in critical incidents. In D. Carson (ed.), *Applying psychology to criminal justice*. Chichester: Wiley, pp. 211–232.Fahsing, I. A. (2016). *The making of an expert detective: Thinking and deciding in criminal investigations*. Unpublished PhD thesis, University of Gothenburg, Sweden.

Fahsing, I. & Ask, K. (2013). Decision making and decisional tipping points in homicide investigations: An interview study of British and Norwegian detectives. *Journal of Investigative Psychology and Offender Profiling*, 10(2), 155–165.

Fyfe, N., Stevenson, O. & Woolnough, P. (2015). Missing persons: The processes and challenges of police investigation. *Policing and Society*, 25(4), 409–425. doi:10.1080/10439463.2014.881812

Gawande, A. (2010). *The checklist manifesto: How to get things right* (Vol. 200). New York: Metropolitan Books.

Gibb, G. & Woolnough, P. (2007). *Missing persons: Understanding, planning, responding – a guide for police officers*. Aberdeen: Grampian Police. Available from: http://www.sipr.ac.uk/downloads/missing_persons_understanding.pdf

Gibson, B. & Goodwin, D. (2009). E learning 101. Canadian Police Knowledge Network. Available at: https://www.stanhopeconference.com/2009/presentations/elearning101.pdf

Gover, A. R., Paul, D. P. & Dodge, M. (2011). Law enforcement officers' attitudes about domestic violence. *Violence Against Women*, 17(5), 619–636.

Greenwood, P., Chaiken, J. & Petersilia, J. (1977). *The criminal investigation process*. Lexington, Mass: D.C. Heath.

Griffiths, A. & Milne, B. (2006). Will it all end in tiers? In T. Williamson (ed.), *Investigative interviewing: Rights, research, regulation*. Cullompton, UK: Willan, pp. 167–189.

Harfield, C. (2008). Criminal investigation. In T. Newburn & P. Neyroud (eds), *The dictionary of policing*. Cullompton, UK: Willan Publishing, pp. 67–69.

Heslop, R. (2006). 'Doing a Maslow': Humanistic education and diversity in police training. *The Police Journal*, 79(4), 331–341.

Her Majesty's Inspector of Constabularies (HMIC). (1999). *Managing learning: A study of police training*. London: HMIC.

Her Majesty's Inspector of Constabularies (HMIC). (2002). *Training matters*. London: HMIC.

Her Majesty's Inspector of Constabularies (HMIC). (2014). *Everybody's business: Improving the police response to domestic abuse*. London: HMIC.

Hoggett, J. & Stott, C. (2010). Crowd psychology, public order police training and the policing of football crowds. *Policing: An International Journal of Police Strategies & Management*, 33(2), 218–235.

Home Affairs Committee (2009). *The Macpherson report ten years on*. London: The Stationery Office.

Home Affairs Committee (2016). *College of Policing: Three years on*. Fourth Report of Session 2016–2017. London: House of Commons.

Honess, R. (2017). *The mandatory delivery of ongoing training within the police service of England and Wales and its relationship to the andragogical principle of self-motivation*. MSc Research thesis, Canterbury Christ Church University, UK. Available at: https://create.canterbury.ac.uk/14999/1/HONESSTHESISv4%20PDF.pdf

Horvath, F., Meesig, R. T. & Lee, Y. H. (2001). *A national survey of police policies and practices regarding the criminal investigation process: Twenty-five years after Rand*. Washington, DC: National Institute of Justice, Office of Justice Programs.

House Standing Committee on Public Safety and National Security (2014). *Economics of policing: Report of the Standing Committee on Public Safety and National Security*. Canada: House of Commons, Library of Parliament. Available at: http://publications.gc.ca/collections/collection_2014/parl/xc76-1/XC76-1-1-412-4-eng.pdf

Huey, L., Cyr, K. & Ricciardelli, R. (2016). Austerity policing's imperative: Understanding the drivers of policing activity in Canada. *International Journal of Police Science & Management*, 18(2), 133–139

Huey, L. & Ricciardelli, R. (2016). From seeds to orchards: Using evidence based policing to address Canadas policing research needs. *Canadian Journal of Criminology and Criminal Justice*, 58(1), 119–131.

Irving, B. L. & McKenzie, I. K. (1989). *Police interrogation: The effects of the Police and Criminal Evidence Act 1984*. London: Police Foundation.

Irving, B. & Dunnighan, C. (1993). *Human factors in the quality control of CID investigations*. Research Study 21. London: HM Stationery Office.

James, A. & Mills, M. (2011). Does ACPO know best: To what extent may the PIP programme provide a template for the professionalization of policing? *The Police Journal*, 85, 133–149.

Jones, D. (2016). *Fatal call: Getting away with murder?* Professional Doctorate thesis, Portsmouth University, UK.

Kahneman, D. (2011). *Thinking, fast and slow*. London: Macmillan.

Kingshott, B. F., Walsh, J. P. & Meesig, R. T. (2015). Are we training our detectives? A survey of large Law Enforcement Agencies regarding investigation training and training needs. *Journal of Applied Security Research*, 10(4), 481–509.

Kolb, D. A. (1984). *Experiential learning*. Englewood Cliffs, NJ: Prentice-Hall.

Levitt, B. & March, J. G. (1988). Organizational learning. *Annual Review of Sociology*, 14, 319–340.

Lum, C. & Koper, C. S. (2017). *Evidence based policing: Translating research into practice*. Oxford: Oxford University Press.

MacDonald, B., Argent, M.J., Elliot, J., May, N., Miller, P., Naylor, J. & Norris, N. (1987). *Police probationer training: The Final Report of the Stage II Review*. London: HMSO.

MacPherson, S. W. (1999). *The Stephen Lawrence Inquiry: Report of an inquiry*. London: The Stationery Office.

Martin, P. & Mazerolle, L. (2015). Police leadership in fostering evidence-based agency reform. *Policing: A Journal of Policy and Practice*, 10(1), 34–43.

McGrory, D. & Treacy, P. (2012). The Professionalising Investigation Programme. In M. R. Haberfield, C. A. Clarke & D. L. Sheridan (eds), *Police organisation and training*. New York: Springer, pp. 113–136.

Meehl, P. E. (1954). *Clinical versus statistical prediction: A theoretical analysis and a review of the evidence*. Minneapolis, MN: University of Minnesota.

Meehl, P. E. (1986). Causes and effects of my disturbing little book. *Journal of Personality Assessment*, 50(3), 370–375.

Moore, C. R. & Rubin, G. R. (2014). Civilian detective doctrine in the 1930s and its transmission to the military police in 1940–1942. *Law, Crime and History*, pp. 1–30. Available at: https://kar.kent.ac.uk/41318/7/Colin%20R%20%20Moore%20and%20Gerry%20R%20%20Rubin%20FINAL.pdf

Morgan, J. B. (1990). *The police function and the investigation of crime*. Brookfield, VT: Avebury.

Mugford, R., Corey, S. & Bennell, C. (2013). Improving police training from a cognitive load perspective. *Policing: An International Journal of Police Strategies & Management*, 36(2), 312–337.

National Research Council (2004). Effectiveness of police activity in reducing crime, disorder and fear. In W. Skogan & K. Frydl (eds), *Fairness and effectiveness in policing: The evidence*. Washington, DC: The National Academies Press.

Neyroud, P. (2011). *Review of police leadership and training*. London: Home Office.

Peace, R. J. (2006). Probationer training for neighbourhood policing in England and Wales: Fit for purpose? *Policing: An International Journal of Police Strategies and Management*, 29(2), 335–346.

President's Task Force on 21st Century Policing (2015). *Final Report of the President's Task Force on 21st Century Policing*. Washington, DC: Office of Community Oriented Policing Services. Available at: https://cops.usdoj.gov/pdf/taskforce/taskforce_finalreport.pdf

Public Safety Canada (2013). *Summit on the Economics of Policing: Strengthening Canada's Advantage*. Summit report of Public Safety Canada. Available at: http://www.publicsafety.gc.ca/cnt/rsrcs/pblctns/smmt-cnmcs-plcng-2013/smmt-cnmcs-plcng-2013-eng.pdf.

Quinlan, A. (2016). Suspect survivors: Police investigation practices in sexual assault cases in Ontario, Canada. *Women & Criminal Justice*, 26, 301–318.

Rossmo, D. K. (2006). Criminal investigative failures: Avoiding the pitfalls. *FBI Law Enforcement Bulletin*, 75(9), 1–8.

Ruff, L. (2012). Does training matter? Exploring police officer response to domestic dispute calls before and after training on intimate partner violence. *The Police Journal*, 85(1), 285–300.

Saunders, E. (2001). *The decision making processes used in operational policing and serious crime investigation.* Unpublished PhD thesis, Warwick University, UK.

Scarman, L. G. (1981). *The Scarman report: The Brixton disorders 10–12 April 1981: Report of an inquiry*. London: Puffin.

Schank, R. C., Berman, T. R. & Macpherson, K. A. (1999). Learning by doing. In C.M. Reigeluth (ed.), *Instructional-design theories and models, volume II. A new paradigm of instructional theory*. London: Routledge, pp. 161–181.

Shawyer, A., Milne, B. & Bull, R. (2009). Investigative interviewing in the UK. In T. Williamson, T. Milne & S. Savage (eds), *International Developments in Investigative Interviewing*, Abingdon, UK: Routledge, pp. 24–38.

Sherman, L. W. (2013). The rise of evidence-based policing: Targeting, testing, and tracking. *Crime and Justice*, 42(1), 377–451.

Sherman, L. W. (2015). A tipping point for "totally evidenced policing": Ten ideas for building an evidence-based police agency. *International Criminal Justice Review*, 25(1), 11–29.

Sklansky, D. A. (2011). The persistent pull of police professionalism. *New Perspectives in Policing*, UC Berkeley Public Law Research Paper No. 1788463. Available at SSRN: https://ssrn.com/abstract=1788463

Skogan, W. & Frydl, K. (eds). (2004). *Fairness and effectiveness in policing: The evidence*, National Research Council of the National Academies. Washington, DC: National Academies Press.

Slothower, M., Sherman, L. W. & Neyroud, P. (2015). Tracking quality of police actions in a victim contact program: A case study of training, tracking, and feedback (TTF) in evidence-based policing. *International Criminal Justice Review*, 25(1), 98–116.

Smets, L. & Rispens, I. (2014). Investigative interviewing and training: The investigative interviewer apprentice. In R. Bull (ed.), *Investigative interviewing*. New York: Springer, pp. 147–165.

Snook, B. & Keating, K. (2011). A field study of adult witness interviewing practices in a Canadian police organization. *Legal and Criminological Psychology*, 16(1), 160–172.

Snook, B., Eastwood, J., Stinson, M., Tedeschini, J. & House, J. C. (2010). Reforming investigative interviewing in Canada. *Canadian Journal of Criminology and Criminal Justice*, 52(2), 215–229.

Snook, B., House, J.C., MacDonald, S. & Eastwood, J. (2012). Police witness interview training, supervision, and feedback: A survey of Canadian Police Officers 1. *Canadian Journal of Criminology and Criminal Justice*, 54(3), 363–372.

Stanko, E. & Dawson, P. (2016). *Police use of research evidence: Recommendations for improvement.* New York: Springer.

Stelfox, P. (2006). *The factors that determine outcomes in the police investigation of homicide.* Doctoral dissertation, Open University, UK.

Stelfox, P. (2007). Professionalising criminal investigation. In T. Newburn, T. Williamson & A. Wright (eds), *Handbook of criminal investigation.* Cullompton, UK: Willan Publishing, pp. 628–652.

Stelfox, P. (2009). *Criminal investigation: An introduction to principles and practice*. Cullompton, UK: Willan Publishing.

Tong, S., Horvath, M., & Bryant, R. (2009). *Understanding criminal investigation*. Oxford: Wiley-Blackwell.

Werth, E. P. (2011). Scenario training in police academies: Developing students' higher-level thinking skills. *Police Practice and Research*, 12(4), 325–340.

White, D. (2006). A conceptual analysis of the hidden curriculum of police training in England and Wales. *Policing and Society*, 16(4), 386–404.

White, M. D. & Escobar, G. (2008). Making good cops in the twenty-first century: Emerging issues for the effective recruitment, selection and training of police in the United States and abroad. *International Review of Law, Computers & Technology*, 22(1–2), 119–134.

Williamson, T. (2007). Psychology and criminal investigation. In T. Newburn, T. Williamson & A. Wright (eds), *Handbook of criminal Investigation*. Cullompton, UK: Willan Publishing, pp. 68–92.

Willis, J. J. (2013). *Improving police: What's craft got to do with it? Ideas in American policing*. The Police Foundation. Available online at: http://www.policefoundation.org/docs/library.html.

Willis, J. J. & Mastrofski, S. D. (2018). Improving policing by integrating craft and science: What can patrol officers teach us about good police work? *Policing and Society*, 28(1), 27–44.

Willis, J. J., Mastrofski, S. D. & Weisburd, D. (2004). COMPSTAT and bureaucracy: A case study of challenges and opportunities for change. *Justice Quarterly*, 21(3), 463–496.

Wright, A.M. & Alison, L. (2004). Questioning sequences in Canadian police interviews: Constructing and confirming the course of events? *Psychology, Crime and Law*, 10(2), 137–154.

Wyatt, S. & Bell, N. (2014). Perspectives on police training and education: The Canadian experience. In P. Stanislas (ed.), *International perspectives on police education and training*. Abingdon, UK: Routledge, pp. 72–90.

Conclusion

Andy Griffiths and Rebecca Milne

The 12 chapters of this book have shown that there is a wealth of established psychological research and theory across numerous areas of criminal investigation, but that the depth of this research varies across individual areas or disciplines. The differing amounts of research is in part due to the relative prominence of each area, caused primarily by high-profile miscarriages of justice cases, and world changing historical events (e.g. 9/11 World Trade Center attacks), which have driven both research and change agendas. In the past, prominent areas of research have been those associated with reactive investigations (i.e. those conducted into reported or discovered crimes) and there has been less published research on pro-active investigations (those commenced in response to information that a crime may be committed, to either prevent the crime or catch the offenders *in the act*). As a result, areas such as investigative interviewing and eyewitness identification have seen decades of psychological research dedicated to them. For example, identification procedures have been part of the criminal justice system for 150 years (Naughton, 2013) and scrutinised for almost as long (Borchard, 1932), resulting in a wealth of real-life and experimental data. This has resulted in a substantial body of knowledge, which in turn has provided research driven processes to help improve the reliability of criminal justice system.

There is also a strong correlation between the level of controversy surrounding the questioning of suspects and the amount of research interest. However, the degree of change that this has produced in real-life practice varies from country to country (Walsh et al., 2016), even though there is widespread research agreement on what constitutes effective practice (HIG, 2016; Milne & Powell, 2010). There appears to be an equally strong causal link between the level of legislative and procedural change and a decrease in miscarriages associated with confession evidence. Legislation and police practice transformations in Britain (Griffiths & Milne, 2006; Clarke & Milne, 2016) and Norway (Fahsing & Rachlow, 2009) have coincided with a consequent decrease in controversy. In contrast, the U.S. has not implemented any *national* changes to its legislation or training protocols and the numbers of miscarriage exonerations are rising (Garrett, 2015); although we acknowledge that the federal system of government is another factor in this equation. These are just two examples (investigative interviewing and identification procedures) where research has had a potential to inform practice, and in some countries has substantially influenced what happens in the field.

In contrast to both these subjects, there is a relative paucity of specific research in the area of human intelligence (HUMINT). Although law enforcement have used criminal informants since time immemorial, HUMINT's formalisation as a distinct discipline, as opposed to a heuristic craft, is much more recent. The role of science in developing practice is vital if we are to progress in this field. Unlike eyewitness identification and questioning of suspects, intelligence has only recently come under scrutiny at trial with examination of the processes involved, and so far fewer miscarriages have been attributed to this area of police work. There is a crossover between HUMINT processes and the investigative interviewing literature but there is a compelling case for more research in this area to produce empirical knowledge that will develop evidence-based practice in the intelligence discipline. This is especially important, given the global threat posed by terrorism, where reactive investigation will not save lives lost in bombings and attacks. There is no doubt that increased judicial examination will result in more failed cases from this area of policing in just the same way as it did for eyewitness identification and the questioning of suspects. Collaborative research in HUMINT at an earlier stage of its evolution represents an opportunity to break the criminal justice pattern of reacting only to critical failure.

The result of change, in either legislation or practice, is less obvious when considering witness/victim interviewing, as it is more difficult to attribute direct causation between these factors and criminal justice outcomes (Poyser, Nurse, & Milne, in press; Clarke & Milne, 2001, 2016; Griffiths, Milne & Cherryman, 2011). It is thus important for legislators and practitioners to consider the wealth of the research on this subject that has been consistent in demonstrating both the frailty of human memory and the negative effect of poor interview practice (Milne, Griffiths, Clarke & Dando, in submission). The extent to which human memory is fragile in its natural state is exacerbated by vulnerability, and in this area recent legislative (Youth Justice and Criminal Evidence Act, 1999) and policy (Achieving Best Evidence, 2001, 2009, 2011) changes in the UK seem to have responded to scientific knowledge (Smith & Milne, 2017). However, what is not so clear is whether actual practice has improved, either in relation to the collection of evidence or the way in which it is used at trial, allowing decision makers (whether this be under the adversarial or inquisitorial systems) to make better decisions (Davies, Bull & Milne, 2016).

Lie detection is another area where the strong body of psychological research has been particularly influential (Vrij & Fisher, 2016). This time in de-bunking widely held beliefs among law enforcement that liars can be detected through their non-verbal behaviour (Vrij, 2008), and on proposing practice based on empirical research, which supports lie detection based on verbal cues rather than previous heuristic traditions. There is no doubt that training is an essential ingredient in developing investigative skills. Indeed, a common response to the identification of a problem within any single area of the criminal justice process is to implement training. However, this training is often process based with little attempt to tackle the underlying cognitive issues.

The common element that underpins all the areas of criminal investigation is the human factors that underpin thinking and decision making and which are the root cause of most miscarriages of justice. The answer to what drives an investigator to pressure a confession from a suspect who they believe to be guilty, or to ask leading questions of a witness, or to over-estimate the accuracy of witness identification is to be found in the *way* in which an investigator thinks and decides (Ask & Granhag, 2005; Fahsing, 2016). This behaviour has its origin in our basic human psychology but has been nurtured in the investigative domain by the heuristic and craft basis of investigation, still prevalent in some criminal justice systems. It is clear that knowledge derived from research is in battle with cultural beliefs established over generations and it will take more than logic and reason to prevail. Tackling the way in which investigators think generally (Fahsing, 2016) represents a change from the classic criminal justice response to the identification of a problem by amending the legislation, or implementing extra training for *that* area of the process. For example, the way in which investigators utilise individual tactics, such as the use of evidence within an interview with a suspect, is approached completely differently dependent on the *prevailing thinking* of the investigator. If the investigator is guilt focused then the tactic becomes one of lie detection, whereas if they are open-minded, it becomes one of exploring various hypotheses that might explain the evidence supporting suspicion.

This brings us to the main point of the book: How much of the available psychological theory is used in practice? The answer to this question is that it varies, dependent on the individual area of investigation, the level of scrutiny applied by the trial process and the general evolution of that discipline. However, what is equally apparent is that the strength of psychological research is *not* the determining factor in whether it is utilised in practice.

Therefore, in concluding this book we wanted to address not the issues arising from each individual chapter of the book but instead examine several themes that transcend them all, and that appear to be fundamental to improving criminal investigation, as a discipline, going forward. These are: (i) How do we actually harness all this research-based knowledge and make it work in the field? and (ii) How do we produce open-minded investigators? This book has shown that, time and time again, research-based techniques/concepts are developed, even in partnership with stakeholders, but that full transference is elusive (e.g. the cognitive interview, Milne et al., in submission). Why is it so difficult to introduce research-based initiatives into real-life practice? Why are organisations and governments able to ignore research evidence so often? We often get asked these questions by organisations that are responsible for investigations and that ask our advice; we found ourselves repeating ourselves, and a mantra developed. In reality, factors such as culture, politics and organisational groupthink appear more dominant than pure or applied knowledge, as shown by the content of the previous chapters. This situation is regrettable, represent a considerable obstacle to the success of Evidence Based Policing (Sherman, 2013), which seeks to establish an evidence base for all areas of policing that can be shared globally, and will perpetuate the situation where criminal justice failures in the form of miscarriages remains as the single most influential driver of change within the system. We need to now be more *proactive* in driving change.

As a result, we developed a framework, each factor of which needs to be present if organisations are to achieve a goal of conducting professional and evidence based criminal investigations, contributing to a fair and effective criminal justice system, by professional open-minded investigators, seeking justice for victims and avoiding miscarriages caused through identifiable errors. We will outline here, for the first time, the Framework for Investigative Transformation (FIT). FIT can be applied to investigations as a whole or any individual area of investigation; for example, FIT for *investigative interviewing*, allowing organisations to create the correct environment for professional criminal investigations. FIT consists of eight factors that are either enablers of, where they are all present, or barriers to, where they are absent, skilled criminal investigations. The first factor is **leadership**, which also impacts upon all the following elements. Leaders set organisational culture and will influence all levels of an organisation through both formal and informal communication. Leadership is not just about seniority within a hierarchy, as leaders can be found at all levels of successful organisations where the pre-dominant culture is influenced by skill. Leadership is critical in creating an organisation that recognises the need for change and constant evolution, as part of high performance (Beckard & Harris, 1977). Good leaders foster a learning culture, providing opportunities to apply new skills and giving workplace support (managers, subordinates, peers and supervisors; Griffiths & Milne, in preparation). Skilled practitioners are also leaders as subject matter experts, with a role to not only use their skills as investigators, but also to influence others. Within policing, however, it is rare to see self-initiated change. Usually, the driver is external, more often than not related to miscarriages of justice, where an organisation is forced to change, often through legislative intervention, to demonstrate to its populous that such atrocities will never happen again, justice will be done and the equilibrium regained. Even where governments impose change through new legislation (e.g. *Police and Criminal Evidence Act, 1984*) ground level policing will often resist this change deriding it as 'soft'. However, regardless of the driver, an organisation needs to be a learning organisation with proficient leadership. An example of this would be the publication of the *Seven Principles of Investigative Interviewing* (ACPO, 1992) by chief police officers in Britain, which publicly stated the commitment to fair treatment of all interviewees. Senior leaders within an organisation must also recognise their role in shaping a balanced legislative framework, and communicate directly with legislators to devise workable legal protocols. We contend that, at a strategic level, it is incumbent on law enforcement organisations to engage with legislators in building criminal justice systems that are fair to all sections of society and balance state powers and individual rights, which takes us to the second factor.

There must be an appropriate **legislative framework** in place, and enforced by other parts of the criminal justice system. It is unrealistic to expect investigators to adopt moral standards that are not reflected in law. For example, where legislation only requires a confrontation as an identification procedure it is impractical to expect the police to arrange a sequential procedure utilising numerous foils, as recommended by research. Therefore, legislators must commit to creating evidence-based statutes that demonstrate balance between the powers of the state and the recognition of individual rights. Sanctions and safeguards within legislation must be clearly laid out. In addition, the law must encompass all types of investigation and ensure that there is transparency and fairness in the process.

With the prior two enablers in place, investigators must adopt an appropriate **investigative mind-set or cognitive style** (e.g. open-mindedness or exploration of alternative hypotheses) to conduct professional investigations. The correct attitude throughout an investigation is key to successful and just outcomes. Attitudes of individuals within law enforcement organisations are often heavily influenced by organisational culture, which takes a long time to change. Thus, the pit-falls of cognitive heuristics (e.g. cognitive bias and premature closure) and how they impact upon the investigative approach and outcomes must be taught from the ground up at each strata of an organisation. This element is strongly linked to leadership and example setting.

The correct mind-set goes hand in hand with **investigators' knowledge base**, in that they must have the right knowledge to perform their role. Contemporary theory and research literature (e.g. memory) must be at the heart of training, policy and also practice. It has been demonstrated that practitioner–academic partnerships work well to help foster change. Indeed, partnerships help to shape concepts to ensure that innovations developed in the laboratory can be used and adapted to fit different circumstances in the field. Thus, the perceived and actual flexibility of the innovation needs to be realised (e.g. the cognitive interview – see Milne et al., 2018 for how the CI has been tailored to suit different circumstances), so that it can be adapted to suit the circumstances. Knowledge is a key derivative of training; the next factor.

Organisations need to have a **training and knowledge regime** that is optimal for transference to real life practice. This means a commitment to scenario-based training, with small classes, and a high ratio of practicals with expert feedback (Powell, 2008), including sessions that are immersive and reflect the real world that the investigators are about to face. Hoffman, Andrews, Flore, Feltovich, DiBello, & Ward (2014, p. 51) note that training success can be characterised as:

> When knowledge, skill or strategy in one context or learned from one problem/task type is successfully utilized in learning or performance in some other context or for some other problem task/type, where either the context or problem/task types have both important similarities and substantive differences.

This definition captures some of the complexity of investigation (Milne et al., 2018), which requires one to consider the context, differences, personal perceptions (bias) and a range of appropriate tools when conducting every investigation. It is essential that training methods successfully embed the required skills and resist fade. This is not unique to investigation. For example, military training research has identified gradual post-training performance decline (Hoffman et al., 2014). This leads us onto the next enabler: the establishment of meaningful **quality assurance mechanisms**. To ensure continuance of standards after the training, there needs to be sufficient processes in place for both support and supervision in the workplace, appropriate evaluation tools, and a refresher training programme to combat the skills fade.

Evaluation must be more than checking the mere application of a process and must be focused on both the quality of an investigation and the personal performance of the individual, the latter linked to personal development (Shepherd & Griffiths, 2013). Unfortunately, both these areas are often overlooked as they are costly in terms of time and money, and can be viewed as unimportant in the task-focused expedient world of policing (Shepherd, 1988). However, one has only to consider the cost of one miscarriage of justice to realise the fallacy of this logic; the State of Illinois has paid $214,000,000 in compensation over 85 wrongful conviction exonerations (Bowers, 2013). Any short-term savings gained by ignoring the importance of quality assurance will be more costly in the long run.

In order for training to be effective, trainers need to have the correct people in the 'training room' in the first place. This leads us to the next factor or enabler – **the ability/ skill set of investigator**; i.e. how ***able*** are investigators at acquiring the knowledge, assimilating the content and applying the skills taught, each individual having differing levels of natural ability, and different levels of skill (Milne et al., 2018)? In the past, investigation by police officers has been considered to be an inherent skill that all officers possess and which could be developed merely by learning from more experienced colleagues. Research has shown us that that is not the case, as outlined above. Indeed, communication has been seen to be key to differentiating skilled and less skilled investigators (O'Neill & Milne, 2014; Westera, Kebbell, Milne & Green, 2016). Furthermore, Griffiths, Milne and Cherryman (2011) also found that not everyone has the ability to attain the Advanced Level of interviewing, only those with 'potential' seem to reach this standard. 'Having potential' is an interesting concept, and raises the question – what is this potential? Further research is currently under-way (by the editors of this book) to examine what this 'potential' actually is. The key here is selection processes need to be clearly outlined and based on what is currently known to be necessary pre-requisites for candidates on investigator and interviewing training courses.

The final factor is **technology**. We are living in the age of accessible technology and it has the potential to improve the transparency and fairness of investigations, performance of individuals and organisations, *and* the research effort. The implementation of mandatory audio recording for every suspect interview in Britain (since 1984) is an excellent example of this. Initially, there were frequent challenges to the conduct of the interviews, but these faded as confidence in the process grew. The recordings of the interviews, when reviewed by skilled practitioners and researchers, identified performance and skills issues (e.g. Williamson, 1993; Baldwin, 1993; Clarke & Milne, 2001) and contributed to both the implementation of initial training (Central Planning and Training Unit, 1992), and then evolution of that process (Griffiths & Milne, 2006). Finally, the publication of research papers from relevant studies has informed and influenced the global debate on the most effective way to question suspects. There is no question that technology is also the researchers' dream, as it allows a window into actual practice, which in turn helps the researcher to study uninterrupted what actually happens so that innovations can be developed around real-world problems. Technology however, can hinder development if not introduced with well thought out policy and procedure.

Adopted comprehensively, we believe these FIT factors will drive the change required. This book has shown that there is a considerable body of psychological knowledge that can assist investigators, but that its use in practice is limited by contextual factors. Consistent, thorough and meaningful application of psychological theory into the discipline of criminal investigation requires management of a range of factors beyond the quality of the empirical knowledge, and needs the collaborative efforts of the academic community and a critical mass of practitioners across all parts of criminal justice systems, at all levels and across nations. Only in this way will criminal investigations break the reactive cycle of responding to failure.

References

ACPO (1992). *Principles of Investigative Interviewing (HOC 22/1992).* London: Home Office.

Ask, K., & Granhag, P. A. (2005). Motivational sources of confirmation bias in criminal investigations: The need for cognitive closure. *Journal of Investigative Psychology and Offender Profiling*, 2, 43–63.

Baldwin, J. (1992). *Video taping police interviews with suspects – an evaluation.* Police Research Series, Paper 1. London. Home Office.

Beckhard, R. & Harris, R. T. (1977). *Organizational transitions: Managing complex change* (1st edn). Reading, MA: Addison-Wesley Publishing.

Borchard, E. M. (1932). *Convicting the innocent: Sixty-five actual errors of criminal justice.* Garden City, NY: Doubleday.

Bowers, M. (2013). The cost of wrongful convictions. *Forensics and Law in Focus*. https://csidds.com/2013/08/12/bad-forensic-experts-police-and-prosecution. Accessed 1 November 2017.

Central Planning and Training Unit (1992). *A guide to interviewing*. Harrogate: CPTU.

Clarke, C. & Milne, R. (2001). *National evaluation of the PEACE investigative interviewing course*. London: Home Office.

Clarke, C. & Milne, R. (2016). Interviewing suspects in England and Wales: A national evaluation of PEACE interviewing: One decade later. In D. Walsh, G. Oxburgh, A. Redlich & T. Mykleburst (eds), *International developments and practices in investigative interviewing and interrogation, vol 2. Suspects*. London: Routledge.

Davies, G., Bull, R. & Milne, R. (2016). Analysing and improving the testimony of vulnerable witnesses interviewed under the 'Achieving Best Evidence' protocol. In P. Radcliffe, A. Heaton-Armstrong, G. Gudjonsson & D. Wolchover (eds), *Witness testimony in sexual cases: Investigation, law and procedure*. Oxford: Oxford University Press.

Fahsing, I. A. (2016). *The making of an expert detective*. Phd thesis, University of Gothenburg, Gothenburg.

Fahsing, I. & Rachlew, A. (2009). Investigative interviewing – the Nordic region. In T. Williamson, R. Milne & S. P. Savage (eds), *International developments in Investigative Interviewing*. Devon: Willan. pp. 39–65.

Garrett, B.L. (2015). Contaminated confessions revisited. *Virginia Law Review*. 101 Va. Rev. 395 Provided by: University of Virginia Law Library, pp. 395–454

Griffiths, A. & Milne, R. (2006). Will it all end in tiers? In T. Williamson (ed.), *Investigative interviewing: Rights, research, regulation*. Cullompton, UK: Willan.

Griffiths, A., Milne, R. & Cherryman, J. (2011). A question of control? The formulation of suspect and witness interview question strategies by advanced interviewers. *International Journal of Police Science and Management*, 13(3), 255–267.

HIG (2016) *Interrogation: A review of the Science*. https://www.fbi.gov/file-repository/hig-report-interrogation-a-review-of-the-science-september-2016.pdf/view. September. Accessed 4 August 2017.

Hoffman, R. R., Ward, P., Feltovich, P. J., DiBello, L., Fiore, S. M. & Andrews, D. H. (2014). *Accelerated expertise: Training for high proficiency in a complex world*. New York: Psychology Press.

Milne, R. & Powell, M. (2010). Investigative interviewing. In J. M. Brown & E. A. Campbell (eds), *The Cambridge handbook of forensic psychology*. Cambridge: Cambridge University Press.

Milne, R., Griffiths, A., Clarke, C., & Dando, C. (in submission). The cognitive interview – a tiered approach in the real world. Chapter to appear in B. Schwartz, J. Dickenson, N. Schreiber Compo, M. McCauley (eds), *Evidence-based investigative interviewing*. Routledge.

Ministry of Justice (2001, 2009, 2011). *Achieving best evidence in criminal proceedings: Guidance on interviewing victims and witnesses, and guidance on using special measures*. London: Ministry of Justice.

Naughton, M. (2013). *The innocent and the criminal justice system: A sociological analysis*. Basingstoke, UK: Palgrave.

O'Neill, M. & Milne, B. (2014). Success within criminal investigations: Is communication still a key component? In R. Bull (ed.), *Investigative interviewing* (pp. 123–146). New York: Springer.

Powell, M. (2008). Designing effective training programs for investigative interviewers of children. *Current Issues in Criminal Justice*, 20, 189–208.

Poyser, S., Nurse, A. & Milne, R. (in press). *Miscarriages of justice*. Bristol: Policy Press.

Shepherd, E. (1988). Developing interviewing skills: A career span perspective. In P. Southgate (ed.), *New directions in police training*. London: HMSO. Chapter 13.

Shepherd, E. & Griffiths, A. (2013). *Investigative interviewing: The Conversation Management Approach*. Oxford: Oxford University Press.

Sherman, L. (2013). *The rise of evidence based policing: Targeting, testing and tracking*. http://cebcp.org/wp-content/evidence-based-policing/Sherman- TripleT.pdf. 20 May. Accessed 1 June 2017.

Smith, K. & Milne, R. (2017). Vulnerable witnesses: the investigation stage. In H. Norton & R. Cooper (eds), *Vulnerable people and the criminal justice system*. Oxford: Oxford University Press.

Vrij, A. (2008). *Detecting lies and deceit: Pitfalls and opportunities* (2nd edn.). Chichester: John Wiley & Sons.

Vrij, A. & Fisher, R. P. (2016). Which lie detection tools are ready for use in the criminal justice system? *Journal of Applied Research and Cognition*, 5, 302–307.

Walsh, D., Oxburgh, G. E., Redlich, A. D. & Myklebust, T. (2016). *International developments and practices in investigative interviewing and interrogation: Volume 2: Suspects*. Routledge Frontiers of Criminal Justice

Westera, N., Kebbell, M., Milne, R. & Green, T. (2016a). The prospective detective. *Policing and Society*, 26, 197–209.

Westera, N., Kebbell, M., Milne, R. & Green, T. (2016b). Towards a more effective detective. *Policing and Society*, 26, 1–17.

Williamson, T. (1993). From interrogation to investigative interviewing: Strategic trends in police questioning. *Journal of Community and Applied Psychology*, 3, 89–99.

Index

Note: page references in italic refer to figures; page numbers followed by 'n' refer to note numbers.

Printed in Dunstable, United Kingdom

80098389R00174